ADVANCES IN
MOTIVATION AND
ACHIEVEMENT

Volume 7 • 1991

ADVANCES IN MOTIVATION AND ACHIEVEMENT

A Research Annual

Editors: **MARTIN L. MAEHR**
PAUL R. PINTRICH
School of Education
University of Michigan

VOLUME 7 • 1991

 **JAI PRESS INC.**

Greenwich, Connecticut   *London, England*

CONTENTS

LIST OF CONTRIBUTORS

Nancy Cantor

Department of Psychology
University of Michigan

William Fleeson

Department of Psychology
University of Michigan

Martin E. Ford

School of Education
Stanford University

Teresa Garcia

School of Education
University of Michigan

Judith M. Harackiewicz

Department of Psychology
University of Wisconsin at Madison

Frederick H. Kanfer

Department of Psychology
University of Illinois
  at Urbana-Champaign

Ruth Kanfer

Department of Psychology
University of Minnesota

Mary M. McCaslin

Department of Curriculum
  and Instruction
University of Missouri

Judith L. Meece

School of Education
University of North Carolina,
  Chapel Hill

Tamera B. Murdock

Department of Educational Studies
University of Delaware

Richard S. Newman

School of Education
University of California at Riverside

C. W. Nichols

School of Education
Stanford University

Lawrence A. Pervin

Department of Psychology
Rutgers University

Paul R. Pintrich

School of Education
University of Michigan

Richard M. Ryan

Department of Psychology
University of Rochester

Carol Sansone

Department of Psychology
University of Utah

Dale H. Schunk

School of Education
University of North Carolina,
Chapel Hill

Jerome Stiller

Department of Psychology
University of Rochester

Kathryn R. Wentzel

Department of Psychology
University of Illinois at
Urbana-Champaign

PREFACE

Volume 7, like previous volumes in this series, reflects current trends in motivation research and theory. The importance of a social cognitive perspective persists, but the research agenda has shifted, new variables and constructs have emerged and the emphases have changed. It is hazardous to specify trends in research, but there does seem to be an important and notable shift from a virtually all-consuming concern with cognitions that focus on the persons' perception of control and competence to thoughts about purpose, goals, and perhaps value, in performing an achievement act. Increasingly, the focus of motivational research is on the individual's personal construction of meaning, or purpose, for achievement and on the nature of the strategies that lead to achievement.

This volume provides sterling examples of the shifting dialogue in the study of achievement. A social cognitive perspective is assumed or accepted as a background for much of the research and theory that is reported in this volume. It is, however, a widened social cognitive framework over that which held sway when this series began. The social cognitive perspective has given rise to a rich variety of useful constructs, measures, and applications. In line with this trend the papers in this volume are not confined to a limited set of cognitive constructs or one particular research paradigm. Even so, there is continuity across the chapters and the stated theme, "Goals and Self Regulation," seems to adequately encompass the variation in argument and fact.

The reader will note that there is at least a hint of duality in the theme. On the one hand, there is the focus on goals and with that an associated concern with success, failure, incentives, and purposes for achieving. On the other hand, there is a concern with strategies and styles that foster success or, in unfortunate instances, lead to failure. In short, the theme reflects the fact that this volume deals both with the "why" and the "how" of achievement. Such duality of emphasis, not surprisingly, gives rise to differing emphases across the papers; but underlying this varying interest in the why and how of achievement is an inherent unity. The two facets are basically complementary in nature. They reflect and reinforce a growing trend which is serving to break down older cognition-volition or skill-will categories. Thus, for example, Pervin argues for a theory that emphasizes the affective properties of goals and indicates how these properties are linked to individuals' problems in self-regulation and volition. Kanfer and Kanfer argue that motivational and cognitive processes have been separated for too long and propose a resource allocation framework that provides a mechanism by which goals and self-regulatory strategies are integrated within the individual.

The integration of both cognitive and motivational constructs is still a goal for most research in this area, so there is still evidence of a differential emphasis on the "why" and the "how" of achievement in the papers. We suggest that this provides not only variety but also spice. Some authors have chosen to focus especially on goals. Key issues in the consideration of goals include questions of definition, content, and number. Much of the literature, especially that relating to achievement in school settings, has tended to concentrate on two goals (e.g., "intrinsic" vs. "extrinsic") and for all practical purposes has treated these two goals not only as different but as mutually exclusive. The papers by Ford and Nichols and by Wentzel take a distinctly different tact. Sharing a similar theoretical perspective, both stress not only the importance of considering a multiplicity of goals but suggest that any given goal does not exist to the exclusion of another. In classroom and in life; in achievement as well as other contexts, multiple goals not only operate simultaneously but also in concert. Ford and Nichols define the range of values that may be operative and suggest how these can be defined and measured. In addition, they present a model which defines more precisely how these various goals function in guiding behavior. They also present data on their assessment instruments that support their assumption that individuals can pursue a multiplicity of goals, albeit at different levels of intensity. Focusing more specifically on the classroom context, Wentzel argues that students can pursue both intrinsic (or "mastery") as well as extrinsic ("performance") goals. Not only does she show how a multiple goals perspective represents a more accurate description of students in school contexts, she presents data that indicate that holding both intrinsic and extrinsic goals are beneficial for classroom achievement and social adjustment.

A number of the authors touch on the generalizability or specificity of goals. Harackiewicz and Sansone make an important distinction between general or global goals and more situation or context specific goals. They then propose a model of how these two types of goals may interact with internal motivational process (e.g., perceived competence) as well as contextual factors (e.g., criteria for evaluation) to influence the individuals' eventual intrinsic motivation for a task. The paper by Cantor and Fleeson likewise reflects a concern with the generality-specificity problem. This paper emerges from an enduring program of research on how more general personal orientations interact with specific contexts in determining achievement patterns. This program of research attends particularly to the construct of "Life Tasks," the individual's personal construction of a developmental task, that is set in general by the sociocultural context, but is defined and accomplished by the person in specific situations. Cantor and Fleeson not only suggest how general personal and specific situational characteristics interact but present new data that illustrate the nature of this interaction. Incidentally, as 'a kind of by-product of the presentation of basic research, this paper provides an interesting vignette and unique insights into the life of undergraduates—a form of life in which many readers should have some interest.

The second theme of Volume 7, self-regulation, concerns how individuals translate goals into plans and strategies for achievement. Although all the papers in the volume in some sense are concerned with this problem, several of them address the issue of cognitive and self-regulatory strategies directly. In his paper, Schunk, highlights the importance of several processes, including the procedures individuals use in setting goals, their strategies for evaluating progress vis-a-vis these goals, and how they redirect their efforts upon self-evaluation of goal progress. Kanfer and Kanfer are likewise concerned with self-regulation. The primary venue in this case is the workplace which not only expands the illustrative material contained in this volume but also serves to enlarge the theoretical dialogue. Thus, they call attention to the role and nature of the task and then relate goals and self-regulation processes to performance on workplace tasks. They also incorporate the extensive research in industrial and organizational psychology on goal setting into a conceptual framework that interfaces with literature on motivation, cognition, and achievement more generally. The paper by Pintrich and Garcia not only interlocks with and complements papers that are concerned with self-regulation, it expands the dialogue in significant ways. Proceeding from a general information processing framework, the authors first of all delineate the cognitive strategies college students use to improve their academic performance. Second, they report recent and previously unpublished results on how learning strategies can be and are used—and with what effects. Among these results is the finding that academic performance and students' use of learning strategies varies as a function of an interaction between intrinsic and extrinsic goals. In particular, their results suggest that an extrinsic goal orientation may have a positive influence on student self-regulation in the absence of intrinsic goals. This appears to be further evidence in support of a multiple goal perspective alluded to earlier in regard to the work of Wentzel, Ford, and Nichols. The paper by Newman is unique in that it attends to a seldom-noted aspect of self-regulation and achievement: help-seeking. In a sophisticated and detailed analysis of the self-regulatory strategy of help-seeking, Newman shows how students' help-seeking behavior is influenced by motivational factors, including goals, self-perceptions of ability, attitudes and beliefs as well as general developmental and contextual factors. His paper lays the groundwork for an expanded research agenda on how motivational, cognitive, developmental, and contextual variables work together to influence help-seeking behavior.

Although several of the papers already reviewed discuss how individuals might derive their goals from contextual and situational constraints, most do not directly address the problem of how different environments influence students' goal adoption. However, three papers included in this volume are concerned in a special way with how school and home environments do affect goals and self-regulatory patterns.

Meece, using a case study approach, presents a detailed analysis of how different characteristics of the classroom can result in the adoption of intrinsic or extrinsic orientations to learning. Most important, she notes that it is not just the structural features of the classroom that are typically thought to influence students' goals (e.g., competition, cooperation), but also the nature of the instructional methods, tasks, and strategies that teachers use that can result in positive motivational outcomes. Both Ryan and Stiller and McCaslin and Murdock address how teachers and parents can influence the internalization of intrinsic goals for learning and self-regulation by students. Ryan and Stiller, working from an intrinsic motivation framework, assume that all students are motivated by needs for competence, autonomy, and relatedness. They then analyze the research on teacher and parental practices, highlighting the different practices that can either facilitate or forestall the process of cognitive and motivational development. McCaslin and Murdock, utilizing a Vygotskian framework and in-depth analysis of two case studies, show how students' motivational goals and beliefs and cognitive processes are linked not just to each other, but also to events that occur in interactions with teachers and parents. These three papers provide an excellent starting point for our efforts to conceptualize how specific interactions with teachers and parents shape students' goals and self-regulation. Clearly, these papers provide a number of enticing hypotheses about the relationships between home and school contexts and individuals' goals and self-regulation that should serve as an incentive for many of us to pursue research on these issues.

Without question, the papers contained in this volume not only reflect the lively debates that exist at the moment in the study of motivation and achievement. More than this, they push the argument and inquiry in new and novel directions. They not only contain fresh new insights on research of the past, but each paper is in effect a point of entry to an important, ongoing program of research that will lead to the dialogues of the future. The authors characteristically provide an extended comment on their own research that can not be found elsewhere. In a number of notable instances, papers contain new and previously unpublished results. As editors we have, of course, spent countless hours working through the materials with the authors. There were moments of pain and concern and wonder, as there always are. But in spite of our focused task, we experienced a special freshness of insight that we believe that you the reader will also experience. Stimulation aplenty awaits you. These papers are evidence that the study of motivation and achievement, never lacking enthusiastic adherents, now possesses new sources of energy, as well as a wealth of new ideas. An occasional reader may choose to sample only a paper here or there, but to catch the spirit of current research, the dialogues, the themes at work, one would do well to work through all papers. We did, first admittedly because we had to. But ours is a case where extrinsic constraint eventuated in intrinsic interest. On the basis of this experience we commend the following papers to you for whatever uses you might have. We are confident that you will find much that will inform and interest you. On more than one occasion there will be something that surprises and challenges you.

Martin L. Maehr
Paul R. Pintrich
Series Editors

SELF-REGULATION AND THE PROBLEM OF VOLITION

Lawrence A. Pervin

If we compare the outward symptoms of perversity together, they fall into two groups, in one of which normal actions are impossible, and in the other abnormal ones are irrepressible, Briefly, we may call them respectively the obstructed and the explosive will.

—James (1892, p. 436)

The study of the mechanisms through which the human is able to control his behavior brings us to the problem of will. One may state without the fear of contradiction that no other psychological question has a history so fraught with errors; the actual history of the study of will is a history of mistakes, and the inventory of contemporary psychological conceptions concerning will is a cemetery of fallacies, of loosely put questions and trivial investigations.

—Luria (1932, p. 397)

Advances in Motivation and Achievement, Volume 7, pages 1-20.

It is my *intention* in this paper to discuss problems in self-regulation or, as I shall refer to them, problems of will or *volition*. I will be referring here to a broad range of phenomena including all cases in which the person wishes, desires, or intends to behave in some way and cannot, as well as those cases in which the person wishes, desires, or intends to *not* behave in some way and cannot avoid doing so. These inhibitions and compulsions or addictions, what James (1892) referred to as cases of obstructed and explosive will, represent disturbances in self-regulatory functioning or disturbances in volition. In the broad terms defined above, almost everyone suffers from momentary or recurrent disturbances in volition!

In this paper problems in self-regulation and disturbances in volition will be discussed within the context of a theory of goals. I will not discuss the history of concepts of motivation, purposive behavior, intention, will and volition because this history can be found elsewhere (Boden, 1972; Brody, 1983; Eacker, 1975; Kimble & Perlmutter, 1970; Kuhl & Beckmann, 1985; McMahon, 1973; Pervin, 1984; Prusyer, 1967; Westcott, 1985). Suffice here to say that although these concepts were present in the early days of psychology, the behaviorist influence virtually swept them from the field. As I have noted elsewhere (Pervin, 1984), the concept of motivation almost disappeared from the field with the demise of the drive concept and the inauguration of the cognitive revolution. Yet, in an interesting way, the cognitive revolution permitted a return to mentalistic concepts and purposive views of behavior (Miller, Galanter, & Pribram, 1960; Simon, 1967). Though at first these models appeared to leave the person left in thought, just as Guthrie (1935) suggested of Tolman's (1925, 1932) views, affect and motivation have increasingly become a part of cognitive and social cognitive thinking (Cantor & Zirkel, 1990).

WILLIAM JAMES AND THE CONCEPT OF WILL

Before proceeding with discussion of disturbances of volition within the context of a theory of goals, it may be useful to consider the views of James (1892) in his chapter on will. As we will see, James considered many of the phenomena that will be of interest to us, and elaborated upon many of the issues and concepts that will be involved in the discussion that follows.

James (1892, p. 415) began his chapter on will with an analysis of voluntary acts:

> Desire, wish, will, are states of mind which everyone knows, and which no definition can make plainer . . . If with the desire there goes a sense that attainment is not possible, we simply *wish*; but if we believe that the end is in our power, we *will* that the desired feeling, having or doing shall be real; and real it presently becomes, either immediately upon the willing or after certain preliminaries have been fulfilled.

James suggested that sometimes the bare idea of a movement's effects is sufficient to produce the movement itself, what he called *ideo-motor action*. In this case conception leads to execution—"we think the act, and it is done" (p. 423)—and there is no involvement of consent, resolve, or "fiat." Much of our habitual, daily activity (e.g., walking, talking, tying our shoes) is of this sort. In such cases there is the absence of other ideas or of conflicting ideas. In other cases, however, resolve or fiat is required. Here we have James' famous description of getting out of bed in the morning:

> We know what it is to get out of bed on a freezing morning without a fire, and how the very vital principle within us protests against the ordeal. Probably most persons have lain on certain mornings for an hour at a time unable to brace themselves to the resolve. We think how late we shall be, how the duties of the day will suffer; we say, " I *must* get up, this is ignominious," etc.; but still the warm couch feels too delicious, the cold outside too cruel, and resolution faints away and postpones itself again and again just as it seemed on the verge of bursting the resistance and passing over into the decisive act. Now how do we ever get up under such circumstances? . . . This case seems to me to contain in miniature form the data for an entire psychology of volition. (pp. 424-425)

According to James, ideas automatically lead to action unless the process is disturbed by competing ideas—we get up at the thought of getting up unless such action is blocked by the thought of staying in the warm bed. In this sense, "consciousness is in its very nature impulsive" (p. 426). In the case of getting out of bed on a cold morning, our resolve or *voluntary fiat* enters in the form of neutralization of the antagonistic or inhibitory idea.

James went on to consider various types of decision and then, most interestingly from our standpoint, cases of *unhealthiness of will*. It is here that we come to the quote with which I began the paper, and to James' consideration of the cases of *obstructed will* and *explosive will*. According to him, action may involve the interplay between *impulsive* and *inhibitory forces*. These two forces are always operating in conjunction with one another and the consequence represents the outcome of the balance between these opposing forces. Obstructed will, then, occurs where the impulsion is insufficient or inhibition is in excess, while the explosive will occurs where impulsion is exaggerated or inhibition is defective. Thus, drinking or drug behavior, where there is a "gnawing, craving urgency to act," may be due to exaggerated impulsion while violent behavior may occur in the absence of scruples or inhibitory forces. In sum, in any particular case of the breakdown of volition there may be too much or too little impulsion and too much or too little inhibition.

INHIBITIONS AND COMPULSIONS-ADDICTIONS: THE PHENOMENA OF PROBLEMATIC VOLITION

One semester I asked students in a large introductory personality course to indicate any problem in volition that concerned them and the reasons for it.

As noted above, almost every student listed one or more such difficulties, the most frequent being the problems of procrastination and overeating. Almost all could list some reason for the difficulty but generally these were merely statements of the problem rather than causal analyses. Thus, for example, a student might report "I feel that I should write the paper but I just can't get myself to sit down and do it." or "I know how many calories that food has and how I want to lose weight but I just feel as if I have to have it."

The problem of procrastination I take to be illustrative of what James called obstructed will or, as I shall refer to it, the problem of *inhibition*. The problem of overeating I take to be illustrative of what James called explosive will or, as I shall refer to it, the problem of *addiction*. The term compulsion might also be used for the latter. However, this term has been taken to refer to specific neurotic symptoms, such as a handwashing compulsion, and my effort here is to consider the problem within a much broader context. The term addiction has the unfortunate connotation of drugs. However, I choose to use it because it connotes the power of desiring, wanting, or "craving" something. Although consideration often has been given to one or the other set of problems, rarely have the two been considered in the same context, exceptions being Shapiro's (1981) discussion of the problem of individual autonomy within the framework of a psychoanalytic theory of action and Block and Block's (1980) discussion of the concepts of ego-control and ego-resiliency in the organization of behavior.

What are the phenomena with which we are concerned? Let us consider briefly the difficulties of five patients. The first patient struggled with the problem of lateness—of turning things in on time and of being on time. When he began as a patient his professional career was in jeopardy because often he did not show up for work on time and could not turn projects in on time. The problem was a longstanding one. In college he struggled with getting papers in on time and periodically only did so under the threat of flunking and being thrown out of school. This itself raises an interesting question, which is why in some cases the threat of a deadline is what is needed to spur the person to action while in other cases the threat of a deadline leads to immobilization.

In any case, this person made it through college and graduate school through the charity of some professors, the selection of courses that would not be problematic, and the mobilization effort (will?). Now, however, the problem was particularly serious and threatening. It was expressed in the therapy as well as in the workplace. Thus, although he would very rarely miss a session, he might come anywhere from two minutes to forty-eight minutes late, a session lasting fifty minutes. At times this seemed to have a deliberate quality to it. More generally, however, he would bemoan the lack of control he had over the difficulty. At times he would struggle with whether to get out of bed or continue to enjoy his sexual fantasies, whether to get to a place on time or have his second cup of coffee, whether to work on his project or finish reading the book he was enjoying. Often these were experienced as driven acts, beyond his control. However, even when he was able to override them something else even more clearly beyond his control would interfere with his being on time— his alarm would not go off, he would oversleep, he wouldn't be able to find something, his car would break down, his mind would go blank, or he would fall asleep. The problem was not everywhere in his life but neither was it specific to one domain or kind of interaction. The dynamics and treatment of the case are quite interesting, involving as one might imagine issues of authority and the meaning of time for him, but let us put these aside for the sake of focusing on the phenomenon itself—his inability to control being on time.

A second case illustrates the problem of inhibition in relation to social interaction. The patient here was a quite successful man in his thirties who had a long history of inhibition in relation to women. As a teenager he dated frequently but never felt comfortable with women. After a period of relative happiness in marriage and success in business he experienced some difficulties in control of his erections. This led to a pattern of increased withdrawal, culminating in divorce. For a year or two thereafter he did not date but then decided that he was lonely and started to have more interaction with women. However, this interaction was characterized by a pattern of avoidance and delay, staying within what came to be known as the comfort zone. Behaving somewhat like people described by Dollard and Miller (1950) as caught in an approach-avoidance conflict, he would delay calling women for dates, finally do so and generally have a good time, only to then delay in arranging further dates or avoid dating altogether because he was so busy with his business. When not with women he was lonely, when with them he was uncomfortable. Even in ending a relationship there was avoidance and delay, not being able to tell a woman he did not want to see her anymore. Often the struggle was enormous as he would find all kinds of excuses for not calling, berate himself for being a coward when he ran out of excuses, but in any case find himself unable to pursue the relationship or to end it if he did not want it to continue. Although the problem was most evident in relation to women, it did appear in a more subtle and less disruptive form elsewhere as well. Thus, he would sometimes delay confronting an employee about a problem or would delay writing a letter while struggling with the best way to put things.

The third case involves the problem of compulsion. In this case the patient felt compelled to work increasingly hard and set increasingly high standards. From his earliest years he had a record of always earning money and meeting responsibilities. He was such a good worker that his company gave him increased responsibility as well as increased pay, until the point where he felt that he wasn't sure that he could do all that was asked of him and wasn't sure that he was earning his salary. His attempts at control involved establishing lists and trying to organize priorities. However, the lists of things to do became so extensive that they themselves became a source of anxiety. Although it seemed reasonable to cut down on the number of tasks and ask for more assistance, he felt compelled to do everything asked of him and to earn every dollar given him.

The fourth case involves the problem of compulsion, impulsion or addiction. This involves a patient who felt driven to act upon sexual feelings that he found shameful and abhorrent. At times of stress he found himself driven to rent pornographic movies that he felt brought him to the lowest level of existence. At other times he felt *driven* to visit prostitutes. His partner would gladly participate with him in the acts he found so arousing in the pornographic movies and in his visits to prostitutes. However, with her such interaction was abhorrent. On the other hand, at times he found the arousal and compulsion of the wish to view a tape or visit a prostitute so enormous that he could think of nothing else but that until the wish was satisfied. Once more the point to be emphasized here is the tremendous amount of conflict and struggle that is experienced by the person; that is, how shameful and abhorrent these acts seemed to him and how compelled he felt to act upon them when the urge was there, how shameful and abhorrent they could appear to be while also being associated with tremendous pleasure that could not be obtained elsewhere in his life. Although the compulsive-addictive nature of his difficulties has been emphasized it should be noted that he suffered from severe inhibitions as well. Thus, for example, he could not allow himself to cry and more generally experience an inhibition of acting naturally or himself in social situations.

The final case also includes elements of both inhibition and compulsion, both avoidance and addiction. In terms of the former, this young woman often found herself procrastinating and unable to complete tasks that she wanted to do. For example, she would not clean the house, write letters, or file health insurance claim forms despite the negative consequences such inaction had for her. I am reminded here of a patient with similar difficulties who only had to return a malfunctioning article to get a refund on his expensive purchase but found himself unable to get himself to do it. Here too this person would experience tremendous anxiety about *not* taking care of things, berate herself for being so irresponsible, yet let weeks elapse before completing the task— if it was completed at all.

On the other side of the coin, she was bulimic and found herself compelled to eat fattening foods that also were destructive to her health. Gaining weight and eating certain foods were problematic for her heart condition yet this was not enough to dissuade her from eating them, not unlike the smoker who cannot quit smoking despite the destructive impact upon the lungs and heart. Vomiting then was a way of undoing all of the destructive consequences of eating and there was the usual cycle of commitments to dieting, violation of the commitment through binging, followed by remorse and vomiting, to be followed by binging and the repeat of the cycle. Again, the point here is to illustrate the general phenomena rather than to present the case in sufficient detail to understand the particular factors involved. In relation to this, once more it is important to emphasize the depth of struggle involved for the individual, a struggle which at times becomes paralyzing and certainly threatens the possibility of any real gratification. As noted, this case is of particular interest because there is evidence of both inhibition and addiction; in fact, this interplay touches upon another strong component of her life—the need to always be on the edge of existence. When things were going poorly she would mobilize herself to get back on an even keel, yet when things were going well she became uncomfortable and did something to create difficulties and tension. In a certain sense the ability to keep these two forces in a delicate balance called for tremendous self-regulation, yet at the same time it had a driven quality to it.

The above cases may seem extreme in their disruptive impact but the essence of them is no different than what the vast majority of people report in relation to one or another part of their existence—the experience of some force that either prevents them from doing what they want and intend to do or compels them to do what they do not want or intend to do. The phenomenology of the latter is particularly striking as given in some recent analyses of "urges" and "craving":

> Any young clinician who attempts to do both applied and research work with substance abusers will probably notice a curious anomaly. Although researchers pay very little attention to urges, they are a chief topic when addicts discuss their addiction. In fact, urges might be viewed as the principal phenomenological manifestation of addiction, and some theorists have viewed them as a sine qua non (Baker, Morse, & Sherman, 1987, p. 257). A fundamental issue that needs to be addressed about alcoholism is why otherwise reasonably intelligent and competent men and women should find it so difficult to resist the temptation to drink and, once they have surrendered to it, should be unable to stop consuming alcohol before reaching the state of intoxication or stupor. What is this seemingly irresistible urge which eventually gives way to an unquenchable thirst, even in individuals who struggle to remain sober? (Ludwig, 1988, p. 33)

Although these accounts relate to the problems of drug and alcohol addiction, the phenomenology is no different than that found in other addictions (e.g., gambling, smoking, sex, eating). In all cases a strictly physiological explanation can be rejected as not fitting the data. And, in all cases there appears to be a powerful struggle between urges or cravings seeking expression and inhibiting forces seeking to retain control, with action reflecting the outcome of the struggle between these opposing forces, much as James (1892) described the issue in terms of the relative balance in strength between competing ideas and impulses to action. Whether or not we like such terms as urges, craving, desires, and forces, the phenomena are there to be accounted for. And, in terms of theoretical interest in the question of self-regulation, these phenomena present serious challenges to any theory of self-regulation. In sum, any theory of self-regulation must include an analysis of problems in volition, including cases of inhibition and addiction such as those described above.

Purposive Behavior and a Theory of Goals

Having considered phenomena illustrative of blockages of will and preparatory to theoretical consideration of the problem, I would like to present, in summary form, a theory of goals that has provided the basis for my thinking over the past decade. In its emphasis on purposive behavior and the goal concept it is similar to other past and current views (Carver & Scheier, 1982; Klinger, 1977; Pervin, 1989; Scheier & Carver, 1988). At the same time, it contains a number of distinctive elements, some of which are directly tied to consideration of the problem of disturbances in volition.

The framework to be presented evolved from efforts to consider the ways in which people remain stable and vary across life situations (Pervin, 1976). For one week a number of students and I logged our behavior in terms of the situations we encountered. The resultant data impressed on me the observation that within the great diversity of situations encountered and behaviors expressed, there seemed to be pattern, organization, and direction. People do not get bumped from situation to situation, nor do they follow a simple path. There is, however, a process or flow to behavior and the following six principles were suggested in an effort to capture the dynamic processes observed as people live their daily lives in the natural environment (Pervin, 1984):

1.   The patterned, organized quality of behavior suggests that it is directed toward end-points or goals; that is, behavior is motivated and the concept of goals is suggested as a useful motivational concept.

2.   Goals, and their implementation through plans, include cognitive, affective, and behavioral components. The primary motivational component, as emphasized by Tomkins (1970) and others, is affective. However, cognition is important in terms of the mental representation of goals and plans for achieving goals, and behavior is important in terms of the enactment of plans. In addition, cognition is important in terms of self-efficacy judgments concerning one's ability to preform tasks necessary for goal achievement (Bandura, 1986) as well as in cost-benefit computations of alternative outcomes. It should be clear, however, that such cognitions and cognitive processes need not be conscious; that is, one may not be aware of some goals or of the judgment processes associated with action decisions.

3.   A person's goals are organized in a hierarchical structure which at the same time provides room for fluid, dynamic functioning. In other words, while

people retain an overall goal structure, providing for stability in system functioning, goals can move higher and lower in the hierarchy, becoming temporarily superordinate or subordinate, thereby providing for flexibility in system functioning and adaptation to varying internal and external demands. As a system, goals can be integrated or in conflict with one another.

4. Goal system functioning involves multiple causes within a dynamic system. Goals are stored and may be activated by internal or external stimuli. Selection among goals is made in terms of their place in the hierarchy and the potential for realization. Long-term behavior is maintained through the serial organization of goals and by self-reinforcement in terms of affects such as pride. Specific goal-directed activities are terminated when the goal is achieved to a satisfactory extent, when achievement seems impossible, or through disruption of system functioning. Such system concepts as multidetermination, equipotentiality, and equifinality are seen as particularly applicable to goal systems; that is, complex behavior is seen as involving multiple goals that may be integrated or in conflict with one another (multidetermination), the same goal may lead to many different end-points (equipotentiality), and the same end-point may be expressive of different goals (equifinality).

5. Goals are acquired primarily on the basis of the association of affect with people, objects, events, symbols, and behavior. Development involves increased elaboration of the goal system in terms of greater diversity and interconnectedness among goals and plans, as well as increased development of self-regulatory capacities. In terms of development, behavior that is part of a plan may become so associated with affect that it itself becomes a goal; that is, Allport's (1961) concept of functional autonomy makes sense within the context of the present framework.

6. Psychopathology can be understood in terms of the absence of goals, goal conflict (e.g., conflicts between wishes and fears), or problems in goal implementation; that is, disturbances can appear in the cognitive, affective, or behavioral components of goal systems or in the relations among the parts of the system. The essence of therapy is the reorganization of the goal system, in particular the affective nature of specific goals (i.e., wishes and fears and the conflicted relationships among specific goals).

The essence of the above is a dynamic, purposive system in which parts are in constant interaction with one another and action reflects the functioning of the system as a whole rather than any single element. Another important component is the emphasis on affect as a major feature of goals and goal system functioning. In contrast with other points of view, affects are seen as inherent in goals and the representation of goals rather than just in the process of approaching goals (Bandura, 1989; Carver & Scheier, 1990). It is these elements which are seen as critical to our effort to understand problems in self-regulation, to which we now turn.

FRAMEWORK FOR A THEORY OF ACTION AND PROBLEMS IN VOLITION

Self-regulation, as well as problems in volition, are merely aspects of the more general problem of action and thus should be considered in the context of a theory of action (Frese & Sabini, 1985; Halisch & Kuhl, 1986; Kuhl & Beckmann, 1985; Miller, Galanter, & Pribram, 1960; Scheier & Carver, 1988). For our purposes here we will consider steps in the process of action and blockages of action. However, it is not suggested that all steps in the process are considered in all action or that action reflects a rational decision-making process.

The first step in the action process is the activation of a goal, either by an external or an internal stimulus. When food is place in front of my dog a goal is activated by external stimuli. However, as the time of her regular feeding approaches, she demonstrates clear behavior suggestive of internal stimuli having been activated. There is evidence that such stimuli can be activated without reaching consciousness (Libet, 1985, 1987). At this point, activation of the goal can lead directly to behavior, as in a habit or automatized act, or to inaction because of a fault in the system or blockage of the action path. Behavior is purposive in this case because it is goal-directed. Such behavior can range from the simple to the complex and includes the action of robots and most animals (e.g., bees, ants), as well as most of the action of infants and some of the action of adults (Gallistel, 1980). Feedback control systems are used to keep the organism or machine on its predetermined path (Powers, 1973). A fault in the system can be due to a structural problem, as in a problem in the action apparatus, or to overwhelming of the action system by a competing response-action, as in the case of a rat that freezes out of fear and thus cannot proceed toward the goal box.

It is important to emphasize that at this point it is considered appropriate to refer to such behavior-action as purposive and goal-directed but not as intentional or volitional. The status of the concept of intention has concerned philosophers for centuries and there are those who argue for the utility of considering all action as being at one or another level or intention (Dennett, 1988; Irwin, 1971; Lewis, in press). However, the view represented here is that intention involves selection among goals and/or plans as opposed to a fixed action pattern directed toward some goal.

Following the process along, activation of a goal may then lead to deliberation among goals and plans. Within the proposed framework, intentionality is a part of this phase of the process though consciousness may or may not be characteristic of the phase. At the intentional phase of the action process we are concerned with selection among goals and strategies or plans for achieving goals. As emphasized in the earlier theory of goals, the system is viewed as being organized in a hierarchical fashion such that some goals are more superordinate and important than others. Thus the organism must decide which of the activated goals are more or less important *under the current circumstances*. In addition, estimates are made of the probability of achieving the goal through various routes, these estimates in part reflect self-efficacy judgments (Bandura, 1986, 1989). In many ways at this point we have an expectancy-value model of action (Ajzen, 1985; Atkinson, 1981; Feather, 1982; Rotter, 1954; Vroom, 1964). However, the model goes beyond most expectancy-value models in emphasizing the interplay among goals and plans as opposed to the operation of a single goal or plan, or, in other words, the principle of multidetermination. Emphasis also is placed on the serial organization of goals so that a time frame is given to the decision-making process.

As I have indicated, goals are affective in nature and in the broadest terms consist of things to be obtained (wishes) and things to avoided (fears). These wishes and fears are expressive of perceptions of the inner world and the outer world; that is, the person considers what is desired and feared internally as well as externally. For example, the human organism considers what is wanted and how to go about getting it in relation to internal standards concerning right and wrong (Higgins, 1987, 1990; Mischel, 1973, 1983). Such standards are of great importance in the self-regulatory process: "The essence of self-regulatory systems is the subject's adoption of contingency rules that guide behavior in the absence of, and sometimes in spite of, immediate external situational pressures" (Mischel, 1973, p. 274). These standards themselves are goals and affective in nature, consisting of such feelings as pride for meeting the standards and guilt or shame for violating them. In addition, there is the perception of the surrounding norms and standards and consideration of the rewards and punishments associated with meeting or violating these standards. Strategies and decisions concerning action also involve perception of the goals and intentions of others (Heider, 1958; Read & Miller, 1989; Trzebinski, 1989; Wyer & Srull, 1986). Thus, there is good evidence that social interaction involves the perception of others in terms of their goals and the processing of information in terms of goal categories and action scenarios.

With the many possible goals and plans entering into any complex decision, there is room for integrative action as well as conflict. In the former case, a single action may lead to the attainment of multiple goals, in the latter case there is the potential for conflict (Dollard & Miller, 1950; Emmons, 1989; Lewin, 1951; Luria, 1932). The issue of conflict has been neglected in many current views, in particular social cognitive views, reflecting in part the lack of a system emphasis. Yet, potential conflict is an important part of goal system functioning and plays an important role in how situations are experienced (Pervin, 1984). Illustrative goal conflicts would be Express Anger or Annoyance versus Avoid Conflict, Relax and Enjoy Self versus Do What Should Do, Assert Self versus Gain Approval, and Strive For Intimacy versus Avoid Risks of Intimacy.

It is clear that within this model there is considerable room for individual differences in goals, plans, mechanisms of delay, goal conflicts, and ways of handling goal conflicts. Thus, for example, Dweck (1986) demonstrates the importance of distinguishing between learning and performance goals, Cantor and Langston (1989) discuss the various strategies individuals use to accomplish life tasks, Lazarus and Folkman, (1984) describe various coping strategies, and Funder and Block (1989) emphasize the traits of ego-control and ego-resiliency.

At this point in the action process a decision is made to go or not to go, the latter involving a decision to delay or to disengage from goal-directed action (Scheier & Carver, 1988). It is here that we meet up with the issue of will or *volition*—the translation of an action decision into action or the translation of a delay or disengagement decision into inaction or substitute action. If the system is functioning well a decision for action leads to specific efforts toward goal attainment. Presumably a command, control decision is made and attention is directed toward the relevant goal and plans-strategies. Goal-directed action then continues until the goal has been achieved, satisfactory progress has been made, or the person becomes impatient or discouraged (Simon, 1967). On the other hand, action can be blocked by a command, control decision to delay or inhibit action (Libet, 1985, 1987; Powers, 1973). Presumably disengagement and delay are facilitated by the activation of inhibiting and competing goals-plans. The invocation of standards-norms and the direction of attention toward alternative goals and plans would be illustrative mechanisms.

In terms of the question of self-regulation, the emphasis has been on goals, including internal and external standards, the affects (pride, shame, guilt, fear) associated with the representation of these goals, and the direction of attention toward relevant goals and plans. When we ask the question of what allows the person to stay on course toward a goal over an extended period of time we answer it in terms of concepts such as serialization of goals, self-reward and rewards from others for staying on course, and the ability to maintain representation of the desired end-point over extended periods of time (Bandura, 1986). The mental representation of the goal and associated affect provide the incentive for remaining on course. In addition, positive expectancies of success and ongoing internal and external rewards for meeting standards-norms provide the mechanism for staying on course.

Alternatively, when we ask the question of what allows the person to delay action or disengage from the goal-directed action we answer it in terms of concepts such as inhibitory responses and the direction of attention to alternative competing goals. Inhibitory responses may be produced and maintained because of negative affect associated with the pursuit of the goal (i.e., anxiety, guilt) and positive affect associated with the delay process and the following of internal and external norms for delay (i.e., pride, relief from anxiety or guilt). In addition, there may be positive expectancies concerning future goal attainment after a period of delay as well as positive affect associated with substitute goals pursued during the period of delay or following disengagement. The delay of gratification literature, whether conceived in trait or social cognitive terms, is relevant to this aspect of the action process (Funder & Block, 1989; Mischel, 1990).

It is important to note here that just as the theory of goals emphasizes affective, cognitive, and behavioral components, so too is this true of our consideration of self-regulatory processes. Self-regulation involves cognitive and behavioral skills in relation to the maintenance of goal-directed activity as well as the activation of delay-disengagement activity. However, it is the associated affect that is seen as crucial to the entire motivational process, including self-regulation. When we speak of standards and self-evaluative processes we are emphasizing concepts that are affective in nature.

It is time now to turn our attention toward the breakdown of volition and to address the questions of why it is that a person should not be able to implement a decision to pursue a goal and why it is that a person may be unable to delay pursuit of a goal or be unable to disengage from a goal—the problems of inhibition (obstructed will) and compulsion-addiction (explosive will). To return to our case examples, why is it that a person cannot be on time or turn things in on time, that a person cannot stay involved in goal-directed activity such as working on a paper, or initiate goal-directed activity such as asking a woman out or turning in a medical claim form, or that a person feels compelled to engage in abhorrent or self-destructive activities? It would seem clear that the problem is not merely one of skill since in many cases these same people are quite competent at maintaining extended goal-directed activity and at inhibition, delay, and disengagement. Rather, it would appear to be necessary to focus on the affective struggle that goes on in the breakdown of volition. This emphasis on affective processes is part of what distinguishes this conceptualization from trait and social cognitive models.

An explanation for certain cases of inhibition would appear to be reasonably straightforward. In these cases, inhibition is activated by fear and the goal of relief from fear. In the patient who delays and avoids asking women out it is the fear of rejection and humiliation that looms large and the goal of avoidance of these blows to his self-esteem that governs action. We must keep in mind, however, that this is not a rational process that we are considering. If you ask him about the probabilities of success versus failure and the values of success versus failure, he will tell you that the odds clearly come out in favor of asking women out. Yet, often he finds himself unable to do so and this is partly because his experiences of success have not altered his self-efficacy judgments and outcome expectancies. Thus, an important question in this regard is why some individuals can retain poor self-efficacy representations and remain low in self-confidence despite records of success and accomplishment (Bandura & Dweck, 1985). In addition to unrealistic self-efficacy judgments and outcome expectancies, there is the problem of the value of the alternative outcomes. In fact, even if rejection or humiliation is unlikely, the potential emotional cost is experienced as enormous. When he thinks back to times of past rejection and humiliation he recalls the experiences as being so devastating that exposure to further risk hardly seems worthwhile. It is not his rational assessment that is driving the inhibition but rather the conditioned affective response associated with earlier traumas. In sum, the inhibitory forces, primarily fear, outweigh the impulsive or expressive forces.

But what of the inhibition of work, being on time, and turning in a medical claim form? Here we may again consider the involvement of fear as well as another competing goal. In terms of the inhibition of work, there is the fear that performance will be below expectations or standards. At times this is sufficient to result in inhibition until the greater fear of failure overrides this and the person completes the work. In this case fear operates as a motivating force rather than an inhibitory one. At other times failure due to not turning in the paper is considered a better alternative than failure due to turning in a poor paper. In addition, other goals may enter in, such as that of defying authority or preserving autonomy. In this case, the behavior of turning in the paper does not occur both because of an inhibitory force (fear of failure) as well as an expressive force (defiance of authority, preservation of autonomy). In this latter case, it has at least some of the properties of an expressive, active act, as well as those of an inhibitory behavior. In sum, the same behavior can be the outcome of competing forces or expressive of multiple forces, both inhibitory and expressive. People do things to avoid losses and create gains at the same time. In the case of the medical claim form there may be the low self-efficacy expectations concerning filling out the forms correctly, a generalized expectancy of little success in dealing with bureaucracies, and a wish (demand) that effort should not be necessary to receive what one is due.

In each of these cases, then, inhibition is due, in total or in part, to the presence of a competing, stronger goal, often one associated with fear or anxiety, and often with low self-efficacy judgments concerning the potential for achieving the intended goal. In addition to the inhibitory power of anxiety, blockage of a behavior may be due to interference from a competing, stronger response which itself represents an expressive force (e.g., rather go out and play than write a paper). In such a case, however, it seems unlikely that the person will experience the turmoil and struggle that generally is associated with the inhibition of volition. Finally, it has been suggested that what appears to be blockage due exclusively to inhibition may also be due to an expressive component to the behavior (e.g., not turning in a paper due to fear of failure and expression of defiance). This latter case represents an illustration of what in psychoanalytic terms has been described as the overdetermination or multidetermination of behavior.

Finally, let us consider two other factors. First is the possibility that the intended goal does not have the value it is presumed to have. This would not seem to provide an acceptable explanation for many of these cases since often there is evidence of considerable effort and struggle. Second is the possibility of depression due to generalized negative expectancies and beliefs (Beck, 1976; Peterson & Seligman, 1984; Weiner, 1985). This would not appear to be an acceptable explanation because these individuals do not appear to be generally depressed and are capable of considerable effort in other areas.

In sum, if goal-directed activity is contingent upon positive affect associated with the mental representation of the goal as well as positive outcome expectancies and self-efficacy judgments, then inhibition may be explained in terms of negative outcome expectancies and self-efficacy judgments as well as the presence of competing goals that interfere with voluntary action in the pursuit of the intended goal. It is, then, often a case of competing goals and conflict, in particular a case of approach-avoidance conflict where the fear response and avoidance goal predominates (Dollard & Miller, 1950).

But what then of the addictions? Why is it that the person cannot delay or disengage despite the negative affect, often including anxiety, associated with pursuit of the goal? Is it that the urge is so great or the inhibition so weak? It is this case of the breakdown of volition that is even more puzzling than that of inhibition since it would appear to contain many of the elements that ordinarily would lead to inhibition—negative affect (anxiety, shame) associated with the outcome.

My sense is that we must take the phenomenological reports seriously and seek to understand the compelling power of urges and cravings. Two elements appear to be key here, the first involving the flight from negative affect and the second the pursuit of a goal charged with enormous positive affect (Baker et. al., 1987; Ludwig, 1988). In most, though not all, cases of action upon a forbidden urge or desire there is a state of negative affect preceding the action. Thus, for example, the patient who felt compelled to see pornographic movies or visit a prostitute often experienced these urges when feeling distressed by anxiety or depression. These activities then were seen as a relief from the negative affective states of anxiety and depression. On the other hand, this was not always the case and clinical reports suggest that often such activities are preceded by a state of positive affect. For example, if this patient engages in some off-color, titillating conversation he will be tempted to pursue the forbidden goal.

Thus, the flight from negative affect alone does not appear to be a satisfactory explanation for this breakdown in volition and we must consider the power of the addiction in terms of the positive affect associated with it—the power of the craving or urge which dominates the attention of the person and compels action. In all cases that I have seen of this sort, at the point of breakdown in volition or enactment of the addiction the person reports a heightened state of arousal associated with some tension and considerable pleasurable affect— either actual at the time or anticipated in terms of the mental representation of the goal. I believe that this is for two reasons. First, the goal itself is associated with powerful positive affect—the high of the drug, the warmth of the alcohol, the fullness associated with eating, the orgasm associated with the pornographic movie or prostitute. This does not mean that the action will in all cases lead to that affective experience or that the person even expects it to, but rather that the experience is possible and that is enough. Thus, the addict does not necessarily expect to get high each time a drug is used but it is enough to imagine the high that once was experienced and to wish for it to occur again. As Ludwig (1988) and others note, this is why punishment programs generally do not work. The person may associate specific actions with negative affect but retain the image of the positive affect associated with the goal.

In addition to the powerful positive affect associated with the goal there is, I believe, a heightening of arousal due to the tension associated with the forbidden activity. As one person put it: "It's more fun eating the cookie stolen from the cookie jar than the one given to you." Obviously this is not always the case and for many people the negative affect (anxiety, guilt) associated with the theft would interfere with the pleasure. However, in some cases the tension serves to heighten the pleasurable arousal associated with the forbidden goal, and perhaps is joined by some pleasure in violating a norm as well.[1]

To return to the model of self-regulation, delay and disengagement are assumed to occur when inhibitory responses are invoked, where internal and external rewards for such activity are present, and where substitute goals are available. In the case of addictions, internal and external rewards for delay or disengagement are available but efforts to invoke inhibitory responses ("Don't drink," "Don't eat.") generally are unsuccessful and substitute goals, at least of the magnitude of the forbidden goal, are not experienced as available. Overriding the efforts at delay and disengagement are the expectancies of escape from negative affect and, even more importantly, the expectancies of the positive affect experienced as necessary and only possible in association with the forbidden goal. In particularly strong addictions the goals of escape from negative affect and the desire for positive affect come together in the form of a substance or act that will accomplish both; that is, the negative affect (e.g., guilt, shame) associated with the forbidden substance or behavior itself contributes to the power of the addiction.

In sum, it is suggested that both problems of inhibition and problems of addiction be understood in terms of competing goals, with the breakdown in volition primarily being due to the affective power of goals competing with the intended goal. Though not suggesting that skills are unimportant, the emphasis is placed on the affective nature of goals and motivational processes. All complex behavior is seen as involving multiple goals, with some promoting approach action (wishes) and others promoting avoidance or inhibitory action (fears). The process of action involves the interplay among the affective, cognitive, and behavioral components of these goals, with the final result expressing the integration of many goals into one action, a compromise among competing goals, inaction due to competing goals, or the dominance of some goals over others.

SUMMARY AND CONCLUSION

Self-regulatory processes are part of the more general question of motivation and should be understood in the context of a more general theory of action. The framework for a theory of goals has been presented with an emphasis on the affective properties of goals. An effort has been made to consider self-regulatory processes as part of goal-directed, purposive behavior and as particularly important in relation to volitional behavior. Attention has focused on problems of volition—problems of inhibition (obstruction of will) and problems of addiction (explosion of will). The question asked was why are we sometimes unable to follow an intended course of action and sometimes compelled to pursue an unintended course of action. It has been suggested that all complex action involves the interplay among goals which may be integrated with one another or in conflict with one another. Breakdowns in volition are seen as involving cases of conflicting goals with strong affective associations that override efforts at cognitive and behavioral control. Understanding volitional behavior, including self-regulatory processes, represents a considerable challenge to us. Even greater is the challenge of understanding breakdowns in volition and self-regulation. Yet, it is such understanding that is key to our efforts to come to grips with the human psychological problems that give us the greatest difficulty.

NOTE

1.   Since completion of the original version of this paper, a cognitive model of drug use behavior has been presented which emphasizes automatized action schemata relative to affects associated with urges (Tiffany, 1990).

REFERENCES

Ajzen, I. (1985). From intentions to actions: A theory of planned behavior. In J. Kuhl & J. Beckman (Eds.), *Action-control: From cognition to behavior* (pp.11-39). Heidelberg: Springer.

Allport, G.W. (1961). *Pattern and growth in personality.* New York: Holt, Rinehart, & Winston.

Atkinson, J.W. (1981). Studying personality in the context of an advanced motivational psychology. *American Psychologist, 36,* 117-128.

Baker, T., Morse, E., & Sherman, J.E. (1987). The motivation to use drugs: A psychobiological analysis of drugs. *Nebraska Symposium on Motivation, 34,* 257-323.

Bandura, A. (1986). *Social foundations of thought and action.* Englewood Cliffs, NJ: Prentice Hall.

————. (1989). Self-regulation of motivation and action through internal standards and goal systems. In L.A. Pervin (Ed.), *Goal concepts in personality and social psychology* (pp.19-85). Hillsdale, NJ: Erlbaum.

Bandura, M., & Dweck, C.S. (1985). *Self-conceptions and motivation: Conceptions of intelligence, choice of achievement goals, and patterns of cognition, affect, behavior.* Manuscript submitted for publication.

Beck, A.T. (1976). *Cognitive therapy and the emotional disorders.* New York: International Universities Press.

Block, J.H. & Block, J. (1980). The role of ego-control and ego-resiliency in the organization of behavior. *Minnesota Symposia on Child Psychology, 13,* 39-101.

Boden, M.A. (1972). *Purposive explanation in psychology.* Cambridge, MA: Harvard University Press.

Brody, N. (1983). *Human motivation: Commentary on goal-directed action.* New York: Academic.

Cantor, N., & Langston, C.A. (1989). Ups and down of life tasks in a life transition. In L.A. Pervin (Ed.), *Goal concepts in personality and social psychology* (pp.127-167). Hillsdale, NJ: Erblaum.

Cantor, N., & Zirkel, S. (1990). Personality, cognition, and purposive behavior. In L.A. Pervin (Ed.), *Handbook of personality: Theory and research* (pp. 135-164). New York: Guilford.

Carver, C.S., & Scheier, M.F. (1982). Control theory: A useful conceptual framework in personality-social, clinical and health psychology. *Psychological Bulletin, 92,* 111-135.

————. (1990). Origins and functions of positive and negative affect: A control-process view. *Psychological Review, 97,* 19-35.

Dennett, D.C. (1988). The intentional stance. *Behavioral and brain sciences, 11,* 495-546.

Dollard, J., & Miller, N.E. (1950). *Personality and psychotherapy.* New York: McGraw-Hill.

Dweck, C.S. (1986). Motivational processes affecting learning. *American Psychologist, 35,* 867-881.

Eacker, J.N. (1975). *Problems of philosophy and psychology.* Chicago: Nelson-Hall.

Emmons, R.A. (1989). The personal striving approach to personality. In L.A. Pervin (Ed.), *Goal concepts in personality and social psychology* (pp. 87-126). Hillsdale, NJ: Erblaum.

Feather, N.T. (1982). *Expectations and actions: Expectancy-value models in psychology.* Hillsdale, NJ: Erlbaum.

Frese, M., & Sabini, J. (Eds.). (1985). *Goal directed behavior: The concept of action in psychology.* Hillsdale, NJ: Erlbaum.

Funder, D.C., & Block, J. (1989). The role of ego-control, ego resiliency and IQ in delay of gratification adolescence. *Journal of Personality and Social Psychology, 57,* 1041-1050.

Gallistel, C.R. (1980). *The organization of action: A new synthesis.* Hillsdale, NJ: Erblaum.

Guthrie, E.R. (1935). *The psychology of learning.* New York: Harper.

Halisch, F., & Kuhl, J. (Eds.). (1986). *Motivation, intention, and volition.* New York: Springer-Verlag.

Heider, F. (1958). *The psychology of interpersonal relations.* New York: Wiley.

Higgins, E.T. (1987). Self-discrepancy: A theory relating self and affect. *Psychological Review, 94*, 319-340.

———. (1990). Personality, social psychology, and person-situation relations: Standards and knowledge activation as a common language. In L.A. Pervin (Ed.), *Handbook of personality: Theory and research* (pp. 301-338). New York: Guilford.

Irwin, F.W. (1971). *Intentional behavior and motivation: A cognitive theory.* Philadelphia: Lippincott.

James, W. (1892). *Psychology: A briefer course.* New York: Holt.

Kimble, G.A., & Perlmutter, L.C. (1970). The problem of volition. *Psychological Review, 77*, 361-384.

Klinger, E. (1977). *Meaning and void: Inner experience and the incentives in people's lives.* Minneapolis: University of Minnesota Press.

Kuhl, J., & Beckman, J. (Eds.). (1985). *Action control: From cognition to behavior.* Berlin: Springer-Verlag.

Lazarus, R.S., & Folkman, S. (1984). *Stress, appraisal, and coping.* New York: Springer.

Lewin, K. (1951). Intention, will, and need. In D. Rapaport (Ed.), *Organization and pathology of thought.* New York: Columbia University Press.

Lewis, M. (In press). The development of intentionality and the role of consciousness. *Psychological Inquiry.*

Libet, B. (1985). Unconscious cerebral initiative and the role of conscious will in voluntary action. *Behavioral and Brain Sciences, 8*, 529-566.

———. (1987). Awareness of wanting to move and of moving. *Behavioral and Brain Sciences, 10*, 320.

Ludwig, A.M. (1988). *Understanding the alcoholic's mind: The nature of craving and how to control it.* New York: Oxford University Press.

Luria, A.R. (1932). *The nature of human conflicts: On emotion, conflict, and will.* New York: Liveright.

McMahon, C.E. (1973). Images as motives and motivations: A historical perspective. *American Journal of Psychology, 86*, 465-490.

Miller, G.A., Galanter, E., & Pribram, K. (1960). *Plans and the structure of behavior.* New York: Holt.

Mischel, W. (1973). Toward a cognitive social learning reconceptualization of personality. *Psychological Review, 80*, 985-1010.

———. (1983). Delay of gratification as process and as person variable in development. In D. Magnusson & V.L. Allen (Eds.), *Human development: An interactional perspective* (pp. 149-165). New York: Academic.

———. (1990). Personality dispositions revised and revisited: A view after three decades. In L.A. Pervin (Ed.), *Handbook of personality: Theory and research* (pp. 111-134). New York: Guilford.

Pervin, L.A. (1976). A free-response description approach to the analysis of person-situation interaction. *Journal of Personality and Social Psychology, 34*, 465-474.

———. (1984). The stasis and flow of behavior: Toward theory of goals. In M. Page (Ed.), *Personality: Current theory and research* (pp. 1-53). Lincoln: University of Nebraska Press.

———. (Ed.). (1989). *Goal concepts in personality and social psychology.* Hillsdale, NJ: Erlbaum.

Peterson, C., & Seligman, M.E.P. (1984). Causal explanation as a risk factor for depression: Theory and evidence. *Psychological Review, 91*, 347-374.

Powers, W.T. (1973). *Behavior: The control of perception.* Chicago: Aldine.

Pruyser, P.W. (1967). Problem of will and willing. In J. Lapsley (Ed.), *The concept of willing.* New York: Abingdon.

Read, S.J., & Miller, L.C. (1989). Inter-personalism: Toward a goal-based theory of persons in relationships. In L.A. Pervin (Ed.), *Goal concepts in personality and social psychology* (pp. 413-472). Hillsdale, NJ: Erlbaum.

Rotter, J.B. (1954). *Social learning and clinical psychology.* Englewood Cliffs, NJ: Prentice Hall.

Scheier, M.F., & Carver, C.S. (1988). A model of behavioral self-regulation: Translating intention into action. In L. Berkowitz (Ed.), *Advances in experimental social psychology* (pp.303-346). New York: Academic.

Shapiro, D. (1981). *Autonomy and rigid character.* New York: Basic Books.

Simon, H.A. (1967). Motivational and emotional controls of cognition. *Psychological Review, 74,* 29-39.

Tiffany, S.T. (1990). A cognitive model of drug urges and drug-use behavior: Role of automatic and nonautomatic processes. *Psychological Review, 97,* 147-168.

Tolman, E.C. (1925). Purpose and cognition: The determiners of animal learning. *Psychological Review, 32,* 285-297.

_____. (1932). *Purposive behavior in animals and men.* Berkeley: University of California Press.

Tomkins, S.S. (1970). Affects are the primary motivational system. In M.B. Arnold (Ed.), *Feelings and emotions: The Loyola symposium.* New York: Academic.

Trzebinski, J. (1989). The role of goal categories in the representation of social knowledge. In L.A. Pervin (Ed.), *Goal concepts in personality and social psychology* (pp. 363-411). Hillsdale, NJ: Erlbaum.

Vroom, V. (1964). *Work and motivation.* New York: Wiley.

Weiner, B. (1985). An attributional theory of achievement motivation and emotion. *Psychological Review, 92,* 548-573.

Westcott, M.R. (1985). Volition is a nag. In F.R. Brush & J.B. Overmier (Eds.), *Affect, conditioning, and cognition: Essays on the determinants of behavior* (pp. 353-367). Hillsdale, NJ: Erlbaum.

Wyer, R.S., Jr., & Srull, T.K. (1986). Human cognition in its social context. *Psychological Review, 93,* 322-359.

GOALS AND INTRINSIC MOTIVATION:

YOU *CAN* GET THERE FROM HERE

Judith M. Harackiewicz and Carol Sansone

People generally begin an activity with some idea about what they are trying to do or accomplish. A person may start a game of pinball planning to show off for his or her friends, to practice for the next pinball competition, to improve skills, or to kill time. Within the context of these general goals that characterize the "purpose" of task engagement, players may pursue more specific goals or "targets." For example, they might try to achieve a particular score on the machine, outperform their friends, improve over their last game, or simply try to keep the ball in play for as long as possible. Target goals guide an individual's behavior, and purpose goals suggest the reasons for the behavior. Both kinds of goals may influence how a person approaches and experiences an activity, how well they perform, and how much they enjoy the activity. Our primary interest is in the effects of these goals on a person's continuing interest in an activity. In particular, we are interested in the effects of externally provided goals on intrinsic motivation.

Advances in Motivation and Achievement, Volume 7, pages 21-49.
Copyright © 1991 by JAI Press Inc.
All rights of reproduction in any form reserved.
ISBN: 1-55938-122-1

Intrinsically motivated activities are interesting and enjoyable activities that we engage in for their own sake, rather than as a means to an end (Lepper, 1981; Lepper, Greene, & Nisbett, 1973). According to many theories of intrinsic motivation, interest in an activity is derived from the opportunity it provides to effectively control or master the environment (deCharms, 1968; Deci, 1975; Harter, 1981; White, 1959). Thus, feelings of efficacy and autonomy are proposed to enhance intrinsic interest, making us more likely to engage in an activity again in the future (Bandura, 1986, Deci & Ryan, 1985).

Of course, activities differ in the level of challenge they afford. Those that offer optimal challenges have the greatest potential to promote involvement and intrinsic interest, because it is in those situations that pleasure in mastering the environment is maximized (Csikszentmihalyi, 1975; Deci & Ryan, 1985; Locke & Latham, 1990; Malone, 1981; Pittman & Heller, 1987; White, 1959). Optimal challenge is often defined as the point where task demands are just within the upper limits of an individual's ability to satisfy them (Csikszentmihalyi, 1990; Harter, 1981; White, 1959). Task demands can therefore be considered the specific goals for performance implicit in an activity. For example, the game of pinball involves several clear goals: the object of the game is to hit as many targets as possible, accumulate points, and keep the ball in play as long as possible. When these goals are attained, an individual should experience a sense of task mastery, which should in turn promote subsequent interest in the task.

On one level, then, goals can be thought of as task-specific guidelines for performance. They are performance standards to aim for, and they motivate and guide ongoing task performance. They also facilitate self-generated feedback, allowing individuals to assess whether they have successfully mastered an activity, and thereby experience a sense of competence and autonomy (Bandura, 1986; Carver & Scheier, 1981; Locke & Latham, 1990). We refer to these task-specific guidelines for performance as target goals.

On another level, however, goals can be thought of as the more general purpose that an individual has when engaging in a particular activity. Target goals can guide individuals toward task mastery, but they may also facilitate the attainment of higher order purpose goals that are not necessarily task-specific (cf. Vallacher & Wegner, 1987). For example, successfully meeting a specific target goal of scoring 1500 points on the next ball can provide immediate satisfaction, but it can also contribute to meeting the more general goal of being a "pinball wizard," or being competent. In fact, one type of purpose goal that people often consciously pursue, especially in achievement situations, is to develop, attain or demonstrate competence at an activity (Dweck, 1986; Nicholls, 1984; White, 1959). We refer to this class of purpose goals as competence purpose goals.

Competence purpose goals may promote personal involvement and intrinsic achievement strivings, resulting in feelings of competence and accomplishment when these goals are attained (Maehr & Braskamp, 1986; White, 1959). This level of involvement can promote continuing intrinsic interest in the activity (Deci & Ryan, 1985; Harackiewicz, 1989; Spence & Helmreich, 1983), and has the potential to generalize beyond the specific activity. When purpose goals are attained, an individual experiences satisfaction, and this sense of personal accomplishment can promote intrinsic interest in an activity.

The effects of task-specific target goals may depend on the purpose goals that individuals hold in particular situations. For example, task mastery may have the strongest influence on intrinsic motivation when individuals hold the purpose goal of attaining competence. In other words, target goals that facilitate such mastery may be most effective in enhancing task interest when individuals are personally involved in the pursuit of competence. Individuals do not automatically pursue competence purpose goals, however. Even in achievement situations, where competence issues are typically highly salient, people may not always have a general competence goal uppermost in mind (Maehr & Braskamp, 1986). Because of this interdependence of target and purpose goals, it is important both to examine the determinants of purpose goals in achievement situations, and to examine how these two levels of goals may work in concert to affect intrinsic motivation.

GOAL-SETTING AND INTRINSIC MOTIVATION

The interdependence of target and purpose goals becomes particularly important when we try to set goals for other individuals. As teachers, supervisors, and parents, we often want to help students, employees, and children develop skills and improve performance on activities. Ideally, we would like to make the pursuit of competence at these activities interesting and rewarding in its own right. To this end, we often provide, suggest, or assign goals for performance. We can suggest purpose goals that prompt individuals to approach activities in particular ways or to adopt more specific target goals on their own. Alternatively, we can communicate specific performance goals that allow individuals to monitor their progress and develop skills. Thus, it should be possible to influence both target and purpose goals with external interventions. If we could socially engineer conditions that foster challenge-seeking and promote feelings of efficacy and self-determination, external goal-setting would seem to have the potential to support and enhance intrinsic motivation.

Because considerable research shows that providing individuals with specific goals reliably improves task *performance* (see Locke, Shaw, Saari, & Latham, 1981 and Locke & Latham, 1990, for review), goal-setting appears to represent an ideal strategy with which to program a series of mastery experiences for another individual. However, the effects of assigned goals on intrinsic motivation may be more complex than their effects on performance. On the one hand, the assigned goals may serve several functions that should promote interest. In particular, these goals can make competence salient and valued, work to orient people to the task at hand, help them concentrate on performance, and provide ongoing competence feedback as an individual monitors his or her progress with respect to goals (Locke & Latham, 1990).

On the other hand, some goals may represent external intrusions into an otherwise absorbing and involving activity. Whenever we try to set goals or standards for others, we risk interfering with their feelings of self-determination (deCharms, 1968; Deci & Ryan, 1985). Goals, even when self-set, may be perceived as constraints and interfere with a person's ongoing task involvement (Ryan, 1982; Shalley, Oldham, & Porac, 1987). These factors may undermine continuing intrinsic interest in an activity. And, in fact, several studies suggest that assigned performance goals can interfere with task satisfaction and interest (Kirschenbaum, Humphrey, & Malett, 1981; Manderlink & Harackiewicz, 1984; Mossholder, 1980; Shalley & Oldham, 1985; Umstot, Bell, & Mitchell, 1976; White, Mitchell, & Bell, 1977). Thus, target and purpose goals may also have negative properties with respect to intrinsic motivation.

Clearly, several processes can be initiated by externally set goals, and these processes may have conflicting implications for intrinsic motivation. Moreover, the same assigned goal may affect both what individuals do (target) and why they are doing it (purpose). It is therefore important to examine the specific processes through which both target and purpose goals have their effects.

TARGET AND PURPOSE GOALS PLACED IN A BROADER CONTEXT

Before we consider the particular effects of target and purpose goals on intrinsic motivation, it is important to place our target versus purpose goal distinction in the context of other theoretical perspectives on goals. Goals can range in a hierarchy from broad, global aims ("I want to be the best I can be, every day, in every way"), down to the specific and mundane ("I want to score 2500 points on this ball"). However defined, goals afford meaning and future perspective to human behavior (Cantor & Zirkel, 1990; Carver & Scheier, 1981; Emmons, 1986; Vallacher & Wegner, 1987). Target and purpose goals fall toward the lower end of this hierarchy of goal types. At the highest and most general level of this hierarchy, researchers have examined individuals' possible selves (Markus & Nurius, 1986) and self guides (Higgins, 1987). At a somewhat lower, or mid-level, other researchers have focused on relatively more specific goals, such as current concerns (Klinger, 1987), personal strivings (Emmons, 1986), personal projects (Little, 1989), or life tasks (Cantor, Norem, Niedenthal, Langston, & Brower, 1987), which are conceptualized as idiographic units of study for personality research. Goals at these highest and mid-levels transcend particular situations or contexts and reflect individuals' general concerns or goals at a particular period of time (Cantor & Zirkel, 1990). They can be expressed and pursued in different ways by different individuals (Cantor & Kihlstrom, 1987). Goals held at these two higher levels may also affect the relatively lower order purpose goals that an individual holds in a particular situation.

In contrast to focusing on individuals' global or long-term goals, other researchers have examined the general kinds of goals implicit in particular domains, especially achievement domains (Ames, 1984; Butler, 1987; Dweck & Leggett, 1988; Maehr & Braskamp, 1986; Nicholls, 1984). These researchers have identified the different types of goal orientations elicited in classes of situations sharing the common theme of achievement, and examined the motivational processes associated with them. For example, Nicholls (1984) distinguishes between ego and task involving situations that invoke different goals; ego-involving conditions promote a desire to demonstrate competence whereas task-involving situations invoke a desire to develop competence. Dweck and Leggett (1988) distinguish performance goals from learning goals, where performance goals involve demonstrating ability, and learning goals involve mastering something new. Ames and Archer (1988) have reviewed this literature, noting the similarities among the theoretical approaches, and characterized these different goal orientations as performance versus mastery goals (cf. Butler, 1989).

These performance and mastery goals may also be influenced by an individual's personality characteristics and general goal orientations. For example, individuals differ in the extent to which they characteristically value and pursue competence (Harter, 1981; McClelland, 1961). Moreover, recent research suggests that the type of competence goals individuals hold in achievement contexts can vary according to individual differences in goal orientation (Dweck & Leggett, 1988; Nicholls, Patashnick, & Nolen, 1985; Pintrich & DeGroot, 1990). In other words, individuals differ in the extent to which they hold general competence goals, and they can also differ in what kind of competence goals they hold.

Thus, there is growing consensus that there are two distinct types of goals (performance and mastery) that may be important in achievement situations. These goals are roughly equivalent to the purpose of task engagement in a particular situation. In other words, they reflect what the individual is trying to accomplish with his or her performance of the activity. In our model, then, both the performance and mastery goals identified by other researchers (e.g., Dweck, 1986; Nicholls, 1984) are purpose goals that operate at the same level; our distinction is between purpose goals at one level, and target goals at a lower, more specific level.

Achievement situations are often "strong" enough to suggest, prompt, or impose purpose goals. However, these goals may also vary as a function of subtle contextual factors. For example, the availability of performance feedback (Sansone, Sachau, & Weir, 1989), the presence of a video camera (Elliott & Dweck, 1988), the focus of performance evaluation (Harackiewicz, Abrahams, & Wageman, 1987), or the announcement that skill tasks are being used (Nicholls, 1984) may be enough to change a person's general goals in an achievement context. Thus, it should be possible for contextual factors to influence the purpose goals that an individual adopts in an achievement situation.

In addition to addressing purpose goals in achievement contexts, there has been considerable interest in the effects of even more specific goals on performance and motivation. For example, the large goal-setting literature emphasizes the use of clear, task-based standards for performance. These goals are often expressed in terms of work units ("Try to solve at least three problems") or specific behaviors ("Try to stuff 14 envelopes"). These goals represent "targets" for performance and seem closer to the challenge-based mastery goals discussed by intrinsic motivation theorists. One important difference between these target and purpose goals is that purpose goals tend to be relatively implicit; they can be instantiated with rather subtle cues or experimental manipulations, or they might even reflect characteristic values and goals that individuals bring into situations. Target goals, on the other hand, tend to be explicit communications with clear behavioral referents.

The lower order performance standards act as targets for performance, and are necessarily specific to the task. Thus, target goals are clearly at the lower, more specific end of the overall goal hierarchy (Cantor & Zirkel, 1990; Vallacher & Wegner, 1987). Purpose goals establish the particular situational context in which activities are performed, but these goals may also fall into the higher order categories of goals studied by other researchers. For example, outperforming peers at pinball (a situationally specific purpose goal) may satisfy the higher goal (or personal striving) of excelling in all domains of pursuit (Emmons, 1989), or may represent one component of the ideal self (Markus & Nurius, 1986). However, for the purposes of our analysis, it is helpful to consider purpose goals as operative within a specific situation. Because intrinsic motivation is typically defined in terms of an individual's interaction with a particular activity, an examination of the goal structures which operate at the levels closest to that interaction (i.e., target and purpose goals) should prove most fruitful in understanding intrinsic motivation processes.

A PROCESS MODEL OF INTRINSIC MOTIVATION

We have recently developed a theoretical model of the motivational processes that mediate the effects of evaluative contingencies on intrinsic motivation

(Harackiewicz, 1989; Harackiewicz & Sansone, 1990). This model identifies the processes through which external communications about task performance and competence affect intrinsic motivation, and it also specifies how contextual factors and individual difference variables can moderate these processes. We refer to external interventions or incentives that concern performance quality as "performance constraints." We call them constraints because the person who communicates them is typically trying to influence or direct a person's performance. For example, people usually assign goals to motivate better performance and facilitate performance feedback during task performance. In so doing, they are essentially imposing an external evaluative structure onto an individual's experience. Externally conveyed target and purpose goals may therefore function as performance constraints, and our model can account for their effects on intrinsic motivation.

Constraints are usually communicated in two stages: the external agent initiates the intervention before the individual performs a task, and then provides feedback about the adequacy of performance in relation to the constraint. For example, in the case of goal-setting, individuals are first assigned goals and then eventually learn whether they have met them. Individuals may gauge their progress while they work, and by task conclusion, they obtain clear feedback about their overall performance with respect to the goals. This feedback may be entirely self-generated or the external agent may also provide feedback about goal attainment. Researchers have tended to focus on the feedback function of goals, and their capacity to provide individuals with feelings of self-determined competence. As a result, most research attention has concentrated on this second stage, with an emphasis on factors that promote goal attainment and the resulting feelings of self-efficacy (Bandura, 1986; Locke et al., 1981).

However, we have found it important to distinguish the motivational processes invoked by the introduction of a performance constraint from those processes affected by its outcome. For example, goals can affect motivation immediately in the process of task performance by determining the initial approach to the activity, and by providing individuals with specific targets to aim for. The motivational processes associated with goal-generated feedback tend to operate later in the process of task engagement, when individuals draw conclusions about their competence. Thus, goals may affect an individual's motivational orientation going into a task as well as their reactions to a task following performance feedback.

We propose that the processes initiated by a particular goal can affect subsequent motivation in both positive and negative directions, sometimes simultaneously. For example, a performance constraint (such as an assigned target goal), by definition, establishes an evaluative context for task performance. As a result, individuals may become more interested in the pursuit of competence or care more about doing well than they would otherwise. This positive orientation toward competence may amplify the effect of succesful goal attainment on intrinsic motivation. In other words, positive feedback may be particularly effective in enhancing subsequent interest when individuals care about doing well.

On the negative side, however, the salience of competence may also arouse concerns about external evaluation. To determine whether an individual has attained a performance goal requires that someone evaluate performance. Individuals may experience performance pressure or worry about their performance throughout the performance period. The test anxiety literature suggests that people anticipating evaluation can become anxious about their performance (Geen, 1980) and that they may become distracted from the task if they ruminate about their inadequacies (Wine, 1971). These findings come from studies conducted in academic testing situations, where performance evaluation can be quite stressful. However, milder levels of evaluation may still produce cognitive interference (Wine, 1971), which could disrupt task involvement and interest during performance (Harackiewicz, Manderlink, & Sansone, 1984). Over the long-term, then, we might discover negative effects on performance from even milder levels of evaluation, as a consequence of diminished interest in an activity.

Performance goals (operating at either the target or purpose level) therefore have the potential to initiate both positive and negative motivational processes during task engagement, as well as at task conclusion. Our model explains how these processes can be differentially affected by target and purpose goals, and it also explains how the two kinds of goals work together to influence intrinsic motivation. Figure 1 presents a schematic version of our process model. The model accounts for the effects of contextual and individual factors operating at the beginning of task engagement in terms of the motivational processes initiated during performance. More specifically, we illustrate the processes by which performance constraints (in this case, assigned purpose and target goals), other contextual factors, and individual differences influence subsequent intrinsic motivation for a task. We propose that these characteristics of the person or situation influence the purpose and target goals that individuals adopt or accept as they begin a task in a particular achievement situation (the "A" paths in Figure 1).

Although performance constraints are features of the situational context, we make a distinction between them and other contextual factors to highlight those situational factors that are explicitly related to the evaluation of individual performance. Other contextual factors may affect the purpose and target goals that people adopt, but they are more likely to do so implicitly, by influencing the context in which particular performance constraints have their effects.

According to our model, the goals that an individual adopts in a situation will subsequently affect motivational processes (the "B" paths), which may in

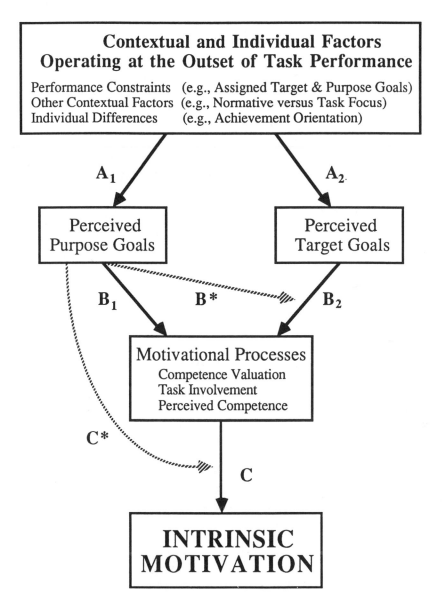

Figure 1. A Schematic Version of Our Process Model of Intrinsic Motivation

turn have beneficial or detrimental effects on subsequent interest in the activity (the "C" paths). Three processes have proven critical in our prior research: competence valuation (personal investment in the pursuit of competence), task involvement (attention and absorption in the activity) and perceived competence (judgments of performance level). We do not mean to imply that other processes identified in achievement literature (e.g., performance anxiety) cannot influence intrinsic motivation. Rather, these are the processes that have proven most relevant in our laboratory studies of intrinsic motivation, where individuals engage in initially interesting tasks that are within their performance capacities.

As illustrated by our model, these three processes can be initiated during the process of task engagement by assigned target goals or higher order purpose goals. Assigned target goals (when accepted as goals by the individual; path A_2) can affect these processes directly by changing the way that an individual interacts with and experiences a task (the B_2 path). A specific performance standard may help a person concentrate attention on an activity, or, over the course of time, make them feel more competent. Assigned target goals may also affect these processes by influencing an individual's perceived purpose goal (the A_1 path).

Perceived purpose goals, whether determined by contextual cues (e.g., an ego-involvement manipulation), particular performance constraints (e.g., an assigned goal) or characteristic values (e.g., achievement motivation) may affect these processes in a more complex manner. Specifically, perceived purpose goals can directly affect motivational processes (the B_1 path), or they may moderate the effects of target goals on these processes (the B^* path). We also propose that perceived purpose goals may serve a moderating function at a second point in the temporal process; that is, they may moderate the relationship between the three motivational processes and intrinsic motivation (the C^* path). Direct effects are represented by solid arrows in Figure 1. The dashed arrows (or * paths) indicate the effects that may be moderated by the purpose goals held by the individual. By moderate, we mean that the B_2 or C path will differ as a function of purpose goals. In a path analysis, we would report two or more values for the B_2 path; for example, the relationship between perceived competence and subsequent task interest might be strongly positive when individuals hold a general competence goal, but near zero when they do not.

Our model therefore makes several important distinctions in accounting for the effects of target and purpose goals on intrinsic motivation. First, it distinguishes externally assigned goals, or performance constraints (i.e., situational factors) from the goals actually adopted by the individual in the situation (i.e., perceived goals). Second, it suggests that the determinants of adopted goals may include more than the performance constraints explicitly conveyed by an external agent. In other words, these determinants may also include the characteristic goals that a person brings to the situation, as well as the goals implicitly conveyed by contextual cues. Third, it distinguishes between target and purpose goals in terms of their level, such that higher order purpose goals can moderate the effects of lower order target goals. And finally, it suggests that these two levels of perceived goals may serve different functions, operating simultaneously in the overall process.

These distinctions are important because they help us understand why goal-setting techniques, even when they have reliable effects on task performance, may have unreliable effects on any particular individual's intrinsic motivation. For example, an achievement oriented individual, committed to the pursuit of competence (and presumably holding a competence purpose goal; an A_1 effect), may value competence in a particular situation regardless of the constraints present (a B_1 effect on the competence valuation process). Alternatively, they may respond to particular constraints, and care even more about doing well when assigned a performance goal, whereas individuals low in achievement motivation (who presumably do not share the competence purpose goal) might not (a B^* effect, showing that achievement orientation moderates the effects of target goals on competence valuation). Or, assigned target goals might make individuals feel more competent in ego-involving contexts (e.g., testing situations) that invoke general competence purpose goals, but have no effect in neutral conditions (a B^* effect). Thus, target goals may have different effects depending on the purpose goals held by an individual in a situation.

Furthermore, the relationship between a particular process and intrinsic motivation (the C paths) may vary as a function of contextual factors or individual differences, through their effects on the purpose goals adopted by the individual (C^* effects). For example, even when specific target goals enhance perceived competence, perceived competence might only influence interest in conditions where individuals also hold the higher order purpose goal of attaining competence.

It is also possible that the different goal levels affect one of these processes more than the others. In general, competence valuation is the process that captures an individual's commitment to the pursuit of competence, and so may reflect involvement at the level of purpose goals. Task involvement, on the other hand, is a process that reflects involvement at the more task-specific level of target goals, where individuals may become immersed in the task-intrinsic features of an activity without reference to higher order goals. These involvement processes seem to parallel the distinction between performance and mastery orientations made by other theorists (e.g., Ames, 1984; Dweck, 1986; Nicholls, 1984). Rather than consider them as alternative ways to approach an activity, however, we consider the distinction to be in terms of the level at which involvement occurs. Performance and mastery purpose goals may therefore have their primary effects at different levles of involvement.

For example, in a competitive squash game, a player might desperately want to outperform their opponent (their general competence purpose goal), and they might also want to hit the ball into the corner effectively (their target goal).

These goals are not necessarily incompatible, but each might invoke different motivational processes. The desire to win might make players care more about doing well, or the performance pressure could distract them from the game. Target goals might help players concentrate on the mechanics of their game, or gauge their progress throughout the match, but they might also provide negative feedback, or interfere with enjoyment of the game.

Previous research in achievement domains suggests that performance and mastery goals can be held simultaneously (Ames & Archer, 1988; Elliott & Dweck, 1988; Nicholls, Chung Cheung, Lauer, & Patashnick, 1989). Our model (supported by our research program, described below) suggests that (as influenced by the purpose and target goals held by the individual) both levels of involvement may be critical to continuing intrinsic motivation. Thus, one goal of our research program has been to identify the conditions under which each of these processes is most relevant to intrinsic motivation.

SUPPORT FOR THE MODEL

Perceived Competence

As mentioned previously, specific target goals have frequently been used in the intrinsic motivation literature because they allow the individual the clearest feedback concerning his or her competence. The emphasis has been on discovering the optimal way to present these target goals to maximize goal attainment and positive feedback, with the assumption that enhanced efficacy and interest will result. In terms of our model, then, goals would be assigned or suggested in hopes that they would be accepted as perceived target goals (path A_2) that would then enhance perceived competence (B_2), which should in turn enhance interest (C). Although many studies have found positive effects on motivation from the receipt of positive feedback (Anderson, Manoogian, & Reznick, 1976; Boggiano & Ruble, 1979; Enzle & Ross, 1978; Harackiewicz, 1979; Karniol & Ross, 1977), only a few of these studies have actually assessed perceived competence, the process assumed to mediate these effects. When perceptions of competence are measured and tested as mediators of feedback effects, the relationship between perceived competence and intrinsic motivation is not as clear as proposed (Harackiewicz & Larson, 1986; Harackiewicz & Manderlink, 1984; Sansone, 1986).

For example, Bandura and Schunk (1981) hypothesized that a specific target goal should optimize performance and subsequent interest when presented as a series of proximal subgoals, rather than as one distal or overall goal. Their reasoning was that proximal goals allow individuals to monitor their performance as they work on an activity, and when attained, they provide frequent indications of competence. To test this, they assigned proximal or distal target goals for math performance to students who initially had deficits in math skills and did not find math interesting. Although the distal goal ultimately provided the same level of overall competence feedback, only the proximal target goals enhanced students' self-efficacy in solving math problems relative to the no-goals control group.

Moreover, these proximal goals promoted greater intrinsic interest in math, measured at the conclusion of the performance period. The proximal subgoals may have been particularly effective in enhancing interest in this study because they provided frequent opportunities for mastery experiences for students with a prior history of math skills deficits. These results suggest that the ability of some target goals to enhance perceived competence may be associated with greater intrinsic motivation.

In contrast, Manderlink and Harackiewicz (1984) used word puzzles that students found initially interesting, and compared the effects of assigning proximal or distal goals on both perceptions of competence and subsequent interest. Although proximal goals enhanced perceived competence relative to distal goals and no-goal controls, individuals assigned distal goals showed the highest levels of subsequent interest in the task. These results suggest that even though the proximal goals allowed the clearest assessment of competence they may have interfered with task involvement during performance, thereby reducing task interest. Congruent with this interpretation were the results from a "reminder" control group in which students were given a distal goal, but reminded of this goal periodically during task engagement. In this case, the distal goal had no advantage over proximal goals in promoting interest.

A study by Harackiewicz, Sansone, and Manderlink (1985) also suggested limits on the degree to which perceived competence may serve as the primary mediator of the effects of performance goals on interest. They varied the timing of specific standards for performance on a series of interesting word puzzles. These standards, or target goals, eventually conveyed positive feedback because all subjects managed to surpass them. Although the standards presented earlier in the course of task performance enhanced perceived competence or self-efficacy, as predicted by Bandura (1982), self-efficacy only mediated subsequent interest for those individuals who began the task with lower perceptions of efficacy. Thus, the perceptions of competence that result from attaining specific target goals may not always be enough to enhance intrinsic motivation, especially when individuals begin a task with reasonably high expectations for their performance.

Overall, these studies suggest that the ability of specific target goals to provide clear assessments of individual competence may be important to interest primarily when tasks are relatively difficult (or at least perceived as such by a particular individual). When individuals have already achieved a certain moderate level of efficacy, however, the process of comparing one's performance against a standard may interfere with task involvement. These studies contributed to the generation of the present model in several ways. Specifically, these results suggest that processes other than perceived competence may be important in determining subsequent interest, particularly when a certain threshold level of competence has already been attained (Bandura, 1982; Pittman, Boggiano, & Ruble, 1983).

They further suggest that the primary purpose for engaging in enjoyable activities may not always be to acquire competence feedback, or at least not the particular type of competence feedback available in these studies. The higher level purpose with which individuals engaged in activities appeared to moderate the role of perceived competence, and this purpose seemed to differ between individuals and according to cues in the context. Thus, the ability of target goals to provide competence feedback may not be the sole function of goals that affects subsequent interest.

Competence Valuation

It is not always enough to know that we are competent; sometimes what matters is whether we *want* to be competent, or whether we are motivated to perform well in a particular situation. Many of our results suggest that being aware of competence at an activity is not always enough to guarantee that intrinsic interest will be maintained or enhanced. This seems to be especially true in cases where individuals have achieved a certain threshold level of competence at an interesting activity. When perceived competence does not account for intrinsic motivation, other processes associated with individual competence may be relevant. Specifically, how much individuals care about doing well in a situation may be more critical than whether they perceive themselves as competent at it. Competence *valuation*, then, is a motivational process that reflects the degree to which individuals care about doing well. We typically measure it at the outset of task performance by asking subjects how concerned they are about doing well in the upcoming session, and how important it is for them to do well. Thus, the measure reflects commitment to the general purpose goal of achieving competence at the activity.

Our model suggests that certain contextual and individual factors may affect motivational processes by suggesting a purpose goal of pursuing competence at the activity. A person starting a task may care more about doing well as a result of holding a general competence purpose goal, and the more they value competence, the more they will enjoy a task after they receive positive feedback. This process represents an active, positive orientation toward achieving competence at the task, but it may also amplify the effects of negative feedback if individuals fail to meet goals.

We have found that a variety of performance constraints can influence this process. These constraints may or may not include specific performance standards or targets. For example, some studies have examined constraints paired with specific targets for performance, such as a competition accompanied by specific information about an opponent's performance (Epstein & Harackiewicz, in press). In other studies, the availability of normative standards themselves served as performance constraints (Harackiewicz et al., 1985; Sansone, 1989; Sansone & Voisard, 1990). Other performance constraints without explicit standards have also proved to increase competence valuation. For example, the promise of a reward for doing well (Harackiewicz et al., 1987; Harackiewicz & Manderlink, 1984; Harackiewicz et al., 1984) and the communication of a positive expectancy for future performance (Harackiewicz et al., 1985) are both factors that made competence more salient and enhanced competence valuation.

Competence valuation can also be influenced by stable individual differences, representing a characteristic goal orientation that people bring to situations. That is, some individuals are typically more oriented toward competence across situations; these are individuals who approach many tasks with a greater interest in doing well. We measure achievement motivation with the Achievement Orientation Scale from the Personality Research Form (Jackson, 1974), which was developed according to Murray's (1938) theory of needs. People scoring high on this scale are described as challenge-seeking, purposive, and maintaining high standards. Depending on the experimental conditions we run, we see the effects of achievement orientation on competence valuation either as a main effect, a B_1 path (Harackiewicz et al., 1987), or in interaction with contextual cues, a B^* effect (Harackiewicz, Manderlink, & Sansone 1991; Sansone, 1989).

For example, Harackiewicz et al. (1985) conducted a study in which high school students were given (or not) positive expectancies for their upcoming performance on a series of interesting word puzzles. All subjects eventually received positive feedback about their performance. The expectancy manipulation raised competence valuation for achievement oriented individuals, who presumably hold a general competence purpose goal, but did not for low achievers, who do not share this purpose goal (a B^* effect).

We have also documented that competence valuation mediates the effects of these variables on subsequent intrinsic interest according to the logic and statistical procedures for mediation analysis developed by Judd and Kenny (1981). We have conducted several studies using a variety of performance constraints (e.g., performance-contingent rewards) in which we measured the process hypothesized to mediate interest, and satisfied the requirements outlined by Judd and Kenny (1981). We have found that in evaluative situations resulting in positive feedback, competence valuation enhances subsequent interest (Epstein & Harackiewicz, in press; Harackiewicz & Manderlink, 1984; Sansone, 1989). In other words, the more that individuals value competence going into a task, the more they enjoy it following positive evaluative outcomes.

We have also found that the effects of competence valuation on interest can differ as a function of individual difference variables (a C* effect). In the Harackiewicz et al. (1985) study discussed above, we found that competence valuation was an important mediator of the expectancy manipulation for high achievers, but not for individuals low in achievement orientation. The expectancy manipulation raised competence valuation for high achievers (B*), who presumably held a general competence purpose goal, and it enhanced their subsequent intrinsic interest through this mediating process (C*). These results suggest a "matching" of process to the characteristic goals of the individual. In other words, high achievers only enjoyed the task when they were committed to the higher goal of attaining competence in this specific situation.

Task Involvement

Our research examining the competence valuation process illustrates the positive consequences of adopting the purpose goal of attaining competence at an activity. However, this particular purpose goal may also have negative consequences, as illustrated by our work with another process, task involvement. Task involvement is a process that reflects an individual's concentration and absorption in an activity, and concerns a person's direct experience with a task. We hypothesize that an evaluative focus (no matter how triggered) may exert negative effects on task involvement, because people may worry about their performance and become distracted from a task (Wine, 1971). As they become less involved in the activity, they may come to enjoy it less. Even if they end up learning that they did well, their experience of the task has been clouded by disruptive cognition and distraction.

In this case, having lower level target goals in addition to the purpose goal of attaining competence may work to prevent these negative effects. If performance standards or target goals provide clear, positive feedback early in the process of task performance, they may help offset the worry and anxiety individuals would otherwise experience, and might actually facilitate concentration and attention to the task at hand.

In our research we have demonstrated both the negative effects of performance evaluation on intrinsic motivation (Harackiewicz et al., 1984, 1987) and the ability of task-specific performance standards to offset these negative effects (Harackiewicz et al., 1984, 1985). We have also collected some supportive process data. For example, in one study (Harackiewicz et al., 1984, Study 3) we collected a cognitive measure of task involvement during the process of playing pinball, loosely based on Sarason's (1980) measure of cognitive interference. We asked subjects how frequently they thought about the ongoing game (e.g., "I thought about keeping the ball in play," "I concentrated on manipulating the flippers"). The results paralleled those on intrinsic motivation, and indicated that subjects in evaluation conditions concentrated less on the pinball game than did no-evaluation control subjects. In another study, we found that low achievers were the ones most likely to show this effect, which suggests that they may be particularly vulnerable to the distracting effects of evaluation (Harackiewicz et al., 1987).

These findings suggest that the evaluative focus on individual performance can have negative effects on intrinsic motivation by interfering with task involvement. However, in other studies, our findings suggest that the provision of a specific target goal can promote task involvement and offset the negative effects of evaluation. For example, in one study (Harackiewicz et al., 1984, Study 3), we manipulated a factor that we hoped would prevent the distracting effects of performance evaluation. We exposed pinball players to an evaluation manipulation ("The experimenter will evaluate your performance and tell you whether you scored above the 80th percentile") or not, and provided half of the players with a specific numerical standard before they began the task. This performance standard was posted on the machine so that subjects would have it available during the course of play (much in the same way that pinball machines often have "Best score ever" posted).

We found that performance evaluation without the standard distracted subjects from the task (on a task thoughts measure) and undermined subsequent intrinsic motivation relative to the no-evaluation control. However, when subjects were given the performance standard before play, evaluation did not distract players from the game, and did not undermine interest. Thus, it seems that providing subjects with a specific score to concentrate on and aim for helped them to remain focused on the game, and prevented the usual negative effects of evaluation.

Thus far we have discussed the ability of specific performance standards to offset the negative effects of performance evaluation. In other words, we may be able to restore the level of concentration and involvement that an individual would have on their own, if purpose goals did not intrude and distract them from the task. However, an important question is whether assigned target goals can promote intrinsic motivation by enhancing task involvement above and beyond that engendered by the task itself in no-goal control groups. This question is especially important in the case of interesting activities in which individuals have already established reasonably high levels of perceived competence, because it is in these cases that we have found target goals to be ineffective in enhancing interest through the perceived competence process (e.g., Manderlink & Harackiewicz, 1984).

Consistent with our analysis, Locke and Latham (1990) have recently suggested that target goals may promote intrinsic interest by facilitating concentration and strengthening the intensity of focus on the task, thereby leading individuals to discover the pleasurable aspects of the task. In support of this hypothesis, they cite one correlational finding (Bryan & Locke, 1967) that specific, challenging target goals lead to increases in both the self-reported degree of mental focus and intrinsic interest in math problems. However, other studies have failed to reveal a consistent pattern for the effects of assigned goals on intrinsic motivation (Hirst, 1988; Jackson & Zedeck, 1982; Mossholder, 1980; Shalley & Oldham, 1985), and most investigators have failed to examine mediating processes (Locke & Latham, 1990). If anything, many of the negative results obtained to date suggest that the target goals used in these studies may have interfered with attention to the task (as in the case of the proximal goals in the Manderlink and Harackiewicz [1984] study).

In a recent study, however, we examined the effects of specific target goals on intrinsic motivation and measured the processes hypothesized to mediate their effects. Harackiewicz, Abrahams, Earleywine, and Manderlink (1990) assigned (or not) target goals for an interesting building task. The goals used in this study were specific standards for performance, expressed in terms of the number of pieces to use. These standards were suggested as goals to aim for, and cognitive measures of task involvement (collected during the performance process) revealed that these goals were effective in enhancing attention to the task. The assigned goals, which all subjects managed to attain, raised subsequent intrinsic motivation above no-goal controls. Furthermore, mediation analyses (Judd & Kenny, 1981) documented that the goals raised interest through this task involvement process.

Moreover, although these goals also enhanced perceptions of competence, measured throughout the performance period and at task conclusion, perceived competence did not prove to mediate subsequent intrinsic motivation. What mattered most was how absorbed subjects became in the building activity during the performance period. Those who became involved in the task were most likely to enjoy the task.

CONTEXT EFFECTS

Up to this point, we have reviewed research documenting the role of each of the three motivational processes in our model, including how we expect purpose and target goals to affect these processes (the B paths), and how the processes should affect intrinsic motivation (the C paths). We have also discussed how individual factors can moderate the effects of performance constraints on these processes, and how they can also moderate the effects of the processes on intrinsic motivation (the A_1, B*, and C* paths). However, we have yet to discuss the consequences of the larger context in which performance takes place. In this section, we review research suggesting that different purpose goals may be adopted as a function of the larger context in which target goals are provided. These purpose goals may differ not only in terms of whether or not a general competence purpose goal is pursued, but also in terms of the *type* of competence purpose goal pursued. We also consider the possibility that competence may not be a central component of all purpose goals, even in achievement situations. Thus, purpose goals may also vary in terms of whether competence is relevant at all, as in the case of amusement, fantasy, curiosity, or even time-killing purpose goals.

As we start to differentiate purpose goals beyond those general competence purpose goals considered earlier, we see more evidence of moderation effects. In other words, we find that purpose goals can moderate effects on motivational processes (the B* effects), and that they can moderate the relationship between these processes and subsequent intrinsic motivation (the C* effects). Although our consideration of mediating process has so far primarily emphasized the direct effects of each process on intrinsic motivation, our results also suggest that different purpose goals, resulting from the larger context, can influence whether and how each of the three processes is related to intrinsic motivation in a particular situation.

Are General Competence Goals Salient in the Situation?

When an activity allows some variability in the types of purpose goals that might be relevant to interest, we may be more likely to see the effects of context on the purpose goals that are adopted in a particular situation. Accordingly, Sansone (1986, 1989) created an activity (a trivia game) that aroused curiosity about correct answers as well as uncertainty about individual performance. She found that feedback satisfying curiosity (providing the correct answers to the trivia questions) enhanced interest to the same degree as positive normative feedback (providing information about individual performance level compared to others), relative to no feedback controls. This was the case even though positive normative feedback resulted in higher perceptions of competence. Thus, attaining competence did enhance subsequent interest, but it did not seem to be the *only* purpose goal relevant to interest.

Sansone (1986) then varied the larger context in which subjects played the trivia game. To do so, she employed an ego-involvement communication which emphasized the importance of attaining competence at the activity. By linking performance to important skills and abilities, individual competence becomes more salient than it might otherwise be (Harackiewicz & Manderlink, 1984), and according to our model, could promote the adoption of general competence purpose goals. Although some researchers have suggested that ego-involvement can be antithetical to intrinsic motivation (e.g., Ryan, 1982), other studies suggest that ego-involving contexts may serve several functions, some of which may actually foster interest. The issue seems to be the intensity of the evaluative threats to self-esteem. If threats to self-esteem are strong, either because of the manipulation used (e.g., an IQ test), or because individuals doubt their ability to perform competently, then concerns about performing poorly may interfere with enjoyment (Butler, 1987; Koestner, Zuckerman, & Koestner, 1987; Nicholls et al., 1989).

In Sansone (1986), however, the ego-involvement manipulation was relatively mild. It suggested that doing well at the trivia game was associated with intellectual flexibility and creativity, and was used to emphasize positive competence purpose goals. The results suggested that this was in fact the primary effect of the ego-involvement manipulation. In particular, the ego-involvement cue did not affect interest directly, but instead served as the context in which perceived competence was positively related to interest. In contrast, perceived competence was unrelated to interest in the absence of the ego-involving cue. These results suggest that situational cues can influence the adoption of a higher order purpose goal of attaining competence (A_1 path), which then moderates the relationship between perceived competence and intrinsic motivation (the C^* effect).

What Kind of Competence Goals are Salient?

We have also found that the mediating role of competence valuation can differ as a function of contextual factors, specifically those that influence how competence is defined in a situation. Our measure of competence valuation does not specify how competence should be defined; rather, we ask subjects how much they care about "doing well." However, given that adolescents and adults usually define competence in terms of normative comparisons (Boggiano & Ruble, 1986; Jagacinski & Nicholls, 1984; Nicholls, 1984), competence valuation is more likely to reflect attitudes and feelings about normatively-based competence, as opposed to task mastery. Task mastery, of course, is probably closer to the kind of task-intrinsic perceptions of competence that White (1959) discussed (cf. Maehr & Braskamp, 1986), but it is the higher order; or "more differentiated" (Nicholls, 1984) definition of competence that seems to characterize the purpose goals under consideration. And, in fact, in the intrinsic motivation literature, external evaluation and performance feedback have almost always been based on normative definitions of competence.

In one study (Harackiewicz et al., 1987), we varied the focus of evaluation by emphasizing normative standards or task-specific criteria as the basis for judgments about competence. High school students played an enjoyable word game and evaluated their scores relative to standards ostensibly based on normative testing (outperforming 50% of their peers) or a particular criterion score for the puzzles. This manipulation of evaluative focus created a context in which the competence valuation process, if normatively based, should have been much more relevant to intrinsic motivation in normatively focused conditions. Presumably, in the conditions emphasizing task-focused evaluation, task involvement should have been the more important process. We found strong evidence for the contextual moderation of process:

competence valuation mediated interest very strongly in conditions stressing normative competence, but only weakly in situations emphasizing more task-focused evaluation. These results again support a matching of process to the higher order goals held by the individual, which in this case were affected by a contextual manipulation.

More recently, Harackiewicz and Lee (1990) varied the evaluative context in which performance goals were assigned. Specifically, they manipulated the focus of performance evaluation, as in the Harackiewicz et al. (1987) study, and assigned specific performance goals for an interesting building game. Subjects assembled a series of models from small pieces and were assigned normatively or task-based goals. In normative conditions, the specific performance targets (expressed in terms of the number of pieces to try to use) were based on normative testing (65th percentile scores). In task-based conditions, subjects were given the same specific scores to aim for, but these scores were ostensibly based on task criteria, and defined as "moderately challenging goals for this particular model." Thus, both goals were specific target goals with clear behavioral referents, but the normative goals were defined in a context emphasizing performance relative to others, whereas the context of evaluation for task-focused goals was specific to the task.

We also measured the achievement orientation of subjects and found, as did Harackiewicz et al. (1987), that across experimental conditions, achievement oriented individuals showed higher levels of competence valuation in the situation. Furthermore, high achievers responded most favorably to the normatively defined target goals, showing large increments in subsequent interest after working toward and attaining these goals. Low achievers, on the other hand, responded especially negatively to the normatively focused goals, which actually undermined their subsequent interest, suggesting that they were distracted by evaluation. This decrement in interest occurred despite the fact that these individuals attained their normative target goals. In contrast, task-focused goals did not undermine interest for low achievers, but maintained interest relative to no goal control groups.

In this study, normative goals seemed to make competence salient, and enhance interest for individuals who characteristically value competence. Thus, we find additional evidence of a matching phenomenon where target goals may work best for individuals when they correspond to the general purpose goals established by the context. Although we did not collect process data in this study, the results seem to mirror the Harackiewicz et al. (1985) findings by suggesting that the competence valuation process may be most relevant for achievement oriented individuals. The results also extend the Harackiewicz et al. (1987) findings suggesting that contextual factors can influence how specific constraints are perceived.

Together, these studies suggest that characteristics of the situation and the individual can both be critical in determining the relevance of specific motivational processes to intrinsic motivation. In particular, achievement motivation seems to have promoted the adoption of a general competence purpose goal in the situation, while the larger context influenced the particular type of competence purpose goal pursued. In combination, these contextual and individual factors subsequently influenced the role of competence valuation in determining intrinsic motivation.

Are Other Purpose Goals Relevant in the Situation?

Thus far we have discussed what may happen to intrinsic motivation as the situation varies in terms of whether a competence purpose goal is adopted, and if adopted, the type of competence goal it may be. However, we have not yet addressed the possibility of other purpose goals, specifically, non-competence purpose goals. This issue is particularly important because non-competence purpose goals may promote an orientation toward a task that conflicts with the orientation fostered by target goals. For example, what happens if we assign target goals hoping to facilitate mastery and perceptions of competence, and the individual holds not a competence purpose goal, but another purpose goal altogether? Our model suggests that these two levels of goals may conflict, with negative implications for intrinsic motivation.

Sansone, Sachau, and Weir (1989) used an activity in which the task demands established a salient purpose goal other than developing or demonstrating individual competence. Specifically, they used a computer fantasy game, and then explicitly manipulated the purpose of involvement by emphasizing individual performance level (a competence purpose) or emphasizing the fantasy aspects of the game (a task-specific purpose). They crossed this manipulation with an instructional manipulation that provided hints and tips to facilitate competent performance. When individuals were told that the goal of the game was to score as many points as possible (the competence goal), these instructions proved beneficial for intrinsic motivation. However, when individuals were told that the purpose of the game was to explore the fantasy adventure world (the fantasy goal), the same instructions proved to be detrimental for subsequent intrinsic motivation.

Thus, the effect of specific target goals (in this case, the instructions for performance) depended on the "match" with the larger context. The instructions were effective in promoting interest only when the context emphasized the purpose goal of performing well. The instructions seem to have been at odds with the more task-oriented purpose of exploring the fantasy world of the game. These results, more than any others that we have collected to date, show how the levels of target and purpose goals can work together. They suggest that only when target goals are consistent with purpose goals will they optimize intrinsic motivation.

Furthermore, Sansone et al. (1989) found that this matching effect was mediated by an affective task involvement measure, obtained midway through task engagement. Specifically, in the absence of further instruction, individuals given the competence purpose goal reported a less positive mood than the subjects given the fantasy purpose goal. Thus, the competence purpose goal seems to have disrupted positive task involvement, relative to the fantasy goal (a B_1 path). However, when individuals given the competence goal received instructional guidelines that ostensibly would help them towards that goal, they reported positive mood levels equivalent to the fantasy goal subjects (a B^* effect).

Conversely, individuals with the fantasy purpose goal had higher levels of task involvement relative to those with competence goals (a B_1 path), but when they received instructions about how to attain competence at the task, their task involvement decreased (a B^* effect). For both purpose goals, this affective measure of task involvement proved to mediate subsequent interest in the task, such that higher levels of positive mood promoted interest at task conclusion (a C path). These results suggest that the evaluative focus established by the competence goal manipulation may have interfered initially with task involvement, but that this disruption was overcome by specific information that might help them work toward and attain competence. Moreover, the effects of specific instruction in the competence purpose conditions parallel the effects in the Harackiewicz et al. (1984) study described earlier, where pinball players were less distracted by evaluation when they were given specific scores that could help them work toward their higher level purpose goal of attaining competence.

These results suggest that target goals can have negative effects on intrinsic motivation when they are in conflict with purpose goals. Although target goals may direct involvement in the task at a lower level, the nature of this involvement may sometimes conflict with the involvement prompted by higher level goals (cf. Vallacher, Somoza, & Wegner, 1989; Vallacher & Wegner, 1987). Evidence for the conflict between levels of involvement only emerges when we explicitly consider the other kinds of purpose goals individuals might hold in a situation. These results indicate the importance of taking a larger view of the context in which we assign goals to people performing enjoyable activities.

GENERAL CONCLUSIONS

Setting performance goals for ourselves and for others is often a critical component of self-regulation. Goals provide guidelines for our behavior, serve to direct attention, and allow ongoing feedback from which we discover whether to correct or continue our present course of action (Bandura, 1986; Carver & Scheier, 1981; Locke & Latham, 1990). Unfortunately, these same goals can adversely affect our intrinsic motivation to continue engaging in an activity. When assigning goals, then, we need to carefully consider the constellation of functions these goals may serve. In the present chapter we have attempted to outline a model of the complex effects of performance goals on the intrinsic motivation process. By distinguishing between goals as targets and as purpose, we are able to examine involvement in an activity at more than one level. This distinction also allows us to integrate the effects of individual differences and the larger context into the overall motivational process.

One implication of our model is that certain factors that have previously been identified as either promoting or disturbing intrinsic motivation may in fact do both, depending on the match between purpose and target goals. For example, previous researchers have suggested that ego-involving contexts or competition should be detrimental for intrinsic motivation. Our model suggests that these factors will affect the particular purpose goal adopted by an individual in the situation. Whether this purpose goal results in positive or negative effects on subsequent interest, however, may depend on whether specific target goals allow the person to feel competent without worrying about evaluation (satisfying their higher order goals), or whether target goals help an individual concentrate attention on the task at hand and become involved in the activity for its own sake.

In this paper we have presented a model that describes a process of task engagement that occurs over a fairly limited period of time. Of course, we often engage in activities over much longer periods of time, and as the process is extended to include these situations, revisions to the model will be required. In particular, additional paths may become important. For example, in the present model we illustrate the effects of the initial goals held by individuals as they enter a situation, and begin engagement in an activity, but we do not consider changes in perceived goals over time. As a result, we do not indicate a path through which perceived target goals may affect perceived purpose goals, or a path through which purpose goals may affect target goals. However, it is possible that over time this type of effect may occur.

Purpose goals might influence the specific target goals that an individual pursues. If squash players hold mastery goals, they may find themselves a series of increasingly challenging partners to play with. If their purpose is to demonstrate competence, however, they may select partners who afford them a higher probabilty of winning each week. Conversely, target goals may influence and modulate our higher order purpose goals over time. In the attempt to reach a particular target goal, feedback may suggest that the target is unreasonable, or that we have little chance of making it. At this point we may then change or adjust our purpose goal to include something that we have some chance of attaining. For example, as we play a series of pinball games aiming for specific target scores, we may decide to strive to be the best player on a very small block, and abandon our goal of attaining true pinball wizardry.

Finally, the studies described in this paper have used interesting and involving activities, games and puzzles in the laboratory to examine the intrinsic motivation process, and as such their findings may appear limited to those times in which we engage in activities purely for recreation, and outcomes are relatively unimportant. However, as educators, we should never lose sight of the fact that much of what we teach has the potential to be interesting, involving, and intrinsically motivated. Furthermore, we believe that our results may in fact generalize to real world contexts. For example, much of the research in the achievement domain has focused on the impact of strong, formal evaluations of students' performance on their motivation in the classroom. When these evaluations are made, they may initiate certain processes (such as performance anxiety) that override intrinsic involvement in the task. Although these periods of formal evaluations are an important part of educational environments, there are also many times when evaluation may be present, but in milder forms. The latter are closer to the kinds of evaluative contexts we have studied in the laboratory, and our results suggest that it may be possible to maintain motivation in the face of these milder forms of evaluation. The key may be the degree to which performance goals are able to promote involvement at both the specific target and more general purpose levels; if they do, and the two levels are in match, our model suggests that intrinsic motivation can not only survive, but thrive.

ACKNOWLEDGMENTS

We thank Andy Elliot, Carolyn Morgan, Carolin Showers, and Julie Zuwerink for their helpful comments on earlier versions of this chapter. Preparation of this paper was supported by a grant awarded to Judith Harackiewicz by the Wisconsin Alumni Research Foundation, and by a grant awarded to Carol Sansone and Cynthia Berg from the National Institute of Child Health and Human Development and National Institute on Aging (HD25728). Much of the research reported in this chapter was supported by grants from the Spencer Foundation to each author.

REFERENCES

Ames, C. (1984). Competitive, cooperative, and individualistic goal structures: A cognitive-motivational analysis. In R. Ames & C. Ames (Eds.), *Research on motivation in education: Vol. 1. Student motivation* (pp.177-207). New York: Academic Press.

Ames, C., & Archer, J. (1988). Achievement goals in the classroom: Students' learning strategies and motivation processes. *Journal of Educational Psychology, 80*, 260-267.

Anderson, R., Manoogian, S. T., & Reznick, J. S. (1976). The undermining and enhancing of intrinsic motivation in preschool children. *Journal of Personality and Social Psychology, 34*, 915-922.

Bandura, A. (1982). Self-efficacy mechanism in human agency. *American Psychologist, 37*, 122-147.

_____. (1986). *Social foundations of thought and action: A social cognitive theory.* Englewood Cliffs, NJ: Prentice Hall.

Bandura, A., & Schunk, D. H. (1981). Cultivating competence, self-efficacy, and intrinsic interest through proximal self-motivation. *Journal of Personality and Social Psychology, 41*, 586-598.

Boggiano, A. K., & Ruble, D. N. (1979). Competence and the overjustification effect: A developmental study. *Journal of Personality and Social Psychology, 37*, 1462-1468.

_____. (1986). Children's responses to evaluative feedback. In R. Schwarzer (Ed.), *Self-related cognitions in anxiety and motivation* (pp. 195-227). Hillsdale, NJ: Erlbaum.

Bryan J. F., & Locke, E. A. (1967). Goal setting as a means of increasing motivation. *Journal of Applied Psychology, 51*, 274-277.

Butler, R. (1987). Task-involving and ego-involving properties of evaluation: Effects of different feedback conditions on motivational perceptions, interest and performance. *Journal of Educational Psychology, 79*, 474-482.

_____. (1989). On the psychological meaning of information about competence: A reply to Ryan and Deci's comment on Butler (1987). *Journal of Educational Psychology, 81*, 269-272.

Cantor, N., & Kihlstrom, J. F. (1987). *Personality and social intelligence.* Englewood Cliffs, NJ: Prentice Hall.

Cantor, N., Norem, J. K., Niedenthal, P. M., Langston, C. A., & Brower, A. M. (1987). Life tasks, self-concept ideals, and cognitive strategies in life transition. *Journal of Personality and Social Psychology, 53*(6), 1178-1191.

Cantor, N., & Zirkel, S. (1990). Personality, cognition, and purposive behavior. In L. A. Pervin (Ed.), *Handbook of personality theory and research.* New York: Guilford.

Carver, C. S., & Scheier, M. F. (1981). *Attention and self-regulation: A control-theory approach to human behavior.* New York: Springer-Verlag.

Csikszentmihalyi, M. (1975). *Beyond boredom and anxiety.* San Francisco: Jossey-Bass.

_____. (1990). The flow experience and its significance for human psychology. In M. Csikszentmihalyi & I. S. Csikszentmihalyi (Eds.). *Optimal experience: Psychological studies of flow in consciousness.* New York: Cambridge University Press.

deCharms, R. (1968). *Personal causation: The internal affective determinants of behavior.* New York: Academic Press.

Deci, E. L. (1975). *Intrinsic motivation.* New York: Plenum.

Deci, E. L., & Ryan, R. M. (1985). *Intrinsic motivation and self-determination in human behavior.* New York: Plenum.

Dweck, C. S. (1986). Motivational processes affecting learning. *American Psychologist, 41*, 1040-1048.

Dweck, C. S., & Leggett, E. L. (1988). A social-cognitive approach to motivation and personality. *Psychological Review, 95*, 256-273.

Elliott, E. S., & Dweck, C. S. (1988). Goals: An approach to motivation and achievement. *Journal of Personality and Social Psychology, 54*, 5-12.

Emmons, R. A. (1986). Personal strivings: An approach to personality and subjective well-being. *Journal of Personality and Social Psychology, 51*(5), 1058-1068.

_____. (1989). The personal striving approach to personality. In L. A. Pervin (Ed.), *Goal concepts in personality and social psychology* (pp. 87-126). Hillsdale, NJ: Erlbaum.

Enzle, M. E., & Ross, J. M. (1978). Increasing and decreasing intrinsic interest with contingent rewards: A test of cognitive evaluation theory. *Journal of Experimental Social Psychology, 14*, 588-597.

Epstein, J.A., & Harackiewicz, J.M. (in press). Winning is not enough: The effects of competition and achievement orientation on intrinsic interest. *Personality and Social Psychology Bulletin.*

Geen, R. G. (1980). Test anxiety and cue utilization. In I. G. Sarason (Ed.), *Test anxiety: Theory, research, and applications* (pp. 253-259). Hillsdale, NJ: Erlbaum.

Harackiewicz, J. M. (1979). The effects of reward contingency and performance feedback on intrinsic motivation. *Journal of Personality and Social Psychology, 37,* 1352-1363.

————. (1989). Performance evaluation and intrinsic motivation processes: The effects of achievement orientation and rewards. In D.M. Buss & N. Cantor (Eds.), *Personality psychology: Recent trends and emerging directions.* New York: Springer-Verlag.

Harackiewicz, J. M., Abrahams, S., & Wageman, R. (1987). Performance evaluation and intrinsic motivation: The effects of evaluative focus, rewards, and achievement orientation. *Journal of Personality and Social Psychology, 53,* 1015-1023.

Harackiewicz, J.M., Abrahams, S., Earleywine, M., & Manderlink, G. (1990). *Goal-setting, task involvement, and intrinsic motivation.* Manuscript in preparation.

Harackiewicz, J. M., & Larson, J. R., Jr. (1986). Managing motivation: The impact of supervisor feedback on subordinate task interest. *Journal of Personality and Social Psychology, 51,* 547-556.

Harackiewicz, J. M., & Lee, J. (1990). *Goal-setting and intrinsic motivation: the effects of goals, evaluative focus, and achievement orientation.* Manuscript in preparation.

Harackiewicz, J. M., & Manderlink, G. (1984). A process analysis of the effects of performance-contingent rewards on intrinsic motivation. *Journal of Experimental Social Psychology, 20,* 531-551.

Harackiewicz, J. M., Manderlink, G., & Sansone, C. (1984). Rewarding pinball wizardry: Effects of evaluation and cue value on intrinsic interest. *Journal of Personality and Social Psychology, 47,* 287-300.

————. (1991). Competence processes and achievement orientation: Implications for intrinsic motivation. In A. K. Boggiano & T. S. Pittman (Eds.), *Achievement and motivation: A social-developmental analysis.* New York: Cambridge University Press.

Harackiewicz, J. M., & Sansone, C. (1990). *A process model of intrinsic motivation: The case of performance-contingent rewards.* Manuscript in preparation.

Harackiewicz, J. M., Sansone, C., & Manderlink, G. (1985). Competence, achievement orientation, and intrinsic motivation: A process analysis. *Journal of Personality and Social Psychology, 48,* 493-508.

Harter, S. (1981). A model of mastery motivation in children: Individual differences and developmental change. In W. A. Collins (Ed.), *Aspects of the development of competence: The Minnesota symposium on child psychology* (Vol. 14, pp. 215-255). Hillsdale, NJ: Erlbaum.

Higgins, E.T. (1987). Self-discrepancy: A theory relating self and affect. *Psychological Review, 94,* 319-340.

Hirst, M. K. (1988). Intrinsic motivation as influenced by task interdependence and goal setting. *Journal of Applied Psychology, 73,* 96-101.

Jackson, D. N. (1974). *Personality Research Form Manual.* Goshen, NY: Research Psychologists Press.

Jackson, S. E., & Zedeck, S. (1982). Explaining performance variability: Contributions of goal setting, task characteristics, and evaluative contexts. *Journal of Applied Psychology, 67,* 759-768.

Jagacinski, C. M., & Nicholls, J. G. (1984). Conceptions of ability and related affects in task involvement and ego involvement. *Journal of Educational Psychology, 76,* 909-919.

Judd, C. M., & Kenny, D. A. (1981). Process analysis: Estimating mediation in treatment evaluations. *Evaluation Review, 5,* 602-619.

Karniol, R., & Ross, M. (1977). The effect of performance-relevant and performance-irrelevant rewards on children's intrinsic motivation. *Child Development, 48*, 482-487.

Kirschenbaum, D. S., Humphrey, L. L., & Malett, S. D. (1981). Specificity of planning in adult self-control: An applied investigation. *Journal of Personality and Social Psychology, 40*, 941-950.

Klinger, E. (1987). Current concerns and disengagement from incentives. In F. Halisch & J. Kuhl (Eds.), *Motivation, intention and volition* (pp. 337-347). New York: Springer-Verlag.

Koestner, R., Zuckerman, M., & Koestner, J. (1987). Praise, involvement, and intrinsic motivation. *Journal of Personality and Social Psychology, 53*, 383-390.

Lepper, M. R. (1981). Intrinsic and extrinsic motivation in children: Detrimental effects of superfluous social controls. In W. A. Collins (Ed.), *Aspects of the development of competence: The Minnesota symposium on child psychology* (Vol. 14, pp. 155-214). Hillsdale, NJ: Erlbaum.

Lepper, M. R., Greene, D., & Nisbett, R. E. (1973). Undermining children's intrinsic interest with extrinsic reward: A test of the overjustification hypothesis. *Journal of Personality and Social Psychology, 28*, 129-137.

Little, B. R. (1989). Personal projects analysis: Trivial pursuits, magnificent obsessions, and the search for coherence. In D. M. Buss & N. Cantor (Eds.), *Personality psychology: Recent trends and emerging directions* (pp. 15-31). New York: Springer-Verlag.

Locke, E.A., & Latham, G.P. (1990). *A theory of goal setting and task performance.* Englewood Cliffs, NJ: Prentice Hall.

Locke, E. A., Shaw, K. N., Saari, L. M., & Latham, G. P. (1981). Goal setting and task performance: 1969-1980. *Psychological Bulletin, 90*, 125-152.

Maehr, M. L., & Braskamp, L. A. (1986). *The motivation factor: A theory of personal investment.* Lexington, MA: D.C. Heath.

Malone, T. W. (1981). Toward a theory of intrinsically motivating instruction. *Cognitive Science, 4*, 333-369.

Manderlink, G., & Harackiewicz, J. M. (1984). Proximal vs. distal goal setting and intrinsic motivation. *Journal of Personality and Social Psychology, 47*, 918-928.

Markus, H., & Nurius, P. (1986). Possible selves. *American Psychologist, 41*(9), 954-969.

McClelland, D. C. (1961). *The achieving society.* Princeton, NJ: Van Nostrand.

Mossholder, K. W. (1980). Effects of externally mediated goal setting on intrinsic motivation: A laboratory experiment. *Journal of Applied Psychology, 65*, 202-210.

Murray, H. A. (1938). *Explorations in personality.* New York: Oxford University Press.

Nicholls, J. G. (1984). Achievement motivation: Conceptions of ability, subjective experience, task choice and performance. *Psychological Review, 91*, 328-346.

Nicholls, J. G., Chung Cheung, P., Lauer, J., & Patashnick, M. (1989). Individual differences in academic motivation: Perceived ability, goals, beliefs, and values. *Learning and Individual Differences, 1*, 63-84.

Nicholls, J. G., Patashnick, M., & Nolen, S. B. (1985). Adolescents' theories of education. *Journal of Educational Psychology, 77*, 683-692.

Pintrich, P. R., & DeGroot, E. V. (1990). Motivational and self-regulated learning components of classroom academic performance. *Journal of Educational Psychology, 82*, 33-40.

Pittman, T. S., Boggiano, A. K., & Ruble, D. N. (1983). Intrinsic and extrinsic motivational orientations: Interactive effect of reward, competence feedback, and task complexity. In J. Levine & M. Wang (Eds.), *Teacher and student perceptions: Implications for learning* (pp. 319-340). Hillsdale, NJ: Erlbaum.

Pittman, T. S., & Heller, J. F. (1987). Social motivation. *Annual Review of Psychology, 38*, 461-489.

Ryan, R. M. (1982). Control and information in the intrapersonal sphere: An extension of cognitive evaluation theory. *Journal of Personality and Social Psychology, 43*, 450-461.

Sansone, C. (1986). A question of competence: The effects of competence and task feedback on intrinsic interest. *Journal of Personality and Social Psychology, 51*, 918-931.

————. (1989). Competence feedback, task feedback, and intrinsic interest: An examination of process and context. *Journal of Experimental Social Psychology, 25*, 343-361.

Sansone, C., Sachau, D. A., & Weir, C. (1989). The effects of instruction on intrinsic interest: The importance of context. *Journal of Personality and Social Psychology, 57*, 819-829.

Sansone, C., & Voisard, B. (1990). *Effects of performance norms and health benefits on motivation for an interesting or uninteresting task*. Unpublished manuscript.

Sarason, I. G. (1980). Introduction to the study of test anxiety. In I. G. Sarason (Ed.), *Test anxiety: Theory, research, and applications* (pp. 3-14). Hillsdale, NJ: Erlbaum.

Shalley, C. E., & Oldham, G. R. (1985). Effects of goal difficulty and expected external evaluation on intrinsic motivation: A laboratory study. *Academy of Management Journal, 28*, 628-640.

Shalley, C. E., Oldham, G. R., & Porac, J. F. (1987). Effects of goal difficulty, goal setting method, and expected external evaluation on intrinsic motivation. *Academy of Management Journal, 30*, 553-563.

Spence, J. T., & Helmreich, R. L. (1983). Achievement-related motives and behaviors. In J. T. Spence (Ed.), *Achievement and achievement motives: Psychological and sociological approaches* (pp. 7-74). San Francisco: W. H. Freeman.

Umstot, D. D., Bell, C. H., & Mitchell, T. R. (1976). Effects of job enrichment and task goals on satisfaction and productivity: Implications for job design. *Journal of Applied Psychology, 61*, 379-394.

Vallacher, R. R., Somoza, M. P., & Wegner, D. M. (1989). That's easy for you to say: Action identification and speech fluency. *Journal of Personality and Social Psychology, 56*(2), 199-208.

Vallacher, R. R., & Wegner, D. M. (1987). What do people think they're doing? Action identification and human behavior. *Psychological Review, 94*, 3-15.

White, R. W. (1959). Motivation reconsidered: The concept of competence. *Psychological Review, 66*, 297-333.

White, S. E., Mitchell, T., & Bell, C. (1977). Goal setting, evaluation apprehension, and social cues as determinants of job performance and job satisfaction in a simulated organization. *Journal of Applied Psychology, 62*, 665-673.

Wine, J. (1971). Test anxiety and direction of attention. *Psychological Bulletin, 76*, 92-104.

USING GOAL ASSESSMENTS TO IDENTIFY MOTIVATIONAL PATTERNS AND FACILITATE BEHAVIORAL REGULATION AND ACHIEVEMENT

Martin E. Ford and C. W. Nichols

Goals:	Thoughts about desired states or outcomes that one would like to achieve.
Self-regulatory processes:	Psychological processes that assess progress and facilitate "staying on track" toward a goal, especially in the face of distractions and obstacles.
Achievement:	The attainment of a personally or socially valued goal in a particular context or domain.

Advances in Motivation and Achievement, Volume 7, pages 51-84.
Copyright © 1991 by JAI Press Inc.
All rights of reproduction in any form reserved.
ISBN: 1-55938-122-1

In an effort to avoid the miscommunication that so often results from the imprecise or ambiguous use of psychological concepts, we begin this paper by providing definitions of the key terms organizing this volume. These simple definitions also summarize our basic purpose in writing this paper, namely, to improve our ability to understand and promote motivation and achievement through the assessment of a person's goals.

RATIONALE

Our work is guided by a systems theoretical framework that assumes that most human behavior is goal-directed (D. Ford, 1987). These goals may not always be conscious, and they may not always be in a form that can be verbalized, but they are almost always present as a motivational force directing and organizing the stream of a person's activity.

This assumption implies that the most informative way to grasp the coherence and meaning in a pattern of behavior is to begin with an understanding of what the person is trying to accomplish (Emmons, 1989). For several years we have been engaged in a process of trying to construct assessment tools designed to identify the kinds of accomplishments that have the most value and significance for a particular individual. Having such information can enhance efforts to regulate the person's behavior toward the pursuit of these goals, especially when these goals are vaguely conceived or poorly articulated. This in turn can help people achieve the outcomes that have the greatest fundamental importance in their lives.

This rationale underlying our theoretical and empirical work indicates that we subscribe to the view that humans are self-organizing, self-constructing living systems who are capable of autonomous decision making and change, especially when the person's contexts and developmental potentials facilitate new opportunities and possibilities. However, we also recognize that biological, contextual, and developmental conditions often place significant constraints on a person's capacity for self-direction and self-regulation. For example, biologically based information processing limitations and the pervasive influence of cultural norms and values can significantly constrain the range of goals a person is able to conceive. Similarly, the tendency for people to persist in the use of unproductive behavioral habits (because they lack more effective options), or to engage in goal-directed behavior that produces unintended negative consequences can sometimes make a person's behavior appear to be illogical or counterproductive. Nevertheless, it is our assumption that personal goals play a central role in determining patterns of motivation and achievement, and that this role will increase as biological, contextual, and developmental limitations become less constraining (e.g., as the person becomes older and increasingly responsible for and capable of making significant life choices).

SPECIFIC OBJECTIVES

We have organized this paper around three interrelated goals:

1. A *theoretical* objective, namely, to introduce and explain a way of thinking about goals and self-regulatory processes based on Donald Ford's *Living Systems Framework* (D. Ford, 1987; M. Ford & D. Ford, 1987).

2. A *practical* objective, namely, to explain how goal assessments, as illustrated by the *Assessment of Personal Goals* (APG) and *Assessment of Core Goals* (ACG), can help (1) researchers in their efforts to predict behavioral choices and outcomes, and to explore and test hypotheses about the role of motivational processes in competence development; (2) practitioners and employers in their efforts to understand their clients/students/employees and to promote effective self-direction and self-regulation; and (3) ordinary people in their efforts to better understand their personal goals and priorities, make wise decisions, and achieve a sense of balance in their lives.

3. An *empirical* objective, namely, to provide initial empirical evidence for the reliability, validity, and utility of the APG and ACG.

CONCEPTUAL FRAMEWORK

Overview of the Living Systems Framework

The Living Systems Framework (LSF) is a comprehensive theory of human functioning and development designed to integrate scientific and professional knowledge about the characteristics of people in general (nomothetic knowledge) and the functioning of individual persons (idiographic knowledge) (D. Ford, 1987). The LSF not only provides a way of thinking about particular component processes of the person (e.g., goals, emotions, perceptions, memory, motor behavior), it also describes how these components function as part of a larger unit (the person) in coherent "chunks" of goal-directed activity (i.e., behavior episodes). It also explains how specific behavior episode experiences "add up" over time and across contexts to produce a unique, self-constructed history and personality (i.e., through the construction, differentiation, and elaboration of behavior episode schemata, or BES). Finally, it describes a diversity of change processes that help maintain stability and flexibility in the organized behavior patterns represented in a person's repertoire of BES (D. Ford, 1987; D. Ford & M. Ford, 1987).

The Functional Organization of Human Behavior

A key assumption of the LSF is that the person always functions as a unit. This is the *Principle of Unitary Functioning.* D. Ford (1987) has developed the concepts of behavior episode and behavior episode schemata to describe how unitary functioning occurs.

A *behavior episode* is a context-specific, goal-directed pattern of behavior that unfolds over time until one of three conditions is met: (1) the goal organizing the episode is accomplished, or accomplished "well enough" (sometimes called "satisficing"); (2) the person's attention is preempted by some internal or external event, and another goal takes precedence; or (3) the goal is evaluated as unattainable, at least for the time being. The goal (i.e., the person's cognitive representation of what they would like to achieve) provides direction for the episode, and triggers an organized but usually flexible pattern of cognitive, emotional, biological, and motor functioning that, in coordination with the opportunities and constraints in the environment, is designed to make the desired consequence actually occur. This activity is often varied and complex, since many behavior episodes involve the simultaneous pursuit of multiple goals in somewhat unpredictable environments.

Behavior episodes are typically organized in nested hierarchies. Within a given episode one can usually identify embedded subepisodes organized by increasingly concrete, context-specific subgoals. For example, a golfing episode guided by the goal of winning a match can be broken down into 18 subepisodes (each representing one hole of play). One could also take each of these smaller episodes and break them down into subepisodes representing each time a shot was played. Depending on how the person approached these shot-making episodes with regard to their goal setting, it might be appropriate to break these episodes down into an even smaller set of subepisodes (e.g., the planning, preparation, and execution components of the shot-making episode). Similar analyses can easily be made for other complex activities, such as writing a book, painting a house, having a dinner party, or pursuing a Ph.D.

The proximal sub-goals directing smaller behavior episodes provide immediate, concrete guidance and feedback regarding progress toward a goal. For this reason they play a very important role in facilitating motivation and learning (Bandura, 1986; Bandura & Schunk, 1981). However, the focus of this paper is on the identification of broader goals that organize large or recurring behavior episodes across many different contexts. In other words, our primary interest is in identifying *pervasive, temporally stable goals of fundamental and intrinsic value to the individual* rather than more transient or context-specific goals. In most cases these latter goals are of value primarily because they serve the person's broader purposes.

Since even large behavior episodes are temporary phenomena, it is necessary to have some concept representing how behavior episode experiences can have a lasting impact on the individual. The concept of *behavior episode schema* serves this purpose. This is similar to but broader than related concepts such as cognitive schema, motor schema, or self-schema (e.g., Markus, Cross, & Wurf, 1990). A BES is an integrated internal representation of a particular kind of behavior episode experience or, more commonly, a set of related behavior episode experiences (including episodes that have only been imagined or observed). A BES represents the functioning of the whole person in context, since that is what is involved in any given behavior episode. For example, a child who has a consistent history of successful experiences at school is likely to develop multiple school BES characterized by a diversity of academic and social goals, an impressive array of school-relevant skills, positive emotions, and strong expectations for success in the school environment. In contrast, a student who experiences occasional success but also failure and social rejection in certain contexts is likely to develop a differentiated repertoire of school BES that produces inconsistent patterns of motivation and achievement.

Describing this repertoire of BES can provide a rich understanding of the individual in that particular context, especially if the conditions under which different BES are activated can be identified. However, this can be a challenging task since some BES components may not be observable, consciously available to the person, or represented in verbal form. For example, goals are unobservable—because they are cognitions—and are often not represented in a form that can be easily accessed by the individual or clearly communicated to others. Thus, a primary purpose of goal assessments is to enable people to put their directive thoughts into a form that meets these criteria.

The concept of *personality* is defined in the LSF as the person's *repertoire of stable, recurring BES*. Since BES are anchored by goals and contexts (like the behavior episode constituents from which they are constructed), an individual's personality is likely to be multifaceted and varied in its manifestations. Indeed, the richer a person's life in terms of the diversity of contexts involved, the range of goals being pursued, and the outcomes experienced, the richer and more complex the individual's personality is likely to be. Nevertheless, goals provide the primary psychological "glue" for the processes that become organized into broad, stable BES. This implies that a broad, comprehensive goal assessment may be a particularly informative and useful method for describing an individual's personality. Moreover, by identifying an individual's most pervasive and fundamental goals, it should be possible not only to discern the major organizing themes in their past and current behavior, but also to make good predictions about the kinds of future circumstances they are likely to find particularly motivating or distressing.

Processes Associated With Achievement

Achievement was defined earlier as the attainment of a personally or socially valued goal in a particular context or domain. In other words, achievement is a concept representing the successful completion of a behavior episode (recall the three criteria for terminating a behavior episode described earlier). Some writers restrict the definition of achievement to particular kinds of contexts (e.g., classroom or testing contexts); however, from our point of view this is overly restrictive and introduces a subtle bias into the concept of achievement (i.e., the only achievements that count are those that are valued within a particular social context). We prefer a generic definition of achievement that treats the normative problem of determining what particular achievements should be valued for particular purposes as a separate matter. Achievement is thus similar to the concept of *competence* as defined by M. Ford (1985), except that the latter is a more complex concept that introduces ethical and developmental boundary conditions into the process of evaluating a person's effectiveness in accomplishing personally or socially desired outcomes:

> **Competence** = The attainment of relevant goals in specified environments, using appropriate means and resulting in positive developmental outcomes.

Thus, according to this definition, a person could be a high achiever in some domain but not be regarded as competent if desired outcomes are being achieved using immoral or illegal methods, or if the attainment of these goals produces negative long-term consequences for the person (e.g., health problems or damage to valued social relationships).

Regardless of the particular states or outcomes that one is trying to achieve, goal attainment requires the effective functioning of the person as a whole in cooperation with an environment that is responsive to the individual's achievement efforts. By classifying (somewhat crudely) the variety of component processes described in the LSF into three broad categories, it is possible to represent the processes contributing to achievement in the following manner:

> **Achievement** = Motivation × Skill × Responsive Environment

In other words, achievement requires a motivated, skillful person and an environment that has the contingencies, resources, and supports needed to facilitate (or at least permit) goal attainment. If *any* of these components is missing or inadequate, nothing will be achieved.

The Concept of Motivation

An examination of the history of motivational theorizing reveals that three different sets of processes have been emphasized in definitions of motivation: *directive processes* (i.e., goals or goal-related constructs such as needs or interests); *arousal processes* (especially emotions); and *regulatory processes* (i.e., processes responsible for the maintenance of goal-directed activity) (Cofer & Appley, 1964). However, most definitions have equated motivation with just one (or in rare cases two) of these processes. Even contemporary theories of motivation that have attended to all three of these elements tend to emphasize a single set of processes (usually self-evaluative thoughts and/or other aspects of self-regulation). In contrast, M. Ford (forthcoming) offers a more comprehensive definition that includes all three sets of processes:

Motivation $=$ Goals $\times$ Emotions $\times$ Personal Agency Beliefs

In other words, *motivation is the organized patterning of an individual's goals, emotions* (i.e., anticipatory arousal processes that regulate behavior), *and personal agency beliefs* (i.e., expectancies about whether one has the personal capabilities and responsive environment needed for goal attainment—also called capability and context beliefs in the LSF). Thus, *motivation is an integrative construct* representing the direction a person is going, the amount and flow of energy being used to move in that direction, and the expectancies the person has about whether they can ultimately reach their destination. Motivation is *not* primarily one or another of these processes. As the preceding equation implies, a person's motivation will be zero if *any* of these elements are missing.

Because the concept of motivation is so broad, it is easy to use it in ambiguous or imprecise ways (D. Ford, 1987). Nevertheless, the concept of motivation provides a uniquely valuable way of describing the *integrated patterning* of a set of intimately related processes.

The Role of Goals in Motivational Patterns

It is tempting to assert that goals are the core component in any given motivational pattern. After all, goals (along with contexts) organize the individual's behavior episodes and the BES that guide them. However, this simple deduction fails to recognize the exquisite interdependence of the three basic motivational components. For example, people often fail to pursue goals that are important to them because other, less important goals are more attentionally salient (e.g., completing daily chores or reacting to ongoing events). Similarly, negative personal agency beliefs can truncate behavior episodes involving important goals by leading to the evaluation that these goals are unattainable. A lack of energy resources (e.g., due to fatigue or depression) may also lead to the inhibition or premature termination of potentially rewarding behavior episodes.

Emotions and personal agency beliefs also play a critical role in the *development and elaboration* of goals. This is because the primary mechanism by which new goals are formed is the (cognitive and emotional) evaluation of current experiences. Thus, for example, a behavior episode directed by a curiosity or compliance goal ("try this activity") may lead to the development of new goals around that previously unfamiliar experience if it stimulates interest, excitement, or a sense of personal competence.

Nevertheless, goals do play a fundamental role in motivational patterns by defining their *content and direction*. If there is no goal in place, no activity or attentional energy will be allocated and no emotions will be triggered. Extant energy from the arousal processes will be expended aimlessly and unproductively, like a car idling in neutral. Similarly, capability and context beliefs about a particular kind of achievement will have no impact or significance if the person has no desire to achieve in that area. In other words, goals provide the meaning and coherence in an individual's behavior episodes, and they set the stage for all of the other components of the person to function in a purposeful and coordinated manner.

Problems With the Goal Concept

In our view, the goal concept has suffered in the literature from three major problems that have distorted its meaning and limited its use to an unnecessarily narrow range of applications. The first problem is the tendency to define goals, usually implicitly, as characteristics of external activities rather than characteristics of people. Since different people often have very different desired outcomes for the same activity (e.g., a person might engage in sex to experience pleasant bodily sensations, attain a state of intimacy, earn money, fulfill a social obligation, or make a baby), it is clearly misleading and perhaps even egocentric to define goals in terms of behaviors or activities, as if what a person is doing automatically reveals what they are trying to accomplish. Although some activities may afford the attainment of a relatively narrow range of possible goals, very few (if any) activities will afford the attainment of only a single goal.

A second, related problem is the tendency to restrict the goal concept to context-specific task goals such as completing an experimental task or performing well on a test. As a consequence, many people equate goals with very concrete or even trivial behavioral objectives. This is a painfully limiting definitional constraint. A goal can refer to *any* desired state or outcome that a person is capable of conceiving, no matter how broad or abstract that conception may be. Indeed, many goals have nothing to do with external tasks, but instead represent desired consequences of social interaction or desired cognitive or emotional states within the person (Emmons, 1989; M. Ford & Nichols, 1987). Moreover, task goals often become important precisely because they are linked in some way to these other kinds of goals (Nichols, 1990a, 1990b).

A third problem of a somewhat more semantic nature is the tendency to restrict the goal concept to directive thoughts that have produced or are currently producing significant cognitive, affective, and/or motor activity. In our view this is an unnecessary constraint that makes the concept harder to define and operationalize. We prefer the simpler conception of a goal as simply any cognition of a desired consequence. The question of whether such thoughts have actually triggered activity designed to achieve the desired consequence is a more complex matter involving regulatory and arousal processes acting in combination with the goal. We therefore prefer the related but more restrictive concept of *intention* to refer to goals that have been infused with energy and prioritized by regulatory processing. This is similar to Klinger's (1977) concept of a "current concern."

Our distinction between goals and intentions is an important one for researchers studying the impact of goals on a person's functioning. Whereas intentions should be directly and reliably associated with behavioral outcomes, the relationship between goals and outcomes will be more subtle and complex (M. Ford, 1984, 1986; Markus & Ruvolo, 1989; Pervin, 1989). Yet, it is precisely because intentions are more closely tied to the opportunities and constraints of current or impending behavior episodes that it is useful to have a conceptually "purer" construct that can reflect not only those desired consequences that are currently being attended to, but also those that have been "put on the shelf," "lost in the shuffle," or not yet conceptualized in concrete, practical terms.

Different Kinds of Goals

Throughout the history of psychology there have been many attempts to identify and label the different kinds of goals or motives that direct and organize behavior (e.g., Buhler, 1964; Cattell, 1957; Maslow, 1943; McDougall, 1933; Murray, 1938; Pervin, 1983; Rokeach, 1968; Wicker, Lambert, Richardson, & Kahler, 1984). This fascination with the directive function persisted even during the lengthy period in which concepts such as goal and purpose were unpopular or controversial (Silver, 1985). Unfortunately, these motivational taxonomies have suffered from a variety of problems that have limited their utility. Early taxonomies failed to clearly distinguish between behavior patterns and the desired consequences of these behavior patterns. As a result, lists of basic motives often were no more than tautological and arbitrary lists of different kinds of behaviors (e.g., sex, aggression, food-seeking, nurturance, play, etc.), and thus were of little explanatory value. Maslow (1943, 1970) was able to avoid this problem with his hierarchy of "needs," and consequently this taxonomy has endured for a much longer period of time in textbooks, business seminars, and the like. However, despite the usefulness of certain motivational categories in this taxonomy (e.g., Physiological, Safety, and Belongingness needs), Maslow failed to explicate the great diversity of goals that may be involved in seeking "Self-Actualization," or in trying to satisfy the less familiar categories of Aesthetic and Cognitive needs.

More recent motivational taxonomies have been more conceptually precise in terms of defining goals as purely cognitive phenomena and separating these from the behavior patterns they direct; however, none of these taxonomies has been sufficiently broad in scope or applicable to the full range of contexts that people may encounter. Thus, there is still a need for a general, comprehensive goal taxonomy that can serve as a useful heuristic device for researchers and practitioners who seek to understand the direction and organization of human behavior.

M. Ford and Nichols (1987) have developed such a taxonomy over the course of several years of research and clinical work with a variety of students, clients, and professionals. The *Ford and Nichols Taxonomy of Human Goals* builds on and extends the tradition of seeking some way to describe the fundamental content and direction of people's motivational patterns, and successfully avoids many of the problems that have plagued earlier efforts. This does not mean that the categories in this taxonomy represent "ultimate truths" about the nature of human motivation; any goal taxonomy will necessarily be limited by the fact that a person's thoughts about desired outcomes will generally be idiosyncratic, context-specific, and highly personal. Indeed, one might question whether it makes sense to conceptualize goals in any other way—after all, most contemporary approaches to goal assessment have moved away from standardized taxonomies in favor of an idiographic strategy (e.g., Emmons' [1989] "personal strivings," Klinger's [1977] "current concerns" and "ultimate incentives," Cantor's "life tasks" [Cantor & Langston, 1989], Markus' "possible selves" [Markus & Ruvolo, 1989], Little's [1983] "personal projects"). Nevertheless, a standardized classification scheme can facilitate the process of making comparisons across individuals and social groups, and it can serve as a conceptual anchor in classifying goals within an individual's hierarchy of goals (Emmons, 1989). Our taxonomy is thus offered as a potentially useful starting point for describing and classifying people's goals in a succinct, efficient, and comprehensive manner.

The Ford and Nichols Taxonomy of Human Goals is summarized in Table 1. Each goal is defined by a primary label and several additional words and phrases that help explicate the intended meaning of each goal label. Because there are an unlimited number of variations on these goals that people may conceive of at the behavior episode level of analysis, the categories in this taxonomy are intended to represent *classes* of goals at a relatively abstract or decontextualized level of analysis (i.e., at the "personality" level of broad, stable BES, or "Level 1" of Emmons (1989) four-level motivational hierarchy). Thus, each goal category can be interpreted as a conceptual "prototype" representing a set of desired states or outcomes that are similar in meaning.

At the most general level of analysis, the taxonomy is divided into two types of goals: goals that represent desired consequences within the person, and goals that represent desired consequences with respect to the relationship between

Table 1.   The Ford and Nichols Taxonomy of Human Goals

Desired Within-Person Consequences

Affective Goals

Entertainment	Experiencing excitement or heightened arousal; Avoiding boredom or stressful inactivity
Tranquility	Experiencing serinity or peace of mind; Avoiding stressful overarousal
Happiness	Experiencing feelings of joy, satisfaction, or well being; Avoiding feelings of distress, dissatisfaction, or lack of fulfillment
Bodily Sensations	Experiencing pleasurable physical sensations; Freedom from physical pain or discomfort
Physical Well Being	Feeling strong, healthy, or physically robust; Avoiding feeling weak or fatigued

Cognitive Goals

Exploration	Satisfying one's curiosity, perceiving new information; Avoiding circumstances in which there are no secrets or novelties to discover
Understanding	Gaining knowledge or making sense out of something; Avoiding feelings of ignorance or confusion
Intellectual Creativity	Formulating or expressing new ideas; Avoiding routine or familiar ways of thinking
Positive Self-Evaluations	Feeling capable, responsible, or worthy; Avoiding feelings of incompetence, guilt, or worthlessness

Subjective Organization Goals

Unity	Experiencing a sense of harmony, coherence, or oneness; Avoiding feelings of psychological disunity or disorganization
Transcendence	Experiencing extraordinary, idealized, or spiritual states; Avoiding feeling trapped within the boundaries of ordinary experience

Desired Person-Environment Consequences

Self-Assertive Social Relationship Goals

Individuality	Feeling unique, special, or different; Avoiding similarity or conformity with others
Self-Determination	Experiencing a sense of freedom or personal control; Avoiding feeling constrained or manipulated by others
Superiority	Comparing favorably to others in terms of winning, status, or success; Avoiding losing or unfavorable comparisons with others
Resource Acquisition	Obtaining approval, support, assistance, advice, or validation from others; Avoiding social disapproval or rejection

Integrative Social Relationship Goals

Belongingness	Building or maintaining attachments, friendships, intimacy, or a sense of community; Avoiding feelings of social isolation or separateness
Social Responsibility	Keeping interpersonal commitments, meeting social role obligations, following social and moral rules; Avoiding social transgressions and unethical or illegal conduct
Equity	Promoting fairness, justice, reciprocity, or equality; Avoiding unfaire or unjust actions
Resource Provision	Giving approval, support, assistance, advice, or validation to others; Avoiding selfish or uncaring behavior

(continued)

Table 1.   (Continued)

Task Goals	
Mastery	Meeting a standard of achievement, improving one's performance; Avoiding incompetence, mediocrity, or decrements in performance
Task Creativity	Constructing or inventing new processes or products; Avoiding repetitious or mindless tasks
Management	Maintaining order, organization, or productivity in daily life tasks; Avoiding sloppiness, inefficiency, or disorganization
Material Gain	Having money or tangible goods; Avoiding the loss of money or material possessions
Safety	Being unharmed, physically secure, and free from risk; Avoiding threatening, depriving, or harmful circumstances

a person and their environment. These two categories are, by definition, exhaustive of all possible goals involving the person.

There are three different kinds of within-person consequences that a person might desire: affective goals, cognitive goals, and "subjective organization" goals. Affective goals represent different kinds of feelings or emotions that a person might want to experience or avoid, such as being happy, avoiding boredom, feeling relaxed, avoiding pain, or experiencing pleasant bodily sensations. Cognitive goals refer to different kinds of mental representations that people may want to construct or maintain, such as acquiring information to satisfy one's curiosity, constructing accurate or novel thoughts about some phenomenon, or maintaining positive thoughts about the self. Subjective organization goals represent special, extraordinary states that people may seek to experience (or avoid) that involve a combination of different kinds of thoughts and feelings (e.g., a subjective sense of unity with nature or an undesired state of psychic disorganization within the self).

There are two broad categories of desired person-environment consequences in the taxonomy: social relationship goals and task goals. Within the former category, four goals represent the desire to maintain or promote the self (i.e., self-assertive goals), and four goals represent the desire to maintain or promote the well being of other people or the social groups of which one is a part (i.e., integrative goals). Task goals represent desired relationships between the individual and various objects in the environment (including people when they are being conceived of in impersonal terms).

It is beyond the scope of this chapter to provide detailed definitions of each goal in the taxonomy (see Ford & Nichols, 1987 for this additional level of explication). However, the essential meaning of each goal in the taxonomy should be interpretable from the descriptions in Table 1.

Different Kinds of Goal Assessments

In this paper we focus on goal assessments that provide an indication of the strength or importance of different kinds of goals, such as those described in the Ford and Nichols Taxonomy of Human Goals. These are assessments of *goal content*. However, it is useful to note that there are two other kinds of goal-related phenomena that one can assess. If the concern is with the method or style a person uses to conceptualize a goal rather than with the content of the goal per se, an assessment of *goal-setting processes* or *goal orientation* would be needed. For example, researchers in the field of industrial and organizational psychology specializing in goal-setting processes have focused on differences in the methods people use to represent goals in behavior episodes involving contextually defined tasks (e.g., in specific or vague terms, with hard or easy standards for goal attainment, or with regard to short-term or long-term desired consequences) (Lee, Locke, & Latham, 1989).

On the other hand, if one were primarily interested in the more general style with which a person thinks about goals (i.e., at the broader "personality" level of analysis), a goal orientation assessment would be needed. Ford and Nichols (1987) have outlined several dimensions along which people may differ in their general orientation to goal setting. *Approach-avoidance* refers to whether a person tends to conceptualize goals in terms of positive consequences to be achieved or negative consequences to be avoided (e.g., wanting to succeed on a task versus wanting to avoid failure; seeking social approval versus fearing social disapproval). *Active-reactive* refers to the extent to which goal-directed activity is initiated by the person or by ongoing events. This is a potentially important distinction because assessments of goal content that tap broad, stable motivational patterns may be more predictive of behavioral choices and outcomes for people with an active than a reactive goal orientation (contextual information, which represents the other major organizing force in behavior episodes, is likely to be more predictive for individuals with a reactive goal orientation). *Maintenance-growth* refers to whether a person's goals reflect more of a self organizing (i.e., stability maintaining) orientation or self-constructing (i.e., change-seeking) orientation (e.g., Dweck's [1986] distinction between performance and learning goals). One can also combine this dimension with the other two to define an even broader pattern, which Winnell (1987) labels *coping* versus *thriving* (i.e., a reactive, avoidant, stability maintaining orientation versus an active, positive, growth-oriented pattern).

The distinction between *intrinsic* and *extrinsic* goals, which has been a major topic in the fields of educational and social psychology, provides another example of a goal-related dimension that may be assessed at the broad goal orientation level, although it is also a relevant distinction at the level of a specific behavior episode. An intrinsic or *terminal* goal (Ford & Nichols, 1987) is a desired consequence that is valued primarily for its own sake and not because its attainment helps a person reach some other goal. An extrinsic or *instrumental* goal is a desired consequence that is valued primarily because its attainment provides a means to achieving some other goal. Unfortunately, this distinction has been conceptually muddled by the tendency of researchers to treat particular categories of goal *content* as extrinsic (e.g., material gain, social approval) or intrinsic (e.g., task mastery, creativity goals). This confusion has occurred because most studies of intrinsic and extrinsic motivation have had task completion or creative output as the (externally defined) outcome of interest. However, *any* goal can be intrinsic, extrinsic, or both. Indeed, behavior episodes directed by goals with both intrinsic and extrinsic properties will generally yield the most powerful motivational outcomes due to the amplifying effect of aligning multiple, mutually facilitative goals.

The Role of Self-Regulatory Processes in Motivation and Achievement

It is impossible to understand how goals facilitate behavioral regulation without first understanding the concept of regulation and how self-regulatory processes work in conjunction with directive processes to promote motivation and achievement. According to the LSF (D. Ford, 1987), three interrelated regulatory mechanisms have evolved in humans: biochemical, affective, and cognitive. In each case, regulation refers to processes that help a person evaluate progress and stay "on track" in their efforts to achieve a goal.

Biochemical regulatory mechanisms are relatively automatic processes that help maintain a diversity of biological variables within preset boundaries, a process called homeostasis by Cannon (1939). These processes generally operate outside of awareness and are therefore not of primary interest for the purposes of this paper (i.e., the goals being served are at a different level of analysis and are qualitatively different phenomena than goals at the psychological level of functioning).

An affect is a consciously perceived manifestation of some neural, biochemical, or body state (D. Ford, 1987). All emotions are experienced as affects, but so are non-emotional states such as fatigue and pain. Positive affective states regulate behavior by facilitating the continuation or repetition of behavior episodes in which such states are experienced. Negative affective states regulate behavior by inhibiting the continuation or repetition of behavior episodes involving these affects or by activating behavior designed to change the conditions that are producing the negative affect. Affective regulation is a powerful mechanism for three reasons: (1) the immediacy of affective experience (i.e., it commands attention and is hard to ignore); (2) the capability of humans to link emotional states with almost any conceivable context; and (3) the fact that cognitive regulatory mechanisms depend on the energy supplied by emotional processes to translate thought into action.

Although emotions provide a very potent mechanism for regulating behavior, evaluative thoughts provide the primary mechanism by which emotional patterns are activated (Arnold, 1960; D. Ford, 1987; Lazarus, 1982, 1984). Therefore, one must again resist the temptation to view one or the other of these intimately related processes as being superior or more fundamental. Cognitive regulation is arguably more complex, however. There are three different mechanisms involved in this kind of regulation:

1. *Feedback mechanisms*: monitoring and evaluation of goal-related progress against relevant (and often implicit) standards for goal attainment, including evaluations of the goals being pursued and the strategies being contemplated or used to pursue them.
2. *Feedforward mechanisms*: expectancies about one's capabilities for effective action (capability beliefs), as well as expectancies about the responsiveness of the environment to one's goal attainment efforts (context beliefs), i.e., personal agency beliefs.
3. *Activation of control processes*: triggering of relevant planning and problem-solving activity, including strategies designed to maintain the integrity of the behavior episode over time in the face of competing goals and obstacles.

Thus, *cognitive regulation involves the coordinated patterning of one motivational mechanism* (personal agency beliefs) *and two skill-related mechanisms* (collection and evaluation of feedback information and the triggering of a different cognitive function, the control process). If one adds affective regulation to this list of mechanisms, it is evident that *self-regulation is a complex, integrative construct that overlaps with the complex, integrative construct of motivation.* Perhaps it is no wonder that people often find the theoretical and empirical literatures on these topics rather confusing!

The explicated definition of regulation just described clarifies how goal assessments might be expected to facilitate behavioral regulation and achievement. With regard to affective regulation, goal assessments may provide an important foundation for intervention by helping to explain why people tend to become emotionally active or agitated in particular kinds of circumstances. For example, someone who experiences stress and frustration in a diversity of contexts involving disorganization, messiness, or procrastination probably feels this way because they have a strong management goal (see Table 1). Similarly, someone who tends to avoid stimulating situations that many people would find pleasurable or exciting probably has a pervasive tranquility goal as a major personality component. In contrast, someone who enjoys highly arousing, even dangerous activities is probably being guided by a potent entertainment goal. People who become agitated about various forms of social injustice probably have equity as a salient concern, whereas those who tend to feel empathic and concerned about people in distress are likely to have resource provision as a major goal. Of course, a particular kind of emotion pattern may be linked to many different kinds of goals (recall the earlier warning about equating goals and activities). The point here is that an individual's emotional experience may become much more comprehensible (and alterable) if both the goals and contexts anchoring the person's experience are well understood.

Given the intimate connection between strong goals and strong emotions, a sound goal assessment that can identify motivational patterns such as these may also give an interventionist (parent, teacher, counselor, manager, director) a powerful tool in helping a person stay "on track" in the face of emotional obstacles and distractions associated with the activation of competing goals. For example, people with strong self-determination goals may respond antagonistically to interventions designed to promote social responsibility if these interventions do not provide some choices and options. People with strong tranquility or happiness goals may respond poorly to interventions that produce acute distress as part of the therapeutic process. People with unusually strong superiority goals may reinterpret interventions designed to promote task mastery or cooperative teamwork into social comparison terms if there is no explicit attempt to prevent this. In short, it is probably commonplace for interventionists to think they are creating one kind of experience when in fact something else is happening. This suggests that without some kind of goal assessment it may be difficult for interventionists to recognize and deal with discrepancies between the intended and actual outcomes of their interventions.

In addition, a goal assessment can help identify the source of more general patterns of anxiety and depression. These emotions are associated with uncertain or negative expectations for goal attainment. By comparing an individual's goal profile with their emotional experience, it may become evident why they feel the way they do, and consequently why they behave the way they do. For example, a person with a large number of very important goals may have difficulty attaining all or even many of these goals, which may lead to considerable negative affect even though the person has achieved a great deal by normative standards. Alternatively, a person may experience negative affect because of a severe mismatch between their personal goals and the opportunities for goal attainment afforded by their current life circumstances.

Goal assessments can also facilitate behavioral regulation and achievement by enabling a person (or interventionist) to become more focused on feedback information of direct relevance to the person's most important goals. This feedback can then be used to help the person "get back on track" in terms of underdeveloped priorities. For example, a person with strong creativity goals and a low score on material gain may want to reconsider a decision to pursue a business career. A young man with strong integrative goals who has been primarily focused on self-gratification and personal advancement may decide to reorganize some aspects of his life as a consequence of a comprehensive goal assessment. Conversely, a woman who has spent most of her time helping others achieve their goals may begin to think about ways to achieve a better balance between her self-assertive and integrative goals.

A goal assessment can also pinpoint the life domains for which personal agency beliefs are of greatest current concern. Capability and context beliefs will generally have more impact in regulating behavior when there is a strong goal in place. For example, if an elderly woman doubts her ability to achieve a thorough understanding of world affairs, but has little interest in achieving this goal, the motivational consequences of her negative capability beliefs are likely to be insignificant. In contrast, if this same woman is pessimistic about her ability to maintain a safe environment and has safety as a dominant concern, her personal agency beliefs are likely to be of great significance in trying to understand the decisions she makes and the actions she takes in her everyday life.

Summary

A prerequisite for understanding the role of goals and self-regulatory processes in motivation and achievement is a clear and precise conception of each of these phenomena and their relationship to each other. The LSF provides such a conception. In it, goals are defined as thoughts about desired consequences, and achievement is defined as the attainment of those consequences (or in the case of socially defined achievements, consequences that are valued by the person's context). Self-regulation refers to the cognitive and affective processes that help a person continue potentially productive behavior episodes (i.e., those that are likely to lead to goal attainment) and discontinue unproductive episodes. Goals and self-regulatory processes are intimately connected in motivational patterns consisting of directive thoughts (goals), emotional arousal processes, and expectancies about goal attainment (personal agency beliefs).

From this conceptual framework one can hypothesize that a particularly useful kind of knowledge to have about an individual would be information about their most fundamental and pervasive goals—that is, the thoughts that are likely to guide many of their life episodes and to become a central force in determining what they try to achieve and what they in fact achieve. Such information may be useful not only in terms of reaching a deeper understanding of an individual's motivational patterns and "personality," but also in very practical ways in terms of designing environments and experiences that will facilitate the individual's achievement of personally and/or socially desired outcomes.

INTERVENING TO FACILITATE
MOTIVATION AND ACHIEVEMENT

The Principle of Unitary Functioning

Because the person always functions as a unit, efforts to facilitate or improve a person's functioning will have an impact on the whole person, not just on some isolated part of the person. For example, if a teenage girl begins to wear eyeglasses to improve her vision, this may alter her reading skills, motor activity, and self-evaluative thoughts. A parent who severely punishes a child for misbehavior at home is likely not only to change the child's behavior, but also to shape the child's thoughts and feelings about his relationship with his parents. If a math teacher repeatedly assigns drill-and-practice exercises to teach computational skills, she will probably also be influencing students' math-related goals, emotions, and personal agency beliefs in predictable ways. A manager who insists on drug testing of employees is likely to influence not only his employees' drug use, but also their thoughts and feelings about working under his management.

These examples illustrate a basic corollary of the Principle of Unitary Functioning that is of particular relevance to interventionists:

The basic units that must be altered are the person's enduring functional patterns, that is, their behavior episode schemata.

One might try to accomplish this by modifying the characteristics of an existing BES or by replacing a problematic BES with a different BES. In either case, *change is accomplished by designing specific behavior episode experiences that have the properties of the desired BES, and then repeating these kinds of experiences until an enduring BES with these properties has been formed.* The number of repetitions needed may range from one to many depending on such factors as the complexity of the BES to be learned, the person's capabilities, and the strength of potentially competing BES that are already in the person's repertoire.

The Problem of Creating Transferable BES

Recall that behavior episodes and the BES that guide them are anchored by *goals* and *contexts*. This property of functional organization has two major implications for interventions designed to facilitate motivation and achievement. First, transfer of training to new or different contexts is unlikely to occur unless the motivational patterns and skills learned in the training context are explicitly tied to the alternative contexts of interest (Goldstein & Glick, 1986). In other words, BES that have been developed in one context (e.g., a classroom, a counselor's office) must be anchored to other relevant contexts if transfer is to occur in a reliable manner. Second, and perhaps less well understood, is a similar phenomenon in which BES organized around one set of goals are unlikely to be activated when a different set of goals is in place. For example, a boy who practices the piano in order to comply with his parents' wishes is unlikely to think about playing the piano when he feels like having fun or wants to take on a new challenge. Similarly, a high school student who is studying a history lesson to earn a passing grade on a test will probably activate a rather different BES than if she were to study this same lesson for the purpose of trying to achieve a depthy understanding of the material.

These considerations suggest that interventions to facilitate motivation and achievement will be more effective in producing powerful, lasting results if the interventionist is sensitive to the range of goals that may be activated by the intervention and is able to identify the particular goals that different individuals may bring to the intervention context. This point was made earlier in the discussion of how people may interpret and respond to interventions in unexpected ways. However, it is also an important issue when people respond to an intervention precisely as intended—even when an intervention is successful (i.e., desired BES have been created), people may not subsequently use what they have learned if their goals in future, "real-life" behavior episodes are incongruent with the goals anchoring the learned BES. For example, a student who learns to think creatively may rarely demonstrate this capability in the classroom if her primary concern is with avoiding negative evaluations from her teacher or friends. A teenager who successfully learns why and how to use a condom in a behavior episode guided by an understanding or social responsibility goal may fail to apply this knowledge in an episode dominated by a bodily sensation or entertainment goal. An executive who has learned sound ethical principles through daily experience with clients and associates may not activate this BES in a relatively impersonal episode dominated by a material gain goal (e.g., a tax computation or accounting episode). Thus, goal information can play a vital role in facilitating the design of sound interventions and clarifying the limitations of one's intervention procedures.

The Crucial Role of Attention/Consciousness in Altering BES

According to the LSF, most cognitive processing occurs outside of awareness in the context of partly or fully automatized BES (D. Ford, 1987). Langer (1989) uses the concept of *mindlessness* to describe this phenomenon. On the one hand, automaticity can enable a person to function in a highly organized and efficient manner—so much so that Sternberg (1985) has made automaticity one of the cornerstones of his triarchic theory of intelligence. On the other hand, the mindless execution of habitual BES can reduce the effectiveness of a person's functioning if the goals organizing these BES are vague, inappropriate for the person's current circumstances, or poorly integrated with the person's "intrinsic," "terminal," or "core" goals. These are conditions for which a goal assessment might be particularly useful for an individual or interventionist attempting to facilitate that individual's motivation and achievement.

The logic underlying this use of a goal assessment is as follows. According to the LSF, learning can only occur if a person *attends* to relevant information (D. Ford, 1987). Thus, it would be impossible to improve the clarity or situational appropriateness of a person's goals without that person first attending to them. However, *people can only be conscious of information that is in perceptible form* (e.g., pictures or other images, words or other symbols) (D. Ford, 1987). Since most people have little experience in putting their basic goals into easily perceptible forms, goal assessments that help people accomplish this function will often be a basic and necessary step in the process of helping people alter problematic BES.

For example, a counselor or therapist could use a goal assessment as a device for interpreting the meaning of a client's problems, communicating this interpretation to the client, and then using this shared understanding to evaluate therapeutic progress. As the focus of therapy moved from the resolution of immediate problems to a more general effort to enhance the client's capabilities for self-direction and self-regulation, goal information could be used to help the client clarify, shape, and prioritize their goals within and across important life contexts (cf. Winell, 1987).

Teachers and other education professionals could use goal assessments to try to achieve a deeper understanding of their students' diverse interests and needs and to facilitate discussions with students and parents about major issues affecting the educational process (e.g., teaching strategies, motivational problems, career decision making). Goal information might also enhance the ability of educators to collaborate with students in designing rich and varied instructional environments and activities that are personally relevant and motivating for as many students as possible.

Similarly, business professionals could use goal assessments to better coordinate work requirements with the personal goals of their employees. For example, goal information could help managers and supervisors organize the work environment in such a way that the pursuit of personal goals would be instrumental to the attainment of the organization's goals. Work environments that clearly communicate goals, rules, and feedback, but that also offer flexibility, choice, and autonomy are particularly likely to achieve this productive state of goal alignment. Goal information might also help employers avoid errors in the selection and assignment of personnel by assisting them in determining the extent to which a person's goals were congruent with the opportunities for goal attainment afforded by a particular work environment (e.g., Behravesh, Karimi, & Ford, 1989).

Finally, goal assessments can help people deal with stressful problems and circumstances in their everyday life, and increase the frequency with which they engage in highly rewarding activities. For example, we have found the information derived from goal assessments to be extremely useful in helping people evaluate the meaning and significance of their emotional reactions to daily life events. Patterns of anxiety and frustration involving dissimilar events often become interpretable in terms of a common goal theme. Seemingly disconnected experiences characterized by high levels of interest and satisfaction can often be understood in terms of underlying similarities in the goals being attained. Such insights can then be used to guide future behavior. Indeed, the process of representing a person's goals in conscious, perceptible form can be a highly empowering experience—not only can it help the person make choices about how to direct or redirect their behavior, it can also promote recognition of the ways in which the person's environment may need to be changed if core goals are to be successfully pursued.

GOAL ASSESSMENT STRATEGIES

Two Strategies for Assessing Goal Content

There are essentially two different methods that can be used to assess goal content. The first method involves the classification of a person's responses into standardized categories that do not vary across individuals. These categories are described using verbal labels that simplify the problem of describing a person's goals (because the menu of possible descriptions is predetermined). This strategy is particularly useful when groups of people are being assessed (i.e., data must be aggregated across individuals) or when comparisons across individuals need to be made.

A second method for assessing goal content is to use the vocabulary or mental images of the individual being assessed to describe the person's desired consequences. This requires an individualized procedure (e.g., a clinical interview or open-ended questionnaire) in which the person is guided through a process designed to yield rich, precise representations of their goals. Because this strategy yields idiosyncratic goal descriptions, it is primarily useful in research designs and applied settings involving the individual case.

In the final sections of this paper we describe two measures of goal content that illustrate the two goal assessment strategies just described, and present some initial empirical evidence for the reliability, validity, and utility of these measures.

The Assessment of Personal Goals (APG)

The APG, which exemplifies the first method for assessing goal content, is a self-administered paper-and-pencil measure designed to assess the strength of each of the 24 categories of goals listed in the Ford and Nichols Taxonomy of Human Goals (Ford & Nichols, 1987, forthcoming). The APG is composed of 24 5-item scales. These items are somewhat unique in that they are presented in behavior episode form rather than in a more traditional propositional or trait label format. For example, one of the belongingness items presents the following hypothetical scenario: "A friend of yours is moving across the country to take a new job. Would it be important to you to stay in close touch with this friend by mail or phone?" For each item in the APG, respondents are asked to indicate on a 9-point scale how likely they would be to desire a particular outcome or to be bothered by a failure to attain that outcome.

The logic underlying this assessment strategy is as follows. We assume that the best way to index the strength of a goal is to determine the probability that the goal will be activated within and across contexts that explicitly afford the attainment of that goal. In other words, we try to control the context component of the behavior episode and then look for variance in the goal component. Each item provides an estimate of the probability that the goal will be activated *within* a particular context—specifically, when asked if goal activation would occur respondents can say "No, definitely not," "Probably not, but perhaps under some circumstances." "Hard to say, it depends on the circumstances," "Probably, but not necessarily in all circumstances," or "Yes, definitely" (in-between responses are also permitted, thus yielding nine response options). In addition, by averaging across the five context-specific items in a scale, one can infer the strength of the abstract goal category *across* contexts. A diversity of item content is included in each scale in an effort to insure that the overall estimate of goal strength is representative of the broadest possible range of contexts.

Crucial to this logic is the assumption that each behavior episode in the APG clearly and unambiguously affords the attainment of just one major goal. Because many situations afford the attainment of several different kinds of goals (as noted earlier), it is a surprisingly difficult task to write items that meet this criterion. Moreover, each item must be familiar to respondents in the sense that one can assume there is a BES in the respondent's repertoire that will enable them to recognize the goal that the item is designed to measure. This does not mean that respondents need to have actually experienced each episode, but it does mean that they must be able to draw on their past observations and experiences in a way that leads them to interpret the item in the intended way.

One way to test whether or not such items can be constructed is to evaluate the internal consistency reliability of the 24 scales in the APG. Thus far we have obtained reliability estimates from three groups: a sample of 482 college and graduate students and professionals from university communities in California, Nevada, Minnesota, New York, Pennsylvania, Ohio, and Georgia, representing a diversity of fields (eduation and business were the two largest)

Table 2. Means, Standard Deviations, and Alpha Coefficients
for the 24 APG Scales in Three Different Samples

Sample	Means			Standard Deviations			Alpha Coefficients		
	1	*2*	*3*	*1*	*2*	*3*	*1*	*2*	*3*
Scale									
Entertainment	5.08	6.39	5.53	1.95	1.65	1.94	.72	.69	.69
Tranquility	5.96	5.84	5.74	1.63	1.61	1.84	.72	.74	.78
Happiness	6.70	7.04	6.66	1.18	1.23	1.26	.51	.63	.51
Bodily Sensations	4.95	5.63	5.05	1.65	1.55	1.57	.62	.51	.49
Physical Well Being	6.64	6.81	6.74	1.54	1.33	1.57	.74	.69	.72
Exploration	6.25	6.51	6.38	1.47	1.31	1.52	.62	.48	.61
Understanding	6.80	6.83	7.04	1.14	1.19	1.18	.53	.64	.54
Intellectual Creativity	5.39	6.42	6.23	1.38	1.34	1.63	.53	.54	.67
Positive Self-Evaluations	6.69	6.73	6.72	1.43	1.44	1.44	.70	.72	.65
Unity	5.19	5.13	5.94	1.87	1.80	1.74	.81	.83	.74
Transcendence	4.91	5.02	5.78	1.74	1.69	1.75	.72	.71	.69
Individuality	5.27	5.58	5.48	1.65	1.66	1.64	.64	.69	.58
Self-Determination	5.29	5.31	5.33	1.44	1.36	1.52	.65	.59	.65
Superiority	4.37	4.80	4.50	1.68	1.57	1.43	.68	.60	.45
Resource Acquisition	6.33	6.36	6.16	1.46	1.57	1.69	.64	.71	.72
Belongingness	7.04	7.01	6.93	1.09	1.14	1.14	.55	.59	.43
Social Responsibility	6.08	5.29	5.86	1.53	1.69	1.60	.68	.72	.62
Equity	6.78	6.22	6.42	1.18	1.25	1.42	.54	.50	.59
Resource Provision	5.67	5.89	5.43	1.48	1.71	1.54	.70	.82	.63
Mastery	6.01	6.35	6.71	1.31	1.14	1.09	.58	.48	.35
Task Creativity	5.90	6.31	6.16	1.82	1.74	1.76	.76	.75	.71
Management	6.87	6.40	7.14	1.39	1.44	1.31	.65	.63	.54
Material Gain	5.07	5.89	5.11	1.51	1.44	1.63	.53	.52	.56
Safety	6.91	6.41	6.68	1.45	1.59	1.53	.63	.69	.59

and ranging in age from 18 to 67 (Sample 1); a sample of 177 high school
students from an ethnically diverse middle- to upper-middle class community
in the San Francisco Bay Area (Sample 2); and a Los Angeles area community
college sample ($N = 176$) ranging in age from 17 to 60 (Sample 3). These
findings are presented in Table 2.

Overall, the moderate to high levels of internal consistency indicate that the
APG is capable of providing reliable estimates of the strength of the goal
categories represented in the Ford and Nichols Taxonomy of Human Goals.
Indeed, given the diversity of item content and the relatively small number
of items in each scale, these results are generally quite impressive. However,
the variability in the alphas across scales suggests that some goal categories
may be more heterogeneous than others (e.g., Mastery, Bodily Sensations,
Material Gain). On the other hand, another reason for the lower alphas in
some scales is the reduced variability that is characteristic of scales representing
goals that are highly important to most people (or at least most of the people

in these samples, e.g., Belongingness, Happiness, Understanding; see Table 2). This illustrates another property of these scales that we discovered as we attempted to write items that would elicit variability across subjects, namely, that for the most important human goals it is virtually impossible to create reliable items that are not skewed toward the positive end of the scale. Thus, scale means are permitted to vary, and scores for individual subjects can be interpreted in two different ways: in terms of the verbal anchors on the nine-point scale and/or in terms of how other people tend to score on that scale. For example, a score of 6.0 for Belongingness would indicate that this is a fairly important goal for that individual, but not as important as is the case for most people. In contrast, a score of 6.0 for Superiority would be an unusually high score compared to other people despite the fact that, for that individual, activation of a superiority goal in social comparison situations would still depend fairly heavily on the particular circumstances involved.

We have attempted to evaluate the validity of the APG in several ways. First, we have examined age and gender differences to see if predictable patterns of group differences are manifested in the data across the 24 scales. Such differences have emerged for both age and gender. Table 3 summarizes the gender difference results in Sample 1 that were statistically significant and replicated at a significant level in at least one of the other two samples. As one might expect, males tend to score higher than females in the self-assertive goal category of Superiority, whereas females score higher than males in the integrative goal categories of Belongingness, Social Responsibility, and Resource Provision. Females also appeared to be more concerned about their personal health and safety (i.e., they scored higher on Physical Well Being and Safety), their mental and emotional health (i.e., Positive Self-Evaluations and Happiness), and their access to social support and approval (i.e., Resource Acquisition). Perhaps the most interesting aspect of these results is the apparent tendency of females to be highly concerned about a relatively broader range of goals than are males. This may represent a potentially productive avenue for future research seeking to identify the processes underlying gender differences in motivational phenomena such as anxiety and depression, goal conflicts, and patterns of personal agency beliefs.

Table 4 presents age difference results from Sample 1 that were statistically significant and replicated in Sample 3 (sample 2 spanned only a very narrow age range). For the most part, there was a linear decrease in the importance of goals representing relatively immediate or perceptually salient outcomes such as experiencing positive affective states (i.e., Entertainment, Bodily Sensations, Physical Well Being), satisfying one's curiosity (Exploration), looking and feeling unique and special (Individuality), and having money or material possessions (Material Gain). However, there was a tendency for these goals to peak in the 20-21 year old age group. Precisely the reverse pattern was observed for four other goals reflecting what might be regarded as more

Table 3. Means and Standard Deviations for Males and Females in Sample 1 for Scales With Consistent Gender Differences Across Samples

	Males		Females			
	Mean	SD	Mean	SD	T	p
Scale						
Superiority	5.00	1.76	4.13	1.58	5.23	<.001
Safety	6.37	1.64	7.12	1.30	−5.23	<.001
Positive Self-Evaluations	6.19	1.63	6.88	1.28	−4.80	<.001
Belongingness	6.74	1.25	7.18	.98	−4.10	<.001
Social Responsibility	5.70	1.69	6.26	1.41	−3.64	<.001
Resource Provision	5.31	1.53	5.84	1.43	−3.55	<.001
Resource Acquisition	5.98	1.48	6.45	1.42	−3.20	.001
Physical Well Being	6.31	1.57	6.80	1.49	−3.12	.002
Management	6.63	1.36	6.99	1.38	−2.60	.010
Happiness	6.51	1.33	6.79	1.11	−2.27	.024

Table 4. Means for Five Age Groups in Sample 1 for Scales With Consistent Age Differences Across Samples

Age Group	18-19	20-21	22-29	30-39	40-67
Scale	(N = 39)	(N = 211)	(N = 111)	(N = 59)	(N = 41)
Entertainment	5.88a	5.91a	4.94b	3.56c	2.85d
Material Gain	5.00abc	5.49a	5.12b	4.60c	3.82d
Physical Well Being	6.73ab	6.97a	6.71a	6.15bc	5.59c
Exploration	6.19ab	6.66a	6.05b	5.71bc	5.49c
Individuality	5.42ab	5.64a	5.04bc	4.67c	4.63c
Bodily Sensations	4.89ab	5.22a	4.95ab	4.63b	3.93c
Social Responsibility	6.04ab	5.80a	6.08a	6.58bc	7.08c
Equity	6.77ab	6.46a	6.93b	7.09bc	7.51c
Safety	6.85a	6.74a	6.83a	7.09ab	7.65b
Self-Determination	4.70a	5.30b	5.35b	5.40b	5.45b
Unity	5.05ab	4.97a	5.31ab	5.48ab	5.73b

Note: Means that do not share a subscript are significantly different at $p < .05$ based on a Duncan's Multiple Range Test.

fundamental concerns about the well being of self and others: Social Responsibility, Equity, Safety, and Self-Determination. Unity was also somewhat more compelling to older respondents.

Another way in which we sought to explore the validity of the APG was to examine the relationships among the 24 scale scores to see if interpretable patterns emerged. We used several different univariate and multivariate correlational procedures in each of the three samples to try to determine the most replicable patterns. The existence of several such patterns provides initial evidence for the construct validity of the APG. These patterns are summarized in Table 5.

Table 5.   Replicable Patterns of Scale Intercorrelations Expressed in Terms
of Scale Clusters With Central and Contributing Components
(Central Components Are Denoted by UPPERCASE lettering)

CLUSTER 1:   MENTAL AND EMOTIONAL HEALTH

HAPPINESS   TRANQUILITY

Self-Determination   Safety   Positive Self-Evaluations

CLUSTER 2:   SELF-ENHANCING THOUGHTS AND EXPERIENCES

POSITIVE SELF-EVALUATIONS   RESOURCE ACQUISITION

Individuality   Superiority   Exploration   Bodily Sensations

CLUSTER 3:   LOW TOLERANCE FOR DISCREPANCY

MANAGEMENT   SAFETY   BELONGINGNESS   POSITIVE SELF-EVALUATIONS

CLUSTER 4:   TASK ACCOMPLISHMENT

MASTERY   MANAGEMENT

Social Responsibility

CLUSTER 5:   INTELLECTUAL DEVELOPMENT

UNDERSTANDING   MASTERY

Intellectual Creativity

CLUSTER 6:   CREATIVITY

INTELLECTUAL CREATIVITY   TASK CREATIVITY

Unity

CLUSTER 7:   EXTRAORDINARY EXPERIENCE

UNITY   TRANSCENDENCE

Understanding

CLUSTER 8:   MORAL AND PROSOCIAL BEHAVIOR

EQUITY   SOCIAL RESPONSIBILITY   RESOURCE PROVISION

CLUSTER 9:   CARING RELATIONSHIPS

RESOURCE PROVISION   BELONGINGNESS

CLUSTER 10:   PERSONAL GAIN

MATERIAL GAIN   SUPERIORITY

Entertainment   Low Social Responsibility

We have also obtained some direct evidence for the convergent and discriminant validity of the APG as a result of the respondents in Sample 2 completing a second goal assessment that is also based (in part) on the the Ford and Nichols Taxonomy of Human Goals. This assessment, which is part of a measure designed to assess capability and context beliefs, is called the *Assessment of Personal Agency Beliefs* (APAB; M. Ford & Chase, 1990). In the APAB, goal importance is rated on a seven-point frequency scale ranging from "never important" to "always important" (i.e., respondents are asked, "How important is this goal to you in your everyday life?"). With only one exception, the correlations between conceptually similar pairs of items in the APG and APAB were higher than any of the correlations between dissimilar pairs of items.

Perhaps the most clinically persuasive evidence for the validity of the APG is the subjective sense of accuracy that many respondents report after seeing their profile of scores. Since the APG attempts to describe patterns of thought processes, this is the most direct way to verify that the APG is measuring what it was designed to measure. This does not mean that respondents are able to predict each of their scores in advance, since their personal goal vocabulary may be quite different from that of the Taxonomy of Human Goals, but it does indicate that most people believe there is some fundamental "truth" in the profile of scores yielded by the APG.

In some cases the APG is also capable of helping people gain new insights about the motivational themes underlying their own behavior or that of other respondents. For example, a professor with a reputation for being helpful learned that, although he scored low on Resource Provision (a result consistent with his view of himself as not being a particularly altruistic person), he had a very strong goal to maintain a sense of personal competence and responsibility (i.e., to maintain Positive Self-evaluations)—a goal for which being helpful to students in his field of expertise was clearly instrumental. A graduate student who couldn't understand why she was having such a difficult time coping with school and family life learned that she was highly motivated to avoid circumstances involving even temporary stress and unhappiness (i.e., she had unusually high scores on Tranquility and Happiness). A high school teacher with a brilliant but socially uncaring student was better able to understand this student's unusual personality when he saw that the student scored extremely low on all four integrative goals (Resource Provision, Belongingness, Social Responsibility, and Equity) and extremely high on Self-Determination and Understanding. A husband who was having difficulty understanding his wife's unusually negative reactions to procrastination, lateness, and other seemingly minor transgressions felt highly enlightened when he learned that she had extremely high scores on Management and Social Responsibility. A successful doctor suffering from bouts of anxiety and low self esteem found that she scored in the very high range (7 and above) on 16 of the 24 APG scales—a profile suggesting that her distress may be a function of wanting to accomplish too many goals in too many different kinds of circumstances.

The Assessment of Core Goals (ACG)

The ACG, which exemplifies the second basic goal assessment strategy, uses an idiographic process to accomplish essentially the same purpose as the APG, namely, the identification and verbal labeling of broad, pervasive goals that may often function outside of awareness. However, the ACG differs from the APG in several important ways. Because it focuses only on the goals that are at the "core" of a person's repertoire of BES, it has less breadth but also more depth than the APG. For example, whereas the APG can indicate that Belongingess goals are generally important to a person, the ACG enables one to identify the specific Belongingness goal that is most salient for that person from among many possible Belonginess goals. In addition, although the ACG can be taken in self-administered form, the process of defining one's core goals is sufficiently demanding that a clinical interview or workshop format is sometimes needed to produce optimal results. Such formats provide extensive opportunities for feedback and reflection that are difficult to build into paper-and-pencil measures. Finally, the ACG's use of the respondent's idiosyncratic, emergent vocabulary to label goal themes should, in principle, provide an increment of validity beyond that available from goal assessments using standardized goal labels.

The ACG's selective focus on core goals is based on the clinical observation that people generally have a small set of personal goals that are so important to them that a large portion of their strong feelings of satisfaction and frustration can be traced back to these fundamental terminal goals. The utility of the ACG therefore will vary depending on the extent to which this assumption is met for a particular respondent. In some cases most of the emotionally salient episodes in a person's life can be linked to a few core goals. Indeed, some people have reported being unable to think of any highly satisfying experiences that did not satisfy at least one of their core goals. In other cases the connections between core goals and satisfying and dissatisfying life experiences are harder to establish, either because the person has difficulty with the process of identifying and labeling their core goals, or because their goal hierarchy has many context-specific goals that are not clearly linked to more fundamental terminal goals. In this respect it is useful to think of core goals as being analogous to factors in a factor analysis—usually a small number of them are responsible for a large proportion of "variance" in the person's important life experiences, but in some instances a less interpretatble "factor solution" will emerge.

The ACG is a carefully organized process of structured exercises through which an individual can move in incremental fashion toward a highly specific and personalized definition of their most central and powerful sources of motivation. This process involves four steps. In Step 1, participants recall and list past behavior episode experiences that were exceptionally satisfying or enjoyable. These experiences are the raw materials from which core goals are abstracted. This first step is based on the assumption that strong positive affect signals the attainment of important personal goals (D. Ford, 1987; Nichols, 1990b). The Ford and Nichols Taxonomy of Human Goals is used in this step as a prompt to help insure that a broad range of satisfying experiences is considered in generating the list. In Step 2, participants more carefully examine up to 15 of these experiences and try to identify for each one the moment of peak satisfaction and the specific event that triggered that feeling. This step is designed to help the person focus on the specific behavior episode or sub-episode in which the core goal was actually attained. More than 15 episodes could be examined, but there are usually diminishing returns after this point due to the high probability that core goals will be involved in highly satisfying experiences. In Step 3, participants search for common underlying themes with regard to the goals being satisfied by these 15 experiences and begin the process of trying to construct accurate verbal representations of these themes. This is accomplished by grouping together experiences that seem to have produced the same or a similar ultimate result. This convergence of different experiences that satisfy the same underlying goal is essential to the identification of fundamentally important goals that guide behavior across many different contexts. Finally, in Step 4, participants work to refine and test their initial goal representations until they have defined their unique set of core goals with the greatest clarity and precision possible. Clinical evidence collected thus far indicates that most people define between one and five core goals through this process.

The most rigorous test thus far of the predictive validity of the ACG comes from a recent study comparing the ACG with two other goal assessments for the purpose of identifying the sources of distress in real-life episodes of job dissatisfaction (Nichols, 1990a). In this study nine subjects each kept a written record of distressing episodes that they experienced at work, noting what happened and how they felt as a result of the incident, until they had completed descriptions of 20 such episodes. After finishing this phase of the study they then completed three different kinds of goal assessments: (1) a baseline measure in which they simply listed the things they needed most to be satisfied at work (SELF Goals); (2) the Minnesota Importance Questionnaire, a paper-and-pencil goal measure based on a standardized taxonomy of work needs (MIQ needs, Dawis & Lofquist, 1984); and (3) the ACG, conducted in a clinical interview format. Three independent raters were then asked to judge the degree to which each goal statement from these three measures explained the distress

Table 6.   Number of Episodes in Which Each Type of Goal Statement
Was Judged to be the Most Probable Explanation for the
Reported Distress, by Subject

Subject Number	Core Goals	MIQ Goals	SELF Goals
1	* 10	5	3
2	* 12	1	7
3	3	* 11	7
4	* 8	6	6
5	2	5	* 13
6	* 7	* 7	4
7	* 11	0	9
8	* 7	* 7	6
9	8	0	* 12

Note: An asterisk denotes the type of goal statement judged to have the greatest cross-situational explanatory power for each individual. Discrepancies from 20 episodes per subject represent slight variations in the number of usable episodes provided by each subject.

Source: Nichols (1990a).

reported in each of the subject's 20 episodes. Raters used a probability scale ranging from 1 to 99, with the highest rating indicating that the rater was virtually certain that the reported distress could be explained by the frustration of the goal being considered.

It is important to note that the design of this study intentionally put core goals at a competitive disadvantage. There were 20 MIQ needs and in most cases 7-10 SELF goals that could be selected as the best explanation for each episode of job dissatisfaction, compared to a typical list of only 2-5 core goals. Moreover, whereas core goals are abstract, context-independent goal representations, all of the MIQ needs and SELF goals were formulated in context-specific terms (i.e., with regard to the work context). Nevertheless, in six out of nine cases, core goals were judged to have explanatory power equal to or greater than either the MIQ needs or SELF goals (see Table 6).

Instances in which core goals provided relatively less explanatory power appeared to be attributable to factors that do not compromise the validity of the ACG for most applications. Specifically, one person (Subject #3) had difficulty dealing with the psychological depth of the core goal interview, as evidenced by the fact that an unusually large number of relatively superficial core goals were defined (nine, four more than for any other subject). This is consistent with the general finding that about 90 percent of the people who begin the ACG process are able to complete it successfully (Nichols, 1990b). Another individual (Subject #5) had only one core goal that was so rich and multifaceted that judges seemed to have difficulty recognizing it in single episode form. Finally, judges seemed to be heavily swayed by the context-specific information in the MIQ and SELF goal statements when there were several goal statements that appeared to do a good job of representing the source of the subject's distress. Thus, the cross-situational explanatory power of the ACG was not as apparent in this study as it presumably would have been if the study had been designed to include multiple life contexts.

A great deal of clinical evidence has accumulated to support the validity of the ACG and its component exercises with regard to the "subjective accuracy" criterion noted earlier in the discussion of the APG. Most people who complete the ACG say that it has provided them with a much better understanding of why they are attracted to certain people or experiences, and conversely why they dislike certain situations or find them frustrating. Moreover, many participants feel that the core goal descriptions they have constructed are empowering in the sense of giving them the tools they need to pinpoint sources of satisfaction and dissatisfaction in current jobs or life circumstances, to make wise decisions among alternatives, and to identify new activities and experiences that are likely to generate feelings of energy, meaning, and well being.

In short, the ACG can help people (1) identify stable, fundamentally important goals that are responsible for satisfaction and distress across a wide range of contexts over many years, and (2) personalize the definition of these goals so that they can be used to pinpoint sources of distress and clarify what aspects of the distressing situation need to be changed.

IMPLICATIONS FOR FUTURE THEORY AND RESEARCH

In this paper we have described a way of thinking about goals and self-regulatory processes and their impact on achievement that we hope will be of broad theoretical utility. In particular, the Living Systems Framework provides the conceptual tools needed to clarify complex constructs and to detail how multiple, interrelated processes work together to help produce effective (and ineffective) functioning. The LSF's emphasis on goals as the primary psychological processes organizing and directing behavior episodes provides the key theoretical rationale for the development of goal assessment strategies and tools. However, the LSF is limited by an impoverished empirical base for understanding how to best represent goals and their connections with other psychological processes in theoretical and operational terms.

Our experience suggests that it is quite difficult to construct a goal assessment that can successfully reveal the broad, pervasive goals that underlie much of our everyday activity. Goals at this deeper level often function outside of awareness and are not easily accessible to consciousness when we attempt to think about them, in part because we have little experience in doing so. Moreover, these more fundamental thoughts about desired outcomes are usually embedded in a complex, hierarchically organized network of goals in which the same goal can be represented at different levels of abstraction and context-specificity, where the same goal can alternately serve both instrumental and terminal roles, where multiple goals can be pursued and achieved simultaneously, and where the importance of the goal can vary depending on the current state of the individual and the person's environment. There is therefore an obvious and critical need for sound empirical work on the properties of goal hierarchies at both the behavior episode and behavior episode schema level of analysis. Research explicating the connections between these two levels of analysis would be particularly useful for efforts such as ours in which there is an attempt to understand the implications of specific experiences (e.g., behavior episodes designed by a researcher or interventionist) for broader patterns of learning and development.

One of the cornerstones of psychological science has been and continues to be the understanding of human motivation and its role in competence development. Conceptual explication of goal-related processes and properties, and empirical research in which goals are assessed directly and precisely can provide needed strength to this relatively neglected domain of psychological research.

REFERENCES

Arnold, M. B. (1960). *Emotion and personality, Vol. 2: Neurological and physiological aspects.* New York: Columbia University Press.
Bandura, A. (1986). *Social foundations of thought and action: A social cognitive theory.* Englewood Cliffs, NJ: Prentice Hall.
Bandura, A., & Schunk, D. H. (1981). Cultivating competence, self-efficacy, and intrinsic interest through proximal self-motivation. *Journal of Personality and Social Psychology, 41,* 586-598.
Behravesh, M. M., Karimi, S. S., & Ford, M. E. (1989). Human factors affecting the performance of inspection personnel in nuclear power plants. *Nuclear Plant Journal, 7,* 16-63.
Buhler, C. (1964). The human course of life in its goal aspects. *Journal of Humanistic Psychology, 4,* 1-18.
Cannon, W. B. (1939). *The wisdom of the body* (rev. ed.). New York: W. W. Norton.
Cantor, N., & Langston, C. A. (1989). Ups and downs of life tasks in a life transition. In L. A. Pervin (Ed.), *Goal concepts in personality and social psychology* (pp. 127-167). Hillsdale, NJ: Erlbaum.
Cattell, R. B. (1957). *Personality and motivation structure and measurement.* New York: World Press.
Cofer, C. N., & Appley, M. H. (1964). *Motivation: Theory and research.* New York: Wiley.
Dawis, R. V., & Lofquist, L. H. (1984). *A psychological theory of work adjustment.* Minneapolis: University of Minnesota Press.
Dweck, C. S. (1986). Motivational processes affecting learning. *American Psychologist, 41,* 1040-1048.
Emmons, R. A. (1989). The personal striving approach to personality. In L. A. Pervin (Ed.), *Goal concepts in personality and social psychology* (pp. 87-126). Hillsdale, NJ: Erlbaum.

Ford, D. H. (1987). *Humans as self-constructing living systems: A developmental perspective on behavior and personality.* Hillsdale, NJ: Erlbaum.

Ford, D. H., & Ford, M. E. (1987). Humans as self-constructing living systems: An overview. In M. E. Ford & D. H. Ford (Eds.), *Humans as self-constructing living systems: Putting the framework to work* (pp. 1-46). Hillsdale, NJ: Erlbaum.

Ford, M. E. (1984). Linking social-cognitive processes with effective social behavior: A living systems approach. In P. C. Kendall (Ed.), *Advances in cognitive-behavioral research and therapy* (Vol. 3, pp. 167-211). New York: Academic Press.

————. (1985). The concept of competence: Themes and variations. In H. A. Marlowe & R. B. Weinberg (Eds.), *Competence development* (pp. 3-49). Springfield, IL: Charles C. Thomas.

————. (1986). A living systems conceptualization of social intelligence: Processes, outcomes, and developmental change. In R. J. Sternberg (Ed.), *Advances in the psychology of human intelligence* (Vol. 3, pp. 119-171). Hillsdale, NJ: Erlbaum.

————. (forthcoming). *Human motivation: Goals, emotions, and personal agency beliefs.* Newbury Park, CA: Sage.

Ford, M. E., & Chase, C. (1990). *The Assessment of Personal Agency Beliefs.* Unpublished test, School of Education, Stanford University, Stanford, CA.

Ford, M. E., & Ford, D. H. (1987). *Humans as self-constructing living systems: Putting the framework to work.* Hillsdale, NJ: Erlbaum.

Ford, M. E., & Nichols, C. W. (1987). A taxonomy of human goals and some possible applications. In M. E. Ford & D. H. Ford (Eds.), *Humans as self-constructing living systems: Putting the framework to work* (pp. 289-311). Hillsdale, NJ: Erlbaum.

————. (forthcoming). *Manual for the Assessment of Personal Goals.* Palo Alto, CA: Consulting Psychologists Press.

Goldstein, A. P., & Glick, B. (1986). *Aggression replacement training.* Champaign, IL: Research Press.

Klinger, E. (1977). *Meaning and void: Inner experience and the incentives in people's lives.* Minneapolis, MN: University of Minnesota Press.

Langer, E. J. (1989). *Mindfulness.* Reading, MA: Addison-Wesley.

Lazarus, R. S. (1982). Thoughts on the relation between emotion and cognition. *American Psychologist, 37,* 1019-1024.

————. (1984). On the primacy of cognition. *American Psychologist, 39,* 124-129.

Lee, T. W., Locke, E. A., & Latham, G. P. (1989). Goal setting theory and job performance. In L. A. Pervin (Ed.), *Goal concepts in personality and social psychology* (pp. 291-326). Hillsdale, NJ: Erlbaum.

Little, B. R. (1983). Personal projects: A rationale and method for investigation. *Environment and behavior, 15,* 273-309.

Markus, H., Cross, S., & Wurf, E. (1990). The role of the self-system in competence. In R. J. Sternberg & J. Kolligian, Jr. (Eds.), *Competence considered* (pp. 205-225). New Haven, CT: Yale University Press.

Markus, H., & Ruvolo, A. (1989). Possible selves: Personalized representations of goals. In L. A. Pervin (Ed.), *Goal concepts in personality and social psychology* (pp. 211-241). Hillsdale, NJ: Erlbaum.

Maslow, A. (1943). A theory of human motivation. *Psychological Review, 50,* 370-396.

————. (1970). *Motivation and personality* (2nd ed.). New York: Harper & Row.

McDougall, W. (1933). *The energies of men.* New York: Scribner's.

Murray, H. A. (1938). *Explorations in personality.* New York: Harper & Row.

Nichols, C. W. (1990a). *An analysis of the sources of dissatisfaction at work.* Unpublished doctoral dissertation, School of Education, Stanford University, Stanford, California.

_____. (1990b). *Manual for The Assessment of Core Goals.* Palo Alto, CA: Consulting Psychologists Press.

Pervin, L. A. (1983). The stasis and flow of behavior: Toward a theory of goals. In M. M. Page (Ed.), *Personality: Current theory and research* (pp. 1-53). Lincoln, NE: University of Nebraska Press.

_____. (1989). Goal concepts in personality and social psychology: A historical perspective. In L. A. Pervin (Ed.), *Goal concepts in personality and social psychology* (pp. 1-17). Hillsdale, NJ: Erlbaum.

Rokeach, M. (1968). *Beliefs, attitudes, and values: A theory of organization and change.* San Francisco: Jossey-Bass.

Silver, M. (1985). Purposive behavior in psychology and philosophy: A history. In M. Frese & J. Sabini (Eds.), *Goal-directed behavior: The concept of action in psychology* (pp. 3-17). Hillsdale, NJ: Erlbaum.

Sternberg, R. J. (1985). *Beyond IQ: A triarchic theory of human intelligence.* New York: Cambridge University Press.

Wicker, F. W., Lambert, F. B., Richardson, F. C., & Kahler, J. (1984). Categorical goal hierarchies and classification of human motives. *Journal of Personality, 52*, 285-305.

Winnell, M. (1987). Personal goals: The key to self-direction in adulthood. In M. E. Ford & D. H. Ford (Eds.), *Humans as self-constructing living systems: Putting the framework to work* (pp. 261-287). Hillsdale, NJ: Erlbaum.

GOAL SETTING AND
SELF-EVALUATION:
A SOCIAL COGNITIVE PERSPECTIVE
ON SELF-REGULATION

Dale H. Schunk

Current theoretical accounts of achievement postulate that individuals are active seekers and processors of information (Anderson, 1990; Pintrich, Cross, Kozma, & McKeachie, 1986; Shuell, 1986). People's cognitions are hypothesized to influence the instigation, direction, and persistence of behavior (Corno & Snow, 1986; Schunk, 1989a; Weiner, 1985; Winne, 1985). In particular, various theoretical traditions emphasize the important role played by individuals' beliefs concerning their capabilities to control their lives (Bandura, 1989, Corno & Mandanich, 1983; Rotter, 1966).

In this paper I present theory and research on *self-regulation*, or people's use of self-directive capabilities to influence their thoughts, feelings, and actions. The theoretical framework is Bandura's (1986, 1988, 1989) social cognitive learning theory. The model of self-regulation I discuss focuses on achievement settings and highlights goal setting and self-evaluation of goal

---

Advances in Motivation and Achievement, Volume 7, pages 85-113.
Copyright © 1991 by JAI Press Inc.
All rights of reproduction in any form reserved.
ISBN: 1-55938-122-1

progress as integral components of self-regulation. As used throughout this chapter, a *goal* is what an individual is consciously trying to accomplish, *goal setting* involves establishing a standard for performance, and *self-evaluation* refers to comparing one's progress with one's goal to determine whether progress is acceptable and reacting to that assessment. The topic of self-regulation fits well with the idea that students contribute actively to their learning goals and exercise a large degree of control over the attainment of those goals (Meece, Blumenfeld, & Hoyle, 1988; Nicholls, Patashnick, & Nolen, 1985).

I initially present a theoretical overview of material relevant to social cognitive theory, self-regulation, and goal setting. Research is reviewed that addresses goal setting and self-evaluation in achievement contexts. I conclude with suggestions for future research.

THEORETICAL BACKGROUND

Social Cognitive Theory

Reciprocal Interactions

A fundamental premise of Bandura's (1986) social cognitive theory is that human functioning can be viewed as a series of reciprocal interactions between behaviors, environmental variables, and cognitions and other personal factors. I will exemplify this reciprocality with an important construct in Bandura's theory: *perceived self-efficacy*, or personal beliefs concerning one's capabilities to organize and implement actions necessary to perform behaviors at designated levels. Research in achievement settings shows that students' efficacy beliefs influence such behaviors as choice of tasks, persistence, effort expended, and skill acquisition (Schunk, 1989a). Students' behaviors affect their efficacy beliefs when students work on tasks and note their progress toward such learning goals as solving a set of mathematical problems or reading a book chapter. Progress indicators convey that students are performing well, which enhances self-efficacy for continued learning.

The interaction between self-efficacy and environmental factors has been demonstrated in research on learning disabilities. Many learning disabled students hold low self-efficacy for improving their skills (Licht & Kistner, 1986). People often react to such students based on attributes typically associated with them rather than on what they can do. Teachers may judge learning disabled students as less capable than nondisabled students and hold lower academic expectations for them, even in domains where learning disabled students perform normally (Bryan & Bryan, 1983). In turn, teacher feedback can have an impact on self-efficacy. Persuasory statements (e.g., "I know you can do this") may raise students' efficacy beliefs.

Students' behaviors and classroom environments can influence one another in many ways. Environmental influence on behavior occurs when teachers use eye-catching displays to gain and hold students' attention. Students' behaviors often alter their instructional environments. When students ask teachers questions indicating that they do not understand the material, teachers may forego starting a new lesson and instead review the troublesome material.

Enactive and Vicarious Learning

Learning is a relatively permanent change in behavior or behavioral potential brought about by intervening experiences (Shuell, 1986). In social cognitive theory (Bandura, 1986), these experiences may be enactive (actual performances) or vicarious (observing models). Enactive learning involves learning from the consequences of one's actions. Actions that result in successful consequences are retained; those leading to failures are discarded. Complex skills typically involve some enactive learning. Students learn components of complex skills by observing teachers, but such learning often is incomplete. As students practice skills, teachers monitor their work and provide corrective feedback to remedy skill deficiencies.

Social cognitive theory is distinguished from earlier reinforcement theories by the explanation for learning, not by the fact that people learn by doing. Skinner (1953), for example, postulated that skillful performances are gradually acquired when successive approximations of target behaviors are reinforced. Cognitions accompany behavioral change but do not influence it. Social cognitive theory contends that behavioral consequences inform and motivate people rather than automatically strengthen their behaviors. Consequences inform individuals about which behaviors are likely to produce successes. People engage in cognitive activities (e.g., rehearsing and integrating information) that assist learning of successful behaviors. Individuals are motivated to learn behaviors they value and that they believe will produce positive consequences.

Much human learning occurs vicariously by observing models. Observation accelerates learning and saves people from personally experiencing negative consequences. As with enactive learning, response consequences of behaviors performed by models inform and motivate observers. Observers are more apt to try to learn modeled behaviors leading to successful outcomes than those resulting in failures. The belief that modeled behaviors will prove useful can lead people to attend to models and mentally rehearse their actions.

Self-Regulatory Processes

Investigators working within a social cognitive learning theory framework view self-regulation as involving self-observation, self-judgment, self-reaction

(Bandura, 1986, 1989; Kanfer & Gaelick, 1986; Karoly, 1982; Schunk, 1989b). These processes are not mutually exclusive but rather interact with one another. While observing aspects of one's own behavior, one may judge them against standards and react positively or negatively. One's evaluations and reactions set the stage for additional observations of the same behavioral aspects or of others.

These processes also do not operate independently of the learning environment; environmental influences can assist the development of self-regulation. This point is important, because educators are increasingly advocating that students be trained to self-regulate their academic performances (Paris, Lipson, & Wixson, 1983; Zimmerman, 1989).

Self-observation

Self-observation refers to deliberate attention to aspects of behavior (Mace, Belfiore, & Shea, 1989). People cannot regulate their actions if they are not fully aware of them. Behavior can be assessed on such dimensions as quality, rate, quantity, and originality.

Self-observation serves the important self-regulatory function of providing information to individuals about what they do, which then is used to set goals and evaluate progress (Bandura, 1986). Self-observation is most helpful when it addresses the specific conditions under which the behaviors occur. Such information is valuable in establishing a program of change and evaluating results. Students who notice they accomplish less when they study with a friend than when they are alone may establish a new routine of studying by themselves.

Self-observation serves another self regulatory function because it can motivate behavioral change; keeping a record of what one does often will prove surprising. Many students with poor study habits are not aware that they waste much study time on nonacademic activities. Self-observation can motivate one to embark on a program of change, although desire alone usually is insufficient. Sustained motivational effects depend on establishing goals, evaluating progress, and maintaining a sense of self-efficacy for goal attainment (Bandura, 1988).

Self-observation is aided with the use of self-recording, where instances of the behavior are recorded along with such features as the time, place, and duration of occurrence (Mace et al., 1989). In the absence of recording, one's observations may not faithfully reflect one's behaviors due to selective memory. Important criteria for self-observation are regularity and proximity. Regularity means that behavior is observed on a continuous basis (e.g., hour by hour, day to day). Nonregular observation provides misleading results. Proximity means that behavior is observed close in time to its occurrence rather than long after it. Proximal observations provide clear information to use in gauging goal progress.

Self-judgment

Self-judgment involves comparing present performance with one's goal. Whether performances are judged to be acceptable will depend on the type of standards employed, goal properties (discussed in next section), importance of goal attainment, and performance attributions.

Goals may be cast as absolute or normative standards. Absolute standards are fixed. Students whose goal is to complete six workbook pages in 30 minutes can gauge their progress against this absolute standard. Grading systems often are based on absolute standards (e.g., 93-100 = A, 84 - 92 = B).

Normative standards are based on the performances of others and can be acquired by observing models (Bandura, 1986). When they socially compare their performances with those of others, people determine the appropriateness of behaviors and evaluate their performances. Students have numerous opportunities to compare their work with that of their peers. Absolute and normative standards can be employed together, as when students have 30 minutes to complete six pages and they compare their progress with peers to gauge who will be the first to finish.

Researchers have shown that classroom goal structures affect the extent to which students socially compare their work with that of others. Competitive classroom conditions, for example, reduce the possibility of students receiving rewards when others are successful (Ames, 1984). Competition leads students to focus on how their performances compare with those of others (Ames & Ames, 1984). Students may adopt such performance goals as finishing first or doing more work than others in order to earn rewards. Competitive conditions highlight an attributional focus on ability (discussed in the next section). Successful (unsuccessful) students may believe that their performances are due to high (low) ability. In contrast, in individualistic conditions students' accomplishments are independent of one another and the opportunity to earn rewards is equal across students. Individualistic conditions may lead students to focus on their own performance improvements over time and to adopt learning goals of improving their skills. The initial attributional focus is on effort as a cause of performance improvement, although as skills develop students are apt to place greater emphasis on ability (Schunk, 1989a).

Standards inform and motivate. In learning settings, comparing one's performance with standards is informative of one's goal progress. Students who complete three pages in 10 minutes realize they finished half of the work in less than half of the time. Standards also can motivate. The belief that one is making goal progress can enhance self-efficacy and sustain motivation. Students who find a task easy and realize that they set their goal too low may set it higher the next time. Similarly, knowing that peers performed a task can promote self-efficacy and motivation because students are apt to believe that if others could succeed, they can as well (Schunk, 1989a).

Self-judgments are affected by the importance of goal attainment. When individuals care little about how they perform at an activity, they may not assess their performance or expend effort to improve (Bandura, 1986). Judgments of goal progress are made for valued goals. Occasionally, goals that originally are not valued become more important when people receive feedback indicating they are improving their skills. Many children do not routinely set reading goals for themselves. As their reading skills develop, they may begin to set specific goals (e.g., read certain stories or books) and judge their progress relative to these goals.

Attributions

Attributions, or perceived causes of outcomes (successes, failures), can influence performance expectancies, behaviors, and affective reactions (Weiner, 1985). Achievement outcomes often are attributed to such causes as ability, effort, task difficulty, and luck (Frieze, 1980; Weiner, 1979). Children view effort as the prime cause of outcomes and ability-related terms as closely associated, but with development a distinct conception of ability emerges (Nicholls, 1984). Ability attributions become increasingly important influences on expectancies (Harari & Covington, 1981). Assuming that task conditions remain much the same, success ascribed to stable causes (high ability, low task difficulty) should result in higher expectations of future success than attributions to unstable causes (effort, luck). Failure ascribed to low ability or high task difficulty is apt to result in lower expectations for future success than failure attributed to insufficient effort or bad luck.

With respect to affective reactions, people take greater pride when they attribute success to internal factors (ability, effort) than when they attribute it to external causes (task ease, luck). People also are more self-critical when they believe failure was due to personal reasons (e.g., low effort) than when it was due to circumstances beyond their control. Whether goal progress is judged as acceptable will depend in part on its attribution. Students who attribute success to teacher assistance may hold low self-efficacy for performing well, because they may believe they cannot succeed on their own. They might judge their learning progress as deficient and be unmotivated to work harder because they believe they lack the ability to perform well.

Self-reaction

Self-reactions to goal progress exert motivational effects on behavior (Bandura, 1986). The perception of acceptable progress and the anticipated satisfaction of accomplishing the goal raise self-efficacy for continued improvement and sustain motivation. Negative evaluations will not decrease motivation if individuals believe they are capable of improving (Schunk, 1989b). If students believe they have been lackadaisical and that enhanced effort will promote progress, they are apt to feel efficacious and work harder. If they feel they have been using an ineffective strategy they may adopt a new approach to the task. Motivation will not improve when learners believe they lack the ability to succeed and that increased effort or a new way of working on the task will not help.

Self-reactions show wide individual differences. The same level of performance can be evaluated positively, neutrally, or negatively, depending on one's goals. Some students are content with performing at a B level in a course, whereas others are satisfied only with an A. When people believe they are capable of improvement, higher goals lead to greater effort and persistence than lower goals (Bandura & Cervone, 1983).

People routinely make such tangible consequences as work breaks, new clothes, and nights on the town, contingent on goal progress or attainment. Social cognitive theory postulates that the anticipation of consequences enhances motivation. Self-administered consequences can motivate individuals even when external contingencies are in effect (Bandura, 1986). Grades are given at the end of courses, yet students set subgoals for accomplishing their coursework and reward and punish themselves accordingly.

Tangible consequences also can influence self-efficacy. Rewards are likely to enhance self-efficacy when they are tied to students' actual accomplishments. Telling students they can earn rewards based on what they accomplish can instill a sense of self-efficacy for learning, which is validated as students work at the task and note their progress (Schunk, 1989a). Receipt of the reward further validates efficacy, because it symbolizes progress. When rewards are given noncontingently (i.e., not tied to performances) they can convey negative efficacy information; students might infer they are not expected to learn much because they do not possess the requisite capability.

Goal Setting

Goals refer to quantity, quality, or rate of performance (Locke, Shaw, Saari, & Latham, 1981). Individuals can set their own goals or goals can be established for them by teachers, parents, counselors, or supervisors.

Goals can motivate behavior and inform people about their capabilities (Bandura, 1988; Locke & Latham, 1984). When students are given or establish a goal, they may experience a sense of efficacy for attaining it. As learners pursue goals, they are apt to engage in appropriate activities, attend to instruction, persist and expend effort. These motivational effects increase on-task behaviors and achievement. Students' initial sense of self-efficacy is substantiated as they work at the task and observe goal progress because the perception of progress conveys they are becoming skillful. In turn, heightened capability self-evaluations sustain motivation and lead learners to establish new goals when they master their present ones.

By themselves, goals do not automatically affect performances. The effectiveness of any goal derives from making a commitment to attain it. Goals do not influence behavior when people do not commit themselves to attempting to attain them (Locke et al., 1981). Allowing people to set their own goals may foster commitment. In addition, certain properties of goals heighten their informational and motivational aspects: specificity, proximity, and difficulty level.

Goals that incorporate specific performance standards are more likely to increase motivation and activate self-evaluative reactions than such general goals as, "Do your best" (Locke et al., 1981). Specific goals boost task performance through greater specification of the amount of effort required for success and the self-satisfaction anticipated when accomplished. Specific goals also promote self-evaluations of capabilities because progress is easy to gauge.

Goals can be distinguished by how far they extend into the future. Proximal goals are close at hand and result in greater motivation directed toward attainment than more temporally distant goals (Bandura, 1986). Pursuing proximal goals also conveys reliable information about one's capabilities. When students perceive they are making progress toward a proximal goal, they are apt to feel efficacious and maintain their motivation (Schunk, 1989a). Because progress toward a distant goal is more difficult to gauge, learners receive less-clear information about their capabilities even if they perform well.

Proximal goals are integral components of teachers' lesson planning. Short-term goals are especially influential with young children, who do not represent distant outcomes in thought. They also are helpful for learners of any age with long-term tasks. For example, many students have doubts about writing good term papers. Teachers can assist by breaking the task into short-term goals (e.g., select a topic, conduct background research, write an outline). Students should feel more efficacious about accomplishing the subtasks, and attaining each subgoal helps develop their overall sense of efficacy for producing a good paper.

Goal difficulty refers to the level of task proficiency required as assessed against a standard (Locke et al., 1981). How much effort learners expend to attain a goal will depend on the level at which it is set. People expend greater effort to attain a difficult goal than when the standard is lower. Although students initially may doubt whether they can attain goals they believe are difficult, working toward difficult goals can build a strong sense of efficacy because progress conveys that one possesses the necessary skills to overcome obstacles.

At the same time, difficulty level and task performance do not bear an unlimited linear relation with one other. Positive effects due to goal difficulty depend on individuals having sufficient ability to attain the goal. Difficult goals do not enhance performance in the absence of requisite ability. When learners believe they do not possess the ability to attain a goal, they are likely to hold low expectations for success and not commit themselves to the task. These points have implications for education. In the early stages of skill acquisition, teachers typically give students easier goals so that students experience success and develop a sense of efficacy for further learning. Teachers introduce challenging goals when students' skills develop to the point where students are not dissuaded from attempting the tasks.

Self-efficacy

As noted in the preceding section, goal setting is hypothesized to affect performance in part through the intervening influence of perceived goal progress and self-efficacy. In achievement contexts, self-efficacy can influence choice of activities, effort expended, and persistence (Bandura, 1989). Students who hold low self-efficacy for learning may avoid tasks; those who judge themselves efficacious are more likely to participate. When facing difficulties, self-efficacious learners are apt to work harder and persist longer than students who doubt their capabilities.

Students acquire information about their self-efficacy in a given domain from their performances, observations of models (vicarious experiences), forms of social persuasion, and physiological indexes (e.g., heart rate, sweating). One's own performances offer quite reliable guides for assessing self-efficacy. In general, successes raise efficacy and failures lower it, although once a strong sense of efficacy is developed an occasional failure will not have much effect.

Students acquire capability information from others (Rosenthal & Zimmerman, 1978). Observing peers perform a task can convey to observers that they, too, are capable of accomplishing it. Information acquired vicariously typically has a weaker effect on self-efficacy than performance-based information because a vicarious increase in efficacy is negated easily by subsequent unsuccessful performances.

Students often receive persuasory information that they possess the capabilities to perform a task, such as when they are told by teachers, "You can do this." Although positive persuasory feedback enhances self-efficacy, this increase is apt to be short-lived if individuals' subsequent efforts turn out poorly. Students also derive efficacy information from physiological indexes (e.g., heart rate, sweating). Bodily symptoms signaling anxiety might be interpreted to mean one lacks necessary skills.

Information acquired from these sources does not influence efficacy automatically but is cognitively appraised (Bandura, 1986). Efficacy appraisal is an inferential process; persons weigh and combine personal and situational factors. In assessing self-efficacy, students take into account such factors as perceived ability, effort expended, task difficulty, teacher assistance, and patterns of successes and failures (Bandura, 1989).

I do not wish to convey that self-efficacy always is important or is the only influence on behavior. Efficacy appraisal typically does not occur for well-established skills or behaviors (Schunk 1989a). People are apt to assess their capabilities for accomplishing a task when personal or situational conditions are altered. Students are more likely to assess self-efficacy for learning new material than for accomplishing review exercises. Furthermore, high self-efficacy will not produce competent performances when requisite skills are lacking. Also important are *outcome expectations*, or beliefs concerning the probable outcomes of one's actions. Individuals are not motivated to behave in ways they believe will result in negative outcomes regardless of their level of efficacy for performing those behaviors. Even when anticipated outcomes are positive, people are not motivated to act when they do not value those outcomes. Assuming adequate skills, positive outcome expectations, and valued outcomes, self-efficacy is hypothesized to influence the instigation, direction, and persistence of much human behavior.

Model of Self-regulation

Figure 1 portrays a model of self-regulation that highlights the roles of goal setting and self-evaluation of goal progress. This model assumes that students enter learning activities with such goals as acquiring knowledge, learning how to solve problems, finishing workbook pages, and completing science experiments. It also assumes that students will differ in how efficacious they feel about being able to attain those goals (Schunk, 1989b). Students' initial sense of self-efficacy is influenced by aptitudes and prior experiences (Schunk, 1989a).

Goals and self-efficacy can influence such task-oriented academic activities as information processing (e.g., attending to instruction, processing and integrating knowledge, rehearsing information to be remembered), behaviors (effort, persistence, help seeking), beliefs (perceived task importance, outcome expectations), and affects (feelings of satisfaction and pride), as well as the self-evaluative activities of self-judgments of goal progress and self-reactions (Schunk, 1989b; Zimmerman, 1989). As students work on tasks they determine their progress by comparing their performances with their goals. The belief that they are making progress validates their initial sense of self-efficacy and maintains their productive pursuit of goal attainment. The perception of minimal progress need not negatively affect self-efficacy or academic activities if students believe they are capable of making progress (i.e., by using a better strategy or working harder). Students react to their progress judgments, and set new, challenging goals for themselves once original goals are attained.

The relation of the processes shown in Figure 1 to the social-cognitive theoretical framework discussed in the preceding sections is as follows. Individuals set goals, then engage in those activities that they believe will help

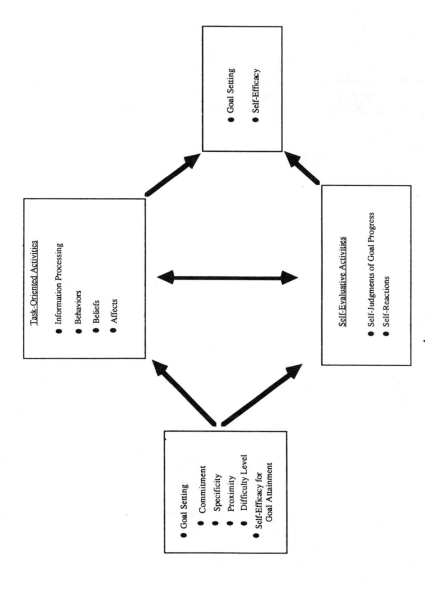

Figure 1. Model of Self-regulation Highlighting Goal Setting and Self-evaluation

them attain their goals. Self-evaluative activities and task-oriented academic activities influence one another. Task-oriented activities help students attain their goals and affect perceptions of progress. In turn, the belief that one is making progress can motivate one to continue working productively. The figure does not portray self-observation preceding the initial goal setting, although that often occurs (e.g., student records number of minutes spent studying over several days).

I have simplified this figure to highlight the roles of goal setting and self evaluation. I have not discussed the antecedent influences on goal setting and self-efficacy or how instructional and social factors associated with the learning context can affect students' goals and progress evaluations. There is evidence, for example, that such factors as teacher feedback, classroom reward structure, and peer comparisons of abilities, can influence students' achievement beliefs and behaviors (Dweck & Leggett, 1988; Levine, 1983; Weinstein, 1989). The effects of some factors associated with learning contexts are discussed in the following section.

LITERATURE REVIEW

In this section I review research on goal setting and self-evaluation in achievement contexts. Although some of these studies did not explicitly focus on self-regulation, they were included because they examined the effects of self-regulatory processes. Many studies used measures of self-efficacy or similar constructs, and investigated the idea that goals and perceived progress in goal attainment influence self-regulation in part by enhancing self-efficacy. This review is comprehensive but not exhaustive. Readers interested in other topics in self-regulation should consult additional sources (Bandura, 1986; Karoly & Kanfer, 1982; Zimmerman & Schunk, 1989).

Goal Specificity

Goal specificity is hypothesized to be an important goal property influencing performance and self regulation (Bandura, 1986). Schunk (1983a) investigated the effects of goal specificity with children lacking mathematical division skills. Students received instruction and practice over sessions. At the start of each session children were given either a specific goal of completing a given number of problems during the session or a general goal of working productively. Within each goal condition, half of the students were told the number of problems other similar children had completed. This number matched the session goal and was designed to convey that goals were attainable. The other half of the children were not given this social comparative information.

Specific goals led to higher self-efficacy and children who received goals and comparative information demonstrated the highest self-efficacy and skill. Comparative information, with or without goals, promoted children's motivation as assessed by the number of problems solved during the independent practice portions of the instructional sessions. These results suggest that providing children with a goal and information it is attainable increases self-efficacy for goal attainment, which raises instructional session performance and leads to greater skill acquisition.

A later study compared the effects of specific goals with those of performance-contingent rewards (Schunk, 1984). Children received division instruction and practice over sessions. Some children were offered rewards commensurate with the number of problems they completed; others pursued specific goals of completing a given number of problems each session; children in a third condition received rewards and goals. The three conditions promoted children's self-regulation of their mathematical performances during the instructional sessions equally well, but combining rewards with goals led to the highest self-efficacy and division performance. Compared with goals or rewards alone, combining goals and rewards may have provided a clearer standard against which to gauge learning progress.

Goal Proximity

Proximity is another important goal property. Bandura and Schunk (1981) tested the idea that proximal goals enhance achievement behaviors better than distant goals, and also investigated the effect of goals on intrinsic interest. Children with low subtraction skills received instruction and practice over seven sessions using seven sets of material. Some children pursued a proximal goal of completing one set each session; a second group received a distant goal of completing all sets by the end of the last session; a third group was advised to work productively (general goal). Proximal goals enhanced motivation, as these children completed the most work during the independent practice portions of the instructional sessions. Proximal goals also resulted in the highest subtraction skill and self-efficacy, as well as the highest intrinsic interest measured by the number of arithmetic problems solved during a free-choice period. The distant goal resulted in no benefits compared with the general goal.

Morgan (1985) found that proximal goals raised academic performance and intrinsic interest among college students over an academic year. Students were assigned to one of four conditions: self-monitoring of proximal goals, self-monitoring of time studying, self-monitoring of distant goals, control (no goals). Students assigned to the self-monitoring of proximal goals condition learned to set subgoals for assigned readings and to monitor subgoal progress. In the time studying condition, students received instruction on setting aside time for studying and on monitoring time spent. Distant goal subjects set a comprehensive goal for each study session.

On the final examination, proximal goal students scored significantly higher than the other conditions. This effect was not due to time spent studying, because students assigned to the self-monitoring of time studying condition spent the most time. Proximal students also judged intrinsic interest in the course higher than students in the other conditions. Though there are some problems with this study (e.g., goal proximity confounded with specificity, perceived competence not assessed), the results show that proximal goals boosted achievement and interest and suggest that proximity may affect self-regulatory processes associated with studying.

Manderlink and Harackiewicz (1984) explored the effects of proximal goals on adults' expectancies, perceived competence, interest and performance on word puzzles. Subjects were given normative information and asked to set either a proximal performance goal (for this puzzle) or a distant goal (for all puzzles). Expectations for goal attainment were assessed during the pretest and twice during the trials; following the experiment, students judged perceived competence. Proximal and distant goals did not differentially affect performance, but compared with the distant goal condition, proximal goal subjects judged expectation of goal attainment and perceived competence higher. Distant goals led to higher ratings of interest.

Some of these findings conflict with those of the preceding two studies. The nonsignificant performance effect may have been due to a ceiling effect, as Manderlink and Harackiewicz report that over 85% of proximal and distant goal subjects attained their goals. Regarding the interest results, Manderlink and Harackiewicz note that subjects displayed high initial interest in the activity. In contrast, Bandura and Schunk studied the development of interest, and it seems likely that the students in Morgan's study also developed interest as a result of participating in the goal setting. Much research shows that offering subjects rewards for performing high-interest activities can lead to decreases in interest (Lepper & Greene, 1978). The mechanism responsible for this effect may involve subjects perceiving that their task performance is controlled by the offer of a reward; that is, that their performance is a means to an end (reward). In the Manderlink and Harackiewicz study it is possible that students viewed the proximal goal setting as a form of extrinsic pressure, which could have decreased interest. Conversely, social-cognitive theory predicts that proximal goals should help develop interest in an activity when they convey to students that they are becoming more competent.

Goal Difficulty

Schunk (1983b) explored the effects of goal difficulty during a mathematical division instructional program. Children received either difficult or easier goals of completing a given number of problems each session. Half of the children in each goal condition were told directly by an adult monitor that they could attain the goal (e.g., "You can work 25 problems") to preclude children from perceiving the goals as too difficult and thereby stifling motivation. The other half of the children received social comparative information indicating that similar peers completed that many problems. Difficult goals enhanced children's motivation during the instructional sessions; children who received difficult goals and direct goal attainment information displayed the highest self-efficacy and division skill.

The role of goal difficulty in brainstorming was explored by Locke, Frederick, Lee, and Bobko (1984). College students participated in multiple timed trials on giving uses for common objects. Some subjects were taught a strategy to generate uses; others were told to give only good uses (anti-brainstorming condition). Midway through the study, half of the subjects in each condition were assigned a difficult goal of 12 uses; other subjects set their own goals. On subsequent trials, all subjects set their own goals. Subjects rated goal commitment and self-efficacy for generating different numbers of uses. Students assigned difficult goals subsequently set higher goals and generated more uses than those initially allowed to set their own goals. When subjects were allowed to set their own goals, self-efficacy was positively related to goal level and commitment. Strategy training had an indirect effect on goal level through self-efficacy. Similar results were obtained in a study by Garland (1985).

Self-Set Goals

We might expect that allowing students to set their learning goals would enhance their goal commitment, which is necessary for goals to affect performance (Locke et al., 1981). Schunk (1985) found that self-set goals promote self-efficacy. Sixth graders classified as learning disabled in mathematics received subtraction instruction and practice over sessions. Some set performance goals each session, others had comparable goals assigned, and children in a third condition did not set or receive goals. Self-set goals led to the highest self-efficacy and subtraction performance. Children in the two goal conditions demonstrated higher motivation during the sessions compared with no-goal subjects. Self-set children judged themselves more confident of attaining their session goals than assigned-goals subjects.

Hom and Murphy (1985) found that self-set goals were beneficial for students low in achievement motivation. College students classified as high or low in achievement motivation were assigned to self-set or assigned goal conditions. Self-set subjects decided how many anagrams they felt they could solve; assigned-goal subjects were given comparable goals. Subjects also judged confidence for goal attainment—a measure similar to self-efficacy. Students high in achievement motivation performed equally well under the two goal conditions, but the performances of those low in achievement motivation were enhanced by self-set goals. The confidence measure yielded nonsignificant differences, perhaps because the variability in this measure was severely restricted.

Goal Progress Feedback

In a series of studies, Schunk and Rice (1987, 1989, 1990a, 1990b) explored the effects on learning and achievement beliefs of providing feedback to remedial readers on their progress in learning a reading comprehension strategy. As used in this paper, a *strategy* is a systematic plan that improves the encoding of information and task performance (Paris et al., 1983). Students were taught to use the following strategy to locate main ideas:

What do I have to do?
1. Read the questions.
2. Read the passage to find out what it is mostly about.
3. Think about what the details have in common.
4. Think about what would make a good title.
5. Reread the story if I don't know the answer to a question.

Participants were fourth and fifth graders placed in remedial classes because they scored at or below the twentieth percentile on standardized reading tests. The strategy was taught during a multi-session instructional program. An adult instructor initially verbalized each step in the strategy prior to applying it to a passage. Students then were given guided instruction and practice using the strategy. They verbalized the strategic steps as they applied them. As the sessions progressed, the instructor occasionally referred to steps and prompted students when they failed to apply them. Instructional materials ranged in difficulty and were appropriate for grades two through four.

Two experiments showed that multiple sources of information stressing the value of the strategy to answer questions benefit achievement outcomes (Schunk & Rice, 1987). The instructor initially provided children with a goal of learning to use the strategy to answer questions. In the first study, children received specific strategy value information, general information, specific and general information (combined), or no strategy value information. The specific information conveyed the value of the strategy for finding main ideas; the general information emphasized strategy value for all reading tasks. In the second experiment, children received strategy effectiveness feedback, specific strategy value information, or feedback and specific information (combined). The feedback linked children's improved performances with strategy use.

In each study, the combined treatment promoted self-efficacy and skill the best. The combined treatments, which integrated strategy training with multiple sources of strategy value information, presented students with the most complete set of influences on reading comprehension. Providing children with strategy instruction and information on strategy usefulness may have engendered a sense of control over comprehension performances, which can raise self-efficacy (Schunk 1989a). As Paris et al. (1983) note, becoming a strategic reader requires combining skills with positive beliefs. The feedback in the second experiment also should have enhanced students' self-efficacy because it informed them about their goal progress (mastering the strategy) with such statements as, "You got it right because you followed the steps in the right order," and, "You've been answering a lot more questions correctly since you've been using these steps."

Schunk and Rice (1989) investigated the effects of process and product goals. A distinction often is drawn between goals reflecting products of learning, which concern what students should know or be able to accomplish as a result of learning, and goals reflecting the processes of learning, which focus on techniques and strategies that students can use to promote learning (Weinstein & Mayer, 1986). Goal-setting research in achievement contexts typically has employed product goals representing quantity of work to be completed. Educators increasingly are emphasizing that students become proficient in the use of learning strategies (Weinstein, Goetz & Alexander, 1988).

During the comprehension strategy instruction, some children received a product goal of correctly answering questions, others were given a process goal of learning to use the strategy, and control students were advised to work productively. Compared with controls, process and product goal children judged self-efficacy higher, and process goal children demonstrated higher skill; the two goal conditions did not differ on either measure. On a measure of children's perceptions of their session goals, process goal children placed greater emphasis on learning to use the strategy compared with children in the other conditions, and judged becoming a better reader more important than product goal children. These latter findings are important, because poor readers develop low expectations for acquiring reading skills (Butkowsky & Willows, 1980). When students believe they can become better readers, they are apt to self-regulate their activities in ways they believe will help them accomplish that goal (Paris & Wixson, 1986).

Follow-up research explored whether providing feedback on students' progress in applying the strategy raises achievement outcomes (Schunk & Rice, 1990a). There were three conditions: product goal, process goal, process goal and progress feedback (combined). During the sessions, each child assigned to the latter condition periodically received feedback linking strategy use with improved comprehension performance.

The combined treatment led to the highest self-efficacy and skill. This treatment included strategy instruction, a goal of learning the strategy, and feedback on goal progress. These factors, which motivate children to learn, teach them a means of improving their achievement, and convey information that they are improving their skills, collectively provide a sense of control over learning outcomes. This seems especially important for children with reading disabilities, who often attribute successes to external factors (e.g., teacher assistance, good luck) (Licht & Kistner, 1986). On a measure of perceived progress in learning the strategy, process goal and combined conditions did not differ but each judged progress higher than product-goal subjects. The goal of learning the strategy was made salient to students in the process goal and combined conditions, and participation in the instructional program likely enhanced progress perceptions.

Recently completed research shows that learning goals and progress feedback promote maintenance of comprehension strategy use (Schunk & Rice, 1990b), which suggests that goals and feedback assist self-regulation by helping students maintain knowledge and use of strategies following completion of strategy instruction. The methodology was similar to that of Schunk and Rice (1987). Children were assigned to three conditions: strategy instruction, strategy value feedback, instructional control. Children assigned to the strategy instruction and strategy value feedback conditions were taught a comprehension strategy to find main ideas; control students received comparable instruction without the strategy. Strategy value feedback was conveyed by periodically giving each child feedback linking strategy use with improved performance.

Combining strategy instruction with strategy value feedback led to the highest self-efficacy and reading skill, and these benefits were maintained on a six-week follow-up test. Subjects in the combined condition also demonstrated the best maintenance of strategy use on the follow-up test.

The benefits of progress feedback with college students were demonstrated by Bandura and Cervone (1983). An ergometer was used, which was operated by alternatively pushing and pulling arm levers and which resisted the individual's effort. Following a baseline evaluation, some subjects pursued a goal of increasing performance by 40%, others were given feedback indicating they had increased performance by 24%, those in a third condition received goals and feedback, and controls received neither goals nor feedback. Goals combined with feedback exerted the strongest effect on performances. Goals and progress feedback instilled a sense of self-efficacy for goal attainment, which predicted subsequent effort.

The goal-feedback discrepancy was varied in follow-up research (Bandura & Cervone, 1986). Subjects received a goal of 50% improvement and false feedback indicating they achieved an increase of 24% (large substandard discrepancy), 36% (moderate), 46% (small), or 54% (small suprastandard discrepancy). Self-efficacy was lowest for the large substandard discrepancy and highest for the small suprastandard discrepancy. Following the goal and feedback manipulation, subjects indicated goals for the next session and performed the task. Effort expenditure was positively related to self-set goals and self-efficacy across all treatment conditions. These results and those of Bandura and Cervone (1983) show that goal setting and self-efficacy contribute to the self-regulation of effort.

Contracts and Conferences

Contracts and conferences employing goal setting have been used to promote students' achievement and self-regulation. Tollefson and colleagues taught goal setting to learning disabled students and explored the role of attributions (Tollefson, Tracy, Johnsen, Farmer, & Buenning, 1984; Tollefson, Tracy, Johnsen, & Chatman, 1986). Attribution training programs often emphasize effort because it is under volitional control and amenable to change. Ascribing prior failures to insufficient effort exerts motivational effects. When students believe added effort will produce success they persist longer and achieve at a higher level (Weiner, 1979). Many training programs attempt to change ascriptions for failure from low ability to insufficient effort (Andrews & Debus, 1978; Dweck, 1975). Effort feedback is a persuasive source of efficacy information. To be told one can achieve better results through hard work raises self-efficacy and motivation because it conveys one possesses the capabilities to succeed.

Junior high learning disabled students were assigned to an experimental or control group (Tollefson et al., 1984). Each week for four weeks, students assigned to the experimental condition selected spelling words or math problems from a list judged by the teacher to be moderately difficult. Students predicted how many they would answer correctly on a test the following week after they had studied the present week. This goal was stated in a written contract, along with a study plan. The contract was intended to help students take personal responsibility for their actions and highlight that effort enhances achievement. The week after each test students charted their scores and made an attribution for the outcome. Compared with students assigned to a no-treatment control condition, experimental students placed greater emphasis on effort as a cause of outcomes and became more realistic in their goal setting as measured by the discrepancy between goals and performance.

In a subsequent study (Tollefson et al., 1986), learning disabled adolescents participated in weekly resource room contracts dealing with work to be completed in-class or as homework. The contracts also specified the study plan, which emphasized effort as a cause of outcomes. Students monitored their progress, and made attributions for successes and failures to attain goals. Students' rate of completing assignments in the resource room increased and generalized to the regular classroom. Following training, students attributed successes to effort and failures to effort, luck, and task difficulty.

Gaa (1973) assigned first and second graders to three conditions: goal setting conferences, conferences without goal setting, no conferences. All children received the same reading instruction. Goal conference children met with the researcher once a week for four weeks. During the conferences, children received a list of reading skills, selected those they would attempt to accomplish, and were given feedback on their previous week's accomplishments. Children who participated in conferences without goals met for the same amount of time but received general information about material covered previously and what would be covered next. All students participated in a goal conference the last week and judged certainty of goal attainment.

Goal-conference children attained the highest reading achievement and the smallest discrepancy between goals set and mastered during the last week, which shows that goal conferences promoted accurate capability perceptions. They also judged certainty of goal attainment lower than the other conditions. This measure (analogous to self-efficacy) may reflect students' greater awareness of the skills involved in reading and the difficulty of attaining some reading goals. Gaa (1979) replicated these achievement results with tenth grade students, and also found that goal-conference students took greater responsibility for their successes.

Conceptions of Ability

Although attribution theorists note that ability levels can fluctuate, ability generally is viewed as a relatively fixed quality (Weiner, 1979). Recent work in achievement motivation, however, has identified individual differences in *conceptions of ability*, or beliefs about the nature of ability and the role it plays in achievement (Dweck, 1986: Dweck & Leggett, 1988; Nicholls, 1984). Some students hold an entity (fixed) view of ability as a global and stable trait. Learning is possible only to the limit set by ability. Such students pursue performance goals of gaining positive judgments and avoiding negative ones. Those with self-doubts about their abilities work lackadaisically and expend little effort on difficult tasks. Those who believe they are capable select tasks at which they can succeed, persist longer, and expend effort, which produce judgments of competence from others.

Other students hold an incremental view of ability: They believe that ability comprises skills and increases with experience. Such students roughly equate ability with learning and strive to increase their competence through learning. Regardless of whether they view their ability as high or low, they persist and expend effort because they believe effort enhances ability.

Research shows that conceptions of ability can have diverse effects in achievement domains. Wood and Bandura (1989) found that ability conceptions influence individuals' goal setting, self-efficacy, and self-regulatory activities. Business school students participated in difficult managerial decision making in which they learned rules on ways to optimize employee performance using goals, feedback, and social rewards. Subjects were told the task represented either an acquirable skill (decision making is developed through practice) or a fixed entity (decision making reflects one's basic cognitive abilities). Subjects set goals for organizational productivity and judged self-efficacy for production levels ranging from 30% better to 40% worse than standard. Over trials, acquirable-skill subjects maintained high self-efficacy, set more challenging goals, demonstrated more efficient use of rules, and produced higher employee performances; entity subjects showed a decline in self-efficacy.

Elliot and Dweck (1988) provided children with goals (learning or performance) and ability assessments (high or low). Children receiving learning goals chose challenging tasks and displayed effort and persistence regardless of ability assessment. Children with performance goals who perceived ability as high selected challenging performance tasks that allowed them to appear competent; those perceiving ability as low selected easier tasks allowing them to avoid judgments of incompetence.

Meece et al. (1988) assessed fifth and sixth graders' goal orientations, perceived competence, intrinsic motivation, and cognitive engagement patterns, during science lessons. Orientations assessed were task mastery (goal is to understand material and learn as much as possible), ego/social (goal is to please others), and work-avoidant (goal is to minimize effort and do as little as possible). Active and superficial patterns of cognitive engagement were distinguished. Active engagement referred to cognitive activities involved in self-regulation (e.g., reviewing material not understood, relating current material to prior material); superficial engagement referred to strategies to complete work with minimal effort (copy answers, skip hard material). The results yielded significant relations between cognitive engagement patterns and goal orientations. Students emphasizing task-mastery goals reported more active cognitive engagement than students in the other conditions. Children reporting greater motivation to learn placed greater emphasis on goals stressing the importance of learning and understanding.

Although these results are correlational, they suggest that altering students' goal orientations may have an impact on their self-regulatory activities. From a social-cognitive theoretical perspective, we might also expect that self-regulatory activities could influence goal orientation. As students work on a task and observe their progress toward their learning goals they are apt to believe they are becoming more skillful and that additional effort will produce further learning. These beliefs, combined with a sense of self-efficacy for learning, could lead students to adopt an incremental view of ability for the task.

CONCLUSIONS AND FUTURE DIRECTIONS

The research reviewed in this chapter supports the point that goal setting and self-evaluative processes help to activate and sustain a variety of self-regulatory processes oriented toward task completion. These processes involve information processing activities, achievement behaviors, achievement-related beliefs and affects. As students work on tasks they evaluate their progress by comparing their performances with their goals and by reacting to those comparisons. The perception of progress validates their initial sense of self-efficacy for achieving and maintains their productive use of self-regulatory activities in pursuit of goal attainment. The belief that progress is inadequate can lead students to work in such a fashion that they believe will produce greater progress. Once goals are attained, students set new goals for themselves.

Research has explored many facets of the goal setting and self-evaluative processes. Much research demonstrates that various properties of goals inform learners of goal progress and motivate them to continue their efforts. Goals that specify performance standards, are relatively close at hand, and are perceived as difficult but attainable, allow learners to gauge progress and convey that learners are capable of improving skills. For goals to enhance performance it also is necessary that learners make a commitment to attempt to attain them. Allowing learners to set their own goals may help foster commitment. Providing learners with feedback on goal progress is important in situations where they cannot derive feedback on their own (e.g., determine whether answers are correct). Explicit feedback also may be important for students who have experienced learning problems and doubt their learning capabilities. Contracts and goal-setting conferences have been employed to help learners develop goal-setting and self-evaluative skills. Recent research has shown that students' beliefs about their abilities can influence their goal choices, achievement beliefs, and motivation.

Many of the points made in this chapter require additional empirical investigation. Most studies have not addressed the mechanism whereby goal setting and self-evaluation influence self-regulation. Although goal setting is hypothesized to affect performance in part through the intervening influence of perceived self-efficacy, there are times when self-efficacy may not be an important influence on self-regulation; for example, the presence of strong external incentives to perform can lead people to behave in given ways regardless of whether they feel particularly efficacious about doing so. In the remainder of this section I address some additional areas that I believe require research attention.

Transfer

There is an urgent need for research examining whether goal setting influences transfer of self-regulatory processes over time (maintenance) and outside of experimental contexts (generalization). We might expect that self-regulatory activities would transfer and that goal setting could facilitate transfer. Students who generally self-regulate their performances may be likely to determine their goals in new learning situations, apply appropriate learning strategies, monitor their performances, alter their approaches if they believe they are making inadequate progress, maintain a sense of self-efficacy for learning, and experience feelings of pride in their work. Based on the theoretical ideas discussed in this chapter, we might predict that students whose goal is to learn to apply a strategy with different tasks would experience a sense of control over achievement outcomes as they observed their learning progress, and would feel efficacious about continuing to improve their skills. Students are likely to use a strategy and apply it in different contexts if they understand how to apply it, believe it will improve achievement, and perceive themselves capable of performing well.

Despite these ideas, little research has addressed how goals influence transfer of self-regulatory activities. In other domains, the research literature is filled with examples of interventions that produced immediate benefits in learners' beliefs and behaviors but whose effects were not evident on transfer tests on similar content or on follow-up assessments some time after completion of the intervention. Research shows, for example, that students who typically perform poorly in school benefit from instruction on learning strategies but that such instruction does not ensure transfer (Borkowski, 1985; Paris, Cross & Lipson, 1984). Lack of transfer can arise from various factors including incomplete learning, inadequate practice opportunities on different content, low motivation, and the belief that the strategy is not as important for success as such other factors as time available or effort expended (Borkowski & Cavanaugh, 1979; Fabricius & Hagan, 1984). Research needs to determine whether goal setting can help to produce better transfer than is often obtained with other experimental treatments.

Longitudinal Studies

A related point concerns a need for longitudinal studies on self-regulation. We might expect that self-regulatory processes, once established, would maintain themselves over lengthy periods. That is important, because many significant achievements in people's lives are long-term in nature: earning a college degree, becoming a corporate executive, coordinating a major fund-raising activity. These types of accomplishments require much decision-making, effort, and persistence, as well as a certain amount of risk taking. Research should address the process whereby people pursue these long-term goals.

For example, researchers might explore such issues as how people subdivide long-term goals into a series of short-term ones, how initially general goals (e.g., graduate from college) become specific (earn a degree in psychology), how goals that at first appear insurmountable become perceived as attainable, which factors (personal, environmental) predict whether people will set difficult goals for themselves, how individuals seek and acquire information pertinent to their goals, and what steps people take to maintain high self-efficacy for goal attainment and positive feelings about the task even in the face of obstacles. Research on these issues will suggest components to include in self-regulation training programs.

Classroom Research

Research is needed on ways to foster self-regulatory skills in educational contexts. Most of the studies reviewed in this chapter were conducted outside of the classroom context. Goal setting and self-evaluative processes are amenable to training to help students become more productive learners. For starters, we might examine how students' goals influence classroom events and are themselves altered by those events. Recent research has shown that students approach classroom tasks with goals, which may not coincide with the goals of teachers (Nicholls et al., 1985; Wentzel, 1989). Students' goals can affect a variety of self-regulatory activities (Meece et al., 1988). Determining the influences on students' goals, especially those goals that relate to more productive self-regulatory efforts, would suggest ways to structure classroom activities to foster self-regulation.

Research is needed on the effectiveness of classroom methods to train students to set realistic goals. Students are unlikely to commit themselves to attempt goals they believe are unreasonable. Realistic goals are challenging but attainable. They require students to monitor progress and decide on a different task approach if their present one seems ineffective. They build self-efficacy as students note progress, attain goals, and take on new challenges. Goals that are perceived as too difficult or too easy do not enhance self-regulatory activities. Students who set goals too high may become demoralized with little goal progress, which lowers self-efficacy and leads them to work halfheartedly and give up readily when they encounter difficulty. When goals are set too low, students do not learn what they are capable of doing, which does not raise self-efficacy.

Realistic goal setting often requires training. Sagotsky, Patterson, and Lepper (1978) had fifth and sixth graders participate in an individualized mathematics instructional program. Children worked on each unit until they reached a given level of accuracy. Goal-setting students set session goals of pages to complete. Self-monitoring students stopped periodically and recorded whether they were working on a unit. Some students received goal setting and self-monitoring; controls received neither treatment. Self-monitoring enhanced time on task and number of problems solved; goal setting offered no advantages. Children may have had difficulty setting realistic goals because problem difficulty varied within and between units.

Goal setting seems more appropriate when task difficulty remains relatively constant. This is especially important when teachers are attempting to train students to set realistic goals. Some methods for training goal setting employed by studies reviewed in this chapter are establishing upper and lower goal limits (Schunk, 1985), using games (Tollefson et al., 1984, 1986), and having students participate in goal setting conferences (Gaa, 1973, 1979). Further research is needed on the effects of these and other methods that can be applied easily in the context of regular classroom instruction.

Affective Reactions

A final research recommendation is to examine the links between goal setting and affective reactions. Affective reactions should depend in part on self-efficacy for goal attainment and the level at which the goal is set. Whether a negative discrepancy between one's goal and present performance level encourages or discourages is likely to involve one's self-efficacy for attaining the goal (Bandura, 1986). The perception of progress toward one's goal should lead to positive feelings; the belief that one's performance has stabilized at an undesirably low level may produce discouragement. In turn, despondency can debilitate performance and lead to lower self-efficacy and future goals.

Attribution theory and research show that internal attributions for success (failure) lead to feelings of greater pride (shame) than external attributions for the same performance (Weiner, 1985; Zaleski, 1988). We might examine whether attributional feedback linking students' goal progress with their abilities and efforts results in more positive feelings than if students make external attributions for progress. Such research would have important implications for teacher-student interaction patterns in classrooms.

ACKNOWLEDGMENTS

The research by Dale H. Schunk was supported by grants from the National Science Foundation, the National Institute of Mental Health, the Donald D. Hammill Foundation, and the University of Houston.

REFERENCES

Ames, C. (1984). Competitive, cooperative, and individualistic goal structures: A cognitive-motivational analysis. In R. Ames & C. Ames (Eds.), *Research on motivation in education. Vol. 1: Student motivation* (pp. 177-207). Orlando, FL: Academic Press.

Ames, C., & Ames, R. (1984). Goal structures and motivation. *Elementary School Journal, 85,* 39-52.

Anderson, J. R. (1990). *Cognitive psychology and its implications* (3rd ed.). New York: Freeman.

Andrews, G. R., & Debus, R. L. (1978). Persistence and the causal perception of failure: Modifying cognitive attributions. *Journal of Educational Psychology, 70,* 154-166.

Bandura, A. (1986). *Social foundations of thought and action: A social cognitive theory.* Englewood Cliffs, NJ: Prentice Hall.

————. (1988). Self-regulation of motivation and action through goal systems. In V. Hamilton, G. H. Bower, & N. H. Frijda (Eds.), *Cognitive perspectives on emotion and motivation* (pp. 37-61). Dordrecht, The Netherlands: Kluwer Academic Publishers.

————. (1989). Social cognitive theory. In R. Vasta (Ed.), *Annals of Child Development* (Vol. 6, pp. 1-60). Greenwich, CT: JAI Press.

Bandura, A., & Cervone, D. (1983). Self-evaluative and self-efficacy mechanisms governing the motivational effects of goal systems. *Journal of Personality and Social Psychology, 45,* 1017-1028.

————. (1986). Differential engagement of self-reactive influences in cognitive motivation. *Organizational Behavior and Human Decision Processes, 38,* 92-113.

Bandura A., & Schunk, D. H. (1981). Cultivating competence, self-efficacy, and intrinsic interest through proximal self-motivation. *Journal of Personality and Social Psychology, 41,* 586-598.

Borkowski, J. G. (1985). Signs of intelligence: Strategy generalization and metacognition. In S. Yussen (Ed.), *The development of reflection in children* (pp. 105-144). New York: Academic Press.

Borkowski, J. G., & Cavanaugh, J. C. (1979). Maintenance and generalization of skills and strategies by the retarded. In N. R. Ellis (Ed.), *Handbook of mental deficiency, psychological theory and research* (2nd ed., pp. 569-617). Hillsdale, NJ: Erlbaum.

Bryan, J. H., & Bryan, T. H. (1983). The social life of the learning disabled youngster. In J.D. McKinney & L. Feagans (Eds.), *Current topics in learning disabilities* (pp. 57-85). Norwood, NJ: Ablex.

Butkowsky, I. S., & Willows, D. M. (1980). Cognitive-motivational characteristics of children varying in reading ability: Evidence for learned helplessness in poor readers. *Journal of Educational Psychology, 72,* 408-422.

Corno, L., & Maninach, E. B. (1983). The role of cognitive engagement in classroom learning and motivation. *Educational Psychologist, 18,* 88-108.

Corno, L., & Snow, R. E. (1986). Adapting teaching to individual differences among learners. In M.C. Wittrock (Ed.), *Handbook of research on teaching* (3rd ed., pp. 605-629). New York: Macmillan.

Dweck, C. S. (1975). The role of expectations and attributions in the alleviation of learned helplessness. *Journal of Personality and Social Psychology, 31,* 674-685.

————. (1986). Motivational processes affecting learning. *American Psychologist, 41,* 1040-1048.

Dweck, C. S., & Leggett, E. L. (1988). A social-cognitive approach to motivation and personality. *Psychological Review, 95,* 256-272.

Elliott, E. S., & Dweck, C. S. (1988). Goals: An approach to motivation and achievement. *Journal of Personality and Social Psychology, 54,* 5-12.

Fabricius, W. V., & Hagan, J. W. (1984). Use of causal attributions about recall performance to assess metamemory and predict strategic memory behavior in young children. *Developmental Psychology, 20,* 975-987.

Frieze, I. H. (1980). Beliefs about success and failure in the classroom. In J.H. McMillan (Ed.), *The social psychology of school learning* (pp. 39-78). New York: Academic Press.

Gaa, J. P. (1973). Effects of individual goal-setting conferences on achievement, attitudes, and goal-setting behavior. *Journal of Experimental Education, 42*, 22-28.

_____. (1979). The effects of individual goal-setting conferences on academic achievement and modification of locus of control orientation. *Psychology in the Schools, 16*, 591-597.

Garland, H. (1985). A cognitive mediation theory of task goals and human performance. *Motivation and Emotion, 9*, 345-367.

Harari, O., & Covington, M. V. (1981). Reactions to achievement behavior from a teacher and student perspective: A developmental analysis. *American Educational Research Journal, 18*, 15-28.

Hom, H. L., Jr., & Murphy, M. D. (1985). Low need achievers' performance: The positive impact of a self-determined goal. *Personality and Social Psychology Bulletin, 11*, 275-285.

Kanfer, F. H., & Gaelick, L. (1986). Self-management methods. In F.H. Kanfer & A.P. Goldstein (Eds.), *Helping people change: A textbook of methods* (3rd ed., pp. 283-345). New York: Pergamon.

Karoly, P. (1982). Perspectives on self-management and behavior change. In P. Karoly & F.H. Kanfer (Eds.), *Self management and behavior change: From theory to practice* (pp. 3-31). New York: Pergamon.

Karoly, P., & Kanfer, F. H. (1982). *Self-management and behavior change: From theory to practice*. New York: Pergamon.

Lepper, M. R., & Greene, D. (1978). *The hidden costs of reward: New perspectives on the psychology of human motivation*. Hillsdale, NJ: Erlbaum.

Levine, J. M. (1983). Social comparison and education. In J.M. Levine & M.C. Wang (Eds.), *Teacher and student perceptions: Implications for learning* (pp. 29-55). Hillsdale, NJ: Erlbaum.

Licht, B. G., & Kistner, J. A. (1986). Motivational problems of learning-disabled children: Individual differences and their implications for treatment. In J.K. Torgesen & B.W.L. Wong (Eds.), *Psychological and educational perspectives on learning disabilities* (pp. 225-255). Orlando: Academic Press.

Locke, E. A., Frederick, E., Lee, C., & Bobko, P. (1984). Effect of self-efficacy, goals, and task strategies on task performance. *Journal of Applied Psychology, 69*, 241-251.

Locke, E. A., & Latham, G. P. (1984). *Goal setting for individuals, groups, and organizations*. Chicago: Science Research Associates, Inc.

Locke, E. A., Shaw, K. N., Saari, L. M., & Latham, G. P. (1981). Goal setting and task performance: 1969-1980. *Psychological Bulletin, 90*, 125-152.

Mace, F. C., Belfiore, P. J., & Shea, M. C. (1989). Operant theory and research on self-regulation. In B.J. Zimmerman & D.H. Schunk (Eds.), *Self-regulated learning and academic achievement: Theory, research, and practice* (pp. 27-50). New York: Springer-Verlag.

Manderlink, G., & Harackiewicz, J. M. (1984). Proximal versus distal goal setting and intrinsic motivation. *Journal of Personality and Social Psychology, 47*, 918-928.

Meece, J. L., Blumenfeld, P. C., & Hoyle, R. H. (1988). Students' goal orientations and cognitive engagement in classroom activities. *Journal of Educational Psychology, 80*, 514-523.

Morgan, M. (1985). Self-monitoring of attained subgoals in private study. *Journal of Educational Psychology, 77*, 623-630.

Nicholls, J. G. (1984). Achievement motivation: Conceptions of ability, subjective experience, task choice, and performance. *Psychological Review, 91*, 328-346.

Nicholls, J. G., Patashnick, M., & Nolen, S. B. (1985). Adolescents' theories of education. *Journal of Educational Psychology, 77*, 683-692.

Paris, S. G., Cross, D. R., & Lipson, M. Y. (1984). Informed strategies for learning: A program to improve children's reading awareness and comprehension. *Journal of Educational Psychology, 76*, 1239-1252.

Paris, S. G., Lipson, M. Y., & Wixson, K. K. (1983). Becoming a strategic reader. *Contemporary Educational Psychology, 8*, 293-316.

Paris, S. G., & Wixson, K. K. (1986). The development of literacy: Access, acquisition, and instruction. In D. Bloome (Ed.), *Literacy and schooling* (pp. 35-54). Norwood, NJ: Ablex.

Pintrich, P. R., Cross, D. R., Kozma, R. B., & McKeachie, W. J. (1986). Instructional psychology. *Annual Review of Psychology, 37*, 611-651.

Rosenthal, T. L., & Zimmerman, B. J. (1978). *Social learning and cognition*. New York: Academic Press.

Rotter, J. B. (1966). Generalized expectancies for internal versus external control of reinforcement. *Psychological Monographs, 80* (Whole No. 609).

Sagotsky, G., Patterson, C. J., & Lepper, M. R. (1978). Training children's self-control: A field experiment in self-monitoring and goal-setting in the classroom. *Journal of Experimental Child Psychology, 25*, 242-253.

Schunk, D. H. (1983a). Developing children's self-efficacy and skills: The roles of social comparative information and goal setting. *Contemporary Educational Psychology, 8*, 76-86.

_____. (1983b). Goal difficulty and attainment information: Effects on children's achivment behaviors. *Human Learning, 2*, 107-117.

_____. (1984). Enhancing self-efficacy and achievement through rewards and goals: Motivational and informational effects. *Journal of Educational Research, 78*, 29-34.

_____. (1985). Participation in goal setting: Effects on self-efficacy and skills of learning disabled children. *Journal of Special Education, 19*, 307-317.

_____. (1989a). Self-efficacy and cognitive skill learning. In C. Ames & R. Ames (Eds.), *Research on motivation in education. Vol. 3: Goals and cognitions* (pp. 13-44). San Diego: Academic Press.

_____. (1989b). Social cognitive theory and self-regulated learning. In B.J.Zimmerman & D.H. Schunk (Eds.), *Self-regulated learning and academic achievement: Theory, research, and practice* (pp. 83-110). New York: Springer-Verlag.

Schunk, D. H., & Rice, J. M. (1987). Enhancing comprehension skill and self-efficacy with strategy value information. *Journal of Reading Behavior, 19*, 285-302.

_____. (1989). Learning goals and children's reading comprehension. *Journal of Reading Behavior, 21*, 279-293.

_____. (1990a). *Learning goals and progress feedback during reading comprehension instruction*. Unpublished manuscript, University of North Carolina, Chapel Hill.

_____. (1990b). *Influence of reading comprehension strategy information on children's achievement outcomes*. Unpublished manuscript, University of North Carolina, Chapel Hill.

Shuell, T. J. (1986). Cognitive conceptions of learning. *Review of Educational Research, 56*, 411-436.

Skinner, B. F. (1953). *Science and human behavior*. New York: Macmillan.

Tollefson, N., Tracy, D. B., Johnsen, E. P., & Chatman, J. (1986). Teaching learning disabled students goal-implementation skills. *Psychology in the Schools, 23*, 194-204.

Tollefson, N., Tracy, D. B., Johnsen, E. P., Farmer, A. W., & Buenning, M. (1984). Goal setting and personal responsibility training for LD adolescents. *Psychology in the Schools, 21*, 224-233.

Weiner, B. (1979). A theory of motivation for some classroom experiences. *Journal of Educational Psychology, 71*, 3-25.

_____. (1985). An attributional theory of achievement motivation and emotion. *Psychological Review, 92*, 548-573.

Weinstein C. E., Goetz, E. T., & Alexander, P. A. (1988). *Learning and study strategies: Issues in assessment, instruction, and evaluation*. San Diego: Academic Press.

Weinstein, C. E., & Mayer, R. E. (1986). The teaching of learning strategies. In M.C. Wittrock (Ed.), *Handbook of research on teaching* (3rd ed., pp. 315-327). New York: Macmillan.

Weinstein, R. S. (1989). Perceptions of classroom processes and student motivation: Children's views of self-fulfilling prophecies. In C. Ames & R. Ames (Eds.), *Research on motivation in education. Vol. 3: Goals and cognitions* (pp. 187-221). San Diego: Academic Press.

Wentzel, K. R. (1989). Adolescent classroom goals, standards for performance, and academic achievement: An interactionist perspective. *Journal of Educational Psychology, 81*, 131-142.

Winne, P. H. (1985). Cognitive processing in the classroom. In T. Husen & T.N. Postlethwaite (Eds.), *The international encyclopedia of education* (Vol. 2, pp. 795-808). Oxford, England: Pergamon.

Wood, R., & Bandura, A. (1989). Impact of conceptions of ability on self-regulatory mechanisms and complex decision-making. *Journal of Personality and Social Psychology, 56*, 407-415.

Zaleski, Z. (1988). Attributions and emotions related to future goal attainment. *Journal of Educational Psychology, 80*, 563-568.

Zimmerman, B. J. (1989). Models of self-regulated learning and academic achievement. In B.J. Zimmerman & D.H. Schunk (Eds.), *Self-regulated learning and academic achievement: Theory, research, and practice* (pp. 1-25). New York: Springer-Verlag.

Zimmerman, B. J., & Schunk, D. H. (1989). *Self-regulated learning and academic achievment: Theory, research, and practice.* New York: Springer-Verlag.

THE SOCIAL CONTEXTS OF INTERNALIZATION:

PARENT AND TEACHER INFLUENCES ON AUTONOMY, MOTIVATION, AND LEARNING

Richard M. Ryan and Jerome Stiller

Education is one of the primary vehicles through which culture is transmitted. On the superficial level schools and teachers communicate specific knowledge that is supposedly central and important to adaptation and participation in the community and in work. Some political leaders claim that students' failure to absorb and master this corpus of knowledge represents a "national crisis," and like-minded educators generate lists of facts that everyone should possess (Hirsch, 1987). Others take the position that the specific contents and facts taught in schools are of little lasting value in a changing world. Instead they emphasize the importance of learning higher order skills that are transferable to absorbing new knowledge and interpreting new experiences and problems (e.g., Broudy, 1988). The educational products of the classroom must have a pragmatic aspect; they are presumably acquired *because* they can and will be utilized in ongoing life.

Advances in Motivation and Achievement, Volume 7, pages 115-149.
Copyright © 1991 by JAI Press Inc.
All rights of reproduction in any form reserved.
ISBN: 1-55938-122-1

On an even deeper level of analysis, schools do more than transmit the facts represented in the curricula and the cognitive tools essential for further learning. Equally central and profound are the affective and behavioral lessons imparted by our educational institutions. Schools are contexts of cultural socialization in which students' behavior is regulated, and orientations toward learning, achievement, and self-expression are developed. In addition, they are the first and primary extrafamilial arena in which children are compared with others, gain a sense of their relative skills and talents, and develop perceptions of their place and worth within a larger social milieu. In other words, schools transmit strong and lasting affective lessons that can affect one's confidence, aspirations, interests, and motivational style long after the classroom years. In addition they convey lessons concerning styles of achievement, competitiveness, and relations with authority that are carried forth into subsequent life within organizations.

While there has been considerable attention and debate concerning the appropriate cognitive agenda of educators, there has been a corresponding neglect of the affective and behavioral curricula that are de facto instilled within the social contexts of schooling. We have an elaborate technology for measuring the acquisition of skills and facts, and there is substantial pressure on educators to meet specified standards on such outcomes. Note, by contrast, how little technology and concern is dedicated to the noncognitive lessons of school—for example, to our relative success in producing curiosity versus boredom, self-confidence versus timidity, or engagement versus alienation in the course of learning. Yet even superficial reflection suggests that such noncognitive outcomes of school probably have more influence on the quality of life of students, their aspirations, and their ultimate adjustment than the whole array of facts and skills acquired along the path leading to graduation.

The affective lessons of schools are taught not through text or lecture, but rather by the functional dynamics of human relationships that surround learning in both homes and classrooms. These relationships provide the social context for the psychological processes we will refer to as *internalization*. Internalization represents the activity within the recipient of socialization through which external regulations, practices, or cultural prescriptions become transformed into internal regulation, values, beliefs and understandings (Ryan, Connell, & Deci, 1985).

Although an educator or parent may value and attempt to communicate the importance of learning and knowledge, it remains a futile effort unless those values or learnings are adopted or "taken in" or internalized by the student. Psychological analysis deals with the aspects of the communication process which make it more or less likely that such internalization will take place. Comprehension of the means through which education ultimately transmits a culture thus requires recognition of the interpersonal dynamics that underlie the activity of internalization and the intrapsychic means through which what is taught and experienced becomes anchored in the minds of the participants.

Today there are many commentators on education who are calling upon teachers to enforce and legislate achievement-oriented outcomes with little regard for the processes that facilitate or forestall the students internalization of the values and orientations that underlie those outcomes. This has resulted in an ultimately paradoxical situation that many astute observers in today's schools have noted: It appears that the more we try to measure, control, and pressure learning from without, the more we obstruct the tendencies of students to be actively involved and to participate in their own education. Not only does this result in a failure of students to absorb the cognitive agenda imparted by educators, but it also creates deleterious consequences for the affective agendas of schools. The absence of results from the strong-arm approach advocated over the past decade, of insuring more learning through more accountability and discipline, provides ample evidence for an increased need to attend to the processes through which internalization proceeds or fails to proceed. In 1991, it is not difficult to argue that our education system is characterized by an excessive rate of failures of internalization among students not only of what is taught, but also of the values of learning and achievement more generally.

In contrast to the idea that education must be enforced from without is an approach which emphasizes the importance of eliciting a willingness and self-determination within the student to learn and to achieve. In the latter approach the central affective goal of education is the fostering of an internalization and integration of the values which support learning, and by achieving this affective goal cognitive outcomes are assumed to follow (Krathwohl, Bloom, & Masia, 1974; Ryan, Connell, & Deci, 1985). As an affective goal, internalization can be defined as the development, on the part of the student, of the perception of his or her activity as not merely obligatory but as useful and worthwhile. It entails an acceptance by the individual of the importance and meaning of his or her activity and thus a shift away from compulsion toward willingness and desire. In short, internalization has as its endpoint a learner whose participation is autonomous and self-regulated.

Many theorists have hypothesized that when learning is characterized by autonomy there are benefits with regard to the cognitive goals of education. The emerging evidence provides some support for these views, and suggests that such learning is more deeply processed, better retained, more transferable, and more integrated with other knowledge. It is also more valued than learning which accrues under more compliance oriented motives. What is intriguing admidst this growing evidence is the recognition of just how deeply entwined the cognitive and affective aspects of education may be. Although the interface between motivational and cognitive outcomes remains largely uncharted territory, some broad sketch of the topography is emerging.

It can also be argued that the goal of self-regulation or autonomy as a motivational style in the context of schools fits with the ideals of a democratic, participative culture. To the extent that education fosters self-regulation in the context of schools and in the larger domain of achievement, it can also help to develop interested, active, and empowered citizens. Ultimately, it seems that our educational institutions can thus play a role in enfranchising developing individuals by facilitating their sense of being able to exercise their talents and their choice and, more generally, to gain the self-confidence required by pluralistic societies.

By contrast to these ideals, however, schools can alternatively fulfill other, less explicit, social mandates when they fail to emphasize and promote experiences of autonomy and competence. Insofar as a predominant focus in schools is the evaluation of individual differences and social comparisons concerning "ability," an inordinate number of students must either internalize a view of themselves as incompetent, or alternatively they must devalue schooling itself. This, in turn, helps to anchor our culture's competitive ideology, and to rationalize economic discrepancies (Fine, 1990). The focus of schools on evaluations, social comparisons, and outcome-oriented criteria also catalyzes students' individualistic motives and minimizes their concerns with or appreciation of social goals and interdependencies (Kohn, 1986). Thus, the extent to which salient evaluations and strong pressures on students constitute a reasonable style of socialization is, in these regards, open to considerable question.

In this paper we examine processes related to students' internalization of values for learning and achievement, and which therefore promote self-regulation in school. We restrict our focus to the dynamics of American schools and families and put the question of cross-cultural generality in abeyance. Our central interest is to explore educational atmospheres that satisfy basic psychological needs in the learner and thus promote an orientation of willingness and desire with respect to educative activities. This, of course, requires that schools offer something potentially meaningful from the students' perspective, and that teachers afford activities and interactions which meet the psychological needs of participants. It is our general hypothesis that, to the extent that schools do not address relevant issues or psychological needs *as experienced by students*, they will foster disengagement or compliance rather than an internalization and valuing of learning and achievement.

There are many ways to conceptualize the psychological needs of students, the potential satisfaction of which would energize and sustain their active involvement and engagement in the educational process. Although no system has proven to be perfectly comprehensive and at the same time parsimonious, we consider three broad needs that function both individually and interactively. These are the psychological needs for *autonomy, competence*, and *relatedness*. The student's experience of volition, self-expression, and initiative as described by the idea of autonomy appears to be a central motivational force in producing engagement. Autonomous action, which occurs in a context wherein challenges are optimal and feedback is effectance relevant, promotes a sense of competence (White, 1963) that in turn encourages further efforts toward effective interactions within one's environment. Finally, the experience of relatedness and mutuality that derives from authentic contact with others appears to play a crucial role in connecting individuals to social tasks and promoting an internalization of valued goals. Primarily, one identifies with and emulates the practices of those to whom one is, or might desire to be, attached. A comprehensive theory of education must deal with how these needs, which are organized in terms of an introspective account of motivation, can be addressed in the social context of schools (see also Connell, 1990; Deci & Ryan, 1991; Ryan 1991; Ryan, Connell, & Grolnick, in press). However, in the current essay our primary focus will be on autonomy because of its centrality to the theme of self-regulation, whereas relatedness and competence will be less directly addressed.

In order to ground this perspective both theoretically and empirically, we proceed as follows: First, we lay out a theoretical framework for understanding and researching the nature of internalization and self-regulation with regard to learning; second, we present research on the social contexts at home and in the classroom that affect internalization and self-regulation; and, finally, we examine some preliminary findings concerning the impact of internalization and self-regulation on the quality of learning per se, that is, on the outcomes related to the cognitive agenda of educators. Ultimately our goal is to explicate the interpersonal and cultural dynamics that are associated with engagement versus alienation in our schools and suggest some reorientations that might begin to redress the all too common failure of internalization evident in schools today.

A MOTIVATIONAL APPROACH TO THE SELF AND INTERNALIZATION

The human organism is certainly unfinished at birth, but prepared by nature with a liberal endowment of interest and motivation toward assimilating the physical and social surround. The propensity to learn, to acquire new skills and to integrate experience is perhaps the most powerful "fact" with which a theory of education must begin. But along side the fact of an assimilatory nature residing within the organism is a social context that supplies both a content to be assimilated and a set of conditions for learning and development that either nurtures assimilation or makes that process more arduous, less satisfying, and, ultimately, less successful. The social-contextual niche of development can thus be either fertile or nutritionally impoverished, but in either case it supplies the ground in which assimilatory processes must take root and take off. Our research into motivational dynamics attempts to examine the characteristics of classroom and home environments that are most conducive to (or alternatively inhibiting of) assimilation and development.

The liberal endowment of curiosity, interest and mastery motivation that nature supplies us with is particularly manifest in the phenomenon of *intrinsic motivation* (Ryan & Connell, 1988). Intrinsic motivation is typically defined as the doing of an activity "for its own sake," or for the satisfactions inherent in action and its effects. Intrinsically motivated activity is both spontaneous (coming from within) and autotelic (an end in itself). Among the inherent satisfactions that accompany intrinsic motivation are the feelings of competence emphasized by White (1963) and the joy of experiencing oneself as a causal agent described by deCharms (1968). Through intrinsically motivated action children thus grow in a sense of both competence and autonomy.

Children begin life with an intrinsic motivation to explore, manipulate and master their surround, and more generally to receive from others practices, knowledge and meanings through mutual interactions (Rogoff, 1990; Ryan, 1991). Caretakers in their early transactions with children may facilitate or dampen this tendency to learn and to do (Grolnick, Frodi, & Bridges, 1984), but typically children entering schools still are highly intrinsically motivated learners, possessing a readiness and willingness to assimilate. Intrinsic motivation thus represents a tremendous inner resource for educators, a resource that can be capitalized on in motivating students to learn. Strategies employed by teachers and parents to motivate students in schools vary in terms of the degree to which they disrupt rather than engage this potential ally (Barrett & Boggiano, 1988; Deci, Nezlek, & Sheinman, 1981; Thomas, 1980).

Intrinsically motivated learning is by definition *self-regulated*. It is characterized by an "internal perceived locus of causality," that is, a feeling of self-determination (deCharms, 1968; Deci & Ryan, 1985). Intrinsic motivation is experienced, that is, as emanating from the self rather than external factors, and it represents a natural and prototypical form of human volition (Ryan, 1991). Intrinsically motivated action thus will occur without external prods, controls, and rewards, and, in fact, is often undermined by their presence. Because motivation for such activity is both innate and spontaneous it cannot be stamped in, prompted, or shaped, but rather must be nourished and nurtured.

In a now voluminous literature, more than a hundred studies have contrasted the effects of external controls and rewards with the absence of such controls or rewards on intrinsically motivated behaviors or interests. The premise has been that when external controls are absent, "internal" regulation will, therefore, be in evidence. In general that assumption has been viable in that intrinsic motivation flourishes only under conditions where external controls or incentives are *not* the salient causes or reasons for acting (see Deci & Ryan, 1987; Koestner & McClelland, 1990, for reviews).

However, there is a serious inadequacy in formulations of intrinsic motivation that rest too heavily on a concrete internal/external dichotomy. Such a dichotomy rests on a metaphor that suggests that forces or controls which are external to the person are therefore necessarily alien to his or her self and conversely that forces which are internal to the person necessarily represent or are congruent with the self. Both of these assumptions are fallacious. In the first instance, external rewards or controls do not always undermine intrinsic motivation; they do so only when they negate or conflict with experienced autonomy or self-determination. There are many instances in which rewards, for example, may aid intrinsic motivation insofar as they are offered and interpreted as positive feedback regarding one's competence or effectiveness at a task (Deci & Ryan, 1985; Harackiewicz, Manderlink, & Sansone, in press; Ryan, Mims & Koestner, 1983). Secondly, the fact that external controls may not be present does not guarantee that the internal controls which, by inference, are regulating behavior are characterized by autonomy or represent *self*-regulation. This is particularly the case when individuals act out guilt, obligation, or compulsion. Here the proximal source of motivation is clearly "internal," in the concrete sense, but is experienced as controlling and coercive. Such behavior is hardly volitional; it is instead better described as heteronomous.

In educational settings the clearest case of internal yet heteronomous forms of motivation is manifest in the phenomenon of *ego-involvement*. In ego involvement, one experiences a contingency between outcomes and self-esteem. Good performance is thus motivated not by choice and value but by a threat to the self (Covington, 1984; Nicholls, 1984; Ryan, 1982). In a culture where a child may perceive his or her value or worth in the eyes of others as determined by how well he or she achieves, ego-involvement is likely to be a pervasive phenomenon. The question becomes not whether ego-involvement motivates (which it does) but what are the cognitive and affective impacts of such motivation.

In a number of studies, the effects of ego-involvement on intrinsic motivation have been explored. Expanding on a discussion by deCharms (1968), Ryan (1982) argued that ego-involvement represents an internally controlling style analogous to being externally controlled and thus should undermine intrinsic motivation. To test this formulation he told college students that their performance on a visual task reflected their creative intelligence, reasoning that this would induce a self-evaluative set and ego-involvement. Results confirmed the prediction, with ego-involved students becoming less intrinsically motivated and more pressured than their task-involved counterparts. Subsequent research has continued to replicate this finding by showing how the hinging of self-esteem on performance outcomes detracts from task interest and enthusiasm (e.g., Butler, 1987; Koestner, Zuckerman & Koestner, 1987; Plant & Ryan, 1985). Later we will review the impact of such motivation on the quality of learning and performance. However, these studies underscore the theoretical point that, despite being "internally" motivated, ego-involved students are neither intrinsically motivated nor autonomous with respect to learning.

The qualitative differences between various "internal" types of motivation come into even starker relief when one examines learning tasks that are *not* intrinsically motivated (Ryan, Connell & Grolnick, in press). Clearly, much of an educator's task concerns not so much offering students what interests them, but rather that which is believed to be in their best interest. Transmitting skills and knowledge which may not be viewed by the student, at least initially, as inherently satisfying, interesting, or valuable thus falls within the domain of facilitating extrinsically motivated learning.

In the past, theorists have made a hard distinction between extrinsic and intrinsic motivation, with the former connoting heteronomy and control and the latter connoting autonomy and self-regulation. However, like the internal/ external dichotomy, the intrinsic/extrinsic dichotomy is more complex than that. While it remains definitionally true that intrinsic motivation is necessarily autonomous or self-regulated, it is not accurate to say that extrinsically motivated behavior cannot be self-determined. Extrinsically motivated actions can vary considerably in their "perceived locus of causality." Extrinsic motivation can be experienced as externally compelled (the classic case); it can be internally compelled (as in ego-involvement or introjection); or it can be relatively self-determined or autonomous (as when one identifies the goals of the behavior as one's own). Here the issue is the extent to which those behaviors that are not intrinsically motivated come to be adopted by the self as valuable, and thus as activities *worth doing*. The more fully an extrinsically motivated behavior is accepted and endorsed as a personal value and as one's responsibility and choice, rather than as something imposed, arbitrary or alien, the more it is characterized by an internal perceived locus of causality, that is, as self-determined (Deci & Ryan, 1985). Together these psychological qualities of acceptance, value, and volition are an endpoint along a continuum of *internalization* (Krathwohl et al., 1974; Ryan et al., 1985), an endpoint that can also be characterized in terms of self-regulation.

In a recently presented set of studies, Ryan & Connell (1989) demonstrated various ways in which achievement behavior could be motivated and also could vary along a dimension of relative autonomy or true *self*-regulation. They asked elementary and high school students to endorse the degree to which various reasons for acting underlie behaviors such as "doing homework," or participating in class. Among the categories of reasons sampled were: *external* (e.g., because I'd get in trouble if I didn't); *introjections* (e.g., because I'd feel guilty if I didn't); *identifications* (e.g., because I think its important to . . .); and *intrinsic* (e.g., because its fun). It was argued that these four classes of reasons were capable of being modeled along a gradient of autonomy, with external reasons being most heteronomous in nature, introjected reasons at an intermediate level, and identified and intrinsic reasons most autonomous in character. Use of an ordered correlational (simplex) analysis supported this view, as did the data from various construct validity studies. Similar findings have also been obtained using this model in other laboratories (e.g., Vallerand, Blais, Briere, & Pelletier, 1989). The implication of such research is that even extrinsically motivated achievement behaviors can be more or less self-determined.

The concepts of autonomy and internalization in education are thus not well captured by a simple contrast between intrinsic and extrinsic motivational approaches. Rather, in our view, the issue concerns promoting self-regulated learning versus learning based on mere compliance or self-esteem related threats. The motivational task, in this conception, is the promotion of learning that *engages the self* of the learner and instills a sense of value and commitment, even for tasks that on the surface are not "fun." It is the engagement of the self, ultimately, that differentiates external forms of regulation from self-regulation in school, and such engagement is dependent on processes and social contexts that promote either intrinsic motivation and/or the internalization and integration of extrinsically motivated regulation.

We have, however, suggested that the internalization of social practices, even those that are not themselves intrinsically motivated, is itself an intrinsically motivated *process*. This means that, given a freedom from superfluous control (Lepper, 1983; Ryan et al., 1985), given an optimal pacing of what is taught, and given reasonable relational contexts and supports (Ryan, 1991), what is originally external will proceed toward being self-regulated. However, this is not to suggest that human nature is infinitely malleable or that just any social values ought to be assimilable. "Human nature" places constraints upon and conditions what people can and want to learn and become, and anyone who works practically (rather than merely abstractly) in social contexts experiences this quite forcefully. A theory of internalization simply allows us to attend more carefully to the process of socialization and to better recognize practices and values that cannot be fully internalized, and that dehumanize and dampen human nature. Our current chapter, restricted to the context of education and achievement, thus falls quite narrowly within a much larger set of questions at the boundaries of psychology and sociology that concern how cultural mores and practices are transmitted and transformed into individual action patterns and beliefs.

A THEORETICAL NOTE ON THE AUTONOMY/COMPETENCE DISTINCTION

Readers familiar with the psychological literature on self-regulation will note how little thus far we have emphasized the concept of *competence*. By contrast, there exists a plethora of research and theory that links competence relevant constructs to the issue of motivation and self-regulation and indeed construes competence as perhaps the central issue. For example, Harter (1982) has linked perceived competence to intrinsic motivation and performance in school. A number of other researchers have related locus of control concepts to achievement (e.g., Connell, 1985; Crandall, Katkovski, & Crandall, 1965; Skinner, Wellborn, & Connell, 1990). Still other lines of research concerned with competence include students' self-efficacy (Bandura, 1989), outcome attributions (Nicholls, 1984; Weiner, 1986), and expectancies for success and failure (e.g., Dweck & Elliot, 1983).

What ties many of these traditions together is a common focus on affects and cognitions regarding academic *outcomes*. They are concerned with students' perceived capacities to produce outcomes (perceived competence); their understanding of the causes of outcomes (locus of control/causal attribution); or their beliefs concerning the probabilities of attaining outcomes (expectancies). Futhermore, many of these approaches focus on competence as the superordinate question pertinent to agency and motivation.

A belief that one can attain or control outcomes or be effective in one's action is, indeed, essential to the motivation of any intentional behavior (Deci & Ryan, 1987; Heider, 1958). Without such beliefs there is no basis for personal causation, effectance, or motivation of any sort. However, in our view, the fact that one *can* attain outcomes, or even that one is motivated to attain them, does not address either the nature of that motivation or more specifically *why* one is so motivated. It is here that the issue of who or what initiates and regulates such motivated behavior becomes salient, and it is in this context that a theory of *autonomy* is necessitated.

One can be motivated, and indeed competent, at a task and yet be completely coerced into doing it. A student, forced by teachers or preoccupied with a parent's contingent approval, may be highly driven and spectacularly efficacious at school work. She would be an agent, in Bandura's (1989) use of the term. But if she does it only for them, and experiences her achievement as having its impetus and sustenance in the control others have over her, then she lacks autonomy, and thus in our view lacks something essential to agency. In contrast the same student could be efficacious and yet autonomous insofar as her achievement is reflective of her personal values and choices.

A theory of autonomy deals with the distinctions, then, not merely between motivated and unmotivated behavior, but *within* motivated behavior, specifically the behavior of "pawns" versus "origins" (deCharms, 1968; Deci & Ryan, 1991). In our view the concepts of agency and self-regulation connote more than mere competence and efficacy but also concern the extent to which one's efficacious actions are also truly volitional, meaning, *self-determined*. Thus, although we view competence or efficacy as a necessary condition for agency, it is not a sufficient criterion. In describing self-regulation, then, we build from the traditions emphasizing issues of competence, but add to their edifice a heavy dose of concern about the left-hand side of that hyphenated term.

THE SOCIAL CONTEXT OF SELF-REGULATION I: IN THE CLASSROOM

In some of our earliest studies, we sought to understand how teaching styles in particular would lead students to feel either engaged and interested in learning or alienated and passive. We made the assumption that in order for students to "want" to learn they would require an atmosphere that encouraged their initiative and self-expression and was sensitive to their internal needs and perspectives. We also assumed that this atmosphere was largely a function of the attitudes and practices of the teacher. In the terms of motivational theory (e.g., Deci & Ryan, 1980, 1985) we expected that teachers who were supportive of autonomy would promote interest and engagement. By contrast we expected that classroom teachers who attempted to enforce and control learning "from without" would produce among students a more passive and less interested orientation towards learning and a diminished experience of autonomy and competence.

To examine this hypothesis, we began by surveying teacher attitudes toward motivating students in the classroom. We (Deci, Schwartz, Sheinman, & Ryan, 1981) created an instrument that assessed the degree to which teachers tended to motivate behavior through the use of external controls, rewards, or comparisons versus through minimizing salient external controls and instead attempting to take the students' internal frame of reference with respect to problems, ideas, and initiatives. Our resulting survey thus tapped teacher styles along a continuum of control to autonomy-support. In an initial study this survey was administered to 35 elementary-school teachers prior to the beginning of a school year. Approximately eight weeks into that year we sampled the 610 children who were taught by these teachers to assess their attitudes and motivation with respect to learning, using measures developed by Harter (1981, 1982). It was found that children in the classrooms of those teachers whose orientations were more autonomy-oriented (versus controlling) reported more curiosity with respect to learning, more desire for challenge, and more independent mastery attempts. In addition, children who were learning from autonomy-oriented teachers experienced greater perceived competence in school. Perhaps most notably, students from classrooms with autonomy-oriented teachers reported greater general self-worth. These findings clearly suggested that teachers' orientations towards autonomy support versus control in the classroom atmosphere impacted not only upon the degree to which students were actively engaged in the learning process and were gaining confidence as a result of their efforts, but also upon how they experienced themselves more generally.

In a subsequent study Ryan and Grolnick (1986) obtained similar findings using different methods. Children from elementary-school classrooms were asked to describe the "climate" of their classroom along an autonomy-supportive versus controlling dimension using a measure developed by deCharms (1976). This measure taps children's perceptions of the teacher's style in fostering either an "origin" versus "pawn" orientation in students. A pawn orientation concerns compliance and passivity, whereas an origin is more initiating, expressive, and self-motivated. It was found that children who experienced the classroom as more origin-oriented were more mastery motivated, had greater perceived competence, and had more understanding of how to attain learning outcomes relative to children experiencing a pawn-oriented climate. Furthermore, when children were asked to write stories about a "neutral" classroom scene depicted in a drawing, students who were currently experiencing pawn-like classroom climates depicted controlling teachers and either passively compliant or rebellious students. By contrast students who reported an origin climate in the classroom tended to write stories involving more active, interested and constructive student-teacher interactions. These findings suggested that not only does autonomy support versus control affect one's current motivational style, it also impacts upon the way classrooms and education may in general be represented and experienced.

Ryan and Grolnick (1986; Grolnick & Ryan, 1989, in press) have additionally argued that students who come to view their interactions with adults as controlling not only act more like "pawns" but may, in fact, lead or pull adults into being more controlling as a reciprocal influence. Similarly students who are relatively self-regulating may facilitate responsiveness and support from adults, which in turn conduces toward greater self-determination. Ryan and Grolnick (1986) provided evidence that a child's perceptions of the classroom climate are determined by both environmental and individual difference elements. Perceptions of classroom climate are a function partially of actual classroom conditions, which are largely shaped by teacher style and orientation, and partially of variations in children's *interpretation* of the ambient environment. It was suggested that such variability in interpretations may result from prior experiences at home and in school and that these prior conditions may dynamically impact upon current teacher-child interactions. Children, for example, who come from authoritarian home atmospheres may transfer this motivational set to the classroom and thus elicit a controlling stance from a teacher.

More direct support for such a reciprocity formulation was recently supplied by Pelletier and Vallerand (1989). They examined how the mere belief that a student is extrinsically oriented can lead a teacher to be more controlling. In this study teachers were led to believe that a student whom they were to instruct was either intrinsically or extrinsically motivated. Teaching sessions were then recorded and rated on content and process dimensions. It was found that teachers who were oriented toward an extrinsic learner were more controlling in their approach, being more directive, contingently praising and critical, and less allowing of participation. Futhermore, the style adopted by teachers as a result of their beliefs about their students' motivation resulted in both motivational and performance differences. Students who experienced control stemming from the extrinsic induction were assessed as less interested and engaged using both self-report and behavioral measures. They also showed a lower quality of learning.

One might wonder why the issue of autonomy support versus control has such broad effects, influencing not only curiosity and motivation but also perceived competence, the quality of one's task engagement, and one's experienced self-worth. One way to comprehend this phenomenon is to imagine yourself in a workplace populated by twenty to thirty others with one boss. In one case your boss listens to you, takes an interest in your perspective, supports your taking of initiative and wherever possible provides you some input and latitude with respect to how you proceed with your work. In a second case your boss appears unwilling to listen to or understand you, sets out agendas without your participation, and uses rewards, punishments, and public evaluations to ensure your compliance. Clearly any adult's motivation, job satisfaction, and sense of effectiveness and organizational value would be differentially affected in these two cases. In fact, our research in adult work settings supports this viewpoint. People who work for controlling managers report less satisfaction with work, less trust in their corporation, and more concern with extrinsic outcomes like pay and benefits than those whose managers are more autonomy supportive (Deci, Connell, & Ryan, 1989). Thus the question is less why is this issue so central, and more why have we focused on it so little in educational practice?

It is interesting to note that, in the context of teacher workshops, findings on the impact of autonomy versus control in the classroom are typically received with little surprise. Most teachers enter the field with an interest in learning and development and are ideologically schooled on such progressive thinkers as Montessori (1917/1965), Dewey (1938), Rogers (1969), and Holt (1964). Thus, on the surface they express a value for autonomy, and such findings make sense to them within this value system. More crucially, however, teachers can also readily detail a number of obstacles that make autonomy support difficult to *practice*. A frequent comment in workshops and discussions is how similar teachers can feel to the children in our studies who work within controlling climates. Teachers often experience the curriculum they teach as imposed upon them, as something they must *cover*. Coverage is then measured through standardized tests and there is pressure both on the teachers and on the school administrators to insure that students are educated up to standards.

Backing up these pressures are increasing methods of surveillance, documentation and accountability. Finally, in many school systems the sheer number and heterogeneity of students in a classroom with one adult makes the structuring of optimal challenges, individualized attention, or empathic interventions a low probability. This is particularly the case in classrooms where a small percentage of children will elicit inordinate teacher attention and management-oriented actions. Such factors, teachers argue, detract from their ability to be facilitative of autonomy, as well as their intrinsic motivation and creativity with respect to teaching per se. They also focus teachers away from attention to the internal processes of the child and toward external criteria and evaluations.

To examine the impact of pressuring teachers to cover externally specified curricula and insure high normative standards, we designed an analog study (Deci, Spiegel, Ryan, Koestner, & Kauffman, 1982). In it we asked two groups of college students to act as teachers in the context of an experiment on spatial problem solving. After familiarizing them with the problems and strategies of importance in the tasks, we assigned each of them a student to whom they were to teach these skills. One group was instructed "to facilitate the student's learning," without a pressure toward performance requirements, whereas the second group was told to "make sure the student performs up to standards." Teaching sessions were then audio taped and later rated by persons unfamiliar with the hypotheses. Teachers in the "standards" group were rated as more demanding and controlling than teachers in the no standards group. Furthermore they talked more, were more directive, used more criticism and praise, and allowed the student less time to explore or independently solve puzzles. This suggests that pressure concerning standards results in a more controlling versus autonomy-supportive style in teachers.

Additional studies have replicated and extended the finding that controlling teaching styles can be readily "induced" by pressure on teachers to produce specified outcomes. In a particularly relevant study, Flink, Boggiano and Barrett (in press) observed actual fourth-grade teachers during sessions in which they had been told either: (a) to facilitate children's learning; or (b) to insure that children perform well (closely paralleling the instructions used in Deci et al., 1982). Results indicated that students of pressured teachers who used controlling strategies performed more poorly than students of nonpressured teachers. In addition their analyses suggested that the performance decrements stemmed directly from the increased use of controlling strategies evidenced by teachers who experienced pressure.

The nature of classroom goals that are established for teachers thus appears to impact directly upon the degree to which they can be autonomy supportive versus controlling. Excessive focus on performance outcomes creates a resultant pressure on teachers towards making students achieve the externally imposed standards, with a corresponding inattention to the internal frame of reference of the learner from which more natural styles and propensities to learn proceed. For this reason, goal orientation and saliency may also be strong determinants of classroom motivational processes.

Much of the literature in this area has focused on contrasting goal orientations such as learning-oriented versus performance-oriented (Dweck, 1986, 1988); task- versus ego-involved (Maehr, 1983; Nicholls, 1984; Ryan, 1982); and mastery-versus performance-focused goals (Ames and Archer, 1988). Learning, task, and mastery orientations all emphasize the intrinsic satisfactions and challenges of learning; the individual is focused on skill development, the process of learning, and the inherent interest of the task. On the other hand, performance goals and ego-involvement emphasize pressure towards normatively high outcomes and the demonstration to others of one's ability. The comparison of the self with others becomes the motivating force for learning, one that is inherently extrinsic and competitive. Whereas learning, task, and mastery orientations focus on self as origin and agent in learning, performance goals and ego-involvement focus on the self as an object of evaluation in the context of learning. Accordingly the former concerns self-regulated learning, whereas the latter conduces toward a perceived external locus of causality with respect to learning.

Early work by Maehr and Stallings (1972) provided substantial support for this view in an experimental examination of the effects of an evaluative, performance-oriented emphasis on students' interest and engagement. Eighth-grade students were asked to complete an easy or difficult pattern-differentiation task under either external or internal evaluation conditions. In the external-evaluation condition, it was emphasized that the task represented a test of the student's ability and that the results would be given to the student's teachers. In the internal-evaluation condition, it was emphasized that the task was being done for intrinsic interest and enjoyment, and that the student's performance would not be evaluated by anyone else. Assessment was then made of the students continued motivation for the task. The results indicated that students in the internal-evaluation condition were more motivated to continue with difficult tasks than students in the external evaluation condition. Maehr and Stallings concluded that because external evaluation is experienced as constraining it leads to decrements in continuing motivation.

More recent research by Ames and Archer (1988) related the salience of mastery-oriented versus performance-oriented goals in the classroom to high-school students' task choices, attitudes, attributions for success and failure, and selection and use of effective learning strategies. Ames and Archer found that students for whom mastery goals were salient in their classroom environment reported using more effective learning strategies, preferred more challenging tasks, liked their classroom more, and were more likely to believe that success and effort are related than students who perceived performance goals to be more salient. Furthermore, they found that the effects of goal saliency remained consistent after the effects of perceived competence were partialled out. Ames and Archer's findings thus further suggest that the pressure on students towards performance outcomes detracts from their willingness and preferences for challenge with regard to the process of learning.

It is interesting to speculate, given the tenor of these findings, on how the "higher standards, more accountability" movement that has swept the nation has really influenced the quality of education in the classroom. Undoubtedly both administrators and teachers are experiencing greater pressure to achieve measurable learning gains in students. The hidden cost of this felt pressure is that it is probably translated into teaching practices that not only fail to incite student interest and involvement, but in fact may even deepen alienation and disengagement among learners. Additionally, such pressures may have a negative impact on *teacher* motivation and enthusiasm.

Although research on the matter of teacher motivation is sparse, there is some evidence emerging that supports the view that, as with students, controlling climates can have a negative impact on teacher motivation. Pajak & Glickman (1984) had teachers rate videotaped supervisory sessions that were varied in terms of being informational versus controlling. As they predicted, using cognitive evaluation theory (Deci & Ryan, 1980), teachers reacted more favorably to less directive, less controlling supervision. More specifically they viewed controlling supervision as less supportive, and they viewed controlling supervisors as less trustworthy, authentic and inspiring of loyalty. Notably, their results also suggested that they would be *less* likely to change their teaching as a result of controlling inputs. It appears that they, like their students and other groups of adults (e.g., Deci et al. 1989) are more motivated when they experience autonomy support. Glickman & Pajak (1986) later replicated and extended this work by having instructional supervisors view videotapes of simulated supervisory sessions that were also varied in terms of being informational or controlling. Again, as predicted, they found supervisors reacted more favorably to sessions that were less controlling and more informational in nature. Their results with supervisors closely paralleled their results with teachers along the dimensions of supportiveness, authenticity, loyalty, trust, and likelihood of change. Taken together, these studies underscore the potential negative impact of surplus control in communication to, and about, teachers.

The general point that can be derived from accumulating research (and from our less systematic observations in school systems) is that the capacity of teachers to promote self-regulation and internalization of value for learning in students is inexorably intertwined with teachers' opportunities to regulate their own activities and thus to be innovative, creative, and intrinsically motivated on a day-to-day basis. The attempt to control teachers, dictate standardized curricula, and "insure" accountability and performance from the outside most typically will translate into classroom practices that are less spontaneous, engaging, and participatory. Accordingly, one will have students whose psychological needs are less addressed and who become less personally engaged and self-regulated in the context of school.

Alternatives do exist. However, given the political and systems constraints, they are most likely to occur in contexts of unusually protective and innovative administrators. These are administrators who can absorb the external pressure toward outcomes while still providing a participative and autonomy-supportive atmosphere for teachers.

It is also worth pointing out that there are considerable individual differences between teachers in the way in which they practice in the classroom and manage to create autonomy-supportive climates within the limitations imposed on them. In a qualitative study, Belenky, Clinchy, Goldberger, and Tarule (1986) described "connected classrooms" in which dialogue and relative autonomy are afforded. Such classrooms were characterized by less salience of evaluation and thus more risk taking; more acceptance and receptivity of participants' viewpoints and thus more disclosure and sharing. In general there was support for gaining a voice.

In another heuristically valuable article, Ingram and Worrall (1987) discuss the concrete practice of autonomy-supportive education within a traditional British primary school. They label their approach the "negotiating classroom," to describe the fundamental feature in which students are given a hearty degree of responsibility for choosing and arranging classroom activities. They also address the anxieties that provision of choice generates in parents and teachers alike, which are considerable. Their discussion suggests that effecting autonomy support requires significant skills and that the advance of self-determination in the classroom is at best, hard won.

THE SOCIAL CONTEXT OF SELF-REGULATION II: IN THE HOME

Although the center of attention with regard to students' motivation and achievement has been upon schools and teachers, it is an obvious point that students' motivational orientations are also shaped and affected in the home. While teachers have a well-documented influence, each teacher is but a temporary figure in the life of a student. No matter what the duration of a given classroom context, a child returns each afternoon, weekend, and summer to caregivers who are the primary regulators of resources, affection, and esteem. The linkage between the social context experienced in the home and the process of internalization with regard to achievement has rightfully been the focus of a growing body of research.

Grolnick and Ryan (1989) investigated the role of relevant parental practices in facilitating academic achievement and the development of attitudes, motives, and self-evaluative outcomes that are associated with student engagement and internalization. More specifically they explored the relations between parental inputs (the social context of the home) and the inner resources that are involved in school adaption. These inner resources primarily involve the capacity to be self-regulating or autonomous with regard to the learning process and the challenges of school.

A central thrust of this study was the investigation of the effects of parental styles characterized by *autonomy support* in contrast to controlling styles of parenting. An autonomy-supportive style reflects the degree to which parents use and value techniques which encourage choice and participation in making decisions and solving problems. Central to autonomy support is an interest and willingness to take the child's frame of reference into consideration when motivating or regulating behavior. At the opposite end of this continuum are parental behaviors and techniques which are controlling, such as dictating outcomes and motivating the child through punishment, rewards, and pressure. Grolnick and Ryan (1989) hypothesized that parental autonomy support provides the foundation for self-regulation and internalization relevant to academic achievement and thus would predict classroom motivation and competence.

Facilitation of children's self-regulation and competence was also hypothesized to be related to parental *involvement*. Involvement was conceptualized as the extent to which the parent is interested in, knowledgeable about, and takes an active part in the child's life. Involvement thus reflects the parents's dedication of resources to the child-rearing process. Grolnick and Ryan argued that more involved parents would provide inputs and resources essential to academic adjustment and achievement.

Finally, parental provision of *structure* was also examined as an input into children's self-regulation and competence in school. Structure concerns the clarity and consistency of parentally set limits, rules, and regulatory inputs. Grolnick and Ryan hypothesized that structure aids a child in the development of intentionality and perceived control. Structure provides predictability and thus should facilitate an understanding of what controls outcomes.

To assess the parenting dimensions of autonomy support, involvement and structure, Grolnick and Ryan separately interviewed mothers and fathers about their child rearing activities. The interview focused on various areas of children's lives, both academic and domestic. For each area, the parent was asked open-ended questions about how he or she motivates their child, whether there are specific rules or expectations, and how he or she responds to positive and negative behaviors. Parents were also asked to describe typical conflicts that occur and how these conflicts get resolved. The interviews were then scored by independent raters on component dimensions that were used to generate in the summary scores for autonomy support, involvement, and structure.

Results showed that parental autonomy support was positively related to children's self-reports of autonomous self-regulation, teacher rated competence and adjustment, and school grades and achievement. Children of autonomy-supportive parents were more likely to report a willingness and interest to engage in the tasks relevant to school, and they were rated by teachers as less likely to act-out or show poor adjustment. They also did better on "objective" indices of performance. Grolnick and Ryan supplied two alternative, but complementary explanations: (1) parents using an autonomy-supportive style promote self-regulation in their children by allowing for the autonomous growth of interest and volition; and (2) children who demonstrate more adjustment and motivational difficulties also elicit greater external control from their parents. These results were thus interpreted in terms of a transactional process in which bidirectional influences by parent and child shape the development of self-regulation in school.

Additional findings showed that, as predicted, parental provision of structure was related to control perceptions. Greater structure in the home was associated with child reports of greater understanding of the sources of control over outcomes within the academic domain (Connell, 1985). Furthermore, maternal involvement was positively related to teacher-rated competence and adjustment, and school grades and achievement. It thus appeared that mothers' provision of resources provided a secure base of operation for children's' classroom regulation and adjustment. By contrast, paternal involvement showed little impact upon children's self-regulation or competence. In the particular sample studied, Grolnick and Ryan interpreted these results in terms of the low absolute level of involvement (time spent) by the interviewed fathers.

In an interesting side note, Grolnick and Ryan also found a strong inverse relation between teacher and parent reports of attention directed towards the child. This negative correlation suggested that teachers may often be expending considerable resources and energies on those children whose parents are not expending much time and energy. However, the time spent by the teachers was not necessarily positive, but rather often focused on management and control rather than learning activities. Insofar as parents are less involved with children, the challenges and demands placed on teachers are raised. This is particularly interesting given that studies of teacher time show that, by late elementary school, teachers are directing more attention to management than to teaching (Thomas, 1980).

In sum, Grolnick and Ryan posited that the autonomy support, structure and involvement dimensions of parental style had identifiable influences on children's classroom self-regulation and competence. Most centrally, they found that an atmosphere of support for autonomy facilitates the internalization of school-related values and the associated development of competence. Such findings emphasize the role of parents in shaping children's internalization as it relates to school functioning. The findings also suggest that the sources of our "problems" in schools may lie less in the practices of teachers and more in the climates and resources available in the student's home.

Working within the same model, Grolnick, Ryan, and Deci (1990) more recently examined the relations between children's perceptions of parental autonomy support and involvement and the children's motivation and performance in school. They hypothesized that children's perceptions of parenting style directly impact and shape the development of the child's inner motivational resources. These inner resources include control understanding (Skinner & Connell, 1986), perceived competence (Harter, 1983), and autonomy (Ryan & Connell, 1989). In turn, it was expected that these resources within the child would predict achievement related outcomes. Grolnick et al. tested this framework using a path analytic strategy. They found that the relationship between perceived parental context and academic achievement was, indeed, mediated by the child's inner resources. Specifically, perceived maternal and paternal autonomy support and involvement positively predicted control understanding, perceived competence, and relative autonomy, all of which predicted both standardized measures of achievement and teacher-rated competence. These findings again demonstrate the impact of the home environment on school-based outcomes and emphasize the role of parents in exerting a pervasive influence on children's competence and autonomy as it relates to school functioning. Moreover they suggest that the impact of interpersonal contexts on outcomes is an indirect one, achieved primarily by the facilitation (or debilitation) of the psychological resources and motives developed within the student.

Research on the relationship between school related motivation and internalization and the social context of the home also highlights the intricate interdependency between school and culture. A child who comes from a background of neglect or overcontrol creates a motivational problem for teachers who in turn may be pulled to respond in ways that yet further alienate or disengage the student. Interestingly, successful programs for such "at risk" students (to use the current buzzword) may achieve their effects mainly through breaking this *interpersonal* cycle of deepening alienation.

Evidence for this was recently provided by Vito and Connell (1989), who examined students' perceptions of an experimental program for students identified as "at risk" for school failure or dropout. They found that gains among at-risk students in self-motivation, confidence, and control were largely a function of changes in their perceptions of teachers' autonomy support, involvement, and provision of structure in their new program. In other words, improvements in students' status could be attributed to the renovation of the interpersonal context afforded to them in the intervention program. In contrast, a control group of at-risk students receiving no intervention changed in neither perception of their context nor in their adjustment to school. Such data help emphasize how the process of internalization in school depends heavily on the character of human exchanges which are salient to the participants, and which either relate to or frustrate important psychological needs.

More specifically, social contexts characterized by autonomy support and involvement probably provide a basis for connectedness between adults and students that facilitates internalization and competence. Ryan, Lynch, and Stiller (1990) recently examined this formulation in a sample of junior high and high school students. They assessed the perceived quality of relatedness students experienced with respect to both parents and teachers. They found that the felt quality of relatedness was in large part a function of the degree to which those adults were perceived as autonomy supportive and involved. Conversely, students reported low security in their attachments and relationships with controlling and/or uninvolved adults. In turn, quality of relatedness and attachment was highly predictive of school-related motivation and attitudes. The more detached a student was to teachers or parents, the less the student reported feeling autonomous, engaged, or competent with regard to school. By contrast, positive attributes to parents and teachers were predictive of greater internalization, engagement, and perceived competence. It thus appeared that autonomy support and involvement facilitate a positive relationship to adults in the social context of learning, which in turn promotes more active engagement, volition, and confidence.

Work by Baumrind (1967, 1971) on parental socialization has also resulted in findings that are consistent with some of our conclusions concerning autonomy support and involvement with respect to educational outcomes. She identified two dimensions of parental style—firm versus lax control and psychological autonomy versus psychological control. Parents high in psychological autonomy and firm control were classified as authoritative; parents high in psychological control and firm control were classified as authoritarian. Baumrind found that children of authoritative parents were more independent and self-reliant whereas children of authoritarian parents were more withdrawn and discontent. A third parenting style, labeled permissive, is characterized as tolerating children's impulses, making few demands for mature behavior, and using sporadic sanctions. Children of permissive parents were found to be immature, lacking in self-reliance and impulse control, and, in a follow-up study, low in both social and cognitive competence.

Applying Baumrind's typology to the study of educational outcomes, Dornbush et al. (1987) examined the relation between child-reported parent style and adolescent academic achievement in a large, heterogenous sample. Indices of parenting style were constructed from students' perceptions of parental behaviors and attitudes, and of family communication patterns. Authoritarian parenting was indexed by the frequency of demands for obedience, use of punishment as coercion to produce good grades, and pressure to constantly do better. The permissive parenting style was indexed by little importance placed on grades, few rules, and lack of parental involvement. Authoritative parenting was indexed by the frequency of open dialogue within the family, participation in decision making, praise for good grades, and support and encouragement as a response to bad grades. Findings of Dornbush et al. indicated lower grades were associated with reports of more authoritarian, more permissive, and less authoritative parenting styles. Furthermore, Dornbush et al. found adolescents who describe their parents as behaving more democratically, more warmly, and more encouraging earn higher grades than their peers. Although there were some minor differences, the positive association between authoritative parenting style and higher grades remained constant across ethnic and socioeconomic groups. This study further underscores the importance of parental styles, especially along the dimensions that we (Grolnick & Ryan, 1989) have labeled autonomy support and involvement, for school-related functioning.

Steinberg, Elmen, and Mounts (1989) extended and elaborated on Dornbush et al.'s findings by examining the role that authoritative parenting plays in facilitating academic success and the mediating role of psychosocial maturity in that process. They hypothesized that the authoritative parenting style is conducive to the development of psychosocial maturity, and that adolescents high in psychosocial autonomy are more likely to achieve academic success than their less autonomous peers. Steinberg et al. reasoned that autonomy influences adolescents' academic performance by reflecting the degree to which the developmentally appropriate tasks of self-reliance, self-management, and identity formation are internalized. Utilizing a path-analytic model, they found that adolescents' reports of parental warmth, democratic treatment, and firmness predicted positive beliefs about, and attitudes toward, academic achievement; and that these attitudes and beliefs predicted academic achievement. In sum, Steinberg et al. found psychosocial autonomy mediates the relationship between the authoritative parenting style and academic achievement. Again, we interpret such results as support for the view that contexts which enhance the students' affective and motivational resources not only facilitate psychological health, but ultimately produce more positive cognitive outcomes as well.

Together, research on the issue of autonomy support versus control in the home speaks to the important role played by social contexts in facilitating self-regulated learning. If by definition self-regulation represents initiation from within, then it is conduced by adults who receive, support, and are responsive to such initiation. Home contexts that are controlling and authoritarian appear to stifle initiative and self-regulation in the service of compliance. Moreover, we suggest that the less self-regulation develops, the more likely it is that adults will employ external controls as a management technique, thus exacerbating an external (or non-self-regulated) motivational orientation in the child. As we train children to learn only for external reasons, we in turn are compelled to continually take external responsibility for their motivation and performance. And thus does a deepening cycle of alienation develop.

EFFECTS OF AUTONOMY SUPPORT AND SELF-REGULATION ON LEARNING AND PERFORMANCE

Despite the fact that controlling atmospheres have demonstrable negative effects on both self-esteem and self-motivation, educators and policy makers, focused on the "bottom line" of achievement results, may be unimpressed. The real question from their perspective is not whether students enjoy or gain confidence as a result of their interactions with teachers; it is whether they learn better. Thus bottom-line educators suspect that the humanistic outcry concerning control in the classroom is nothing but a misplaced warm fuzziness that is unrelated to what schools are "really" about, namely cognitive outcomes of the concrete kind. Even those of us who view schools as contexts for human development rather than learning factories must also appreciate the importance of this question, which has been clouded by the relative absence of studies at the interface between motivation and cognition—that is, research examining the quality of learning that results from various motivational sets.

There is little doubt among most educators and developmentalists that significant learning can and does take place without external prompts, controls, or rewards. Recognition of intrinsic motivation to learn is now broad and furthermore is consistent with many theoretical approaches that focus on the active assimilatory nature of human beings (e.g. Piaget, 1971; White, 1963). One motivational question thus concerns how learning differs when it results from intrinsically motivated versus extrinsically motivated processes. A second, and perhaps more practical issue for educators concerns not simply the intrinsic/extrinsic distinction, but rather how learning can be directed from the "outside" (e.g., by a teacher) and still be undertaken by a student with affective qualities that are associated with volition and autonomous engagement. A further issue concerns the dynamic connections between motivational states and learning outcomes. Here we hypothesize that the more internal the perceived locus of causality for learning, the greater will be the depth of processing, retention, integration, and generalization of knowledge. Knowledge acquired autonomously will be more fully internalized. As yet, detailed investigation in this area is relatively sparse.

McGraw (1978) provided an early comprehensive review on the effects of intrinsic versus extrinsic motivation on learning and performance on learning tasks. He suggested based on relatively little evidence available at the time that the impact of extrinsic motivators depended on what aspect of learning outcomes one assessed. More specifically he argued that on algorithmic tasks, that is, tasks where there exists a straightforward, overlearned or rote path to the solution, extrinsic incentives or controls may not only not be problematic, they can even facilitate performance. By contrast McGraw argued that on heuristic tasks, that is, those where innovative, unique, or integrative solutions are required, extrinsic motivational sets tend to have deleterious consequences.

Research by Fabes, Moran, and McCullers (1981) provided support for the McGraw model. Using subtests from the Wechsler Adult Intelligence Scale (WAIS), Fabes, Moran, and McCullers found that, on the WAIS subscales selected as representing heuristic tasks (i.e., the Block Design, Picture Arrangement, and Object Assembly subscales), performance was poorer for those subjects under reward conditions than for subjects who were not rewarded. Furthermore, they found that, on algorithmic tasks (i.e., the Information, Digit Symbol, and Picture Completion subscales), performance did not differ for rewarded and nonrewarded subjects. This undermining effect of reward was found to be consistent across a variety of reward structures (i.e., performance contingent, performance noncontingent, competitive).

A conceptually related line of research has been forwarded by Amabile (1983). She has proposed an intrinsic motivation hypothesis regarding creativity stating that "the intrinsically motivated state is conducive to creativity, whereas the extrinsically motivated state is detrimental" (p.91). In a variety of studies she has shown particularly that conditions conducive to an internal perceived locus of causality or self-determination facilitate creative outcomes, whereas controlling, evaluative conditions undermine creativity. We have obtained similar findings in our own labs (e.g., Koestner, Ryan, Bernieri, & Holt, 1984). Findings relating to creativity and intrinsic motivation further support aspects of McGraw's formulation, insofar as one considers creative activities as heuristic in nature.

Although the importance of intrinsic motivation is fairly well established with regard to interesting or creative tasks, it also has a role in more traditional types of learning, particularly learning which takes place in the absence of external pressures. For example, we recently examined the role of intrinsic motivation in effecting spontaneous learning of traditional textbook-style material. We (Ryan, Connell, & Plant, 1990) asked students to read and rate text passages of an expository nature. In the context of the reading we assessed their ongoing intrinsic interest and sense of competence with respect to the material, as well as other emotional states. However students were led to believe that they would not be tested or assessed concerning their learning of the texts. Thus whatever they learned or assimilated was nondirected or "spontaneous." When students' memory for texts was subsequently assessed, it was found that assimilation of material was largely attributable to factors related to intrinsic motivation. A second follow-up study also found similar results for long-term text retention. It was concluded that intrinsic motivation supplies a crucial noncognitive support for spontaneous learning, and for its integration into long-term knowledge.

There is also a well-documented relationship between students preferences for challenges or complexity and conditions conducive to intrinsic versus extrinsic motivation. Pittman, Emery and Boggiano (1982), for example, showed that subjects who were rewarded for task performances preferred easier tasks. Similar results were also reported by Kruglanski, Stein, and Riter (1977), who found that rewarded subjects tended to put out the minimum effort sufficient to complete a task, consistent with an absence of interest in the task per se. Shapira (1976) reported that when college students were free to work on cognitive tasks they chose challenging problems, whereas rewards led to preferences for easier tasks (to insure a higher probability of receiving rewards).

Finally, in a study of particular relevance to cognitive developmental theory, Danner and Lonky (1981) demonstrated the relationship of intrinsic versus extrinsic motivation to the undertaking of cognitive challenges. Utilizing a Piagetian perspective, Danner and Lonky rated the difficulty level of three tasks according to their cognitive complexity. They then grouped a sample of elementary children according to the three ability levels. When left alone with a choice of tasks, children in each of the cognitive-ability groups spent the most time with and rated as most interesting those tasks that were one step ahead of their current level. Furthermore, children who were rewarded for task engagement evidenced decreased intrinsic motivation for optimally challenging tasks. These results support the notion that self-determination is crucial to intrinsically motivated action, in which people seek challenges and activities that are just beyond, but not altogether out of, their current capabilities.

It is important to note that what seems to impact negatively on innovative outcomes and the desire to challenge oneself in these studies of intrinsic versus extrinsic motivational sets are primarily factors that impact upon self-determination or autonomy. Autonomous engagement is undermined by the controls implicit in rewards (Deci & Ryan, 1987), insofar as they promote a perceived external locus of causality for action. The external control over behavior thus leads to "least output" solutions wherein effort and interest are minimal. As a result, less challenge is sought, and less stretching and development of current capacities will likely occur.

An important facet of this literature is that when controls are not salient people tend to undertake more optimal challenges. By contrast, externally set performance goals will often be out of synchrony with what is currently optimally challenging to the learner from a cognitive-developmental perspective. They are thus highly unlikely to inspire intrinsic interest on the part of the learner, being as it were an unnatural nutriment (Elkind, 1971). In consequence adults may feel it more necessary to force feed the lesson plan, and thus to employ controlling, evaluative or external reward based techniques.

To fight against the grain of intrinsic processes for learning requires a considerable cache of weapons.

It seems likely that classroom practices and learning that occur under salient external pressure or incentives to learn may result in less autonomous student engagement with curricula. This suggests further that less depth of processing and integration of knowledge will result. In contrast, learning which is self-regulated and autonomous will have a qualitative advantage over that which is brought about through external control or reward.

Grolnick and Ryan (1987) examined this conceptualization in a study of reading comprehension and memory among fifth-grade students. They compared three conditions for learning: (a) non-directed or "spontaneous" learning, in which children read a text with no expectation that learning would subsequently be assessed; (b) autonomy supportive, directed learning, in which children read a text and were told that the experimenters were interested in and would assess what children might learn from it, while emphasizing that there were no grades or evaluations attached to their performance; and (c) controlling and directed learning, in which children were told they would be tested on their reading and would be graded. It should be noted that what we labeled controlling in this study is the common form of directing or "motivating" children to learn in many educational settings. After reading the text under these varied conditions, all children were tested for both rote recall of the text and conceptual learning outcomes. In addition, children were also assessed one week later (unexpectedly) in order to evaluate their longer term retention of their rote knowledge.

It was found that the two directed-learning conditions produced superior results in rote learning relative to the nondirected learning condition. Undoubtedly, the directive to learn oriented students to pay more attention to details and perhaps motivated more differentiated encoding. But subjects directed to learn in the more controlling style (i.e., using grades) evidenced a greater deterioration of rote recall over the follow-up period, which suggests that pressured learning may be less likely to be retained. However, in contrast to the results concerning rote learning, conceptual outcomes were significantly *lowest* in the controlling, directive condition. Children who learned under the pressure of evaluation were least likely to glean the main points of the text they read. Grolnick and Ryan suggested that there was less active assimilation and integration of what was read when children's learning was less self-determined. Here again is evidence that points to the failure of external, pressure-oriented techniques in the production of cognitive internalization.

In the context of this research, further evidence for the relationship between autonomous motivation and the quality of learning outcomes was gleaned by assessing individual differences in children's' internalization of achievement motivation using a strategy described in Ryan and Connell (1989). It was found that within spontaneous or non-directed learning conditions children for whom learning and achievement was experienced as more autonomous were much more likely to retain rote knowledge over time, even controlling for intelligence. Put differently, under non-pressured conditions for learning, children who have come to value achievement show better long-term retention than those who have more external orientations. However, individual differences in internalization were significantly less influential under conditions of external pressure.

Grade contingencies were employed in this study because it was reasoned that they would have a functional significance of being controlling rather than informational. It was assumed that grades frequently generate what Ryan (1982) labeled ego-involvement. Students come to attach a contingency between their sense of self-worth and esteem and the grades. This contingency is undoubtedly "backed up" (if not originated) by the contingent approval of parents and teachers that also attends performance. Grades thus may typically have a negative impact on autonomous engagement.

Despite their hypothesized detrimental effects, however, it is clear that grades are pervasively used in schools to motivate performance. Nonetheless, until relatively recently there has been little published research directly examining grades and their impact on motivation and performance in school. Some interesting evidence has however been provided experimentally in the literature growing out of motivational perspectives.

Benware and Deci (1984) found that college students who read material with the expectation of teaching it to other students showed greater conceptual learning than students who read the same material with the expectation of being tested on it. Furthermore, students with the expectation of being tested showed less evidence of intrinsic motivation and reported feeling less active engagement with the material than students who learned the material to teach it. It was suggested that the expectation of being evaluated may have resulted in a decreased intrinsic motivation in relation to the material, which in turn resulted in performance decrements. In contrast, learning material in order to actively use it facilitated a more intrinsically motivated approach.

Butler and her colleagues (Butler, 1987, 1988; Butler & Nisan, 1986) have also explored the effects of evaluation, in the forms of either task-related comments or grades, on intrinsic motivation and performance. She has hypothesized that grades typically have ego-involving significance and hence impede intrinsic motivation and performance. Although Butler has occasionally interpreted her research as contrasting with the approach of Deci and Ryan (1985), we see her results as largely congruent with our perspective and the findings we have offered (see Butler, 1989; Ryan & Deci, 1989; for comments on this issue).

In the first study, Butler and Nisan (1986) randomly assigned sixth-grade children to conditions of no feedback, task-related comments, and grades given after completion of two interesting tasks, one qualitative and one quantitative.

Subsequent assessment of students' performance on both tasks and accompanying intrinsic motivation revealed that (1) the no-feedback group scored low on both tasks and reported varying attributions for success; (2) the task-related comments group scored high on both tasks, and on reported interest, and they attributed internal rather than arbitrary or other-controlled factors as determining success; and (3) the grades group scored low on the qualitative task and high on the quantitative task, and attributed their effort either to desire to succeed or to avoid failure. Butler and Nisan interpreted these findings as suggesting that grades often foster quantitative aspects of learning at the expense of creativity, interest, and active engagement. They also concluded that the normative grading so prevalent in schools is largely control salient, rather than effectance relevant.

In the second study, Butler (1987) demonstrated similar findings that further support the notion that grade-oriented evaluation is experienced as ego-involving and mostly as containing information about one's standing in relation to others, rather than information helpful in self-evaluation. Accordingly grades will typically lead to decrements in intrinsic motivation and in some aspects of learning. In a third study, Butler (1988) found that both high and low achievers who received informational or task-relevant feedback reported greater continued interest and higher subsequent task performance than high and low achievers who received controlling or evaluative feedback. In addition, Butler found that the effects of controlling and informational communications, when presented together, are similar to the effect of controlling communication alone. Of further interest is her finding that continuing ego-involved motivation is especially undermined when opportunities for socially comparative evaluation are withdrawn. The results of these studies clearly implicate the controlling, ego-involving aspect of grades in undermining students' continued motivation and learning.

Despite the demonstration that grades, rewards, and other events that have an ego-involving or controlling significance to learners have a negative impact on certain types of performance, the mechanisms through which this occurs have not been well explicated. Golan and Graham (1990), however, recently speculated that ego-involvement may actually lead students to a more "shallow" processing approach, whereas task involving conditions may promote greater depth of processing. In her paradigm she compared a control group, a task-involved group, and an ego-involved group within a learning paradigm based on Craik and Lockhart's (1974) levels of processing model of learning. Results confirmed that the condition conducive to ego-involvement resulted in a more shallow processing of information, whereas both control subjects and those specifically induced to be task-involved evidenced greater depth of processing in their learning. Much like those of Grolnick and Ryan (1987), her findings suggest that ego-involvement may be especially detrimental to those types of learning that require deeper levels of cognitive processing.

Nolen (1988) presented a study in which the relation between depth of processing and motivational orientation was further explicated. She showed that task- versus ego-involved orientations to learning were associated with greater use of deep processing versus surface processing strategies. Deep processing strategies involved the active use of information, sorting of important from unimportant, and testing the fit with what one knows. Surface strategies included memorizing, rehearsing, reading over and over. Furthermore, Nolen reported that motivational orientation was a stronger predictor of strategy differences than perceived ability or value of the strategy. These relationships remained after an interval of four to six weeks. She concludes that individual differences in motivational orientation shape the metacognitive process of strategy selection such that environmental emphasis on evaluative outcomes lead to use of more superficial and therefore less effective learning strategies.

Pintrich and De Groot (1990) also examined the role of motivational processes in effecting learning strategies. They found that intrinsic value of schoolwork was related to use of cognitive strategies and self-regulation, which in turn predicted academic performance. Seventh-grade students who reported learning-oriented (i.e., intrinsically valued), rather than performance-oriented classroom goals were more cognitively engaged in trying to comprehend material and were more likely to be self-regulating in regard to classroom pursuits. Moreover, the best overall predictor of academic performance in their model was students' self-regulation. Pintrich and De Groot argued that self-regulation is necessary for effective use of cognitive strategies and that the impact of students' perceived competence and goal orientations on academic performance may be mediated by cognitive engagement and, more importantly, self-regulated learning strategies.

It thus appears that there are a considerable number of researchers singing in concert. The harmony here is that externally imposed evaluations, goals, rewards, and pressures seem to create a style of teaching and learning that is antithetical to quality learning outcomes in school, that is, learning characterized by durability, depth, and integration. And, despite the fact that these differences are explained using different theoretical terminologies (e.g. learning versus performance goals, task versus ego involvements, or intrinsic versus extrinsic orientations), there is a common dynamic which underlies their common predictions and results. *We submit that the common underlying principle involves an autonomous engagement of the self in the endeavor of learning.* Such autonomous engagement represents the essence and endpoint of the process of internalization, and the converse of alienation.

Education is thus inexorably embedded in and conditioned by the interpersonal processes through which the self-regulated engagement of learning may be facilitated or forestalled. Ultimately, the student must be the point of origination for making contact with and assimilating the cognitive content of school curricula at a pace and level appropriate to his or her current capacities. In the presence of an active, responsive, and empathic adult not only will internalization of the content of teaching be more likely to occur; moreover the affective goals of education will also be more probably accomplished.

INTERNALIZATION AND EDUCATION IN SOCIAL CONTEXT

We began by noting that education is fundamentally a form of cultural transmission, in which knowledge, skills, and a sense of oneself in a larger social context are acquired. Schools are contexts of social and cognitive development and thus are potent sources of influence concerning what members of a culture internalize, identify with, and become. We have further argued that whether one is concerned with the cognitive agenda of education or the significant lessons that take place on an affective and value plane, the degree to which internalization is successful is dependent upon interpersonal processes. Parents and teachers, through their structure and style of educating conduce toward or obstruct the internalization of what they may intend to transmit, namely, a value for and interest in learning and a sense of competence with regard to acquiring new knowledge. They can also, perhaps without intent, transmit and facilitate the internalization of lessons that are counter to the explicit aims of education, such as a sense of alienation and/or incompetence.

The social context provides, then, either an environment that facilitates cognitive differentiation, development, and the engagement and empowerment of the self in the activities of learning or, alternatively, one that forestalls such processes. Facilitation requires that the psychological needs of autonomy, relatedness and competence be addressed. Thus, facilitating environments are those which are characterized by support for autonomy, provision of interpersonal involvement, and affordance of optimal challenges. Alternatively, excessive controls, evaluation, and neglect of participants' internal frame of reference frustrate psychological needs and thus the autonomous involvement of the self in learning.

It is perhaps most striking, then, to recognize that those students coming from extra-school environments lacking in opportunities for self-regulated learning so often experience further obstacles to absorbing the cultural values transmitted via school-based education. This is the paradox of the bidirectional transactional model elaborated earlier: Those whose needs for autonomy, competence, and relatedness are the most unsatisfied outside of school may elicit the most control and least relatedness from their educational environment. Both in terms of the affective and cognitive agenda of schools, the rich appear to get richer and the poor, poorer.

More optimistically, we believe that students bring to the educational enterprise sufficient energies and direction—the hallmarks of motivation— such that the cognitive and affective goals of education may be fully realized. As we have argued, the contexts of home and school are the places where motivated behaviors take root and, depending on the climate, either grow or wither. Students provide the point of origination for making contact with and assimilating the cognitive content of schools at a pace and level appropriate to their current capacities. Educators, through the qualities of the interpersonal world they provide, either encourage that contact and assimilatory tendency or forestall its exercise. When students can be engaged, and experience such engagement as emanating from within, then not only will internalization of content occur, but the affective goals of education will also be accomplished.

ACKNOWLEDGMENTS

Preparation of this paper was facilitated by a grant from the National Institute of Child Health and Human Development (HD 19914) to the Human Motivation Program, Department of Psychology, University of Rochester, and to the National Institute of Health (MH 18922).

REFERENCES

Amabile, T.M. (1983). *The social psychology of creativity*. New York: Springer-Verlag.

Ames, C., & Archer, J. (1988). Achievement goals in the classroom: Student's learning strategies and motivation process. *Journal of Educational Psychology, 80*, 260-267.

Bandura, A. (1989). Human agency in social cognitive theory. *American Psychologist, 44,* 1175-1184.

Barrett, M., & Boggiano, A.K. (1988). Fostering extrinsic orientations: Use of reward strategies to motivate children. *Journal of Social and Clinical Psychology, 6*, 293-309.

Baumrind, D. (1967). Child care practices anteceding three patterns of preschool behavior. *Genetic Psychology Monographs, 75*, 43-88.

————. (1971). Current patterns of parental authority. *Developmental Psychology Monographs, 4*, 1-102.

Belenky, M.F., Clinchy, B.M., Goldberger, N.R., & Tarule, J.M. (1986). *Women's ways of knowing: The development of self, voice, and mind*. New York: Basic Books.

Benware, C., & Deci, E.L. (1984). Quality of learning with an active versus passive motivational set. *American Educational Research Journal, 21*, 755-765.

Broudy, H.S. (1988). *The uses of schooling*. New York: Methuen.

Butler, R. (1987). Task-involving and ego-involving properties of evaluation: Effects of different feedback conditions on motivational perceptions, interest, and performance. *Journal of Educational Psychology, 79*, 474-482.

————. (1988). Enhancing and undermining intrinsic motivation: The effects of task involving and ego involving evaluation on interest and performance. *British Journal of Educational Psychology, 58*, 1-14.

————. (1989). On the psychological meaning of information about competence: A reply to Ryan and Deci's Comment on Butler. *Journal of Educational Psychology, 81*, 269-272.

Butler, R., & Nisan, M. (1986). Effects of no feedback, task-related comments, and grades on intrinsic motivation and performance. *Journal of Educational Psychology, 78*, 210-216.

Connell, J.P. (1985). A new multidimensional measure of children's perceptions of control. *Child Development, 56*, 1018-1041.

————. (1990). Context, self and action: A motivational analysis of self-system processes across the life-span. In D. Cicchetti and M. Beeghly (Eds.), *The self in transition* (pp. 61-97). Chicago: University of Chicago Press.

Covington, M.V. (1984). The motive for self-worth. In C. Ames & R.E. Ames (Eds.), *Research on motivation in education: Student motivation* (pp. 78-108). New York: Academic Press.

Craik, F. & Lockhart, R. (1974). Levels of processing: A framework for memory research. *Journal of Verbal Learning and Verbal Behavior, 11*, 671-684.

Crandall, V.C., Katkovski, & Crandall, V.S. (1965). Children's beliefs in their control of reinforcements in intellectual academic achievement situations. *Child Development, 36*, 91-109.

Danner, F.W., & Lonky, E. (1981). A cognitive-developmental approach to the effects of rewards on intrinsic motivation. *Child Development, 52*, 1043-1052.

deCharms, R. (1968). *Personal causation: The internal affective determinants of behavior*. New York: Academic Press.

————. (1976). *Enhancing motivation: Change in the classroom*. New York: Irvington.

Deci, E.L., Connell, J.P., & Ryan, R.M. (1989). Self-determination in a work organization. *Journal of Applied Psychology, 74*, 580-590.

Deci, E.L., Nezlek, J., & Sheinman, L. (1981). Characteristics of the rewarder and intrinsic motivation of the rewardee. *Journal of Personality and Social Psychology, 40*, 1-10.

Deci, E.L., & Ryan, R.M. (1980). The empirical exploration of intrinsic motivational processes. In L. Berkowitz (Ed.), *Advances in experimental social psychology* (Vol. 13, pp. 39-80). New York: Academic Press.

————. (1985). *Intrinsic motivation and self-determination in human behavior*. New York: Plenum.

————. (1987). The support of autonomy and the control of behavior. *Journal of Personality and Social Psychology, 53*, 1024-1037.

————. (1991). A motivational approach to self: Integration in personality. In R. Dienstbier (Ed.), *Nebraska symposium on motivation: Vol. 38. Perspectives on motivation* (pp. 237-288). Lincoln, NE: University of Nebraska Press.

Deci, E.L., Schwartz, A.J., Sheinman, L., & Ryan, R.M. (1981). An instrument to assess adults' orientations toward control versus autonomy with children: Reflections on intrinsic motivation and perceived competence. *Journal of Educational Psychology, 73*, 642-650.

Deci, E.L., Spiegel, N.H., Ryan, R.M., Koestner, R., & Kauffman, M. (1982). The effects of performance standards on teaching styles: The behavior of controlling teachers. *Journal of Educational Psychology, 74*, 852-859.

Dewey, J. (1938). *Experience and education*. New York: Collier.

Dornbush, S.M., Ritter, H.P., Leiderman, P.H., Roberts, D.F., & Fraleigh, M.J. (1987). The relation of parenting style to adolescent school performance. *Child Development, 58*, 1244-1257.

Dweck, C.S. (1986). Motivational processes affecting learning. *American Psychologist, 41*, 1040-1048.

————. (1988). Motivation. In R. Glaser & Lesgold (Eds.), *The handbook of psychology and education* (Vol. 1, pp. 187-239). Hillsdale, NJ: Erlbaum.

Dweck, D.S., & Elliot, E.S. (1983). Achievement motivation. In P.H. Mussen (Ed.), *Handbook of child psychology* (Vol. 4, 4th ed., pp. 643-691). New York: Wiley.

Elkind, D. (1971). Cognitive growth cycles in mental development. In J.K. Cole (Ed.), *Nebraska symposium on motivation* (Vol. 19, pp.1-31). Lincoln, NE: University of Nebraska Press.

Fabes, R.A., Moran, J.D., and McCullers, J.C. (1981). The hidden costs of reward and WAIS subscale performance. *American Journal of Psychology, 94,* 387-398.

Fine, M. (1990). "The public" in public schools: The social construction/constriction of moral communities. *Journal of Social Issues, 46,* 107-120.

Flink, C., Boggiano, A.K., & Barrett,M. (in press). Controlling teaching strategies: Undermining children's self-determination and performance. *Journal of Personality and Social Psychology.*

Glickman, C.D., & Pajak, E.F. (1986). Supervisors discrimination among three types of supervisory scripts. *Educational and Psychological Research, 6,* 279-289.

Golan, S., & Graham, S. (1990). *The impact of ego and task-involvement on levels of processing.* Paper presented at the annual meeting of the American Educational Research Association, Boston.

Grolnick, W., Frodi, A., & Bridges, L. (1984). Maternal control styles and the mastery motivation of one-year-olds. *Infant Mental Health Journal, 5,* 72-82.

Grolnick, W.S., & Ryan, R.M. (1987). Autonomy in children's learning: An experimental and individual differences investigation. *Journal of Personality and Social Psychology, 52,* 890-898.

————. (1989). Parent styles associated with children's self-regulation and competence in school. *Journal of Educational Psychology, 81,* 143-154.

————. (in press). Parental influences on children's autonomy and competence in school. In C. Fisher & S. Redmon-Mann (Eds.), *Connecting families with schools.* Cambridge: Cambridge University Press.

Grolnick, W.S., Ryan, R.M., & Deci, E.L. (1990). *The inner resources for school achievement: Motivational mediators of children's perceptions of their parents.* Unpublished manuscript, University of Rochester.

Harackiewicz, J., Manderlink, G., & Sansone, C. (in press). Competence processes and achievement motivation: Implications for intrinsic motivation. In A.K. Boggiano & T.S. Pittman (Eds.), *Achievement and motivation: A social-developmental perspective.* New York: Cambridge University Press.

Harter, S. (1981). A new self-report scale of intrinsic versus extrinsic orientation in the classroom: Motivational and informational components. *Developmental Psychology, 17,* 300-312.

Harter, S. (1982). The perceived competence scale for children. *Child Development, 53,* 87-97.

————. (1983). Developmental perspectives on the self-system. In E.M. Hetherington (Ed.), *Handbook of child psychology, Vol. 4. Socialization, personality and social development* (4th ed., pp. 275-386). New York: Wiley.

Heider, F. (1958). *The psychology of interpersonal relations.* New York: Wiley.

Hirsch, E.D. (1987). *Cultural literacy: What every American needs to know.* Boston: Houghton-Mifflin.

Holt, J. (1964). *How children fail.* New York: Dell.

Ingram, J., & Worrall, N. (1987). The negotiating classroom: Child self-determination in British primary schools. *Early Child Development and Care, 28,* 401-415.

Koestner, R., & McClelland, D.C. (1990). Perspectives on competence motivation. In L. Pervin (Ed.), *Handbook of personality: Theory and research.* New York: Guilford.

Koestner, R., Ryan, R.M., Bernieri, F., & Holt, K. (1984). Setting limits in children's behavior: The differential effects of controlling versus informational styles on intrinsic motivation and creativity. *Journal of Personality, 52,* 233-248.

Koestner, R., Zuckerman, M., & Koestner, J. (1987). Praise, involvement and intrinsic motivation. *Journal of Personality and Social Psychology, 53,* 383-390.

Kohn, A. (1986). *No contest: The case against competition.* Boston: Houghton Mifflin.

Krathwohl, D.R., Bloom, B.S., & Masia, B.B. (1974). *Taxonomy of educational objectives, handbook II: Affective domain.* New York: David McKay.

Kruglanski, A.W., Stein, C., & Riter, A. (1977). Contingencies of exogenous reward and task performance: On the "minimax" strategy in instrumental behavior. *Journal of Applied Social Psychology, 7*, 141-148.

Lepper, M.R. (1983). Social-control processes and the internalization of social values: An attributional perspective. In E.T. Higgins, D.N. Ruble, & W.W. Hartup (Eds.), *Social cognition and social development* (pp. 294-330). New York: Cambridge University Press.

Maehr, M.L. (1983). On doing well in science: Why Johnny no longer excels; why Sarah never did. In S.G. Paris, G.M. Olson, & H.W. Stevenson (Eds.), *Learning and motivation in the classroom* (pp. 179-210). Hillsdale, NJ: Erlbaum.

Maehr, M.L., & Stallings, W.M. (1972). Freedom from external evaluation. *Child Development, 43*, 177-185.

McGraw, K.O. (1978). The detrimental effects of reward on performance: A literature review and a prediction model. In M.R. Lepper & D. Greene (Eds.), *The hidden costs of reward* (pp. 33-60). Hillsdale, NJ: Erlbaum.

Montessori, M. (1917/1965). *Spontaneous activity in education.* New York: Schocken.

Nicholls, J.G. (1984). Achievement motivation: Conceptions of ability, subjective experience, task choice, and performance. *Psychological Review, 91*, 328-346.

Nolen, S.B. (1988). Reasons for studying: Motivational orientations and study strategies. *Cognition and Instruction, 5*(4), 269-287.

Pajak, E.F., & Glickman, C.D. (1984). Teachers discrimination between information and control in response to videotaped simulated supervisory conferences. Paper presented at the annual meeting of the American Educational Research Association, New Orleans, 1984.

Pelletier, L.G., & Vallerand, R.J. (1989). Behavioral confirmation in social interaction: Effects of teacher expectancies on students' intrinsic motivation. *Canadian Psychology, 30*, 404.

Piaget, J. (1971). *Biology and knowledge.* Chicago: University of Chicago Press.

Pintrich, P.R., & De Groot, E.V. (1990). Motivational and self-regulated learning components of classroom academic performance. *Journal of Educational Psychology, 82*, 33-40.

Pittman, T.S., Emery, J., & Boggiano, A.K. (1982). Intrinsic and extrinsic motivational orientations: Reward-induced changes in preference for complexity. *Journal of Personality and Social Psychology, 42*, 789-797.

Plant, R. & Ryan, R.M. (1985). Intrinsic motivation and the effects of self-consciousness, self-awareness, and ego-involvement: An investigation of internally controlling styles. *Journal of Personality, 53*, 435-449.

Rogers, C. (1969). *Freedom to learn.* Columbus, Ohio: Merrill.

Rogoff, B. (1990). *Apprenticeship in thinking: Cognitive development in social context.* New York: Oxford University Press.

Ryan, R.M. (1982). Control and information in the intrapersonal sphere: An extension of cognitive evaluation theory. *Journal of Personality and Social Psychology, 43*, 450-461.

_____. (1991). The nature of the self in autonomy and relatedness. In G.R. Goethals & J. Strauss (Eds.), *Multidisciplinary perspectives on the self.* New York: Springer-Verlag.

Ryan, R.M., & Connell, J.P. (1988). Mastery motivation. In T. Husen & T.N. Postlethwaite (Eds.), *International encyclopedia of education.* New York: Pergamon Press.

_____. (1989). Perceived locus of causality and internalization: Examining reasons for acting in two domains. *Journal of Personality and Social Psychology, 57*, 749-761.

Ryan, R.M., Connell, J.P., & Deci, E.L. (1985). A motivational analysis of self-determination and self-regulation in education. In C. Ames & R.E. Ames (Eds.), *Research on motivation in education: The classroom milieu* (pp. 13-51). New York: Academic Press.

Ryan, R.M., Connell, J.P., & Grolnick, W.S. (in press). When achievement is not intrinsically motivated: A theory of self-regulation in school. In A.K. Boggiano & T.S. Pittman (Eds.), *Achievement and motivation: A social-developmental perspective.* New York: Cambridge University Press.

Ryan, R.M., Connell, J.P., & Plant, R.W. (1990). Emotions in nondirected text learning. *Learning and Individual Differences, 2,* 1-17.

Ryan, R.M., & Deci, E.L. (1989). Bridging the research traditions of task/ego involvement and intrinsic/extrinsic motivation: Comment on Butler (1987). *Journal of Educational Psychology, 81,* 265-268.

Ryan, R.M., & Grolnick, W.S. (1986). Origins and pawns in the classroom: Self-report and projective assessments of individual differences in children's perceptions. *Journal of Personality and Social Psychology, 50,* 550-558.

Ryan, R.M., Mims, V., & Koestner, R. (1983). Relation of reward contingency and interpersonal context to intrinsic motivation: A review and test using cognitive evaluation theory. *Journal of Personality and Social Psychology, 45,* 736-750.

Ryan, R.M., Lynch, J., & Stiller, J. (1990). *Working models of parents, teachers, and friends as predictors of adolescent adjustment.* Unpublished manuscript, University of Rochester.

Shapira, Z. (1976). Expectancy determinants of intrinsically motivated behavior. *Journal of Personality and Social Psychology, 34,* 1235-1244.

Skinner, E. & Connell, J.P. (1986). Development and the understanding of control. In M.M. Baltes & P.B. Baltes (Eds.), *Aging and the psychology of control* (pp. 35-61). Hillsdale, NJ: Erlbaum.

Skinner, E., Wellborn, J.G., & Connell, J.P. (1990). What it takes to do well in school and whether I've got it: A process model of perceived control and children's engagement and achievement in school. *Journal of Educational Psychology, 82,* 22-32.

Steinberg, L., Elmen, J.D., & Mounts, N.S. (1989). Authoritive parenting, psychosocial maturity, and academic success among adolescents. *Child Development, 60,* 1424-1436.

Thomas, J.W. (1980). Agency and achievement: Self-management and self-regard. *Review of Educational Research, 50,* 213-240.

Vallerand, R.J., Blais, M.R., Briere, N.M., & Pelletier, L.G. (1989). Construction et validation de l'échelle de motivation en éducation (EME). *Canadian Journal of Behavioural Sciences, 21,* 323-349.

Vito, R., & Connell, J.P. (1989). *A longitudinal study of at-risk high school students: A theory based description and intervention.* Unpublished manuscript, University of Rochester.

Weiner, B. (1986). *An attributional theory of motivation and emotion.* New York: Springer-Verlag.

White, R.W. (1963). *Ego and reality in psychoanalytic theory.* New York: International Universities Press.

GOALS AND SELF-REGULATED LEARNING:

WHAT MOTIVATES CHILDREN TO SEEK ACADEMIC HELP?

Richard S. Newman

Self-regulated learners typically are described as individuals who purposefully control their own academic outcomes. Their cognitive activity is intertwined with personal beliefs of efficacy and control. They deliberately monitor their performance and independently apply cognitive resources as tasks demand. At first glance, self-regulated learners might appear to be self-sufficient. It is clear, however, that there is an important, and often ignored, social aspect of self-regulated learning. Students frequently must regulate their cognitive activity through interaction with teachers and classmates. The purpose of this paper is to examine one particular way in which children interact with others in the classroom in pursuit of learning, namely through help-seeking. I argue that a distinguishing characteristic of self-regulated learners is their ability to seek academic assistance in an adaptive way such that the likelihood of learning is optimized. Further, I argue that *adaptive help-seeking* is predicted by motivational and developmental characteristics of the child as well as various characteristics of the classroom.

Advances in Motivation and Achievement, Volume 7, pages 151-183.
Copyright © 1991 by JAI Press Inc.
All rights of reproduction in any form reserved.
ISBN: 1-55938-122-1

The paper is organized in four sections. First, I discuss the concept of self-regulated learning and show why help-seeking can be considered an important strategy of the self-regulated learner. I propose a definition of *adaptive help-seeking*. The adaptive help-seeker seeks assistance for the purpose of learning, restricts questions to necessary situations, and asks questions in the most efficacious way. Second, I discuss motivational aspects of adaptive help-seeking, identifying goals, attitudes, and beliefs that account for the fact that certain children socially regulate their learning in school and others do not. Third, I discuss developmental aspects of adaptive help-seeking, examining in particular, the role of socialization and knowledge. Finally, I discuss how various features of the classroom (e.g., classroom climate, structure of the classroom activity, and type of learning task) set the stage for and facilitate adaptive help-seeking.

SELF-REGULATED LEARNING AND HELP-SEEKING

Self-Regulated Learning: An Integrative View

Self-regulated learning has been defined and discussed in a variety of ways (see Zimmerman & Schunk, 1989). Common to these discussions is the notion that the self-regulated learner promotes his or her own academic achievement. An emphasis on active learning, based on self-understanding and self-control, contrasts sharply with the traditional behaviorist emphasis on a much simpler and more passively-acquired association of stimulus and response. The concept of self-regulated learning is complex and rich because it incorporates with behavior a number of cognitive, metacognitive, motivational, and social processes.

During the elementary-school years, children learn a variety of cognitive and metacognitive skills that form a set of building blocks for self-regulated learning. The child's active, coordinated, and spontaneous use of information-processing techniques such as rehearsal, organization, elaboration, skimming, and self-verbalization is critically important for cognitive performance and cognitive growth (Pressley & Levin, 1983; Weinstein & Mayer, 1986). Metacognitive, or executive, strategies are equally important in facilitating the performance and growth of the child. Self-planning, self-monitoring, self-checking, and self-questioning, for example, allow children to regulate and manage their own learning in a wide variety of domains such as memory, reading comprehension, oral communication, and writing (Brown, Bransford, Ferrara, & Campione, 1983; Flavell, 1979; Paris & Lindauer, 1982; Wong, 1985). These metacognitive strategies involve self-awareness of one's cognitive processing and allow one to direct and, if necessary, redirect cognitive resources in a goal-directed fashion.

Importantly, the spontaneous employment of cognitive and metacognitive strategies is not at all automatic, but rather intentional, deliberate, and goal-directed. This point has been made in experimental research on children's production deficiencies and transfer (see Brown et al., 1983; Pressley, Borkowski, & Schneider, 1987). The same point is dramatically made every day in the average American classroom, where children are commonly observed sitting passively, disengaged from the learning process. Whether or not children spontaneously use strategies, assuming of course that they do possess the requisite knowledge and skills, can be attributed to the children's academic goals, values and beliefs about schooling, and beliefs about themselves regarding competence, control, and self-efficacy (Paris, Newman, & Jacobs, 1985; Skinner, Wellborn, & Connell, 1990).

Goals, values, and beliefs—the motivational component of self-regulated learning—are related to strategies—the cognitive and metacognitive components—in a nonadditive way. They are woven together into children's will to learn (Paris & Byrnes, 1989). Across the numerous descriptions of self-regulated learning that have emerged in the last several years, there is a common theme: Children who are self-regulated learners possess a set of goals, values, and beliefs that shape their intention to learn and promote task involvement. These motivational factors play an equally important role in volitional control, which protects children's commitment to learn from distractions and steers their involvement toward successful task completion (Corno, 1989; Kuhl, 1985).

The role of socialization in self-regulated learning is evident when we try to understand how the interweaving or fusing of cognition, metacognition, and motivation comes about. The development of children's will to learn takes place over the individual's life span, partially as a result of normative processes of development (e.g., see Piaget) and partially—and perhaps predominantly—as a result of social guidance, cultural practice, and apprenticeship in learning with parents, teachers, and peers (e.g., see Vygotsky). The self-regulated learner has been socialized with both skill and will to work independently. Importantly, he or she has also been socialized with the conditional knowledge, volition, and social skills that allow him or her to know when and how to enlist the assistance of others (Diaz, Neal, & Amaya-Williams, 1990; Paris & Newman, 1990).

Help-Seeking as a Strategy of Self-Regulated Learning

Based on an integrative conceptualization of self-regulated learning that incorporates cognitive, metacognitive, motivational, and social processes, I examine a particular learning strategy, namely help-seeking. Kuhl (1985) discusses help-seeking as a way of achieving environmental control in the learning process, that is, as a volitional strategy for dealing with difficulty and potential failure. Rohrkemper and Corno (1988) categorize skills and strategies according to their adaptive use. For example, in order to adapt to challenging situations, self-regulated learners might modify the task, modify themselves, or modify the situation. One particular way of modifying the situation is by seeking assistance from the teacher or a classmate. Nelson-Le Gall (1981, 1985) and Ames (1983) emphasize academic help-seeking as an instrumental strategy for long-term success (i.e., learning and mastery) rather than simply a means for completing assignments or getting a good grade (i.e., performance).

Academic help-seeking is unique among learning strategies because of its social-interactional nature. It necessarily involves other people to whom the child directs requests for assistance and from whom he or she (hopefully) receives that assistance. This is different from other strategies that the child carries out alone or perhaps with the assistance of notes, reference books, or a computer. Help-seeking is also unique because of its executive nature; that is, the compound way in which the child benefits from help. The child who asks questions and obtains needed assistance from teachers and peers not only alleviates immediate academic difficulties but also acquires knowledge, skills, and strategies that can in turn be used for self-help.

In sum, seeking help from a knowledgeable other person can be more beneficial than giving up prematurely, more appropriate than waiting passively, and more efficient than persisting unsuccessfully on one's own. High achievers would seem to be especially aware of the potential value of help-seeking. In fact, one feature that discriminates high from low achievers is the high achievers' tendency to seek information and social assistance from knowledgeable others (Rohwer & Thomas, 1989; Zimmerman & Martinez-Pons, 1986; see similar findings regarding gifted and regular students, Zimmerman & Martinez-Pons, 1990). Students who organize and elaborate their learning material, monitor cognitive performance, and thoughtfully manage study time are likely also to rely on assistance from others when it is needed (Karabenick & Knapp, 1991).

The discussion up to this point implicitly has imputed unidimensionality and instrumentality to the construct of help-seeking. The fact of the matter is, however, that children seek help in many different ways and are motivated by many different goals and intentions. Not all instances of help-seeking can be considered instrumental for learning. Traditionally, in fact, help-seeking has been viewed as a manifestation of dependency, immaturity, and even incompetence (e.g., Sears, Maccoby, & Levin, 1957). In order to consider help-seeking as a strategy of self-regulated learning, it is necessary to focus attention on what might be termed *adaptive help-seeking*.

Adaptive Help-Seeking: A Definition

To define adaptive help-seeking, it is necessary to clarify the domains of help-seeking and question-asking. Then it is necessary to address what is meant by "adaptive."

First, I note that not all questions in the classroom are posed for the purpose of seeking help with academic matters. For example, a child might ask about rules and organization (e.g., "Can I get a drink of water?," "Who lines up first for recess?"), or he or she may ask questions for the purpose of showing off or diverting the teacher's attention from the task at hand. Not all classroom questions that are posed for the purpose of seeking help with academic matters involve obtaining information. For example, a child might ask for emotional support or encouragement. It should also be mentioned that there are ways in which children try to obtain help in class when they have academic difficulties other than by asking a question. For example, children may copy someone else's answer, make statements and demands, or try subtle strategies such as placing themselves in proximity to the helper, making eye contact, frowning, or even crying (Cosgrove & Patterson, 1977; Patterson, Cosgrove, & O'Brien, 1980).

The focus of this paper is the intersection of the domains of informational help-seeking and question-asking. Specifically, I focus on direct, verbal questions (cf. typology of question forms, Kearsley, 1976) that children pose to teachers and classmates in order to obtain information required for the successful completion of school tasks, that is, questions regarding academic matters such as solving problems, understanding class material, and completing assignments. Of this particular subdomain, some questions can be considered adaptive for learning and others not.

Now, in order to address what is meant by "adaptive," it is important to consider both the child's purpose in seeking help and the sequence of mental actions and decisions prior to, and during, the act of seeking help. First, the child's goal or purpose in obtaining information is to learn or master some task. Mere expedient completion of an assignment would be excluded under this definition. Note that asking for an answer is considered adaptive for learning if the child's purpose is to use the answer as a confirmation of, or as a debugging tool for, preceding work. Second, the child follows, in a particular way, a sequence of actions and decisions that make up the help-seeking process. The sequence has been outlined by Nelson-Le Gall (1981, 1985) and Flammer (1981):

1. awareness of a need for help (i.e., awareness that knowledge is lacking or comprehension is incomplete);
2. decision to seek help rather than taking alternative actions (e.g., persevering, trying a new strategy, inferring missing information, waiting for help, or giving up);
3. decision regarding the type of help to seek (e.g., formulation of a particular type of question);
4. decision regarding the target person from whom to seek the help;

5. employment of a help-seeking strategy (e.g., expression of the question at a particular time and with a particular tone and attitude); and
6. processing of the help.

Based on this sequence of actions and decisions, *adaptive help-seeking* can be defined as questioning that:

1. follows the child's awareness of a need for help;
2. involves the child's having considered all pertinent and available information (for example, regarding task demands, personal resources, and costs and benefits) in making the following decisions:
    a. Is it necessary that I ask another person for help? (i.e., a decision regarding the *necessity* of the request);
    b. What should I ask? (i.e., a decision regarding the specific *content* of the request);
    c. Whom should I ask? (i.e., a decision regarding the *target* of the request);
3. involves the child having expressed the request for help in a way that is most suitable to the particular circumstance; and
4. involves the child having processed and considered the help that is received in such a way that the probability of success in subsequent help-seeking attempts is optimized.

Notice that although the definition of "adaptiveness" implies adaptiveness for the *child's* learning, one may have to take into account also the perspective of the *teacher* in actually deciding whether particular help-seeking requests are adaptive. This is because the child might make decisions, for example about the necessity, content, or target of a request, that are contrary to judgments of an individual who may in fact be more knowledgeable and/or objective than the child about such decisions. Also, notice that the definition does not imply that adaptive help-seeking necessarily leads to final success, in terms of the child solving a problem, understanding class material, or completing an assignment. It does imply that the child is goal-directed and that he or she planfully considers the probability of success and strives for success.

Simply put, an adaptive request for help is necessary, well-planned, and well-processed. It involves the child matching to the best of his or her ability the content and target of the request with the specific needs of the task at hand. In a Piagetian sense of "adaptation," there is both assimilation and accomodation. The adaptive help-seeker takes into account the particular situation (e.g., the task, the potential helpers, the available information about consequences and task difficulty) and adjusts himself or herself to the situation so as to maximize the opportunity for learning.

MOTIVATIONAL ASPECTS OF
ADAPTIVE HELP-SEEKING

Clearly there are individual differences in help-seeking attitudes and behavior. Motivational factors are important in explaining why certain children regulate their learning in school by adaptively seeking help while other children do not. Theories linking motivation to task engagement traditionally have emphasized (1) achievement goals and motivational orientation, (2) self-perceptions of ability, and (3) task-specific attitudes, beliefs, and intentions (see Eccles, 1983). Although the focus of the present volume is achievement-related goals, each of these motivational perspectives is examined in an attempt to understand individual differences in children's academic help-seeking.

Achievement Goals and Motivational Orientation

Goal setting has been shown to have numerous positive effects on adults' task performance. For example, setting challenging yet realistic goals for oneself tends to direct one's attention, mobilize effort, increase persistence, and lead to the employment of relevant task strategies (Locke, Saari, Shaw, & Latham, 1981). The question at hand is, "Are there particular goals that have similar positive effects on children's help-seeking efforts?"

Research on goals and help-seeking largely has focused on general rather than specific goals. One such factor that has been shown to be predictive of help-seeking is the child's intrinsic versus extrinsic motivational orientation (Harter, 1981, 1983). Children with an intrinsic orientation to learning are thought to strive toward independent mastery and competence, prefer academic challenge, and show curiosity and interest in their work. In contrast, children with an extrinsic orientation are overly dependent on others, prefer relatively easy assignments and subjects, and do their schoolwork in order to satisfy the teacher and get good grades.

Active cognitive engagement and self-regulated learning, as described by Corno and Mandinach (1983) and Rohrkemper and Corno (1988), have been shown to be positively related to the child's level of intrinsic orientation (e.g., Meece, Blumenfeld, & Hoyle, 1988). As adaptive help-seeking is a strategy of self-regulated learning, it is reasonable to expect that children who have an intrinsic orientation perceive help-seeking as a positive way of attaining skill and knowledge. This expectation is reinforced by research indicating that children's questioning is largely motivated by epistemic curiosity (Berlyne & Frommer, 1966). Children with an extrinsic orientation, on the other hand, may perceive help-seeking as a waste of time or perhaps in a positive yet expeditious way, that is, as an easy guarantee of a good grade.

Nelson-Le Gall and Jones (1990) showed a relationship between help-seeking and one particular component of intrinsic orientation, namely, preference for independent mastery. Third- and fifth-graders who were characterized as intrinsic in their striving for independent mastery were more likely to seek academic help of an indirect type (i.e., hints) than of a direct type (i.e., answers). Children characterized as extrinsic, i.e., dependent on their teacher, showed no such preference. Findings suggest that requests for hints, more than answers, are indicative of an inquisitive, active, and instrumentally-motivated type of learning.

Further evidence of a relationship between intrinsic orientation and help-seeking comes from a recent study of children's intentions to seek help from their teacher in math class. Newman (1990) interviewed children at grades 3, 5, and 7 and examined interrelationships among their perceived academic competence and attitudes about costs and benefits of help (which are discussed in a subsequent section), two components of intrinsic orientation (i.e., preference for challenge and preference for independent mastery), and help-seeking intentions. At all three grades, the greater the child's preference for challenge, the greater was the child's likelihood of seeking help. Preference for independent mastery, however, was related to help-seeking in a more complex, age-related way. At the elementary grades, the greater the child's *dependence* on the teacher, the greater was the likelihood of seeking help, whereas at the middle school, the greater the child's preference for *independence* from the teacher, the greater the likelihood. Thus, for the younger children, two seemingly divergent purposes (challenge and dependency) are important in explaining help-seeking intentions; for the older children, on the other hand, two seemingly convergent purposes (challenge and independent mastery) are important. Findings remind us that asking for help can serve multiple, independent, and even seemingly contradictory purposes. Findings also point to the importance of examining not just general orientations but, in addition, more specific goals in the classroom that might explain children's help-seeking behavior.

In an attempt to understand specific classroom goals, Wentzel (1989) has identified 12 goals that are simultaneously influential in motivating high school students. They have to do with self-assertion (e.g., doing one's best), academic mastery (e.g., learning new things), social responsibility (e.g., getting things done on time), and social interaction (e.g., making friends). Nicholls, Patashnick, and Nolen (1985) similarly have identified nine personal goals important for high school students. Work by Dweck (1986; Elliot & Dweck, 1988) and Nicholls (1979, 1983) provides a framework most helpful for understanding such classroom goals. Goals of *performance*, or *ego-involvement*, are representative of the child attempting to gain positive judgments or avoid negative judgments of competence, whereas goals of *learning*, or *task-involvement*, are representative of the child's attempting to increase his or her competence, or understanding or mastering something new. In order to explore relations among specific classroom goals and help-seeking, I recently asked third-, fifth-, and seventh-graders to rank, from (1) "least important" to (6) "most important," a list of six "things that might be important for you in math class when you are doing an assignment." Three of the goals might be classified as performance-related (to get a high grade, to finish all the problems in the assignment, and to get the assignment done on time) and three as learning-related (to become better at math, to learn something from the assignment, and to be challenged by the assignment). In addition to these rankings of goals, I had available for each child an index representing his or her intentions to seek help from the teacher in math class (for details regarding the sample, see Newman, 1990). Pictured in Figure 1 are mean rankings at each grade.

Three particular goals—to get a high grade, to learn something from the assignment, and to become better at math—are most important. Two grade-related differences in rankings are evident. One of the learning goals, to learn something from the assignment, showed increasing mean rankings and one of the performance goals, to finish all the problems, showed decreasing rankings across grades. Most interesting are the correlations between goal rankings and students' intentions to seek help. At grade 3, an index representing two learning goals, to learn something and to become better at math, was negatively correlated ($r = -.21$) with help-seeking intentions whereas an index representing two performance goals, to finish all the problems and to get the problems done on time, was positively correlated ($r = .29$) with help-seeking intentions. At grade 7, the index of learning goals was positively correlated ($r = .30$) whereas the index of performance goals was negatively correlated ($r = -.25$) with help-seeking intentions. It is noted that neither of the two goals, getting a high grade and being challenged, was significantly correlated with help-seeking at any grade level. Also, at grade 5, none of the six goals was correlated with help-seeking.

So third-graders seem to be motivated to seek help more by several performance-related goals than by learning-related goals whereas the opposite is the case with seventh-graders. These findings involving specific classroom goals agree, at least partially, with findings of Newman (1990) involving general goal orientations. In that study, an extrinsic influence (i.e., dependence on the teacher) on help-seeking was evident among third- and fifth-graders but not seventh-graders. It is noted that an intrinsic influence (i.e., preference for challenge) was evident as well, across all grades. While a portrayal of elementary school children as being motivated by extrinsic and performance-related goals seems counterintuitive with the typical finding that children become more extrinsic and less intrinsic as they progress through the school years (e.g., Eccles, Midgely, & Adler, 1984; Harter, 1981); in actuality, individuals across the lifespan are no doubt influenced by multiple goals.

In summary, purposes or goals are an important element in understanding what motivates children to seek academic help. We are reminded that a given behavior, for example raising a hand and asking for help, can serve very different purposes for different children or, for that matter, for the same child but under different circumstances. In fact, there can be multiple influences—

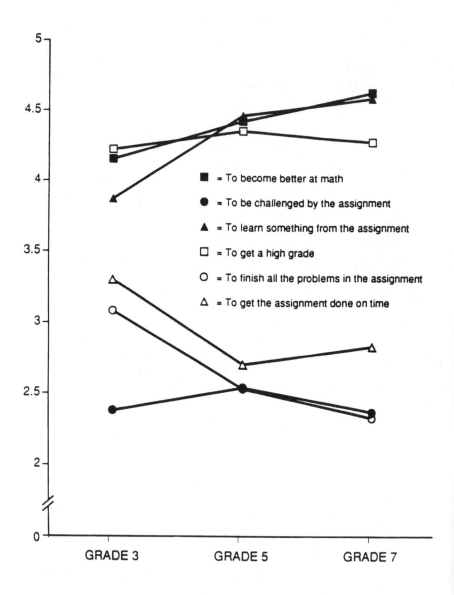

Note: *n*s = 60, 57, and 60 at Grades 3, 5, and 7, respectively. Rankings go from (1) "least important" to (6) "most important."

Figure 1.   Mean Rankings of Goals in Math Class

that are not always consonant with one another—that operate simultaneously in the same child. Furthermore, we are reminded by developmental findings that the relative importance of different goals can vary over the school years.

Self-Perceptions of Ability

A second motivational factor that is predictive of children's help-seeking behavior is self-perceptions of ability. There is consistent evidence of a positive relationship between children's self-concept of ability, perceived academic competence, and perceived self-efficacy on the one hand and actual academic performance on the other (Harter & Connell, 1984; Newman, 1984; Schunk, 1989; Shavelson & Bolus, 1982; Wylie, 1979). Children who perceive themselves as academically competent tend to display high levels of task engagement and have high achievement. It is likely that children who perceive themselves as competent view help-seeking as an instrumental strategy for classroom learning and therefore are likely to seek help when it is needed (Ames, 1983). The key to this prediction is the *necessity* of help. Generally, those with high self-perceptions of ability are high in achievement and/or domain-specific knowledge and do not need much help (Karabenick & Knapp, 1991). However, if the need arises, such individuals would be expected to seek assistance readily and adaptively.

A prediction of a positive relation between perceived academic competence and help-seeking is also based on evidence from a related literature on self-esteem (see Nadler, 1983). According to the "vulnerability hypothesis" of help-seeking, individuals with low self-esteem have a greater need than do those with high self-esteem to avoid threatening situations such as admission of failure, and thus individuals with low self-esteem are expected to be relatively unlikely to seek help. The contrasting "consistency hypothesis" predicts that individuals with high self-esteem have a greater need than do those with low self-esteem to protect themselves from perceptions of failure that are inconsistent with existing self-perceptions, and thus individuals with high self-esteem are expected to be relatively unlikely to seek help.

The resolution of the two competing hypotheses, at least with adults, may actually involve an interaction between self-esteem and the degree of ego-centrality or ego-relevance that the individual places on performance in the particular domain in which difficulty and need for help occur. Research (e.g., Ames & Lau, 1982; Karabenick & Knapp, 1991) shows that the vulnerability hypothesis explains help-seeking behavior in non-ego-central situations (e.g., when one perceives that failure is due to the lack of a specific skill). Here, the individual's ego is presumably not threatened by failure, and he or she is able to interpret help-seeking as a means of resolving problem difficulty and eventually mastering the material. The consistency hypothesis, on the other hand, explains behavior in ego-central situations (e.g., when one perceives that failure is due to the lack of global ability). Here, the individual's ego is threatened by failure, and seeking help presumably would undermine his or her self-perceptions.

Newman (1990) provides evidence supporting (albeit in terms of self-concept of ability rather than self-esteem) the vulnerability hypothesis with children. Across grades 3, 5, and 7, the greater the child's perceived academic competence, the less strongly the child felt that there were personal costs associated with seeking help in math class. In addition, at grade 7, the greater the child's perceived academic competence, the stronger were his or her stated intentions of seeking help. Thus, the child who perceives himself or herself as academically weak is relatively unlikely to seek needed assistance from the teacher.

Attitudes and Beliefs about Help-Seeking

An important link between means to achieve a goal and the spontaneous employment of those means is the individual's sense of *instrumentality* concerning the means (Skinner, Chapman, & Baltes, 1988). Paris, Newman, and Jacobs (1985) argue that at least two aspects of instrumentality are critical in explaining whether children spontaneously use particular strategies: utility and economy. In order for a particular strategic action to be carried out, the individual must understand, as well as personally believe in, the utility or effectiveness of the action (Borkowski, Levers, & Gruenenfelder, 1976; Paris, Newman, & McVey, 1982). Utility, however, is considered by individuals in the context of alternatives. That is, individuals weigh the costs (e.g., effort allocation) of an action in relation to its benefits (e.g., task success). Recent research has examined adults' and children's attitudes about the costs and benefits of academic help-seeking and how these attitudes might influence help-seeking behavior.

Among adults, negative attitudes tend to reflect either a threat to self-esteem due to perceived inadequacy or social-cultural norms that inveigh against question-asking (Nadler, 1983; Rosen, 1983; Shapiro, 1983). Positive attitudes, about the benefits of help-seeking, reflect a recognition of help as an instrumental and pragmatic means for learning and long-term mastery (Ames, 1983; Nelson-Le Gall, 1985).

Most research with children has focused on negative aspects of help-seeking. Children as young as eight years are aware of personal costs. Studies by van der Meij (1988) and Newman and Goldin (1990) indicate that children may be inhibited from asking questions in class because they believe that teachers and classmates are unavailable or unwilling to help, because they fear a negative reaction from the help-giver (especially if there is an expectation that they should not require additional assistance after a lesson has already been explained), and because of resulting fear of embarrassment in the eyes of classmates. Graham and Barker (1990) and Weinstein and Middlestadt (1979) have shown that children as young as 5 and 6 years perceive agemates who receive help from the teacher as having low ability.

On a more positive note, however, there is evidence that elementary school children are also aware of benefits of help-seeking. Children at grades 2, 4, and 6 express the belief that asking the teacher questions helps them learn (Newman & Goldin, 1990). Moreover, the stronger this belief, especially at the upper grades, the greater the tendency for children to like asking the teacher questions.

Attitudes and beliefs influence behavioral intentions and, in turn, actual behavior (Ajzen, 1988; Fishbein & Ajzen, 1975). This causal linkage, pertaining specifically to children's academic help-seeking, has been partially tested by Newman (1990). Third-, fifth-, and seventh-graders' attitudes about help-seeking—both positive (e.g., involving benefits to learning) and negative (e.g., involving costs such as embarrassment)—were hypothesized to mediate between background motivational factors (i.e., perceived competence and intrinsic orientation) and the children's intentions to seek needed assistance in math class.

Findings indicated no mean differences across grade in children's attitudinal ratings nor in children's stated intentions to seek help. That is, younger children were just as aware as older children of both costs and benefits of help-seeking and were just as likely to report that they would seek assistance when needed. However, a grade difference emerged in relations involving attitudes and intentions. At all grades, positive attitudes had an encouraging effect on the expressed likelihood of asking questions. At grade 7, children's negative attitudes had an additional—inhibiting—effect on the expressed likelihood of seeking help. In other words, for older students, individual differences in attitudes about the costs as well as the benefits of help-seeking were predictive of who intended to seek help and who did not. For younger students, on the other hand, individual differences in attitudes about only the benefits of help-seeking were predictive of help-seeking intentions. Findings suggest that, with age, there is increased complexity in the way in which children's attitudes affect help-seeking behavior in the classroom.

In summary, it is clear that motivational factors, for example, achievement goals, self-perceptions of ability, and attitudes and beliefs that pertain specifically to the meaning, utility, and value of help in the classroom, play a critical role in task engagement. These factors are important predictors of individual differences in children's academic help-seeking. Furthermore we see that motivational influences on children's help-seeking vary systematically over the school years.

DEVELOPMENTAL ASPECTS OF ADAPTIVE HELP-SEEKING

Based on a definition of adaptive help-seeking as a strategy of self-regulated learning, we can expect individual differences in its use according to various motivational characteristics of the child. Can we also expect developmental differences? That is, are mature and knowledgeable individuals especially likely to seek help in an adaptive way?

Normative Developmental Factors in the Help-Seeking Process

For a number of reasons, one can expect both age-related and knowledge-related increases in adaptive help-seeking. First, there is clear evidence of a developmental trend in self-regulated learning (see Paris & Byrnes, 1989; Paris & Newman, 1990). For example, we know that, with age and knowledge, children increasingly employ cognitive strategies such as organization and elaboration and metacognitive strategies such as planning, monitoring, checking, and correcting.

Second, we know that in naturalistic settings children tend to show an age-related increase in questioning in general. Van Hekken and Roelofsen (1982) observed, across the elementary years, an increase in the frequency with which children use information-seeking questions with one another in everyday communication, for example during play.

Third, there are age-related differences in specific components of the help-seeking process: concern regarding one's academic performance, awareness of the need for help, identification of potential helpers, and employment of strategies to elicit help (Nelson-Le Gall, 1981, 1985). More specifically, with age, there is increased concern for evaluating one's own academic performance, in particular, in comparison to peers (Frey & Ruble, 1985; Stipek & Tannatt, 1984). There is better comprehension monitoring, increased understanding of task difficulty, and increased awareness of the specific type of help that is needed in various problem-solving situations (Markman, 1981; Nicholls & Miller, 1983; Patterson, Cosgrove, & O'Brien, 1980). With age there is increased knowledge of traits and skills that distinguish effective from ineffective helpers (Barnett, Darcie, Holland, & Kobasigawa, 1982; Nelson-Le Gall & Gumerman, 1984) and an expanded repertoire of communicative skills and strategies to elicit help (Ladd & Oden, 1979; Markman, 1981).

Hoppe-Graff, Herrmann, Winterhoff-Spurk, and Mangold (1985) and Gibbs (1985) discuss two socio-linguistic factors that play an additional part in adults' ability to request and successfully obtain help. These are, respectively, the individual's awareness that the targeted help-giver is available and willing to help and the awareness of social schemas and conventions regarding indirect requests for assistance. Given what we know about the development of children's social cognition (e.g., Flavell & Ross, 1981), I expect that children's awareness along these two dimensions, as well, increases with age.

So there are definite reasons to expect a developmental increase in question-asking and help-seeking. In fact, there is evidence of an increase over the elementary school years in the frequency of children's seeking assistance from teachers, parents, and peers (Kreutzer, Leonard, & Flavell, 1975; Myers & Paris, 1978; Stevenson, Stigler, Lucker, Lee, Hsu, & Kitamura, 1987; Wood, Bruner, & Ross, 1976).

How, though, does one reconcile this picture of a developmental increase with the common observation that students, especially as they get older, ask questions in the classroom very infrequently? Classrooms typically are portrayed as places of passivity regarding question-asking and help-seeking (Dillon, 1988; van der Meij, 1986). This portrayal is reinforced by a recent finding that high school students say they put less effort into achieving the goal of getting academic help than they put into achieving any other classroom goal (Wentzel, 1989). One way of reconciling this seeming inconsistency is to examine individual differences in how children are socialized in the classroom.

Differential Patterns of Socialization

An age-related increase in the frequency of children's help-seeking might be explained according to theories of social interaction (e.g., Vygotsky, 1978; Wertsch, 1985). Children's learning often occurs in social situations in which an adult, that is, a parent or teacher, provides guided participation for the child. That is, the adult can provide tailored prompts, hints, or "scaffolding" for the child in an attempt to help the child learn in a gradual and challenging way (e.g., Ferrara, Brown, & Campione, 1986). One of the things that children potentially learn as a result of guided participation in achievement-related situations is the usefulness of questioning and dialogue (cf. research on reciprocal teaching, Palinscar & Brown, 1984). Ideally, children are socialized in such a way that they come to control their own prompts and hints by asking for them directly. But how often does guided participation and scaffolding occur in the average classroom? The answer, I believe, is not very often. And if it does occur, it probably is not equally effective for all students.

An increase in help-seeking can be expected for some children but not for others. In particular, it is reasonable to predict that as children progress through school there is actually a divergence in help-seeking—both in attitudes and actual behavior—according to the students' level of achievement and the degree of facilitation that exists in the classroom. It is expected that there are different patterns of development such that relatively successful students, over time, develop positive attitudes about seeking help and freely engage in academic questioning whereas relatively unsuccessful students develop negative attitudes and become increasingly inhibited from asking questions (Good, 1981; Good, Slavings, Harel, & Emerson, 1987).

Teachers' expectations and behavior differ for low-achievers in comparison to average- and high-achievers. Teachers call on students perceived to be low-achievers less often, wait less time for them to respond, give them answers rather than guidance when they respond incorrectly, and rarely praise their successes.

Low-achievers may learn not to volunteer questions and answers in order to avoid negative feedback and embarrassment in the classroom (Eccles & Wigfield, 1985; Weinstein, 1985). Also, with age, children show increased sensitivity to social comparison information regarding their academic abilities and correspondingly increased concern about embarrassment. Low-achievers may be especially prone to reacting to this sort of sensitivity with anxiety and reduced task engagement. In sum, individual differences in children's socialization experiences need to be taken into account in understanding the development of adaptive help-seeking. In the last section of the paper, I examine in more detail how classroom factors can influence children's help-seeking efforts.

Suitability of Help-Seeking Requests

In addition to normative developmental factors and individual differences in classroom socialization, an accurate developmental picture regarding adaptive help-seeking requires an in-depth consideration of the suitability of children's questioning. I have chosen to discuss three of the criteria for "adaptiveness" that were outlined earlier: (1) necessity of the child's request, (2) content of the request, and (3) target of the request.

Necessity of the Request

One criterion for adaptiveness of help-seeking is necessity. Self-regulated learners restrict help-seeking to occasions when the assistance is truly needed. On such occasions, the child presumably has recognized that his or her knowledge is lacking or comprehension is incomplete because of some difficulty inherent in the problem or perhaps because of some "bug" in cognitive processing. What evidence is there that children are responsive to need in their seeking of assistance with schoolwork? Is there an age-related or knowledge-related increase in that responsiveness?

First, we do know that children increasingly, with age as well as knowledge, are aware of difficulties they may be having in cognitive processing or academic performance. They become more accurate at monitoring correctness of task performance (Pressley, Levin, Ghatala, & Ahmad, 1987). When faced with an objective need for help, such as an inconsistency or omission inherent in the material, children increasingly are able to detect difficulties (Markman, 1979). There is evidence as well that children become more able to respond appropriately to such needs. For example, when presented with tasks intentionally designed to be ambiguous, preschoolers and elementary-aged children increasingly ask information-seeking questions in order to resolve the ambiguities (Cosgrove & Patterson, 1977).

Failure on initial solution attempts provides an objective measure of need. Accordingly, help-seeking following initial failure is appropriate or necessary, and help-seeking following an initial solution that is correct is inappropriate or unnecessary (Cotler, Quilty, & Palmer, 1970). Utilizing such an approach for examining children's response to need, Nelson-Le Gall (1987) asked third- and fifth-graders to define vocabulary words with the option of requesting help. Children gave a tentative answer, were given the option of requesting help, and then were asked for a final answer. Third-graders tended to make more unnecessary requests for help (i.e., requests following a correct tentative response) than did fifth-graders. Using a similar procedure with fifth-graders, van der Meij (1990) found that children with low knowledge (i.e., relatively poor vocabularies) asked significantly more unnecessary questions and tended to ask fewer necessary questions than did children with good vocabularies.

There is evidence that children increasingly, with age and knowledge, respond appropriately to subjective need, as measured for example, by judgments of confidence. Children become better "calibrated," that is, more realistic, at assessing their confidence in task performance (Newman & Wick, 1987). It can be reasoned that the less confident one is in an initial performance—regardless of objective reality of initial performance—the greater is the perceived, or felt, need for help. Utilizing this approach for examining children's response to need, Nelson-Le Gall, Kratzer, Jones, and DeCooke (1990) followed the same procedure with third- and fifth-graders that was used by Nelson-Le Gall (1987), although children additionally were asked to judge how confident they were that their initial solutions were correct. Children's subjective judgments of need for help then can be compared with objective standards of need. Subjective judgments of need matched objective standards more often among fifth-graders than third-graders. Fifth-graders sought help more often when they perceived an initial solution to be incorrect than when correct; third-graders, on the other hand, were just as likely to seek help when they perceived a solution to be incorrect as when they perceived it to be correct.

In summary, help-seeking is adaptive if it is necessary, that is, if there is cause based on either objective or subjective criteria for a discontinuation of independent effort. With increased age and knowledge, children are more likely to be aware of comprehension difficulty and need for assistance, and based on this awareness, more likely to request help in order to deal with the difficulty.

Content of the Request

An accurate developmental picture regarding adaptive help-seeking is dependent on the type of request for help that the child makes. Given a particular task situation, certain ways of seeking help may be more appropriate, adaptive, and successful than others. The following discussion illustrates how useage of different question formulations can vary according to the experience and knowledge of the individual.

Good, Slavings, Harel, and Emerson (1987) differentiated among four types of informational questions that elementary, junior-high, and secondary students ask in the classroom: requests for an explanation, factual information, clarification of information, and confirmation of an answer. In spite of requests for explanations being relatively infrequent across all grades, the frequency increased with grade level, with ninth-graders ten times more likely and twelfth-graders eight times more likely than kindergartners to ask for explanations. Although one cannot generalize that requests for explanations are necessarily adaptive, without considering the individual's specific needs of the situation, evidence does support the value of explanations in classroom discourse. Webb (1982) and Anderson, Evertson, and Brophy (1979), for example, have shown that students who receive explanations from either classmates or the teacher in response to questions tend to score better on subsequent achievement tests than students who receive just answers or restated solutions without explanations. Although the latter findings involve the type of help received rather than requested, they stress an important element of adaptiveness in children's help-seeking.

Kearsley (1976) discussed two types (actually "forms") of informational requests: open and closed. Open questions (e.g., "What arithmetic operation do I use?" or "How do I do this problem?") are non-specific and require the help-giver to respond with a completion. Closed questions, (e.g., "Does this problem require addition or subtraction?" or "Am I supposed to subtract?" or "This problem requires subtraction, doesn't it?") on the other hand, presuppose some specific proposition and offer the help-giver a choice of alternatives. A distinction between open and closed questions has been noted by van Hekken and Roelofsen (1982). During play, 5- and 7-year olds were observed asking more open than closed questions, while 9- and 11-year olds asked more closed than open questions. Older children presumably are more knowledgeable and have greater capability than younger children to analyze situations and on this basis to formulate one or more alternatives.

Importance of knowledge on questioning is supported by Smith, Tykodi, and Mynatt (1988) who examined the types of questions that adults with different levels of computer background ask when they are learning from a manual how to use a computer text-searching program. More knowledgeable subjects asked relatively more closed questions whereas less knowledgeable subjects asked relatively more open questions. The difference existed, however, only during the early stage of problem solving; as subjects became more knowledgeable over time, the difference in questioning disappeared. Flammer, Grob, Leuthardt, and Luthi (1984) also examined the role of knowledge on questioning. Adults were asked to plan a specific action, that is, the following of a recipe for making a chocolate mousse. Questions posed to the experimenter were categorized according to whether they pertained to: (1) goals of actions, (2) sequential organization or planning of actions, (3) how to carry out individual actions, (4) cooking instruments, or (5) cooking ingredients. Questions about goals and sequencing were considered "higher-level," and ones about individual actions, instruments, and ingredients "lower-level." Experts (experienced cooks) asked more higher-level questions regarding goals and sequential planning than did novices. Novices asked more lower-level questions regarding simple actions and utensils than did experts.

The experimental procedure of Nelson-Le Gall et al. (1990) was used to examine further the effects of age and knowledge on different types of requests for help. Children could select one of two types of help after giving a tentative answer and before giving a final answer. Requests were for either "direct" help (i.e., an answer "from another child who had done well on the task") or "indirect" help (i.e., a hint in the form of the target word used in a sentence). Asking for a hint was presumed to be indicative of a desire to clarify or refine current knowledge whereas asking for a direct answer was indicative of either a lack of knowledge or a desire for expedient task completion. Findings showed that fifth-graders (and children with good vocabularies) asked the experimenter for more indirect than direct help, whereas third-graders (and children with poor vocabularies) showed no preference. Most interestingly, when fifth-graders (and children with good vocabularies) did ask for direct help, these requests were on trials for which the children felt especially unsure of themselves (i.e., their confidence was low). In other words, more experienced learners seem to match the specific type of request to their subjective sense of need.

Finally, consider clarity of the child's request as an indicator of adaptiveness of help-seeking. Wilkinson and Calculator (1982), interested in first graders' classroom communication with one another, found that requests that are directed unambiguously to the listener and that possess a form that makes it explicitly understood what is being requested are especially likely to be successful in eliciting the requested information. Cooper, Marquis, and Ayers-Lopez (1982) similarly showed that kindergartners' and second-graders' help-seeking requests that get the focused attention of a peer (e.g., that first elicit an acknowledgement that the listener is willing to respond ["Hey Bill, are you busy?"—"No"—"What is this called?"]) and that are specific to the task at hand tend to be effective in getting an informative reply. Lack of ambiguity in the content as well as in the communication of a request for help then is indicative of adaptive help-seeking.

In summary, studies indicate patterns or trends of questioning by older, more experienced, and more knowledgeable students. With increased age and knowledge, students seem especially likely in certain situations to request explanations and hints and ask closed and higher-level questions, implying perhaps a desire to learn and an awareness that partial information is already available. It is important to note however that such patterns or trends do not imply that children necessarily generalize help-seeking behaviors across situations. In fact, a mark of the adaptive help-seeker is her or his ability to match particular types of questions to particular task situations.

Target of the Request

A third criterion for adaptiveness of help-seeking is the suitability of the child's choice of help-giver in the classroom. The adaptive help-seeker is able to assess the situation and choose the particular target (for the present discussion, the teacher or a classmate) who is most likely to meet his or her particular needs. Although the child's needs can be both academic (e.g., task completion and mastery) and social (e.g., encouragement and enhancement of friendship), the present discussion focuses on choices based on academic need. What evidence is there that children take into account various characteristics of the helper as they consider the suitability of whom to ask for help? Is there an age-related or knowledge-related increase in children's responsiveness to these characteristics?

We know that, with age, children are increasingly cognizant of characteristics that distinguish effective from ineffective helpers (Barnett, Darcie, Holland, & Kobasigawa, 1982). For example, whereas kindergartners choose helpers whom they say are nice and kind, children in middle and upper grades choose helpers whom they say are competent and willing to help. Similarly, Nelson-Le Gall and Gumerman (1984) have shown that, with age, children increasingly reason about helper selections by focusing on specific attributes of the helper and their relationship with the helper.

We also know that individual differences in children's choice of helpers reflect the children's attitudes and beliefs about those helpers. Newman and Goldin (1990) have shown that, across grades 2, 4, and 6, children believe that asking for help from the teacher is more likely than asking for help from a classmate to result in learning, and that asking the teacher is less likely than asking a classmate to result in that person thinking they are dumb. In fact, children say they prefer to ask the teacher more than a classmate when they need help with an academic problem (see also Nelson-Le Gall & Gumerman, 1984). Correlations among these various beliefs are revealing. At all three grades, there were positive associations between the belief that asking questions of the teacher or peer helps in learning and the child's liking to ask that particular person. However, the expected negative associations between the belief that asking questions of the teacher or peer results in perceptions of dumbness and the child's liking to ask that particular person were not significant. It appears, across the elementary grades, that a positive belief about the benefits of help-seeking may be more instrumental in the child's decision of whom to ask for help than is a negative belief about possible costs. Apparently it is later, at middle school, that attitudes and beliefs about costs of seeking help, for example, potential embarrassment, have a negative impact on children's intentions and behavior (Newman, 1990).

Children's choice of helpers reflects not only the children's beliefs about help per se, but also general achievement-related beliefs with which the children have been socialized. Several examples involve sex differences. First, although elementary school girls are generally perceived by classmates to be more academically competent than boys, girls are not chosen more often than boys as targets for help. Girls prefer asking for help from girls, and boys prefer asking boys (Nelson-Le Gall & DeCooke, 1987). A second sex difference is seen when we consider children's concern about negative reactions to their seeking help. Although elementary school children have relatively little concern that the teacher, in comparison with a classmate, will think they are dumb when they ask a question in class, this concern regarding the teacher is significantly stronger among girls than boys. Interestingly, this sex difference occurs only in the context of math, and not reading, class (Newman & Goldin, 1990). The implications are important: If girls are more reluctant than boys to seek help from their teacher in math class, perhaps they do not get adequate help and therefore do not perform as well as boys in later years (cf. literature on sex differences in math achievement and achievement attitudes, Eccles, 1983).

In summary, the third criterion of adaptive help-seeking is flexibility in the choice of a helper. As children get older, they increasingly are cognizant of characteristics of effective helpers in the classroom and increasingly are influenced by a variety of attitudes, some of which show sex differentiation, regarding costs and benefits of seeking help. Research has dealt largely with children's general comparisons of seeking help from teachers and classmates, and unfortunately no research has examined children's preferences for particular teachers or particular classmates in particular situations. I expect that future studies will show that the self-regulated learner thoughtfully decides among all options, carefully considering the relative utility of each.

IMPACT OF THE SCHOOL CONTEXT ON ADAPTIVE HELP-SEEKING

Most research on children's help-seeking has focused on personal characteristics of the child while very little has examined the role of the school context. Help-seeking is a social act and, as such, is influenced by a number of contextual factors. These factors can be examined on various levels, for example, interpersonal interaction, the classroom, the school, and the culture at large. Whatever the level of analysis, in order to understand help-seeking as an adaptive strategy of self-regulated learning, context needs to be considered. "Adaptiveness" implies a match between the child's needs and capabilities on the one hand and the available resources and constraints in the environment, on the other hand. For present purposes, I have chosen to discuss three characteristics of the classroom: climate, structure or organization of activity, and type of learning task. I attempt to illustrate how these factors set the stage for, and facilitate, adaptive help-seeking.

Classroom Climate

The climate of the classroom, in particular the degree to which the child perceives support and encouragement for questioning and the degree to which positive learning goals are socialized, plays an important role in the likelihood that the child will seek assistance when needed. Classroom climate traditionally has been operationalized in a variety of ways that provide insight into how teachers may encourage children to seek needed assistance.

Moos (1979), for example, has identified several psychosocial dimensions of classroom climate that may help explain how children react when they need assistance. A climate of involvement, affiliation, and support—surrounding the teacher as well as classmates—is expected to provide encouragement for question-asking. According to Deci and Ryan (1985) and deCharms (1976), classroom climate is determined by the teacher's goal orientation. Based on a distinction between autonomy and control, the teacher's behavior is manifest as "originlike" versus "pawnlike." The originlike teacher fosters self-confidence; expresses warmth in the classroom; and encourages internal goal-setting, instrumental behavior, realistic aspirations, and personal responsibility for learning.

Related to the notion of goal orientation toward autonomy versus control is the distinction between *learning* (or *task-involved*) and *performance* (or *ego-involved*) goals. According to Dweck (1986) and Nicholls (1979, 1983), different goals in the classroom have different outcomes in terms of children's achievement-related behavior. In classrooms that emphasize learning, children are socialized with the goal of long-term mastery; there is cooperation; and performance feedback stresses each individual child's intellectual and social development. In classrooms that emphasize performance, children are socialized with the goal of getting good grades; there is competitiveness; and performance feedback stresses social comparison with classmates.

Ames (1983) argues that these classroom goal orientations have associated with them distinctive student attitudes and behaviors regarding help-seeking. Classrooms emphasizing learning goals presumably encourage children to deal with academic difficulty as a challenge—with positive affect, increased persistence, and seeking of assistance when needed. Classrooms emphasizing performance goals and social comparison with classmates, on the other hand, presumably lead to a wide dispersion of help-seeking attitudes and responses within the classroom. Although some children are likely to engage in adaptive help-seeking, other children are likely to deal with academic difficulty by exhibiting negative affect and maladaptive self-attributions and by giving up.

Unfortunately, there is virtually no empirical research on classroom climate in relation to help-seeking. Preliminary work by Schwager and Newman (1991) has begun to address one specific aspect of climate, namely the degree of encouragement and affiliation present in the classroom. Third-, fifth-, and seventh-graders were asked to describe various features of their math class and were asked how likely they were to seek needed help from the teacher. One part of the classroom description involved children's ratings of the degree to which they they liked their teacher, their teacher liked them, and they felt encouraged to ask their teacher questions during math class. Individual differences in both mutual liking and perceived encouragement were strongly predictive of which children intended to seek assistance from the teacher.

In sum, what we know so far leads us to believe that particular aspects of classroom climate such as encouragement, personal warmth, and a learning (versus performance) goal orientation facilitate adaptive help-seeking because of their effect on children's decisions regarding whom to ask for help. Positive affect and lack of anxiety surrounding a particular helper no doubt facilitate both the choice of the "best" helper and the actual carrying out of a request and processing of information from the helper.

Structure of the Classroom Activity

A second factor that affects help-seeking is the structure of the classroom activity. There are three major types of activity structure (see Berliner, 1983). Whole-class activity is characterized by a high level of teacher control in an activity such as presentation of a new lesson, class discussion, or question and answer period. Small-group activity is characterized by a nondirective, supervisory role of the teacher, with students engaged in assigned activities such as small-group discussion or development of group projects. Individual activity is also characterized by a nondirective, supervisory role of the teacher, with students engaged in assigned activities such as silent reading or completion of worksheets.

The structure of the class activity is an important feature around which teachers organize rules of classroom communication, feedback, and student-teacher interaction (Rosenholtz & Simpson, 1984). Differences in classroom structure are expected to be related to students' help-seeking attitudes and behavior. Small-group activity, for example, is designed to promote children's interacting with one another by both giving and receiving help (Cooper et al., 1982; Slavin, 1983). It is not surprising that help-seeking occurs frequently in cooperative small groups in junior high school nor that the frequency of these interactions is positively related to student achievement (Webb, 1982). Findings by Meece, Blumenfeld, and Puro (1989) suggest that in fifth- and sixth-grade classes, students address help-seeking questions to the teacher more often in small-group and individual activities than in whole-class activities. Nelson-Le Gall and Glor-Scheib (1985) observed more help-seeking among first-, third-, and fifth-graders in math and reading classes with either individual or small-group activity than in classes with whole-class activity.

The mechanism by which individual and small-group activity influences adaptive help-seeking would seem to be directly related to the mechanism, namely positive affect and lack of anxiety, by which classroom climate has its facilitative effect. That is, warmth and encouragement on the part of the teacher would seem to be incorporated most easily or naturally into individual and small-group instruction, thereby facilitating student interaction with the teacher. Small-group activity, when designed cooperatively or according to a plan of reciprocal teaching, may be especially facilitative of adaptive help-seeking because of additional effects of modeling, group reward structures, and guided participation (see Palinscar & Brown, 1984; Slavin, 1983). It may be, in fact, that increased help-seeking and help-giving among students in such situations has a positive transfer effect on student-teacher interaction, in particular on the willingness of students to actively seek help from the teacher when it is necessary.

Type of Learning Task

A third classroom factor that affects children's help-seeking is the nature of the learning task and the child's perceptions of work that are associated with the task. Classroom organization, management, and curriculum as well as cultural values shape students' perceptions of work (Blumenfeld, Mergendoller, & Swarthout, 1987; Doyle, 1983). Attitudes toward help-seeking and actual help-seeking behavior are related to these perceptions.

On certain learning tasks children feel comfortable asking for assistance, and on certain other tasks they are reluctant. Attitudes and behavior regarding help may depend, for example, on the academic subject and the child's personal and culturally-based attitudes and beliefs that surround the subject. Important differences exist in children's attitudes and beliefs (e.g., interest, perceived value, perceived task difficulty) regarding different subjects, for example, math and language arts (Newman & Stevenson, 1990; Stevenson & Newman, 1986; Stodolsky, 1988). By high school—but perhaps even earlier according to some studies—students like math less than language-related subjects; they find math more difficult; they more commonly report math anxiety; and they are more likely to attribute success (or failure) to help (or lack thereof) from the teacher. At the elementary level, children report a greater need for help in math than in reading (Newman & Goldin, 1990), and in fact, it has been reported that elementary-school children do seek assistance more frequently in math than in reading class (Nelson-Le Gall & Glor-Scheib, 1985). Perhaps children feel more comfortable seeking help in difficult subjects, in spite of perhaps not liking those subjects, since admitting failure is less damaging in a situation for which there is relatively low expectancy for success (Covington & Beery, 1976).

Differences in children's perceptions and classroom behavior, between math and language-related subjects, may be related to underlying differences in instructional format. Elementary school math classes differ from social studies classes in a number of ways that may be relevant to explaining differences in children's help-seeking (Stodolsky, 1988). For example, there is a rigidity in math lessons; teachers are "experts" who present or "tell" an explanation and then expect students to practice. Very little instruction is provided in math books, and consequently there is little expectation of the child being an independent learner. In all, the student in math class may feel dependent on the teacher for help.

The nature of the lesson itself, that is, whether children are presented new, review, or enrichment material, also affects children's help-seeking. In Schwager and Newman's (1991) study of third-, fifth-, and seventh-graders, children overwhelmingly reported a greater likelihood of asking the teacher for academic help when they were having difficulty with new material than with old material. This finding again suggests that there is relative comfort in asking questions about material for which it is perceived to be "normal" to need help. Similarly, van der Meij (1988) has shown that children feel less inhibited seeking help during instruction when mastery is not yet expected than during lessons when the child is expected to work independently. We can speculate that enrichment activities also provide children a sense of freedom to ask questions. Instructional studies have demonstrated that novel, interesting, and manipulative materials are successful in eliciting students' questions (see reviews in Dillon, 1988, 1990). So children are most likely to ask questions and seek help in situations in which the need for help, defined according to both task difficulty and desire to know, is especially great.

In summary, three contextual factors—classroom climate, structure of the classroom activity, and type of learning task—are related to children's help-seeking behavior. Specific mechanisms by which encouraging and learning-oriented classrooms, small-group activities, and particularly difficult and/or interesting tasks facilitate children's adaptive help-seeking have not been fully researched. However, I expect that all three factors play a role in the child's decisions regarding whom to ask for help. Encouragement from the teacher or classmates, especially in the context of activity structures and learning tasks that are themselves encouraging, makes it easier for the child to approach the helper. In addition to a direct effect on help-seeking, these contextual factors no doubt also have an important indirect effect on task engagement in general because they interact with, and help formulate over time, the child's entire system of goals, values, and beliefs about schooling and about the self.

CONCLUSIONS

Seeking assistance—when assistance is needed—is an obviously important strategy in the repertoire of the self-regulated learner. The child who is comfortable, and capable of, eliciting help from knowledgeable others stands a good chance of not only alleviating immediate academic difficulty but also acquiring knowledge that can be used in the future for self-help.

The prescription sounds simple: When one needs help, one should take the initiative and seek it. Yet often children do not seek needed academic assistance; they seek assistance when it is not really needed; or their requests are not adaptive to the particular situation.

I have discussed a number of reasons why these "non-adaptive help-seeking" events may occur. Since help-seeking is a social-interactional strategy, reasons have to do with both the child and his or her environment. I have focused on three sets of variables: (1) motivational characteristics of the child, in particular, achievement goals, self-perceptions of ability, and specific beliefs and attitudes regarding help; (2) developmental processes, that are age-related and knowledge-related; and (3) characteristics of the classroom, namely, classroom climate, activity structure, and nature of the academic task at hand. I have examined interactions among variables and integrated findings in a framework of self-regulated learning.

Although the present perspective on help-seeking as an instrumental strategy for learning is not new (cf. Nelson-Le Gall, 1981, 1985), I have attempted to emphasize specific strategic and planful aspects of the adaptive help-seeker's behavior. In particular, I have discussed three decisions—necessity, content, and target—in which the self-regulated learner engages prior to making a request for help.

At the heart of the discussion of why children do or do not seek help adaptively are general issues of strategy development. Strategies are behaviors or actions that children coordinate deliberately, planfully, and voluntarily as a means to an end. Over time, children come to use strategies routinely, and as a result, the strategies become automated skills that can be applied involuntarily. In situations of novelty, difficulty, and cognitive disequilibrium, however, the skillful learner often falls back to an "earlier" strategic type of behavior (Paris, Newman, & Jacobs, 1985).

Adaptive help-seekers are both strategic and skillful in the sense that they possess all the skills, both cognitive and social, required to enlist the help of others. They use those skills as a means to a particular end (i.e., learning and task mastery). Importantly, they do not automatically call out for help when they first encounter difficulty. They fall back to a deliberate, planful, and voluntary (i.e., strategic) mode. They are aware of their own competencies and weaknesses and are motivated to address difficulty in an optimal way. They thoughtfully determine if there are reasonable alternatives (e.g., Should I persist on my own? or go to the dictionary?), weigh the costs and benefits (e.g., What will I learn?; Will I be embarrassed?), determine the best way to formulate their request (e.g., Should I ask for a hint? or directly ask for the answer?), and determine who might be the best person to approach. They then act upon these various decisions, expressing their request and processing the results with care.

Where does this body of research and this conceptualization of help-seeking as a strategy of self-regulated learning take us? An understanding of self-regulated learning in general, and adaptive help-seeking in particular, emphasizes the responsibility that students have in controlling their own learning. The role of motivational goals and self-system beliefs is clear. It is equally clear that students must be provided a school environment that actively encourages questioning. Although I discussed just three features of the school environment that affect help-seeking, future research will undoubtedly show the importance of a number of other contextual factors as well, for example, teacher's style of management, type of student evaluation, class size, ability grouping, cultural practice, and support by parents and siblings at home.

How might classroom instruction encourage adaptive help-seeking? Three critical aspects of instruction, that have been discussed in terms of promoting self-regulated learning (see Paris & Newman, 1990), provide at least a partial answer for educators attempting to promote students' adaptive help-seeking. First, effective instruction for self-regulated learning can prompt students to change their goals, personal beliefs of agency and self-efficacy, and commitment to learn. Neither lecturing nor simply modeling the virtues of question-asking is sufficient; students must be convinced that question-asking has personal value. Second, effective instruction can "make thinking public." Group discussions, dialogues, and shared articulation of problems, frustrations, and fears allow teachers to diagnose students' processes of thinking and decision-making (e.g., regarding necessity, content, and target of help-seeking requests) and allow students to understand each other, become aware of alternative problem-solving strategies, and potentially change their personal beliefs about help-seeking. Third, effective instruction can promote active participation and collaboration. Cooperative learning, reciprocal teaching, and peer tutoring are specific ways in which teachers can challenge children to develop an active and intrinsically-directed reliance on questioning of themselves and of others.

In conclusion, I reemphasize the value of considering adaptive help-seeking as a strategy of self-regulated learning. An integrative perspective on help-seeking is informed by a variety of theoretical positions in developmental and educational psychology. Continued research on adaptive help-seeking promises to explain the complexity of how children learn in the classroom. Instructional strategies that follow from this integrative perspective promise to guide students to take a more active role in their own learning.

ACKNOWLEDGMENTS

I would like to express my appreciation to Jim Dillon, Stuart Karabenick, Mahna Schwager, and Hans van der Meij, who provided helpful comments on earlier drafts.

REFERENCES

Ajzen, I. (1988). *Attitudes, personality, and behavior*. Milton Keynes, England: Open University Press.

Ames, R. (1983). Help-seeking and achievement orientation: Perspectives from attribution theory. In B. M. DePaulo, A. Nadler, & J. D. Fisher (Eds.), *New directions in helping* (Vol. 2, pp. 165-186). New York: Academic Press.

Ames, R., & Lau, S. (1982). An attributional analysis of help-seeking in academic settings. *Journal of Educational Psychology, 74*, 414-423.

Anderson, L. M., Evertson, C. M., & Brophy, J. E. (1979). An experimental study of effective teaching in first-grade reading groups. *The Elementary School Journal, 79*, 193-273.

Barnett, K., Darcie, G., Holland, C. J., & Kobasigawa, A. (1982). Children's cognitions about effective helping. *Developmental Psychology, 18*, 267-277.

Berliner, D. C. (1983). Developing conceptions of classrooms environments: Some light on the T in classroom studies of ATI. *Educational Psychologist, 18*, 1-13.

Berlyne, D. E., & Frommer, F. D. (1966). Some determinants of the incidence and content of children's questions. *Child Development, 37*, 177-189.

Blumenfeld, P. C., Mergendoller, J. R., & Swarthout, D. W. (1987). Task as a heuristic for understanding student learning and motivation. *Journal of Curriculum Studies, 19*, 135-148.

Borkowski, J. G., Levers, S. R., & Gruenenfelder, T. A. (1976). Transfer of mediational strategies in children: The role of activity and awareness during strategy acquisition. *Child Development, 47*, 779-786.

Brown, A. L., Bransford, J. D., Ferrara, R. A., & Campione, J. C. (1983). Learning, remembering, and understanding. In P. Mussen (Ed.), *Handbook of child psychology* (Vol. 3). New York: Wiley.

Cooper, C. R., Marquis, A., & Ayers-Lopez, S. (1982). Peer learning in the classroom: Tracing developmental patterns and consequences of children's spontaneous interactions. In L. C. Wilkinson (Ed.), *Communicating in the classroom* (pp. 69-84). New York: Academic Press.

Corno, L. (1989). Self-regulated learning: A volitional analysis. In B. J. Zimmerman & D. H. Schunk (Eds.), *Self-regulated learning and academic achievement: Theory, research, and practice* (pp. 111-141). New York: Springer-Verlag.

Corno, L., & Mandinach, E. (1983). The role of cognitive engagement in classroom learning and motivation. *Educational Psychologist, 18*, 88-108.

Cosgrove, J., & Patterson, C. (1977). Plans and the development of listener skills. *Developmental Psychology, 13*, 557-564.

Cotler, S., Quilty, R. F., & Palmer, R. J. (1970). Measurement of appropriate and unnecessary help-seeking dependent behavior. *Journal of Consulting and Clinical Psychology, 35*, 324-327.

Covington, M. V., & Beery, R. (1976). *Self-worth and school learning*. New York: Holt, Rinehart, & Winston.

deCharms, R. (1976). *Enhancing motivation: Change in the classroom*. New York: Wiley.

Deci, E. L., & Ryan, R. M. (1985). *Intrinsic motivation and self-determination in human behavior*. New York: Plenum Press.

Diaz, R. M., Neal, C. J., & Amaya-Williams, M. (1990). The social origins of self-regulation. In L. Moll (Ed.), *Vygotsky and education*. New York: Cambridge University Press.

Dillon, J. T. (1988). The remedial status of student questioning. *Journal of Curriculum Studies, 20*, 197-210.

————. (1990). *The practice of questioning*. New York: Routledge.

Doyle, W. (1983). Academic work. *Review of Educational Research, 53*, 159-199.

Dweck, C. (1986). Motivational processes affecting learning. *American Psychologist, 41*, 1040-1048.

Eccles, J. (1983). Expectancies, values, and academic behaviors. In J. T. Spence (Ed.), *Achievement and achievement motives: Psychological and sociological approaches* (pp. 75-146). San Francisco: Freeman.

Eccles, J., Midgley, C., & Adler, T. F. (1984). Grade-related changes in the school environment: Effects on achievement motivation. In J. Nicholls (Ed.), *Advances in motivation and achievement* (Vol. 3, pp. 283-331). Greenwich, CT: JAI Press.

Eccles, J., & Wigfield, A. (1985). Teacher expectations and student motivation. In J. Dusek (Ed.), *Teacher expectancies*. Hillsdale, NJ: Erlbaum.

Elliott, E. S., & Dweck, C. S. (1988). Goals: An approach to motivation and achievement. *Journal of Personality and Social Psychology, 54*, 5-12.

Ferrara, R. A., Brown, A. L., & Campione, J. C. (1986). Children's learning and transfer of inductive reasoning rules: Studies of proximal development. *Child Development, 57*, 1087-1099.

Fishbein, M., & Ajzen, I. (1975). *Belief, attitude, intention, and behavior*. Reading, MA: Addison-Wesley.

Flammer, A. (1981). Towards a theory of question asking. *Psychological Research, 43*, 407-420.

Flammer, A., Grob, A., Leuthardt, T., & Luthi, R. (1984). Asking how to act. *Archives de Psychologie, 52*, 103-120.

Flavell, J. H. (1979). Metacognition and cognitive monitoring: A new area of cognitive developmental inquiry. *American Psychologist, 34*, 906-911.

Flavell, J. H., & Ross, L. (1981). *Social cognitive development*. Cambridge: Cambridge University Press.

Frey, K. S., & Ruble, D. N. (1985). What children say when the teacher is not around: Conflicting goals in social comparison and performance assessment in the classroom. *Journal of Personality and Social Psychology, 48*, 550-562.

Gibbs, R. W. (1985). Situational conventions and requests. In J. P. Forgas (Ed.), *Language and social situations* (pp. 97-110). New York: Springer-Verlag.

Good, T. L. (1981). Teacher expectations and student perceptions: A decade of research. *Educational Leadership, 38*, 415-423.

Good, T. L., Slavings, R. L., Harel, K. H., & Emerson, H. (1987). Student passivity: A study of question asking in K-12 classrooms. *Sociology of Education, 60*, 181-199.

Graham, S., & Barker, G. P. (1990). The down side of help: An attributional-developmental analysis of helping behavior as a low-ability cue. *Journal of Educational Psychology, 82*, 7-14.

Harter, S. (1981). A new self-report scale of intrinsic versus extrinsic orientation in the classroom: Motivational and informational components. *Developmental Psychology, 17*, 300-312.

————. (1983). Developmental perspectives on the self-system. In P. Mussen (Ed.), *Handbook of child psychology: Socialization, personality and social development* (Vol. 4, pp. 275-385). New York: Wiley.

Harter, S., & Connell, J. P. (1984). A model of children's achievement and related self-perceptions of competence, control, and motivational orientation. In J. Nicholls (Ed.), *Advances in motivation and achievement* (Vol. 3, pp. 219-250). Greenwich, CT: JAI Press.

Hoppe-Graff, S., Herrmann, T., Winterhoff-Spurk, P., & Mangold, R. (1985). Speech and situation: A general model for the process of speech production. In J. P. Forgas (Ed.), *Language and social situations* (pp. 81-95). New York: Springer-Verlag.

Karabenick, S. A., & Knapp, J. R. (1991). Relationship of academic help seeking to the use of learning strategies and other instrumental achievement behavior in college students. *Journal of Educational Psychology, 83,* 221-230.

Kearsley, G. P. (1976). Questions and question asking in verbal discourse: A cross-disciplinary review. *Journal of Psycholinguistic Research, 5,* 355-375.

Kreutzer, M., Leonard, C., & Flavell, J. H. (1975). An interview study of children's knowledge about memory. *Monographs of the Society for Research in Child Development, 40* (1, Serial No. 159).

Kuhl, J. (1985). Volitional mediators of cognition-behavior consistency: Self-regulatory processes and action versus state orientation. In J. Kuhl & J. Beckmann (Eds.), *Action control: From cognition to behavior.* Berlin: Springer-Verlag.

Ladd, G., & Oden, S. (1979). The relationship between peer acceptance and children's ideas about helpfulness. *Child Development, 50,* 402-408.

Locke, E. A., Saari, L. M., Shaw, K. N., & Latham, G. P. (1981). Goal setting and task performance: 1969-1980. *Psychological Bulletin, 90,* 125-152.

Markman, E. M. (1979). Realizing that you don't understand: Elementary school children's awareness of inconsistencies. *Child Development, 50,* 643-655.

_____. (1981). Comprehension monitoring. In W. P. Dickson (Ed.), *Children's oral communication skills* (pp. 61-84). New York: Academic Press.

Meece, J., Blumenfeld, P. C., & Hoyle, R. (1988). Students' goal orientations and cognitive engagement in classroom activities. *Journal of Educational Psychology, 80,* 514-523.

Meece, J, Blumenfeld, P. C., & Puro, P. (1989). *A motivational analysis of elementary science learning environments.* Paper presented at the annual meeting of the American Association for the Advancement of Science, San Francisco.

Moos, R. H. (1979). *Evaluating educational environments.* San Francisco: Jossey-Bass.

Myers, M., & Paris, S. G. (1978). Children's metacognitive knowledge about reading. *Journal of Educational Psychology, 70,* 680-690.

Nadler, A. (1983). Personal characteristics and help-seeking. In B. DePaulo, A. Nadler, & J. Fisher (Eds.), *New directions in helping* (Vol. 2, pp. 303-340). New York: Academic Press.

Nelson-Le Gall, S. (1981). Help-seeking: An understudied problem-solving skill in children. *Developmental Review, 1,* 224-246.

_____. (1985). Help-seeking behavior in learning. In E. W. Gordon (Ed.), *Review of research in education* (Vol. 12, pp. 55-90). Washington, DC: American Educational Research Association.

_____. (1987). Necessary and unnecessary help-seeking in children. *Journal of Genetic Psychology, 148,* 53-62.

Nelson-Le Gall, S., & DeCooke, P. A. (1987). Same-sex and cross-sex help exchanges in the classroom. *Journal of Educational Psychology, 79,* 67-71.

Nelson-Le Gall, S., & Glor-Scheib, S. (1985). Help seeking in elementary classrooms: An observational study. *Contemporary Educational Psychology, 10,* 58-71.

Nelson-Le Gall, S., & Gumerman, R. A. (1984). Children's perceptions of helpers and helper motivation. *Journal of Applied Developmental Psychology, 5,* 1-12.

Nelson-Le Gall, S. & Jones, E. (1990). Cognitive-motivational influences on the task-related help-seeking behavior of Black children. *Child Development, 61,* 581-589.

Nelson-Le Gall, S., Kratzer, L., Jones, E., & DeCooke, P. (1990). Children's self-assessment of performance and task-related help seeking. *Journal of Experimental Child Psychology, 49,* 245-263.

Newman, R. S. (1984). Children's achievement and self-evaluations in mathematics: A longitudinal study. *Journal of Educational Psychology, 76*, 857-873.

_____. (1990). Children's help-seeking in the classroom: The role of motivational factors and attitudes. *Journal of Educational Psychology, 82*, 71-80.

Newman, R. S., & Goldin, L. (1990). Children's reluctance to seek help with schoolwork. *Journal of Educational Psychology, 82*, 92-100.

Newman, R. S., & Stevenson, H. W. (1990). Children's achievement and causal attributions in mathematics and reading. *Journal of Experimental Education, 58*, 197-212.

Newman, R. S., & Wick, P. L. (1987). Effect of age, skill, and performance feedback on children's judgments of confidence. *Journal of Educational Psychology, 79*, 115-119.

Nicholls, J. G. (1979). Quality and equality in intellectual development: The role of motivation in education. *American Psychologist, 34*, 1071-1084.

_____. (1983). Conceptions of ability and achievement motivation: A theory and its implications for education. In S. Paris, G. Olson, & H. Stevenson (Eds.), *Learning and motivation in the classroom*. Hillsdale, NJ: Erlbaum Press.

Nicholls, J. G., & Miller, A. T. (1983). The differentiation of the concepts of difficulty and ability. *Child Development, 54*, 951-959.

Nicholls, J. G., Patashnick, M., & Nolen, S. B. (1985). Adolescents' theories of education. *Journal of Educational Psychology, 77*, 683-692.

Palinscar, A., & Brown, A. L. (1984). Reciprocal teaching of comprehension-fostering and comprehension-monitoring activities. *Cognition and Instruction, 1*, 117-175.

Paris, S. G., & Byrnes, J. P. (1989). The constructivist approach to self-regulation and learning in the classroom. In B. J. Zimmerman & D. H. Schunk (Eds.), *Self-regulated learning and academic achievement: Theory, research, and practice* (pp. 169-200). New York: Springer-Verlag.

Paris, S. G. & Lindauer, B. K. (1982). The development of cognitive skills during childhood. In B. Wolman (Ed.), *Handbook of developmental psychology*. Englewood Cliffs, NJ: Prentice Hall.

Paris, S. G., & Newman, R. S. (1990). Developmental aspects of self-regulated learning. *Educational Psychologist, 25*, 87-102.

Paris, S. G., Newman, R. S., & Jacobs, J. E. (1985). Social contexts and functions of children's remembering. In M. Pressley & C. J. Brainerd (Eds.), *Cognitive learning and memory in children*. New York: Springer-Verlag.

Paris, S. G., Newman, R. S., & McVey, K. (1982). Learning the functional significance of mnemonic actions: A microgenetic study of strategy acquisition. *Journal of Experimental Child Psychology, 34*, 490-509.

Patterson, C., Cosgrove, J., & O'Brien, R. (1980). Nonverbal indicants of comprehension and non comprehension in children. *Developmental Psychology, 16*, 38-48.

Pressley, M., Borkowski, J., & Schneider, W. (1987). Cognitive strategies: Good strategy users coordinate metacognition and knowledge. In R. Vasta (Ed.), *Annals of child development*, (Vol. 4, pp. 80-129). Greenwich, CT: JAI Press.

Pressley, M., & Levin, J. R. (1983). (Eds.). *Cognitive strategy research: Psychological foundations*. New York: Springer-Verlag.

Pressley, M., Levin, J. R., Ghatala, E. S., & Ahmad, M. (1987). Test monitoring in young grade school children. *Journal of Experimental Child Psychology, 43*, 96-111.

Rohrkemper, M., & Corno, L. (1988). Success and failure on classroom tasks: Adaptive learning and classroom teaching. *The Elementary School Journal, 88*, 297-312.

Rohwer, W. D., & Thomas, J. W. (1989). The role of autonomous problem-solving activities in learning to program. *Journal of Educational Psychology, 81*, 584-593.

Rosen, S. (1983). Perceived inadequacy and help-seeking. In B. DePaulo, A Nadler, & J. Fisher (Eds.), *New directions in helping* (Vol. 2, pp. 73-107). New York: Academic Press.

Rosenholtz, S. J., & Simpson, C. (1984). The formation of ability conceptions: Developmental trend or social construction? *Review of Educational Research, 54*, 31-63.

Schunk, D. H. (1989). Self-efficacy and cognitive skill learning. In C. Ames & R. Ames (Eds.), *Research on motivation in education* (Vol. 3, pp. 13-44). New York: Academic Press.

Schwager, M. T., & Newman, R. S. (1990). *Children's perceptions of the classroom in relation to help-seeking.* Paper presented at the annual meeting of the American Educational Research Association, Chicago.

Sears, R., Maccoby, E., & Levin, H. (1957). *Patterns of child rearing.* Evanston, IL: Row and Peterson.

Shapiro, E. G. (1983). Embarrassment and help-seeking. In B. DePaulo, A. Nadler, & J. Fisher (Eds.), *New directions in helping* (Vol. 2, pp. 143-163). New York: Academic Press.

Shavelson, R. J., & Bolus, R. (1982). Self-concept: The interplay of theory and methods. *Journal of Educational Psychology, 74*, 3-17.

Skinner, E. A., Chapman, M., & Baltes, P. B. (1988). Control, means-ends, and agency beliefs: A new conceptualization and its measurement during childhood. *Journal of Personality and Social Psychology, 54*, 117-133.

Skinner, E. A., Wellborn, J. G., & Connell, J. P. (1990). What it takes to do well in school and whether I've got it: A process model of perceived control and children's engagement and achievement in school. *Journal of Educational Psychology, 82*, 22-32.

Slavin, R. (1983). *Cooperative learning.* New York: Longman.

Smith, K. H., Tykodi, T. A., & Mynatt, B. T. (1988). Can we predict the form and content of spontaneous questions? *Questioning Exchange, 2*, 53-60.

Stevenson, H. W., & Newman, R. S. (1986). Long-term prediction of achievement and attitudes in mathematics and reading. *Child Development, 57*, 646-659.

Stevenson, H. W., Stigler, J. W., Lucker, G. W., Lee, S., Hsu, C. C., & Kitamura, S. (1987). Classroom behavior and achievement of Japanese, Chinese, and American children. In R. Glaser (Ed.), *Advances in instructional psychology.* Hillsdale, NJ: Erlbaum.

Stipek, D., & Tannatt, L. (1984). Children's judgments of their own and their peers' academic competence. *Journal of Educational Psychology, 76*, 75-84.

Stodolsky, S. S. (1988). *The subject matters.* Chicago: The University of Chicago Press.

van der Meij, H. (1986). *Questioning.* The Hague: SVO.

————. (1988). Constraints on question asking in classrooms. *Journal of Educational Psychology, 80*, 401-405.

————. (1990). Question asking: To know that you do not know is not enough. *Journal of Educational Psychology, 82*, 505-512.

van Hekken, S., & Roelofsen, W. (1982). More questions than answers. *Journal of Child Language, 9*, 445-460.

Vygotsky, L. (1978). *Mind in society: The development of higher psychological processes* (M. Cole, V. John-Steiner, S. Scribner, & E. Souberman, Eds.). Cambridge, MA: Harvard University Press.

Webb, N. M. (1982). Student interaction and learning in small groups. *Review of Educational Research, 52*, 421-445.

Weinstein, C. F., & Mayer, R. F. (1986). The teaching of learning strategies. In M. C. Wittrock (Ed.), *Handbook of Research on Teaching* (pp. 315-327). New York: Macmillan.

Weinstein, R. (1985). Student mediation of classroom expectancy effects. In J. Dusek (Ed.), *Teacher expectancies.* Hillsdale, NJ: Erlbaum.

Weinstein, R., & Middlesdtadt, S. (1979). Student perceptions of teacher interactions with male high and low achievers. *Journal of Educational Psychology, 71*, 421-431.

Wentzel, K. R. (1989). Adolescent classroom goals, standards for performance, and academic achievement: An interactionist perspective. *Journal of Educational Psychology, 81*, 131-142.

Wertsch, J. V. (1985). *Vygotsky and the social formation of mind.* Cambridge, MA: Harvard University Press.

Wilkinson, L., & Calculator, S. (1982). Effective speakers: Students' use of language to request and obtain information and action in the classroom. In L. Wilkinson (Ed.), *Communicating in the classroom* (pp. 85-99). New York: Academic Press.

Wood, D., Bruner, J., & Ross, G. (1976). The role of tutoring in problem solving. *Journal of Child Psychology and Psychiatry, 17,* 89-100.

Wong, B. Y. L. (1985). Self-questioning instructional research: A review. *Review of Educational Research, 55,* 227-268.

Wylie, R. (1979). *The self-concept: Theory and research on selected topics* (Vol.2). Lincoln: University of Nebraska Press.

Zimmerman, B. J., & Martinez-Pons, M. (1986). Development of a structured interview for assessing student use of self-regulated learning strategies. *American Educational Research Journal, 23,* 614-628.

————. (1990). Student differences in self-regulated learning: Relating grade, sex, and giftedness to self-efficacy and strategy use. *Journal of Educational Psychology, 82,* 51-59.

Zimmerman, B. J., & Schunk, D. H. (1989). (Eds.) *Self-regulated learning and academic achievement: Theory, research, and practice.* New York: Springer-Verlag.

SOCIAL AND ACADEMIC
GOALS AT SCHOOL:
MOTIVATION AND ACHIEVEMENT IN CONTEXT

Kathryn R. Wentzel

Inherent in any purposeful activity are goals—ideas about what we would like our efforts to result in and that guide and direct our behavior. The education of children is no exception and indeed, if one were to ask students and teachers what they try to accomplish at school, their responses would most likely reflect a wide range of learning objectives. Most typical would be goals such as developing expertise in a particular content area, being challenged and maintaining high levels of interest in learning, or earning high grades. In addition, it is quite likely that teachers as well as students would express desires to achieve a variety of non-intellectual outcomes such as developing positive interpersonal relationships, being dependable and responsible, or displaying cooperative and prosocial forms of behavior.

Often, however, the accomplishment of these social objectives is considered unimportant for understanding students' intellectual progress at school. Yet, the activities of instruction and learning take place within a larger social context defined by social rules and expectations for behavior that regulate the day-

Advances in Motivation and Achievement, Volume 7, pages 185-212.
Copyright © 1991 by JAI Press Inc.
All rights of reproduction in any form reserved.
ISBN: 1-55938-122-1

to-day activities of the classroom. As such, intellectual development is only one of many objectives that guide the educational process, and the achievement of social and task-related goals is most likely an interactive process in which social and cognitive outcomes are mutually dependent and facilitative.

Clearly, taking such a broad perspective on the nature of educational objectives can frustrate attempts to identify precise links between goals and academic outcomes. However, there are several reasons why studying multiple goals—both social and academic—may enhance our understanding of relations between student motivation and subsequent achievement. First, theories and conceptual frameworks used to study task performance and achievement motivation are based on the notion that qualitatively different goals have the potential to influence motivation and performance outcomes. Second, because classroom teachers tend to value socially competent as well as intellectually competent behavior, it is likely that classroom reward structures and evaluations of student progress will reflect these multiple social and academic goals. Finally, given the social nature of the classroom, students have the opportunity to pursue many goals, both academic and nonacademic. Thus, it is reasonable to expect that students will try to achieve multiple goals and that ways in which students coordinate the pursuit of these goals may also be related directly to their competence at school.

In sum, a recognition that goals for classroom life encompass a wide range of social as well as intellectual concerns can perhaps broaden our understanding of links between students' goals and their educational accomplishments. This paper focuses on ways in which taking a multiple goals perspective can enhance our understanding of the relations between motivational processes and student competence. First, a multiple goals perspective for studying links between motivation and achievement in the classroom is presented. Literature linking achievement with task-related as well as social goals is then reviewed. Next, in support of a multiple goals perspective, findings relating adolescents' social and academic goals with classroom competence are presented. Finally, the implications of a multiple goals perspective for studying goals and self-regulation is discussed.

A MULTIPLE GOALS PERSPECTIVE

Personal goals have been of central theoretical importance for explaining motivational patterns of behavior (Pervin, 1982). In this regard, goals have been described with respect to their content (Ford & Nichols, this volume), orientation (Dweck & Leggett, 1988; Nicholls, 1984), levels of challenge, proximity, and specificity (Bandura, 1986), and their relations with each other (Powers, 1978; Winnell, 1987). Central to all of these descriptions is the notion that people do set goals for themselves and, as cognitive representations of future events, these goals can be powerful motivators of behavior.

Research on motivation and achievement has also identified a wide range of processes that regulate goal pursuit. For example, beliefs concerning one's ability to achieve goals (e.g., Bandura, 1986), beliefs concerning control over achievement outcomes (e.g., Weiner, 1985), and theories about how goals can be attained (e.g., Dweck & Leggett, 1988), all appear to influence the degree to which goals are pursued and actually achieved. Similarly, the ability to protect goals from distractions and sustain goal-directed behavior, to monitor progress, and to adjust behavior in light of feedback are important volitional and control strategies that increase the likelihood of successful goal attainment (Kuhl, 1984, 1985). Thus, other self-regulatory processes appear to motivate behavior and performance as well.

The complex nature of these various motivational and self-regulatory processes underscores the importance of clearly defining what is meant when we talk about goals and the role they play in regulating behavior. In this paper, goals are defined as cognitive representations of what individuals would like to achieve, and their function is to direct behavior toward achieving these outcomes. Thus, goals are part of a network of cognitive representations of the self in which goals specify *what* an individual is trying to accomplish and other processes regulate the degree to which that goal is pursued and ultimately achieved.

A focus on goal content departs from traditional definitions of achievement goals as desires to increase or demonstrate levels of competence or ability (Dweck & Leggett, 1988; Nicholls, 1984). Indeed, with respect to classroom functioning, a focus on the content of students' goals might reveal desires to achieve academically-relevant objectives such as to learn or to be evaluated positively for academic accomplishments, but also social objectives such as to make friends, have fun, be cooperative and helpful, or to comply with social rules and norms. Because these goals may be differentially related to academic accomplishments, this focus also implies that to understand classroom behavior, we need to examine not only the psychological processes that regulate goal pursuit but also the degree to which these "desired outcomes" are rewarded and valued within the classroom context.

A multiple goals perspective is especially important for studying behavior in complex social settings such as the classroom. Work in the area of social competence and social development suggests that competence in social settings often requires the achievement of socially defined goals reflecting approval and acceptance by the social group, as well as those reflecting the achievement of personal competence and feelings of self-determination (see, e.g., Ford, 1985). Research on motivation and achievement is typically focused on the latter set of self-assertive goals. However, the pursuit of socially integrative goals should be equally important for understanding competence in the classroom, especially to the extent they direct behavior toward the achievement of socially derived criteria used to evaluate competence.

In sum, investigating the multiple goals that individuals try to achieve may be especially profitable for understanding behavior in complex social settings such as the classroom. Indeed, competence in social settings most often requires the achievement of multiple goals that have been coordinated into an organized system of behavior. In the following section, the academic and social goals that appear to have value for classroom competence are discussed.

UNDERSTANDING COMPETENCE AT SCHOOL: MULTIPLE VERSUS SINGLE GOALS

As noted earlier, the social nature of the classroom requires that school children pursue nonacademic goals by conforming to rules for social conduct and, in general, behaving in socially appropriate ways. Thus, students are expected to achieve goals that reflect appropriate forms of social behavior as well as academic goals that promote learning and intellectual accomplishments. In addition, however, it seems that multiple academic goals are also necessary to explain children's learning behavior at school. For the most part, research on motivation and academic achievement has been experimental work requiring children to solve problems or engage in tasks that are deliberately designed to be challenging, fun, and exciting. This research has underscored the importance of an intrinsic interest in learning for obtaining positive academic outcomes. Unfortunately, however, much of what children are asked to do in the classroom is not challenging, fun, or exciting. In fact, it is often quite dull and boring! As such, we need to account for academically-related goals that direct children to persist at less than interesting tasks as well as those that represent challenge and excitement.

In this section, literature on academic and social competence at school is reviewed and a multiple goals perspective for explaining relations between students' goals and classroom competence is presented.

Academic Goals and Achievement at School

The idea that goals organize and regulate behavior has been central to research linking achievement motivation to academic performance and related outcomes. Students' goals most often associated with academic outcomes are described as concerns with either task-intrinsic or extrinsic outcomes. Task-intrinsic goals such as task-involved (Nicholls, 1984) or learning (Dweck & Leggett, 1988) goals represent outcomes reflecting the actual process of learning. Such goals can take the form of increased knowledge or task mastery. Task-extrinsic goals such as ego-involved (Nicholls, 1984) or performance (Dweck & Leggett, 1988) goals are those derived from social expectations or values associated with the consequences of task performance. In this case, desired outcomes can take the form of praise or tangible rewards.

Mastery Versus Performance Goals

In most cases, research on goal orientations has generated discussions concerning the relative benefits of one type of goal over another. Indeed, these goal orientations have been consistently related to distinct patterns of behavior when initial attempts to learn result in failure. For instance, the pursuit of task-intrinsic goals has been associated with high levels of effort, persistence at finding solutions to problems, and the development of new or alternative learning strategies. Conversely, extrinsic goal orientations have been associated with helplessness, withdrawal from tasks, and negative emotional states that appear to place children at risk for academic failure (see, Dweck & Leggett, 1988; Lepper & Hodell, 1989; Nicholls, 1984). Nolen (1988) has demonstrated that intrinsic goal orientations are associated with deep, holistic learning characterized by critical thinking and the integration of concepts, whereas extrinsic goal orientations are associated with strategic learning characterized by doing only what is necessary to get the highest grade.

Similarly, research on competitive and individualistic reward structures suggests that the task-related goals teachers set for their students can influence learning behavior in very distinct ways (Ames, 1984; Ames & Ames 1984). Competitive reward structures are those in which evaluation criteria are normative. These structures are most likely to promote performance or ego-involved goal orientations in students, with a concomitant focus on ability attributions for success and comparisons of one's own performance with that of others. In contrast, individualistic reward structures—those in which evaluations are based on individual student progress and self-improvement— tend to promote task-involved or mastery goals, a focus on effort as a reason for success and failure, comparisons of current progress with past performance, and the use of self-regulated learning and study strategies (Ames & Ames, 1984; Ames & Archer, 1988; Nolen, 1988). Thus, links between unique patterns of learning behavior and qualitatively different goals can be found when teachers set goals for their students as well as when students set them for themselves.

Mastery and Performance as Complementary Goals

Given that maladaptive learning behavior is often associated with performance goals and normative standards of evaluation, it has been suggested that educators should actively promote the development of mastery goal orientations toward learning and discourage goals or reward structures that focus on outcomes extrinsic to learning or task-mastery. These findings, however, do not preclude the possibility that students pursue goals that are both intrinsic and extrinsic to the task of learning and that these multiple goals can be coordinated in positive ways to jointly regulate achievement behavior. Indeed, the tradition of comparing and contrasting the differential effects of mastery and performance goals on achievement behavior has led us to ignore the fact that in most cases, students must pursue both mastery and performance goals if they are to succeed at school. In other words, performance goals are inextricably linked to learning goals in that it is impossible to obtain positive judgments of ability without first achieving some level of task mastery.

Moreover, from a societal perspective, a high level of intrinsic motivation by itself may not always be the most desirable motivational state to achieve. Indeed, an implicit goal of educational institutions has always been to socialize children into adult society by teaching work- and responsibility-oriented values such as dependability, punctuality, and obedience in conjunction with the learning process (Dreeben, 1968; Jackson, 1968). As such, learning usually takes place within the constraints of socially prescribed rules and norms that will ensure successful integration into adult society. Competence is most often evaluated in terms of culturally-valued consequences that are attached to task performance. In short, whereas we may delight in the fact that our children have developed an intrinsic love of learning, we also expect them to express these interests in productive, responsible, and future-oriented (i.e., extrinsically motivated) ways.

One way that students can pursue both mastery and performance goals is by coordinating them into a system of hierarchically-related, complementary objectives. For instance, learning goals can focus a student's attention on producing actions necessary for task mastery, whereas performance goals can remind them of the long-term consequences of those actions. Linking mastery and performance goals in this manner suggests that motivation to achieve academically can be strengthened if both are pursued. In other words, it is possible that levels of task involvement and mastery-oriented behavior can be enhanced if task-extrinsic goals such as obtaining good grades or other positive forms of social recognition are also being pursued.

Extrinsic rewards may also be necessary at times to initiate and maintain more intrinsic mastery-oriented goals. For instance, the positive motivational effects of extrinsic rewards may be especially salient when a learning task is not particularly interesting in the first place (e.g., memorizing multiplication tables) but nevertheless essential for subsequent learning and higher-order problem solving. Performance on tests, which often requires demonstrations of skills that are presumably well-learned and therefore no longer challenging, may also be enhanced if an extrinsic reward such as a high grade is being pursued.

That multiple goals can interact in complementary ways is supported by findings suggesting that attempts to master tasks and to gain social approval can combine additively to increase the likelihood of achievement behavior (Atkinson, 1974; Reuman, Atkinson, & Gallop, 1986). Similarly, Nakamura and Finck (1973) found that having both social and task-related goal orientations is associated with better performance outcomes in evaluative situations than having only task-related goals. Work by Lepper and his colleagues suggests that when extrinsic rewards are perceived as an added bonus to task mastery, provide informational feedback, or are related in some meaningful way to the task at hand, they can also promote task-involvement (Lepper & Hodell, 1989).

Social Competence at School

Although goals to learn and to achieve task mastery are undoubtedly necessary for learning to take place, the achievement of socially prescribed goals may also have a significant and positive impact on achievement behavior and actual levels of performance. Presumably, this is because evaluations of academic competence reflect not only learning and mastery, but displays of learning and mastery in socially appropriate ways.

In addition, however, students are required to achieve goals that govern social interaction in the classroom, reflecting cooperation, respect for others, and positive forms of group participation. Although adherence to rules and norms for social conduct is a form of social competence valued by both students and teachers, the pursuit of these social goals may also be important for achieving positive academic outcomes. On the one hand, social competence can be a valued educational objective in and of itself. As such, goals to be socially competent may contribute directly to evaluations of classroom performance.

On the other hand, social competence is reflected in the quality of students' social relationships with teachers and peers. In turn, the quality of these relationships often has an impact on instruction and learning. Thus, goals to be socially competent may contribute to achievement indirectly by promoting the development of positive relationships with teachers and peers.

Although little is known about relations between social goals and academic outcomes, objective indices of social responsibility have been associated with various aspects of school performance. For instance, correlational studies have linked positive intellectual outcomes in the elementary years with tendencies to be prosocial and empathic (Feshbach & Feshbach, 1987), positive interactions with peers (Cobb, 1972; Green, Forehand, Beck, & Vosk, 1980), appropriate classroom conduct (Entwistle, Alexander, Cadigan, & Pallas, 1986; Lambert & Nicoll, 1977), and compliance (Cobb, 1972; Kohn & Rosman, 1973). Longitudinal studies linking social competence to academic achievement have been less frequent but have yielded the same general conclusions (Feldhusen, Thurston, & Benning, 1970; Safer, 1986). In the following sections, literature on social competence as a goal for education and as a mediator between academic achievement and relationships with both teachers and peers is described.

Social Competence as a Goal for Education

One form of social competence that appears to be an especially important component of academic accomplishments reflects socially responsible forms of behavior. At the policy level, such behavior in the form of moral character, conformity to social rules and norms, cooperation, and positive styles of social interaction has been a traditional and valued educational objective for American schools. Indeed, character development and social responsibility in general have been stated as explicit objectives for public schools in almost every educational policy statement since 1848, being promoted with the same frequency as the development of academic skills (see Wentzel, 1991a).

The suggestion that social responsibility is an important educational objective is also supported by literature indicating that teachers value socially competent behavior, and spend an enormous amount of time teaching their students how to behave and act responsibly. Indeed, teachers appear to have common social rules and norms that they expect students to follow (Hargreaves, Hester, & Mellor, 1975; LeCompte, 1978a, 1978b). For the most part, these classroom rules are designed to establish classroom order and the hierarchical nature of teacher-student relationships. However, teachers establish norms for peer relationships that also focus on considerate, cooperative, and morally responsible forms of behavior (Hargreaves et al., 1975; Sieber, 1979).

Relationships with Teachers and Academic Performance

For teachers, students' adherence to classroom rules allows them to focus their efforts on teaching rather than classroom management. Presumably, students learn more when this occurs. Relations between student behavior and learning are not well understood. However, it seems that student characteristics can influence the nature of teacher-student interactions and thus, the quality of individual instruction received. Several studies have asked teachers to identify students toward whom they feel attachment, concern, indifference, or rejection (see Brophy & Good, 1974, for an in-depth review of this literature). When observed in the classroom, these students displayed markedly different types of behavior: "attachment" students were typically bright, hardworking, and model students; "concern" students made excessive but appropriate demands for teachers' attention; "indifference" students had few contacts with teachers; and "rejection" students typically displayed problem behavior and made illegitimate demands for attention.

The teachers observed in these studies rarely showed favoritism toward model students. In contrast, however, teachers interacted with the "concern" and "rejection" students in noticeably different ways. Whereas the "concern" students were allowed to approach teachers freely and were given subsequent help and encouragement, "rejection" students were typically criticized and refused help. Thus, this work suggests that students who are socially irresponsible are treated negatively and most likely receive less one-on-one instruction than other students. The effects of behaving appropriately on individual instruction are less clear.

Relationships with Peers and Academic Performance

The dual role of social responsibility in promoting both social and academic competence is also supported by evidence that peer relationships have the potential to influence classroom performance and learning outcomes in positive ways. Within the classroom, students tend to interact with each other more than with their teachers (Nelson-Le Gall & Glor-Scheib, 1987). Because these interactions are typically under constant teacher supervision (Sieber, 1979), they can often complement teacher behavior in ways that directly support the instructional process. First, students can provide each other with valuable resources necessary to accomplish academic tasks. For instance, students frequently clarify and interpret their teacher's instructions, provide mutual assistance, and share various supplies such as pencils and paper (Sieber, 1979). Second, classmates provide each other with information by modeling both academic and social competencies and establishing normative standards for performance (Ruble, 1983; Schunk, 1987).

Relationships with peers can also have a strong influence on a student's emotional and motivational response to school. For example, positive relationships with peers can provide emotional security and incentives to achieve (Ladd & Price, 1987; Schwarz, 1972), whereas the loss of a familiar peer group can have negative effects on self-esteem and general interest in school (Miller, 1983). During adolescence especially, peers can have a direct influence on the degree to which students like school and plan to go to college (Epstein, 1983). Finally, perceived isolation from peers as well as perceived lack of control in obtaining social support at school have been related to low levels of achievement (Epperson, 1963).

Summary

Most research linking academic goals and accomplishments has focused on identifying distinct patterns of behavior associated with mastery and performance goals. As a consequence, discussions of achievement motivation have generated interest in promoting the development of mastery goals and discouraging the pursuit of performance goals. In contrast, a multiple goals perspective suggests that students need to pursue both types of goals in order to succeed at school. Indeed, it appears that at least under some circumstances, pursuing performance goals can enhance motivation and contribute in positive ways to achievement outcomes. In addition, it has been suggested that the pursuit of social goals, in particular those concerned with socially responsible outcomes, may also combine with academic goals in positive ways to enhance learning and performance.

Research that focuses explicitly on students' pursuit of multiple goals has not been widespread. During adolescence especially, when children are expected to achieve a wide range of social and academic competencies, little is known about the types of goals that students actually try to accomplish while they are at school or how the pursuit of multiple goals is related to students' academic and social accomplishments. In the following section, research on adolescents' classroom goals is presented. In particular, the role of multiple goals in predicting both academic and social competence is discussed.

RESEARCH ON CLASSROOM GOALS

Adolescence is a particularly interesting period of development for studying multiple goals in that children at this age become increasingly challenged to achieve a wide range of goals in preparation for adulthood (see e.g., Havighurst, 1972). With respect to schooling, adolescents are expected to master more difficult and abstract academic curricula, often with some future educational or occupational goal in mind, to establish emotional and psychological independence from adults while maintaining a respect and appreciation for adult values and authority, and to form positive and healthy relationships with their peers.

In short, during adolescence, children experience new demands to coordinate a diverse set of social and academic goals in positive and complementary ways. Moreover, adolescents are expected to achieve these goals despite competing demands to do otherwise. Indeed, the critical importance of achieving these goals is perhaps most salient when they are not achieved, that is, when adolescents drop out of school or participate in socially irresponsible forms of behavior such as cheating or vandalism with their classmates.

The predictive utility of a multiple goals perspective is suggested by findings from a series of studies designed to assess the types of goals that adolescents try to achieve at school and how these goals are related to academic success and social competence. In a first study, relations between students' goals and academic achievement were investigated in a group of 203 high school students (see Wentzel, 1987, 1989). In a second study, goals were studied in relation to academic performance, social status among peers, and teachers' preferences for students in a sample of 423 junior high school students and their teachers (Wentzel, 1991b).

Study I: Goals and Academic Achievement

The first study was designed to explore the possibility that academic achievement is related to adolescents' goals to achieve social as well as academic outcomes. As such, this research focused on academic performance as measured by grade-point averages (GPAs) and how often students tried to achieve a set of 12 goals while they were in class at school. The twelve goals were: being a successful student, earning approval from others in the class, having fun, being better than others in the class, getting others to help you, being dependable and responsible, making and keeping friendships, being helpful to others, learning new things, understanding things, doing the very best that you can, and getting things done on time. The goal measure consisted of students' reports of how often they tried to achieve each of these goals. As such, students' goals reflected what they perceived themselves as trying to accomplish at school (see Emmons, 1989, for a similar approach to goal assessment).

Single Goals

As expected, adolescents said they tried to achieve each of the twelve goals to differing degrees. Interestingly, achieving both social responsibility goals and academic mastery goals was of concern to this group of high school students. Students reported trying to make friends and have fun most often, but not significantly more often than trying to learn new things and to be dependable and responsible. In contrast, students reported trying to be better than others and trying to get help from others least often. In addition, effort to achieve seven of the twelve goals was related significantly to student GPAs. Goals positively related to student grades were to be a successful student, be dependable and responsible, learn new things, understand things, do your best, and get things done on time. Trying to have fun was related negatively to academic achievement.

Multiple Goals

Of additional interest was whether the relations between academic performance and student effort could be explained more precisely by examining the sets of goals that students pursued at school. To study these relations, patterns of goal pursuit in a subset of students belonging to achievement-defined groups were analyzed. Specifically, three achievement groups were studied: High GPA students (cumulative GPAs greater than or equal to an A−, $n = 25$), Medium GPA students (cumulative GPAs equivalent to a C+, $n = 25$), and Low GPA students (cumulative GPAs of a D+ or less, $n = 27$).

As shown in Table 1, the patterns of goal pursuit were quite different for each achievement group. The Spearman Rho correlation of goal rankings was .32 for the High and Medium GPA groups, .04 for the High and Low GPA groups, and .59 for the Medium and Low GPA groups. Indeed, each achievement group reported trying to achieve very different types of goals. For example, fewer students in the Low GPA group reported always trying to earn approval and trying to be dependable and responsible than did those in the High and Medium GPA groups. Of particular interest is the finding that as many Low GPA students reported always trying to learn as did Medium GPA students. Thus, these students were unique only in that fewer reported trying to pursue social responsibility goals. In addition, the High GPA group was unique in that fewer of these students reported always trying to have fun than did students in the Medium and Low GPA groups, and more High GPA students reported trying to be better than others, learn new things, understand things, and do their very best than did those in the Medium and Low GPA groups.

Case-by-case analyses were also conducted to identify the sets of goals that individual students pursued. These analyses revealed that 84% of the High GPA students reported always trying to achieve at least three goals: be a successful student, be dependable and responsible, and get things done on time; only 33% of these students indicated they they always try to have fun in classes at school. In the Low GPA group, 69% reported that they always try to have fun and to make or keep friendships. Only 13% of this group said they always try to achieve the three goals that High GPA students reported always trying to achieve (be a successful student, be dependable and responsible, get things done on time). In the Medium GPA group, 76% reported always trying to be dependable and responsible and to make or keep friendships. Thus, within each group, results were relatively homogeneous in terms of the sets of goals students always tried and rarely tried to pursue.

Summary

The results of this first study suggest that adolescents try to achieve a wide range of goals at school that reflect academic and socially responsible objectives as well as concern with having fun and being with friends. Moreover, individual differences in academic achievement were related to unique patterns of goal pursuit. What is particularly interesting about the achievement group data is that although the High GPA students reported frequent pursuit of academic mastery goals (i.e., to learn new things, to understand things), less frequent pursuit of these goals did not distinguish low-achieving students from average students. However, the Low GPA students were unlike other students in that they reported rarely trying to earn approval from others or to be dependable and responsible. Thus, whereas an increase in motivation to learn may improve

Table 1. Percentages of High, Medium, and Low GPA Students Always Trying to Achieve Classroom Goals

High GPA (n = 25)		Medium GPA (n = 25)		Low GPA (n = 27)	
Goal[a]	% always trying	Goal	% always trying	Goal	% always trying
On time	92[b]	Friends	88[c]	Fun	74[d]
Successful	92	Responsible	76	Friends	74
Responsible	84	Fun	72	Learn	56
Do best	80	Approval	64	Understand	44
Understand	80	On Time	56	Be helpful	41
Learn	76	Learn	52	Do best	33
Approval	72	Understand	48	Responsible	30
Friends	68	Successful	48	Approval	26
Be helpful	52	Be helpful	48	On time	22
Fun	40	Do best	40	Successful	19
Be better	24	Be better	12	Get help	11
Get help	12	Get help	12	Be better	11

Notes: [a] Goals: Successful = Be a successful student; Approval = Earn approval from others; Fun = Have fun; Be better = Be better than others; Get help = Get others to help you; Responsible = Be dependable and responsible; Friends = Make or keep friendships; Be helpful = Be helpful to others; Learn = Learn new things; Understand = Understand things; Do best = Do your very best; On time = Get things done on time.
[b] Of the High GPA students, 84% reported always trying to get things done on time, be successful students, and to be dependable and responsible.
[c] Of the Medium GPA students, 75% reported always trying to make and keep friendships and to be dependable and responsible.
[d] Of the Low GPA students, 69% reported always trying to have fun and to make and keep friendships.

Source: Wentzel (1989, p. 135). Reprinted with permission.

the academic performance of both average and low achievers, it appears that failure to try to conform to the social and normative standards of the classroom uniquely characterizes the least competent students.

Study II: Multiple Goals and Multiple Outcomes

In a second study of early adolescents, relations between students' goals and academic outcomes were again investigated. In this case, the social value of students' goals was also investigated by examining relations between the pursuit of goals and students' social status among peers as well as their acceptance by classroom teachers.

Based on the results of the earlier study, scales were developed to assess five academic and social goals. Two academic goals reflected efforts to master new and challenging things (4 items, alpha = .78) and to earn positive evaluations (5 items, alpha = .78). Sample items for the mastery and evaluation goals, respectively, are: "How often do you try to learn things because its a challenge?" "How often do you try to show your teachers how smart you are?" Conceptually, these academic goals correspond to mastery and performance goals as they are typically used in studies of motivation and achievement (e.g., Ames & Archer, 1988; Elliot & Dweck, 1988).

Two social responsibility goals reflected efforts to be prosocial (helpful to others, cooperative and sharing; 6 items, alpha = .84) and compliant (following rules, keeping promises and commitments; 7 items, alpha = .74). Sample items for prosocial and compliance goals, respectively, are: "How often do you try to help other kids when they have a problem?" "How often do you try to do what your teacher asks you to?" One social interaction goal reflected efforts to do things with peers rather than by one's self, for example, "How often do you try to ʋe with other kids rather than by yourself?" (3 items, alpha = .64).

The degree to which students reported trying to achieve the five goals differed significantly depending on goal content. Students reported trying to achieve social interaction goals significantly more often than all other goals, and to achieve the two social responsibility goals and the evaluation goal significantly more often than the mastery goal (Wentzel, 1991b).

Multiple Goals and Academic Performance

As in the first study, goal pursuit differed as a function of student achievement when the goals of High, Medium and Low achievement groups were compared. In this case, students in the High GPA group had cumulative GPAs equivalent to an A— or better ($n = 76$), Medium GPA students had cumulative GPAs equivalent to a C+ ($n = 78$), and the Low GPA students had cumulative GPAs of a D+ or lower ($n = 78$). Results of a series of one-way analyses of variance (ANOVAs) indicated that social interaction goals did not differ significantly as a function of achievement group. This finding is important in its suggestion that trying to interact with peers is not, in and of itself, detrimental to classroom learning. The pursuit of academic and social responsibility goals did differentiate the achievement groups in that the High GPA students reported trying to achieve the two academic goals and the two social responsibility goals significantly more often than did the Medium and Low GPA groups. The goal patterns of the Medium and Low GPA groups did not differ significantly from one another.

With respect to multiple goals, two additional findings are noteworthy. First, combinations of mastery and evaluation goal pursuit differed as a function of student achievement (χ^2 (6, $N = 204$) = 24.00; $p < .001$). Of particular interest is that 59% of the High GPA students reported high levels of effort for both mastery and evaluation goals as compared to 42% of the Medium GPA group and 30% of the Low GPA group. In contrast, only 17% of the High GPA students reported low levels of effort for both mastery and evaluation goals, whereas 45% of both the Medium and Low GPA groups reported low levels of effort for both of these goals. Similar results were obtained for the two social responsibility goals (χ^2 (6, $N = 204$) = 19.14, $p < .01$). High levels of effort to achieve both prosocial and compliance goals were reported by 51%, 35%, and 26% of the High, Medium, and Low GPA groups, respectively. Students reporting low levels of effort to achieve both goals represented 14%, 38%, and 43% of the High, Medium, and Low GPA groups, respectively.

Finally, composite scores representing average academic (mastery and evaluation) and social responsibility (prosocial and compliance) goal scores were computed to compare combinations of academic and social goal pursuit across levels of student achievement. Once again, findings indicated a significant relationship between combinations of goal pursuit and achievement (χ (6, $N = 204$) = 15.60, $p < .01$). In this case, 59% of the High GPA students reported trying to achieve high levels of both social responsibility and academic goals as compared to 21% who reported high levels of only one type of goal, and 20% who reported low levels of effort for both goals. Only 38% of the Medium GPA students and 34% of the Low GPA students reported high levels of effort for both social responsibility and academic goals, whereas 38% and 40% of the Medium and Low GPA students, respectively, reported low levels of effort to achieve both goals. In a follow-up of student achievement one year later, these combinations of social responsibility and academic goals remained significant predictors of academic performance as measured by both grades and standardized test scores (see Wentzel, 1991b).

As in the first study, these results suggest that academic achievement is related to the sets of goals that students pursue at school. Moreover, these goals include social responsibility as well as academic goals. What is particularly important to note in these findings is that mastery and performance goals, and at a more general level, academic and social responsibility goals, appear to have an additive effect on achievement. In other words, pursuing both goals seems to be related to the most optimal achievement outcomes.

Multiple Goals and Social Competence

A second set of analyses was conducted to investigate relations between students' goals and their social acceptance by classmates and teachers. Social acceptance among classmates was measured using sociometric techniques designed to identify popular, rejected, neglected, controversial, and average status children. Briefly, popular children are those with many friends and who are disliked by few of their peers, rejected children have few friends and are disliked by many of their peers, neglected children have few friends but are not disliked by their peers, and controversial children are those with many friends but who are also disliked by many of their peers. (See Wentzel, 1991c, for a description of the procedure used to measure sociometric status.)

Results from ANOVAs suggested that the status groups did not differ in their pursuit of academic mastery and evaluation goals (see Table 2). However, patterns of social goal pursuit uniquely characterized the status groups. For instance, popular children reported trying to achieve social interaction and prosocial goals significantly more often than average status children. Rejected children tried to achieve social interaction goals significantly less often than their average status classmates. Neglected children reported trying to achieve the two social responsibility goals significantly more often than their average status classmates. Finally, controversial children reported trying to achieve compliance goals significantly less often than average status children.

Thus, as with academic achievement, social competence as defined by social status among classmates appears to be related to the unique sets of goals that students try to achieve at school. Moreover, the sets of goals related to social competence overlap with goals related to achievement. In particular, the two social responsibility goals were positively related to acceptance by peers as well as to academic achievement. The significance of this overlap in goals is suggested by findings indicating that popular and neglected students (the two status groups with the highest levels of social acceptance by peers) also earn significantly higher grades than children in other status groups (see Wentzel, 1991c). Thus, the pursuit of social responsibility goals may be a necessary (albeit insufficient) requirement for achievement in both social and academic domains of functioning.

Finally, relations between students' goals and acceptance by teachers were investigated. To assess teachers' acceptance of students, teachers were asked to rate how much they would like to have each of their students in their class again next year. In this case, only a small set of goals was related to teachers' preference for students. As shown in Table 2, students reporting high levels of effort to achieve evaluation and compliance goals were preferred by teachers

Table 2. Social and Academic Goals of Sociometric Status and Teacher Preference Groups

Goals	Status Groups[a]						Teacher Preference Groups[bc]			
	Popular	Rejected	Neglected	Controversial	Average	F	High Preference	Medium Preference	Low Preference	F
Social Interaction	.39[a]	−.51[a]	.12	.04	.07	6.75**	−.15	.02	−.01	.48
Social Responsibility										
Compliance	−.10	−.01	.38[a]	−.47[a]	.03	4.89**	.31[b]	.08[c]	−.31[bc]	5.82*
Prosocial	.26[a]	−.36	.23[a]	−.21	−.07	4.72**	.13	.05	−.19	1.52
Academic										
Learning	−.01	.03	.19	−.30	−.11	1.71	.14	−.12	−.17	1.57
Evaluation	−.07	.01	.05	−.18	−.02	.41	.18[b]	.07[c]	−.30[bc]	3.77*

Notes: Mean standardized scores are shown.
[a] Means are significantly different from the average group at $p < .05$, as determined by planned contrasts.
[bc] Means having the same subscript are significantly different at $p < .05$.
* $p < .01$; ** $p < .001$.

significantly more than other students. The pursuit of mastery, prosocial, and interaction goals was not related significantly to teachers' preference for students. What is intriguing in this set of findings is that the set of goals related to teachers' preference for students is only a subset of the goals related to high levels of achievement. As such, these results suggest that the students most preferred by teachers are not necessarily those with the highest grades. Rather, they are the students who try to comply to social rules and norms and who are concerned with obtaining positive evaluations of their work.

Summary

The results of this second study confirm the potential of a multiple goals perspective for understanding links between motivation and competence at school. First, it appears that both task mastery and more extrinsic, evaluation goals can combine in positive ways to influence achievement outcomes. Moreover, these findings indicate that goals to be socially responsible are positively related to academic performance and may contribute to achievement outcomes independently of academic goals. Finally, this research identified motivational patterns common to positive outcomes in both social and academic domains of functioning. In particular, the pursuit of social responsibility goals appears to be related positively to academic achievement, teachers' preferences for students, and social acceptance among peers.

Summary and Conclusions

This research was designed to identify ways in which multiple goals are related to adolescent competence at school. Of special interest are findings suggesting that both task-mastery and evaluation goals are related positively to achievement outcomes and that students who try to achieve both types of goals earn higher grades than those who try to achieve only one of these goals or neither goal. Social responsibility goals appear to be related to academic performance as well as to competence within the peer group.

These findings are intriguing in that they appear to contradict previous conclusions that students who pursue evaluation goals or more general task-extrinsic goals are at risk for undesirable achievement outcomes. One possible explanation is that maladaptive outcomes typically associated with achievement goals reflect the belief systems and regulatory processes that regulate goal pursuit rather than *what* it is that students are trying to achieve. Indeed, theories of motivation and achievement, have been developed around the notion that goals can and do interact with each other to produce achievement behavior. For instance, in work by McClelland and Atkinson (Atkinson, 1964; McClelland et al., 1953), the relative strength of two competing goals—to approach success and to avoid failure—was hypothesized to predict the strength of achievement motives. Further, it was hypothesized that the relative strength of these emotions would direct subsequent choice of tasks or levels of task difficulty.

In a more recent conceptualization of achievement motivation, Dweck and Leggett (1988) have also used approach and avoidance tendencies to describe links between performance goal orientations and patterns of behavior. These authors suggest that performance goals reflect two concerns: obtaining positive judgments and avoiding negative judgments of competence. When ability is perceived to be high (i.e., success is anticipated), individuals are expected to engage in mastery behavior that will lead to favorable judgments. In contrast, when perceived ability is low (i.e., failure is anticipated), helpless and avoidance patterns of behavior that preclude negative evaluations ensue (see also, Elliot & Dweck, 1988).

These theories suggest that regulatory processes such as emotional control and perceived self-efficacy are instrumental in achieving one's goals. Thus, it is not goals per se, but goals interacting with other processes that explain the maladaptive behavior often associated with the pursuit of task-extrinsic goals. Indeed, research on self-regulated learning (see Zimmerman & Schunk, 1989) and action control (Kuhl, 1984, 1985) has clearly demonstrated that learning behavior is the result of a complex and interactive set of processes that include goals as well as other cognitive, emotional, and environmental factors.

In light of a multiple goals perspective, this work suggests that failure to achieve or debilitation under conditions of failure may reflect ways in which the pursuit of multiple goals is influenced by other self-regulatory processes, in particular, processes that result in an inability to coordinate the pursuit of goals in adaptive ways. In the following section, the ability to coordinate goals into an organized system of functioning is discussed as one form of self-regulation that is particularly important for understanding the effects of multiple goals on behavior.

GOAL COORDINATION AND SELF-REGULATION

As defined earlier, the unique function of goals is to direct behavior toward achieving a particular outcome or set of outcomes. In the classroom especially, children are required to achieve multiple goals that reflect socially-prescribed objectives as well as task-related goals to develop intellectual and academic competencies. The achievement of goals, however, is dependent on other processes and skills that facilitate or constrain goal pursuit. One skill that is particularly relevant for the achievement of multiple goals is the ability to resolve conflicts among competing goals or seemingly incompatible goals.

Negative Consequences of Competing Goals

Conflicts among competing goals can be resolved in many ways, and failure to achieve one's goals does not automatically lead to decreased motivation or maladaptive problem solving. In fact, initial failure most often results in increased efforts and only after repeated unsuccessful attempts are goals abandoned altogether (Kuhl, 1984, 1985). However, pursuing too many goals or placing too much attention on social or performance-related goals may place children at risk for less than optimal achievement outcomes.

Negative academic consequences are most often found when mastery and performance goals conflict with each other. On the one hand, such conflicts may result in students placing an inordinate amount of attention on the pursuit of performance goals. Over time, this focus may undermine the pursuit of more intrinsic, mastery goals and, under conditions of repreated failure to perform well, may overpower and stop the pursuit of matery goals altogether (Dweck & Leggett, 1988). In such cases, abandoning mastery-oriented subgoals would make more abstract performance goals impossible to achieve as well. Conversely, an inordinate amount of attention can also be placed on achieving task-intrinsic goals. At the extreme, this may lead to self-absorbed or socially inappropriate patterns of behavior. Moreover, a lack of long-term performance or socially derived evaluation goals may result in a child's becoming isolated or alienated from the social life of the classroom.

Socially prescribed goals can compete with self-set goals in similar ways. For instance, reward structures that focus on extrinsic rewards can be detrimental to performance when they focus students' attention on the consequences of learning rather than on learning itself. These effects become especially salient when extrinsic rewards are superfluous or prominent relative to intrinsic rewards, or when they provide a reasonable and sufficient justification for task involvement. In particular, the use of extrinsic rewards can be detrimental to motivation and performance when children are engaged in incidental learning tasks, tasks requiring creativity or insight, or tasks for which childrens' intrinsic interest is initially high (see Lepper & Hodell, 1989, for a detailed review of this literature).

In learning contexts where cooperative learning is stressed, social and academic goals such as learning algebra and interacting with peers may combine additively to promote positive social interactions as well as academic achievement. However, students who are unable to coordinate the pursuit of these goals in adaptive ways may have trouble focusing attention on either goal and experience anxiety or frustration when required to do so. As a consequence, these students may abandon more difficult learning goals (e.g., solving an algebra problem) to achieve more easily attainable social goals (e.g., have fun with friends).

Although studied less frequently, students who are unable to coordinate social responsibility goals and academic goals may also display maladaptive learning behavior. The issue of competing social responsibility and achievement goals is especially relevant for children from minority cultures who are expected to behave at school in ways that are inconsistent with those espoused by their families and community. For instance, McDermott (1974) describes how not learning to read can be interpreted by some minority children as an achievement rather than a failure. In such cases, noncompliance with institutional norms and standards for achievement can lead to acceptance within the minority community. Similarly, Sindell (1974) describes how children with traditional attitudes toward compliance and obedience have difficulty adapting to learning situations requiring self-reliant and competitive behavior.

Strategies for Goal Coordination

Trying to achieve too many goals or an inability to resolve competing or incompatible goals can make the pursuit of multiple goals detrimental to classroom learning. The solution, however, does not necessarily have to be to change students' goals or lower expectations for the number of outcomes they are to achieve. Rather, students need to develop strategies that enable them to achieve multiple goals in appropriate and complementary ways.

Organizing goals in hierarchical fashion appears to be one promising strategy for successful goal coordination. For instance, Bandura and Schunk (1981) suggest that setting explicit proximal subgoals in the service of larger but future goals ensures greater persistence, enhanced perceptions of self-efficacy, and increased intrinsic interest for children in learning situations. Studies of future time perspective also suggest that students who perceive their present behavior as facilitating the achievement of long-term objectives show more positive motivational and achievement outcomes than students with more negative attitudes about the future (Raynor, 1974; Wolf & Savickas, 1985).

This research suggests that the tendency to organize goals hierarchically can contribute in positive ways to learning and academic performance. These positive outcomes occur because the setting of proximal subgoals cultivates a greater sense of self-efficacy—positive performance on smaller and easily managed tasks provides immediate feedback and information concerning the likelihood of future success. In turn, the development of self-efficacy generates increased interest in task engagement and mastery that eventually leads to the accomplishment of more distal or future goals (see Bandura, 1986).

With respect to mastery-performance goal hierarchies, this research suggests that maladaptive responses to failure can be changed by focusing children's attention on mastery subgoals and teaching them how to achieve performance goals in an incremental fashion. At a more general level, this research suggests that students need to approach educational tasks with a recognition that academic success requires the achievement of many goals and that the achievement of specific subgoals—the *process* of learning—is as important as earning high grades, attending college, or a future job—the *products* of learning.

Most educators would support the notion that education reflects both the means and ends of instruction and learning. For instance, the development of an intrinsic pleasure in reading is undoubtedly as important as the mastery of the actual mechanics of word recognition and comprehension. Clearly, however, one cannot be easily achieved without the other. Thus, making relationships between subgoals and end products more obvious and explicit may result in more effective instructional strategies as well as provide students with a clearer rationale for much of what they are asked to do at school.

In the case of competing goals, action control strategies may be especially critical for successful goal coordination. Briefly, action control strategies have been defined as metacognitive processes that protect goal-directed behavior from competing goals, including social pressures and other psychological processes that may constrain goal pursuit such as perceptions of low self-efficacy or feelings of helplessness (Kuhl, 1985). In particular, Kuhl has identified five types of control strategies: selective attention or attention control, selective encoding of information or encoding control, inhibition of negative emotional states or emotion control, enhancing the strength of goal priorities or motivation control, manipulating the social environment or environmental control, and parsimonious decision making. Research on these strategies has just begun (Corno, 1989; Kuhl, 1985). However, an understanding of these strategies seems essential for helping students coordinate demands to achieve multiple and often conflicting goals at school.

Finally, educators can create learning environments that deliberately set up competing or conflicting goals for students to resolve. Indeed, research suggests that cognitive conflict and social interactional processes associated with peer learning contexts can contribute in positive ways to cognitive and intellectual development (Damon & Phelps, 1989; Doise, 1985; Webb, 1982). Thus, designing learning environments that require the negotiation and resolution of conflicting interpersonal goals can have a positive and facilitative effect on intellectual development.

FUTURE DIRECTIONS AND CONCLUSIONS

In this paper, it has been argued that goals for classroom life encompass a wide range of social as well as intellectual outcomes. The goals that teachers and students have for schooling are numerous and complex, reflecting both social and intellectual concerns. At the policy level as well, educational objectives have included goals for the development of social competencies as well as scholastic achievements, for producing model citizens as well as scholars. As Dewey observed, "it is well to remind ourselves that education as such has no aims. Only persons, parents, and teachers, etc., have aims . . . . (Brown, 1970, p. 154). Thus, in a discussion of educational goals and achievement, it seems important to recognize that what is accomplished in the classroom reflects goals that serve the needs of many different people. Moroever, it follows that the educational achievements of individual children will reflect ways in which these multiple goals have been negotiated and coordinated to guide the development of intellectual as well as social competencies.

Work on motivation and achievement has paid little attention to the possibility that classroom learning is linked to other aspects of children's development. However, the findings reported in this chapter suggest that the achievement of social and task-related goals is most likely an interactive process in which social and cognitive outcomes are mutually dependent and facilitative. These findings are noteworthy in several respects.

First, goals to be socially responsible and, in particular, to comply to rules and norms for behavior, seem to play a key role in promoting academic achievement as well as social acceptance by peers and teachers. Often, compliance is viewed as a rather undesirable characteristic in that it can undermine feelings of self-determination, creativity, and independent thinking. Moreover, negative sanctions for noncompliance in the classroom can lead to conforming, obedient, and submissive behavior on the one hand, or to even more deviant and defiant behavior on the other. However, in the eyes of the beholder, adherence to rules and norms connotes trustworthiness, loyalty, and respect, characteristics that are not only valued, but necessary for maintaining stable and harmonious social groups. Thus, it seems to be important for children to develop a respect for social rules and expectations for behavior.

As with childrearing, inductive reasoning and positive sanctions for socially responsible behavior may be one way to promote classroom compliance without jeopardizing feelings of autonomy and personal control (see Condry, 1987; Maccoby, 1980). This notion is supported by findings of Hamilton and colleagues in their comparative work on Japanese and American school children. These authors found that Japanese children's reasons for learning were more internalized and empathic than those of American children and reflected an identification with adult authority (Hamilton, Blumenfeld, Akoh, & Muira, 1989a, 1989b). Of special interest is that Japanese teachers were observed to stress the positive consequences of conformity and compliance, whereas American teachers tended to stress the negative consequences of noncompliance (Hamilton et al., 1989b). These findings suggest that classroom behavior management strategies can be developed that do not have the potentially negative consequences typically associated with extrinsic reward structures.

Second, findings reported in this chapter suggest that classroom competence requires the achievement of socially defined goals that result in approval and acceptance by the social group as well as the achievement of more self-assertive goals that reflect task mastery and personal competence. In general, we know very little about how these sets of goals develop over the course of the school years, nor the relative contribution of schooling and family socialization processes to individual differences in children's ability to coordinate these goals.

With respect to social responsibility, it is clear that teachers and students actively promote socially responsible forms of conduct at school. However, the degree to which teachers and peers actually teach social responsibility as opposed to reinforcing social behavior learned at home is not well understood. Furthermore, the contribution of various socialization agents to the development of responsible behavior may also change with age. Whereas parents and teachers may facilitate development in the early years, peers may play an increasingly important role as children reach adolescence.

Achieving a balance between social and academic goals may also change with age. For instance, we know that intrinsic interest in schooling declines as children reach high school (Harter, 1981). On the one hand, this may reflect an increase in demands to achieve social responsibility goals from adults. In addition, however, competing demands from peers may focus attention on other intrinsically interesting (albeit social) tasks such as forming new friendships. Thus, how children's goal priorities change as a function of development and perhaps competing socialization agents is a particularly interesting question for further study.

Finally, we are beginning to understand the important role of other regulatory processes in facilitating and constraining goal-directed behavior. Much of this research has focused on emotions and cognitions related to task performance. However, given the social nature of learning and instruction, the potential for social emotions and social cognitions to influence classroom motivation and performance cannot be ignored. For instance, social emotions such as guilt and trust have been positively related to socially responsible behavior as well as achievement-related outcomes (Ford, Wentzel, Wood, Stevens, & Seisfeld, 1989; Wentzel, 1991c). Similarly, social cognitions such as perceived opportunities to pursue goals and perceived adult and peer expectations for behavior have been linked with effort to achieve both social and academic goals at school (Wentzel, 1987, 1989). Understanding these social processes in relation to classroom motivation and performance presents an intriguing and challenging agenda for future research in this area.

ACKNOWLEDGMENTS

Preparation of this paper was supported by a post-doctoral training grant from the National Institute of Child Health and Human Development to the Department of

Psychology, University of Illinois, Urbana-Champaign. Thanks are due to Martin Ford for his comments on an earlier draft of this paper.

REFERENCES

Ames, C. (1984). Competitive, cooperative, and individualistic goal structures: A cognitive-motivational analysis. In R. Ames & C. Ames (Eds.), *Research on motivation in education* (Vol. 1, pp. 177-208). New York: Academic Press.

Ames, C., & Ames, R. (1984). Systems of student and teacher motivation: Toward a qualitative definition. *Journal of Educational Psychology, 76*, 535-556.

Ames, C., & Archer, J. (1988). Achievement goals in the classroom: Students' learning strategies and motivation processes. *Journal of Educational Psychology, 80*, 260-267.

Atkinson, J. W. (1964). *An introduction to motivation.* Princeton, NJ: Van Nostrand.

_____. (1974). Strength of motivation and efficiency of performance. In J. W. Atkinson & J. O. Raynor (Eds.), *Motivation and achievement* (pp. 193-218). New York: Wiley.

Bandura, A. (1986). *Social foundations of thought and action: A social cognitive theory.* Englewood Cliffs, NJ: Prentice Hall.

Bandura, A., & Schunk, D. (1981). Cultivating competence, self-efficacy and intrinsic interest through proximal self-motivation. *Journal of Personality and Social Psychology, 41*, 586-598.

Brophy, J. E., & Good, T. L. (1974). *Teacher-student relationships: Causes and consequences.* New York: Holt, Rinehart, & Winston.

Brown, L. M. (1970). *Aims of education.* New York: Teachers College Press.

Cobb, J. A. (1972). Relationship of discrete classroom behaviors to fourth-grade academic achievement. *Journal of Educational Psychology, 63*, 74-80.

Condry, J. (1987). Enhancing motivation: A social developmental perspective. In M. L. Maehr & D. A. Kleiber (Eds.), *Advances in motivation and achievement* (Vol. 5, pp. 23-49). Greenwich, CT: JAI Press.

Corno, L. (1989). Self-regulated learning: A volitional analysis. In B. J. Zimmerman & D. H. Schunk (Eds.), *Self-regulated learning and academic achievement: Theory, research, and practice* (pp. 111-141). New York: Springer-Verlag.

Damon, W., & Phelps, E. (1989). Strategic uses of peer learning in children's education. In T. J. Berndt & G. W. Ladd (Eds.), *Peer relationships in child development* (pp. 133-157). New York: Wiley.

Doise, W. (1985). Social regulations in cognitive development. In R. A. Hinde, A. Perret-Clermont, & J. Stevenson-Hinde (Eds.), *Social relationships and cognitive development* (pp. 294-308). Oxford: Clarendon Press.

Dreeben, R. (1968). *On what is learned in school.* Menlo Park, CA: Addison-Wesley.

Dweck, C. S., & Leggett, E. L. (1988). A social-cognitive approach to motivation and personality. *Psychological Review, 95*, 256-272.

Elliot, E. S., & Dweck, C. A. (1988). Goals: An approach to motivation and achievement. *Journal of Personality and Social Psychology, 54*, 5-12.

Emmons, R. A. (1989). The personal striving approach to personality. In L. A. Pervin (Ed.), *Goal concepts in personality and social psychology* (pp. 87-126). Hillsdale, NJ: Erlbaum.

Entwisle, D. R., Alexander, K. L., Cadigan, D., & Pallas, A. (1986). The schooling process in first grade: Two samples a decade apart. *American Educational Research Journal, 23*, 587-613.

Epperson, D. C. (1963). Some interpersonal and performance correlates of classroom alienation. *School Review, 71*, 360-376.

Epstein, J. L. (1983). The influence of friends on achievement and affective outcomes. In J. L. Epstein & N. Harweit (Eds.), *Friends in school* (pp. 177-200). New York: Academic Press.

Feldhusen, J. F., Thurston, J. R., & Benning, J. J. (1970). Longitudinal analyses of classroom behavior and school achievement. *Journal of Experimental Education, 38*, 4-10.

Feshbach, N. D., & Feshbach, S. (1987). Affective processes and academic achievement. *Child Development, 58*, 1335-1347.

Ford, M. E. (1985). The concept of competence: Themes and variations. In H. A. Marlowe, Jr. & R. B. Weinberg (Eds.), *Competence development* (pp. 3-49). New York: Academic Press.

Ford, M. E., Wentzel, K. R., Wood, D. N., Stevens, E., & Siesfeld, G. A. (1989). Processes associated with integrative social competence: Emotional and contextual influences on adolescent social responsibility. *Journal of Adolescent Research, 4*, 405-425.

Green, K. D., Forehand, R., Beck, S. J., & Vosk, B. (1980). An assessment of the relationships among measures of children's social competence and children's academic achievement. *Child Development, 51*, 1149-1156.

Hamilton, V. L., Blumenfeld, P. C., Alcoh, H., & Muira, K. (1989a). Japanese and American children's reasons for the things they do in school. *American Educational Research Journal, 26*, 545-571.

————. (1989b). Citizenship and scholarship in Japanese and American fifth graders. *American Educational Research Journal, 26*, 44-72.

Hargreaves, D. H., Hester, S. K., & Mellor, F. J. (1975). *Deviance in classrooms*. London: Routledge & Kegan Paul.

Harter, S. (1981). A new self-report scale of intrinsic versus extrinsic orientation in the classroom: Motivational and informational components. *Developmental Psychology, 17*, 300-312.

Havighurst, R. (1972). *Developmental tasks and education*. New York: David McKay.

Jackson, P. W. (1968). *Life in classrooms*. New York: Holt, Rinehart & Winston.

Kohn, M. & Rosman, B. L. (1973). Cognitive functioning in five-year-old boys as related to social-emotional and background-demographic variables. *Developmental Psychology, 8*, 277-294.

Kuhl, J. (1984). Volitional aspects of achievement motivation and learned helplessness: Toward a comprehensive theory of action control. In B. A. Maher & W. B. Maher (Eds.), *Progress in experimental personality research* (Vol. 13, pp. 99-171). New York: Academic Press.

————. (1985). Volitional mediators of cognition-behavior consistency: Self-regulatory processes and action versus state orientation. In J. Kuhl & J. Beckman (Eds.), *Action control: From cognition to behavior* (pp. 101-128). New York: Springer-Verlag.

Ladd, G. W., & Price, J. M. (1987). Predicting children's social and school adjustment following the transition from preschool to kindergarten. *Child Development, 58*, 1168-1189.

Lambert, N. M., & Nicoll, R. C. (1977). Conceptual model for nonintellectual behavior and its relationship to early reading achievement. *Journal of Educational Psychology, 69*, 481-490.

LeCompte, M. (1978a). Establishing a workplace: Teacher control in the classroom. *Education and Urban Society, 11*, 87-106.

————. (1978b). Learning to work: The hidden curriculum of the classroom. *Anthropology and Education Quarterly, 9*, 22-37.

Lepper, M. R., & Hodell, M. (1989). Intrinsic motivation in the classroom. In C. Ames & R. Ames (Eds.), *Research on motivation in education* (Vol. 3, pp. 73-106). New York: Academic Press.

Maccoby, E. (1980). *Social development*. New York: Harcourt Brace Jovanovich.

McClelland, D. C., Atkinson, J. W., Clark, R. A., & Lowell, E. L. (1953). *The achievement motive*. New York: Appleton-Century-Crofts.

McDermott, R. P. (1974). Achieving school failure: An anthropological approach to illiteracy and social stratification. In G. D. Spindler (Ed.), *Education and cultural process: Toward an anthropology of education* (pp. 82-118). New York: Holt Rinehart & Winston.

Miller, N. (1983). Peer relations in desegrated schools. In J. L. Epstein & N. Karweit (Eds.), *Friends in school* (pp. 201-217). New York: Academic Press.

Nakamura, C. Y., & Finck, D. N. (1980). Relative effectiveness of socially oriented and task-oriented children and predictability of their behaviors. *Monographs of the Society for Research in Child Development, 45*(3-4).

Nelson-Le Gall, & DeCooke, P. A. (1987). Same-sex and cross-sex help exchanges in the classroom. *Journal of Educational Psychology, 79*, 67-71.

Nicholls, J. G. (1984). Achievement motivation: Conceptions of ability, subjective experience, task choice, and performance. *Psychological Review, 91*, 328-346.

Nolen, S. B. (1988). Reasons for studying: Motivational orientations and study strategies. *Cognition and Instruction, 4*, 269-287.

Pervin, L. A. (1982). The stasis and flow of behavior: Toward a theory of goals. In M. M. Page (Ed.), *Personality-Current theory and research* (pp. 1-53). Lincoln, NE: University of Nebraska Press.

Powers, W. T. (1978). Qualitative analysis of purposive systems: Some spadework at the foundations of scientific psychology. *Psychological Review, 85*, 417-435.

Raynor, J. O. (1974). Future orientation in the study of achievement motivation. In J. W. Atkinson & J. O. Raynor (Eds.), *Motivation and achievement* (pp. 121-154). New York: Wiley.

Reuman, D., Atkinson, J. W., & Gallop, G. (1986). Computer simulation of behavioral expressions of four personality traits. In J. Kuhl & J. W. Atkinson (Eds.), *Motivation, thought, and action* (pp. 203-234). New York: Praeger.

Ruble, D. N. (1983). The development of social comparison processes and their role in achievement-related self-socialization. In E. T. Higgins, D. N. Ruble, & W. W. Hartup (Eds.), *Social cognition and social development: A sociocultural perspective* (pp. 134-157). New York: Cambridge University Press.

Safer, D. J. (1986). Nonpromotion correlates and outcomes at different grade levels. *Journal of Learning Disabilities, 19*, 500-503.

Schunk, D. H. (1987). Peer models and children's behavioral change. *Review of Educational Research, 57*, 149-174.

Schwarz, J. C. (1972). Effects of peer familiarity on the behavior of preschoolers in a novel situation. *Journal of Personality and Social Psychology, 24*, 276-284.

Sieber, R. T. (1979). Classmates as workmates: Informal peer activity in the elementary school. *Anthropology and Education Quarterly, 10*, 207-235.

Sindell, P. S. (1974). Some discontinuities in the enculturation of Misassini Cree children. In G. D. Spindler (Ed.), *Education and cultural process: Toward an anthropology of education* (pp. 333-341). New York: Holt Rinehart & Winston.

Webb, N. M. (1982). Peer interaction and learning in cooperative small groups. *Journal of Educational Psychology, 74*, 642-655.

Weiner, B. (1985). An attribution theory of achievement motivation and emotion. *Psychological Review, 92*, 548-573.

Wentzel, K. R. (1987). *Social, emotional, and cognitive factors associated with classroom-related goals and academic competence in adolescence: A developmental systems approach to the study of motivation.* Unpublished dissertation, Stanford University, Stanford, CA.

_____. (1989). Adolescent classroom goals, standards for performance, and academic achievement: An interactionist perspective. *Journal of Educational Psychology, 81*, 131-142.

_____. (1991a). Social competence at school: The relation between social responsibility and academic achievement. *Review of Educational Research, 61*, 1-24.

_____. (1991b). *Motivation and achievement in early adolescence: The role of multiple classroom goals.* Unpublished manuscript.

_____. (1991c). Relations between social competence and academic achievement in early adolescence. *Child Development*.

Winnell, M. (1987). Personal goals: The key to self-direction in adulthood. In M. E. Ford & D. H. Ford (Eds.), *Humans as self-constructing living systems: Putting the framework to work* (pp. 261-287). Hillsdale, NJ: Erlbaum.

Wolf, F. M., & Savikas, M. L. (1985). Time perspective and causal attributions for achievement. *Journal of Educational Psychology, 77*, 471-480.

Zimmerman, B. J., & Schunk, D. H. (1989). *Self-regulated learning and academic achievement*. New York: Springer-Verlag.

THE EMERGENT INTERACTION OF HOME AND SCHOOL IN THE DEVELOPMENT OF STUDENTS' ADAPTIVE LEARNING

Mary M. McCaslin and Tamera B. Murdock

In this paper we explore some of the dynamics between home and school that are expressed in children's "adaptive learning" in classrooms. We make a case for considering the emergent, interactive relationship between home and school that contributes to children's *internalization* of values and goals, their *motivation* to commit to those goals or to challenge and reform them, and their *competence* to enact and evaluate those commitments. A Vygotskian (Vygotsky, 1978) approach to the development of higher psychological processes guides this perspective.

We begin with a brief description of the Vygotskian approach. Second, we define "adaptive learning" and stress its origins in the social world. Third, we locate this perspective in the study of children's perception of competence through brief review of related research. Fourth, the utility of this perspective for research on the dynamic interplay between home and school in students'

Advances in Motivation and Achievement, Volume 7, pages 213-259.
Copyright © 1991 by JAI Press Inc.
All rights of reproduction in any form reserved.
ISBN: 1-55938-122-1

adaptive learning is illustrated through presentation of two cases selected from a larger investigation conducted by the first author. We close with hypotheses about how the emergent interactive processes of home and school affect the development of students' adaptive learning and suggest some avenues for future research.

VYGOTSKIAN PERSPECTIVE

The research program builds on an elaboration of a Vygotskian perspective that incorporates insights from attribution theory (e.g., Weiner, 1985), information processing theory (e.g., Simon, 1969), social learning theory (e.g., Bandura, 1977), and socialization research (e.g., Baumrind, 1971, 1987). (Other modern social-cognitive theories of motivated self-regulation have also built upon multiple perspectives and have provided contrasting frameworks. See, for example, Corno [1989b, 1990].) We begin with three basic tenets of historical Vygotskian theory: (1) the multiple functions of language, (2) internalization processes and the nature of change, and (3) the unit of psychological analysis. Each tenet is briefly noted. More elaborate discussion can be found elsewhere (see McCaslin Rohrkemper, 1989b, for an overview of historical Vygotskian theory; Wertsch, 1985, for an extensive analysis).

Multiple Functions of Language

Vygotsky maintained, as did other Marxists (Engels, 1890/1972; Marx, 1867/1972) and researchers of his day (e.g., Luria, 1979; Pavlov, 1927), that language was peculiar to humans and was responsible for the human ability to direct and mediate others' and, ultimately, one's own behavior. Thus, language serves two functions: communication with others and self-direction. The first capacity necessarily precedes the second. Vygotsky's particular focus was on how one comes to acquire self-direction. He hypothesized a process in which language initially received from and then directed to others acquires the facility to direct the self. In this progression, speech initially propels action. Subsequently, speech enables cessation of action. Ultimately, speech inhibits action. Covert self-directed (inner) speech regulates one's own action. For example, the process of a child's coming to not "color on the wall" may be understood as a progressive function of father telling his child to stop coloring on the wall. Initially, father's admonition results in more enthusiastic wall coloring. Subsequently, the child is able to stop coloring on the wall mid-picture when father reminds her. Ultimately the child does not color on the wall in the first place. Father has told her not to color; eventually, she will be able to tell herself to not color on the wall.

The developmental sequence of the two functions of language is from social or *inter*personal to self-directive or *intra*personal. The implications of this progression are critical. Not only does language acquire two distinct functions, but the source of self-directive inner speech is the social/instructional environment, the cultural and historical language environment. The structure and function of each type of speech, external communicative and internal self-directive ("inner" speech) differ. Vygotsky argued that ultimately, "the speech structures mastered by the child become the basic structures to his thinking" (Vygotsky, 1962, p.51). Inner speech then is the opposite of external speech. External speech involves turning thought into words, whereas inner speech involves turning words into thought (1962, p.131). Inner speech is the link between the language of the social/instructional environment and the thought of the individual.

Processes of Internalization

As we have noted, the developmental sequence of self-directive inner speech squarely locates the emergent capacity for "self" direction in the interpersonal realm; the social/instructional environment is preeminent. In a Vygotskian perspective, mind is the product of social life; it is originally shared between people and only later becomes a form of behavior in one person (Luria, 1969). "Emergent interaction" is an expression coined by Wertsch and Stone (1985) to capture the dynamics of this internalization process that integrates the multiple social/instructional environments of the child's experience with the child's biologically-based developmental processes. It underscores that the number, form, and structure of social/instructional environments evolve even as the child develops; internalization is a fluid process. It embeds the individual within her or his culture, it blurs the distinction between self and other. The individual is a part of the perceived social world; thus self-knowledge is dependent on knowledge of others.

Elsewhere McCaslin (1990; McCaslin Rohrkemper, 1989b) has argued that reports about self are not interpretable without a context of "perception of other" within which to analyze them. The dynamic interplay between other and self-perception are illustrated in two case studies, selected from the Adaptive Learning Study (McCaslin, in progress), that follow this discussion. Indeed, there are empirical examples to suggest that currently popular motivational phenomena such as "self-perceptions of ability" vary with context and/or comparison group (McCaslin, 1989; Midgley, Feldlaufer, & Eccles, 1989; Reuman, 1989) rather than function as stable individual difference factors.

Consideration of "emergent interaction" in school-aged children demands attention as well to the increased number of social/instructional environments in their lives that coincide with their emerging capacity for self-direction (see

McCaslin, 1990). One must consider the prior and ongoing influences of home and, as children mature (or mothers work [see Scarr, Phillips, & McCartney, 1989]), other social/instructional environments in a child's experience (e.g., child care, school, friends) if we are to understand the values, goals, and self-regulatory strategies that are enacted in school. This appears especially true of the regulation of one's motivation and affect as compared with the regulation of one's task-involved knowledge of school subjects, which is more directly affected by specific school learning for most children (McCaslin Rohrkemper, 1989b).

Exposure to an increased number of social/instructional environments requires adaptive learning. Corno (1989a), for example, discusses just this point in her analysis of classroom literacy. Some social/instructional environments are more supportive, informative, and appropriately challenging, and, thus, facilitate adaptive learning better than others. And gaps in language, social interactional patterns, naive psychology, and managerial styles between the social/instructional environments of home and school can demand adaptive learning of some students more than others. And as is so often the case, students from higher socioeconomic homes are more likely to receive a familiar set of expectancies in school than are their less advantaged peers (Heath, 1982). We return to conceptions of home and school dynamics in our review of related research.

Unit of Psychological Analysis

Vygotsky, writing at the turn of the century, was concerned that psychology had bifurcated important psychological processes and, in so doing, had trivialized the study of the human condition. He anticipated present-day attempts to integrate "will" with "skill" when he called for the integration of the affective with the intellectual, the study of thought within the "fullness of life" (Vygotsky, 1962, p.8).

In short, Vygotsky argued that the basic unit of concern for psychology was the *integration* of the affective with the intellectual and their *emergent* interactional origins with the social/instructional environment(s). He used word meaning as the basic unit of analysis for exploring this integration. Current Soviet psychologists challenge this last position and posit in its place the construct of "activity." Advocates of the activity construct hypothesize that it is not word meaning per se that integrates the affective with the intellectual, rather it is purposeful cognition and behavior in the context of a goal. In their terms, "tool-mediated, goal-directed action" is the appropriate unit with which to examine the integration of the affective with the intellectual (Wertsch, 1985; Zinchenko, 1985).

The research program described below provides some supportive evidence for the activity position that fuses goal with motivation, cognition, and the opportunity for strategic engagement. Indeed, the functions of task difficulty in the enactment of self-directive inner speech was a focus of earlier work (Rohrkemper, 1986; Rohrkemper and Bershon, 1984; Rohrkemper, Slavin, & McCauley, 1983) and continues to influence our current thinking and future directions. One important pursuit for educators is the design of tasks that enhance the integration of the affective and the intellectual, that afford the enactment and thus, *enhancement* of self-involved and task-involved inner speech (see also McCaslin Rohrkemper, 1989b).

A DEFINITION OF ADAPTIVE LEARNING

The primary interest of our research is the development and enhancement of "adaptive learning." We include in this construct the internalization of goals, the motivation to commit, challenge, or reform them, and the competence to enact and evaluate those commitments. In the specific instance, one manifestation of adaptive learning is the ability to take charge of frustration and maintain the intention to learn while enacting effective task strategies in the face of uncertainty—taking charge of one's motivation, emotion, and thinking. Adaptive learning merges the affective and the intellectual (Vygotsky, 1962) and empowers students to initiate and to transform tasks: it enables proactive behavior in either case (see also, McCaslin, 1990; McCaslin Rohrkemper, 1989b; Rohrkemper & Corno, 1988).

In this program of research two types of inner speech are identified that reflect the fusion of the affective and the intellectual and, therefore, the potential enactment of adaptive learning. Inner speech is hypothesized to guide thought and action in nonautomatic "effortful" (Posner, 1979) cognition (McCaslin Rohrkemper, 1989a, 1989b; Rohrkemper, 1986). Self-involved inner speech can inhibit ("I'm never going to get this") or enable ("don't get mad [because] you can do it, just hang in there") control over the self through motivational and affective self-statements. The processes of "staying with" a plan and renewing commitment to a goal—of maintaining and protecting an intention from distractors when recognizing the need to do so—also have been termed "volitional control" through the process of "intention escalation" (see Corno, 1989b, 1990).

Similarly, task-involved inner speech can impede or support control over the task. Task-involved inner speech that interferes with task control in mathematics, for example, would include misidentification of a problem type, employment of a "buggy" algorithm, or a misconception of numeracy that allows unreasonable diagnosis of one's work. Enabling task-involved inner speech includes the deliberate employment of problem solving strategies and procedural algorithms warranted by the task and modification or reformulation of the task as necessary and possible (e.g., "ok, start over on a new piece of paper with a completely new way," "oh, I'm going to change it"). Together, enhancing and mutually supporting self-involved and task-involved inner speech are hypothesized to enable adaptive learning because students not only have the tools to modify, initiate, or transform a task and/or the self, they also use them. The opportunity to employ and, thus, fine-tune these adaptive learning tools is a critical feature of the enhancement of adaptive learning.

Adaptive learning is not yet another euphemism for high ability; it is acquired through experience with a range of tasks within multiple, supportive social/instructional environments. One must have the opportunities to become, and to know oneself, as an adaptive learner. Such enabling opportunities involve both challenging, and therefore potentially informative, tasks and a supportive environment, an "arena of comfort" (Simmons, 1987), within which to extend and perhaps to strain one's emergent capacity to think and to know oneself as a learner.

Function of Task Difficulty

As Rohrkemper and Corno (1988) argue, uninformative success is not educative anymore than is mindless failure. Too readily earned success on tasks that are so furiously designed for success or are not difficult enough, and thus are understimulating, does not allow students to become adaptive learners. Similarly, tasks that are so difficult they merely overwhelm have little to contribute to increased understanding. The development and enhancement of adaptive learning requires that students encounter tasks that enable them to learn how to cope with the stress of uncertainty—to learn about their frustration thresholds, to swallow the lump in their throats, and to go back and try a different way: to engage in "tool-mediated, goal-directed action."

Thus, we hypothesize that an essential aspect of the enhancement of adaptive learning is the opportunity to experience a balance between more and less-easily "learned" tasks and "earned" outcomes. This likely affords a distinction between process and outcome in the first place and, secondly, allows for an understanding of the malleability of the learning process. Such understanding allows elaboration and fine-tuning of a range of enabling self-and task-involved strategies—an expanding and specialized tool kit (Rohrkemper, Slavin, & McCauley, 1983). As has been argued elsewhere (McCaslin, 1990; McCaslin Rohrkemper, 1989a), there is some support for the hypothesis that, given the structure of our classrooms and the diagnostic insensitivity of much classroom work, moderate ability learners are provided more opportunities to become adaptive learners: to recognize that tasks, and the strategies we bring to them, are malleable and to enact this knowledge rather than become undone by a too difficult task or defeated by one that is too easy. Adaptive learning is acquired. It involves a constellation of learned strategies and dispositions that merge the "affective" (i.e., motivated and personal commitment) and the "intellectual" (i.e., purposeful and strategic cognition) in the pursuit of a goal.

Social Origins of Adaptive Learning

Adaptive learning begins in the social world. It is not isomorphic with self-regulation. We stress affording opportunities and the interpersonal antecedents of, and ongoing interaction with, intrapersonal characteristics. Hence, the facility to transform and initiate tasks and self does not reside solely in the individual, it is not purely an "intrinsic" concept. Thus, when a student does not exhibit adaptive learning, we do not confine our explanatory search to the individual. We look as well to the contexts within which the student functions.

We wish students to engage in adaptive learning so that they become more able, even as they are initially able, to profit from experience that helps them attain the goals that we wish them to seek. Adaptive learning is all about the internalization of values and goals and the strategic motivation and competence to commit to or alter them. Adaptive learning involves being a member of a community and transforming that community even as we are transformed by it. A Vygotskian orientation is distinctive in its interest in the emergent interaction of the developing individual within and among the changing contexts of her/his multiple social/instructional environments. Thus, at a minimum, the emergent interaction of experiences within home (e.g., Glazier-Robinson, 1990), within school (e.g., Fetterman, 1990) and between home and school must be considered if we are to fully understand adaptive learning in students' classroom behavior. A specific learning event is not isolated from prior experience; present intrapersonal consequences can be related to former and ongoing interpersonal influences.

RELATED LITERATURE

Literature noted here is meant to locate our focus on the social origins of intrapersonal processes with other perspectives on intrapersonal phenomena. We briefly note research on (1) children's self perception and (2) parental beliefs and managerial practices that are believed to inform children's classroom performance. The first section is meant to be suggestive of differing conceptions of student perception (e.g., cognitive developmental models, contextual approaches) and their import for student mediation of classroom phenomena and motivated learning. The second section records some of the more recent work on parental beliefs and behavior and their believed influence upon students in classrooms. Each section is mutually informative.

Children's Self-Perception of Competence

Cognitive Developmental Approaches

The literature of the past decade is replete with studies of children's self perception of competence based upon cognitive developmental models of achievement motivation. These studies examine the predictive role of self-perceived competence (Bandura, 1981; Frieze & Snyder, 1980; Phillips, 1984; Weiner, 1985) and the behavioral consequences of perceived competence (Blumenfeld, Pintrich, Meece, & Wessels, 1982; Phillips, 1984, 1987; Phillips & Zimmerman, 1990). Results suggest the necessity of understanding children's perceived competence as a requisite to the study of academic motivation and persistence.

Research has shown that early elementary students (K-2) have uniformly high estimates of their academic competence. Beginning in third grade and continuing throughout elementary school, variation in self-perception increases as does the actual relationship between perception and achievement (Eshel and Klein, 1981; Nicholls, 1978, 1979; Stipek, 1981; Stipek & Tannatt, 1984). Explanations within the developmental tradition are highly influenced by the Piagetian conception of cognitive development (Piaget, 1970). Within this framework, changes in student perceived ability are understood as a function of children's difficulty attending to feedback (Ruble, 1983), difficulty integrating evaluative information (Nicholls, 1978; Parsons & Ruble, 1977; Surber, 1984), confusion of wishes with reality (Stipek & Hoffman, 1980), and the complexity of the judgment criteria (Blumenfeld, Pintrich, & Hamilton, 1986).

Within a purely developmental perspective, changing perceptions of competence are viewed as interindividual, mediated by biologically-based cognitive structures. These structures limit the accuracy and abstraction of one's construction of the world. Current research and working theory has called into question a benign, universal development and emphasized the importance of intra- and interindividual contexts in the understanding of self perception (e.g., DiMarino-Linnen, 1990).

Contextual Approaches

Research on contextual factors associated with self perception of competence typically have examined the interplay between environmental factors, particularly school and home, and salient student characteristics, particularly developmental level, aptitude, gender, and social class. These factors clearly are not independent. The communication that children receive about themselves both at home and at school is mediated by both intrinsic and extrinsic factors, in emergent interaction. Even so, research on their interplay is informative. In this section we overview research that examines the interaction of student characteristics and classroom phenomena. Discussion of home and social class in interaction with student self-perception occurs in the final section.

Research conducted on classroom and teacher effects suggests that the type of evaluative information that children are given about their achievement (Stipek & Tannatt, 1984) and about their behavior (Rohrkemper & Brophy, 1980) change across the elementary years. Exposure to differing types of information appears consistent with beliefs about children's capacity to profit from that information. Some studies indicate that, as in a "zone of proximal development" (Vygotsky, 1962), teachers can structure information such that learning precedes developmental progression in self-perceptions of ability (Stipek & Daniels, 1988) and in interpersonal perception and behavior (Rohrkemper, 1984). In both studies, differences in students attributable to classroom structures were confined to early elementary; by fourth grade there were no differences in perception attributable to classroom structure.

Other research indicates the fruitfulness of considering the co-occurence of developmental and classroom structure variables in understanding the dynamics of self perception (Ames, 1984; Marshall & Weinstein, 1984; Rosenholtz & Simpson, 1984). Teacher expectation research examines as well the subsequent effects of interpersonal dynamics on intrapersonal perception and performance (see Brophy, 1983; Good & Brophy, 1987; Harris & Rosenthal, 1985).

Research on the effects of teacher expectation on student mediation of classroom events and self perception has documented that students in early grades perceive differential teacher treatment as a function of student ability and internalize these cues (Brattesani, Weinstein, & Marshall, 1984; Weinstein, Marshall, Brattesani, & Middlestat, 1982; Weinstein & Middlestat, 1979). Students apparently do not *use* this knowledge to understand their own interactions with their teacher, however, until fifth grade (Weinstein, Marshall, Sharp, & Botkin, 1987).

Research on gender differences in student perception of competence consistently finds that girls underestimate their academic abilities while boys overestimate their abilities (Deaux, 1976; Eccles, 1983; Frey & Ruble, 1987; Phillips & Zimmerman, 1990). The age at and the domains in which these differences emerge are less stable findings. Some studies have found differences between boys and girls as early as kindergarten (Frey & Ruble, 1987), others do not locate meaningful differences until junior high (Eccles, 1983; Fennema, 1974; Newman, 1984; Phillips & Zimmerman, 1990). Gender differences in self-perception have been associated with differential attributions for success and failure (Dweck, Goetz, & Strauss, 1980) and sex-role identity (Parsons, Frieze, & Ruble, 1976). Other research examines more directly the environmental contexts such as parental modeling and conveyance of differential expectations (Astin, 1974; Eccles, 1983; Parsons, Kaczala, & Meece, 1982; Phillips & Zimmerman, 1990).

Home Influence

Parental Beliefs

Research has found a relationship between parental expectations and children's academic performance (Gigliotti & Brookover, 1975; Keeves, 1972; St. John, 1972; Seigner, 1983). Parents, like teachers, also have been implicated as major influences upon their children's self-perception of ability. Parent perceptions have been found to be more salient predictors of student perceived self-competence than are ability and achievement scores (Parsons, Adler, & Kaczala, 1982; Phillips, 1987).

Family role in gender differences in self-perception has been hypothesized to result from parental modeling (of differential ability) and parental expectancy (communication of differential expectations for achievement). Several studies have examined both possibilities (Eccles, 1983; Parsons, Adler, & Kaczala, 1982; Phillips & Zimmerman, 1990). The expectation hypothesis appears to receive the most support as a mediating mechanism for children's differential self-perception of ability.

Managerial Styles

Conceptions of "parenting" generally have been understood in terms of two dimensions, control and affect, based on factor analyses of parenting behavior (e.g., Schaefer, 1959). More recent elaborations of the control dimension owe much to the early work of Baumrind (1971). Parental control is typically anchored by "laissez-faire" or "permissive" parenting at one extreme, wherein parents exert little control over, or instruction to, their child. Parents are resources that the child may or may not wish to use. "Authoritarian" parenting anchors the other extreme, wherein parents exert and maintain control over decision making and their child, independent of the child's emerging capacities. These parents are less likely to engage in explanation of parental behavior. They order. Authoritarian parents are obedience-focused and dogmatic. A third control profile, that lies between the anchors, identified by Baumrind (1971) is "authoritative," wherein parents provide explanations for "firm yet flexible" limits on child behavior. Authoritative parents discuss their standards, teach children how to meet them, and value appropriate child behavior that is monitored by self-control.

Parental affection is considered an independent dimension from parental control. Affection is anchored by warmth-hostility (or acceptance-rejection). Essentially all child outcomes that are valued by middle-class parents (and by mental health practitioners and teachers) are correlated with parental warmth (Maccoby & Martin, 1983). The implications of distinguishing parental control from parental warmth are important. Thus, some parents may be permissive with their child out of respect for and valuing of the child's inner goodness;

some because they do not wish to participate in the child's growth. Similarly, some authoritarian parents may wish to protect their child and provide security in an unsafe, unpredictable world; some may exert control because they reject the emerging child. Authoritative parenting can be based in a supportive, loving atmosphere; it can also be rooted in a legalistic enterprise (cf. Baumrind, 1971, 1987).

More recent work by Baumrind (1987) has elaborated upon these styles of parenting as a result of her longitudinal work. She describes four prototypic nonlenient patterns: (1) traditional, (2) authoritarian restrictive, (3) punitive, and (4) authoritative. Two styles, traditional and punitive, represent additions to her work (for more elaborate discussion, see Baumrind, 1987).

Traditional families are defined as those who desire continuity in world view and value judgments that have identified the family over time. Traditional families have a strong belief system and emphasize order more than risk-taking. They are not necessarily authoritarian, however, because traditional families exert strong influence early in the child's life so that the child can develop self-discipline later on. Authoritarian-Restrictive families, in contrast, *keep* their children in a subordinate role; they do not share power as the child develops. Coercive authority interferes with children developing a sense of themselves as moral agents (Hoffman, 1983; Lepper, 1981). Thus, authoritarian parents, in effect, likely create the conditions that "require" their continued coercive function.

Traditional and authoritarian parents are not necessarily punitive. Recall that control is distinct from affect. Baumrind's third level of nonlenient parenting more clearly differentiates parental hostility and harsh punitive measures from issues of control.

Studies of social class and parenting styles locate more authoritarian control in working-class families (e.g., Hess, 1970; Kohn, 1977). Kohn (1977) classified families based on father occupation and found that lower-class children were more apt to be punished on the basis of their misbehavior per se; middle-class children on the basis of the intentions that underlie their behavior. Clearly, this research should be interpreted with caution as much has happened to family structure, parental occupation, and income in the intervening years. In addition, research on parenting has not yet attended to the dynamics of child-rearing when parents differ in managerial style and relative influence. Surprisingly little research has been conducted on situational factors in parent managerial behavior. There is some support, however, for the fruitfulness of constructs like "problem ownership" (Gordon, 1970) in predicting parental responses to children (e.g., Kallman & Stollak, 1974) and teacher responses to students (e.g., Rohrkemper & Brophy, 1983) in specific situations.

In short, conceptions of parenting would benefit from more specific attention to situational factors. Nonetheless, differential home patterns are important to learn more about when we consider that most mentally healthy behavior, including valued behavior in school, is believed to be based in self-regulation rather than obedience. Punishment based on outcome does not promote understanding and, thus, the development of self-regulation and adaptive learning; it simply targets obedience.

Social Class, Ethnicity, and Children's Ability Perceptions

Social class influences on student self-perception essentially are assumed. Despite the frequent implication of social class as a mediating variable to school success and the belief that family-fostered low self-esteem may underlie performance deficits, there have been relatively few recent systematic studies on social class and academic self-concept. Research by Phillips and Ziegler (1980) challenges the hypothesis that economically deprived students have low ideal self-image and, therefore, low achievement striving. Their research highlights the need to consider the social context at many levels of self-esteem measurement and, we would add, the need to consider the functional utility and scope of schooling in self-perception. Eshel and Klein (1981) have made similar qualifications, suggesting that the implications of social class are contextually bound.

Investigations exploring differential effects of parental expectations as a function of social class are mixed. For example, Marcus and Corsini (1978) found that, even though there were no group differences in actual performance, lower class parents of preschool children predicted lower achievement than what their children actually obtained; middle class parents were more accurate in their predictions. In contrast, Entwistle and Hayduk (1978) found that both lower- and middle-class mothers of early elementary school children overestimated their children's school performance, but the discrepancy was larger for lower-class mothers. These studies differed significantly in the type of task evaluation parents were asked to engage. Marcus and Corsini exposed parents to task evaluation criteria that consisted of 15 performance levels for four discrete tasks; a level of specificity likely atypical in parental assessment of children's performance. It would seem that the global assessments made by parents in Entwistle and Hayduk's study are the more typical representations of parental expectation.

Stevenson, Chaunsheng, and Uttal (1990), in a multiracial study, found that black and Hispanic mothers put more emphasis on the importance of achievement, had higher hopes for the long-range value of education, and saw their children as generally enjoying school more than white mothers reported. Black and Hispanic children reported similar high expectations and enjoyment in school, also in contrast to their white peers' reports. This study suggests that parental expectations are not an explanation for low motivation and high drop out rates of minority youth and, in so arguing, is consistent with the position of Phillips and Ziegler (1980).

In brief, research on social class, ethnicity, and parental expectations for children's performance and children's self-perception suggests that, first, social class is not a given differential predictor of parental expectation for child performance. Second, parental belief associated with social class and ethnicity is not a compelling mediator of the decreased academic self-perception and performance rates of lower-class and minority youth.

A RESEARCH EXAMPLE:
THE ADAPTIVE LEARNING STUDY

The research reviewed here supports an integrative approach to the study of intrapersonal processes. In the research program we briefly describe, the construct of student adaptive learning encompasses the emergent interaction of previous and ongoing influences of home, in the context of the influences of school (e.g., principal expectations, teachers, peers, tasks). Multiple social/instructional environments permeate students' development and increased understanding of their culture, themselves, and their relation to and within that culture. Students' interpersonal understandings are an important part of their intrapersonal knowledge. Any given classroom behavior is a constellation of self and other understanding and self and other influence.

The Adaptive Learning Study is a multiphase investigation, conducted by the first author, that seeks to understand the parameters of adaptive learning and the process of emergent interaction through interviews with teachers, parents, and students and classroom observation. A description of the basic research program is provided so that the reader may better interpret the inclusion of the two case studies as exemplars of emergent interaction.

Sample

Teachers in grades 2, 4, and 6 were nominated by their principals for possible participation because of their believed expertise as instructional leaders and classroom managers. The final selection of 12 teachers was based upon principal nomination, interview, and classroom observation. Each teacher was "matched" with a teacher of similar philosophy with similar students. One half of participating teachers were in schools where 10-25% of the students receive lunch aid; one half taught in schools where 35-70% of the students receive lunch support. One hundred and fifty students in these 12 classrooms, their ("outstanding") teachers, and 45 of their parents (15 per grade level) are the primary participants of the study.

Instrumentation

Parent Interview

Parents were interviewed about their child's strengths and weaknesses as a learner; their child's and their own response to mistakes and frustration in home and school learning; and their general managerial style and expectations. Parent interviews ranged from 30 minutes to 2 hours.

Student Interview

Students were interviewed about aspects of classroom learning that one can attempt to influence, that afford the exertion of personal control. The semistructured interview included vignettes constructed to remove stereotypic ability and achievement outcome confounds where students described as low achieving do not succeed and those described as high achieving do. Process and outcome are disentangled so that effortful failure and success occur as do effortless failure and success. Hence the vignettes describe four moderate ability students who get along in the classroom, each engaged with more or less effort and more or less successfully, in a particular task in math. Each vignette was matched to student gender, read to students, and controlled for order effects. After hearing each vignette, students were asked to describe the portrayed event; predict the character's inner speech during the described event and immediately afterward; and predict what was going to happen next. Following presentation of all four vignettes, students were asked a series of self-comparison questions that differentiated general self-perception from contextualized (i.e., as a function of task difficulty) self-perception. Interviews ranged from 30 minutes to one hour.

My Classroom Journal

Two classrooms at each grade level (2, 4, and 6) participated in the experience-sampling phase of the study adapted from Csikszentmihalyi and Larson (1985). For a three-week period beginning in mid-March, students ($N = 100$) recorded their thoughts and behavior at intervals designed to capture the full array of the moment-to-moment of classroom learning. Each entry included

1. *information about the task in progress*—subject (e.g., science), type (e.g., review), and difficulty of work, degree of procedural understanding, self-assessment of performance, and interest level;
2. *description of teacher-student classroom action*—what the teacher is doing; what the student is doing;
3. *metacognitive awareness*—how the student felt; what s/he thought about; said to her/himself; and
4. *concentration/openness to incidental observation*—I "noticed" that . . .

Problem Solving

Finally, a subgroup of 38 students in grades 4 and 6 who were identified as either likely "adaptive" or "effortful" by their teacher, interview, and classroom observation participated in individual problem-solving interviews. Mathematics problem sets were designed with the teacher to include a range of difficult problems that would be experienced as intended (i.e., low, moderate, or high difficulty) by a particular student. In practice, however, problem difficulty does not reside solely in the task, it is coconstructed by the student. Thus, students did not necessarily experience problem difficulty as "objectively" defined and intended.

Students were trained in the "Think Aloud" method while engaged in problem solving; they were observed and tape-recorded. After problem solving, students were immediately interviewed about the experience. One week later they were again asked to recall their problem solving experience. Thus, this segment of the research allows consideration of immediate experience and reconstructions of that experience over time.

Case Analysis

One purpose of this investigation is to allow comparisons among students who differ along dimensions we typically study in classroom research (e.g., grade level, gender, ability, self-perception, SES) in their acquisition of adaptive learning. Another is to examine the role of teachers and tasks in facilitating the development of adaptive learning. A third is to understand potential influences of home learning on adaptive learning in school. In this paper, our purpose is to illustrate what we mean by the emergent interaction of these "factors" at the level of the individual. Thus, two cases are presented that provide two examples of this process.

Criteria for selection as a case in this paper were: (1) a student in sixth grade because this aged student, in general, is more adept at describing internal processes than are younger students; (2) parent participation; and (3) the student participated in each phase of the study. This restricted the possibilities to two sixth-grade classrooms. The classroom more representative of the economic distribution of the city was chosen. Within this classroom, four students qualified. One had been described by the teacher as a high ability student, two as moderate ability, and one as low ability. Parent managerial styles varied such that one parent described what Baumrind (1987) terms authoritarian-restrictive management, one authoritative-conservative, one authoritative-liberal, and one traditional. The two cases selected for inclusion represent the more typical parent managerial styles for this school district: authoritarian-restrictive and traditional.

Case development involved independent analysis of case materials by each author. The first and second author each independently designed cases from the materials. The second author's case construction was designated the reliability assessment for each case. The second, independent case construction served to verify and, in three instances, emphasize assertions in the initial cases.

The first case is an example of a child in an authoritarian-restrictive family structure; the second a child in a traditional family structure. Both children are in working-class families. They live in the same neighborhood and are in the same sixth grade. Each case begins with the parent interview. Student data begins with the student's perception of other learners and achievement and of her- or himself in relation to them. Student contextual self-knowledge is then examined, as is its relation to actual task engagement. Finally, student processing of classroom moments, through "experience sampling" (Csikszentmihalyi & Larson, 1984) journal entries is presented to provide some insights into student reported enactment of perceptions, beliefs, strategies, and goals in the classroom.

CASE ONE: JULIO

Home Learning

Parent Values

Julio's family consists of a sister and working parents. Spanish is the first language of his parents; English is the first language of the children. Julio's father, with whom the interview took place, is comfortable speaking English; Julio's mother is not. Julio's father works the swing shift at a local plant. He took time off work to participate in the interview, concerned that Julio was in trouble or about to be.

Neither parent completed high school in the standard four-year pattern; mother because she needed to help her family financially, father because he was "a little wild" and "didn't really like school." Father subsequently received a G.E.D.; mother completed night school. Both parents value education highly, frequently using themselves as models to their children of what NOT to do, emphasizing that

> it's more important (to complete school) now . . . it's not like it used to be. Before you could have gotten a job, there was a lot of work available. Now if you don't have a diploma or college, you can hardly get a good paying job . . . I told them if I had gone to college, I wouldn't be working like this, swing shifts, nights. . . . So I try to make him understand, by, even if I have to put myself on his part. I do it so they can learn from it, and the same thing with my wife.

Language differences between parents and children cause some difficulties for Julio, particularly with respect to homework. There is a premium on homework at Julio's house, partly because it represents to the parents their role in helping their child do well in school, and partly because it is the punitive link between home and school, something that demonstrates shared authority over their child. And Julio's parents give the school considerable authority. For example, when there is a problem with Julio's achievement OR his behavior at school, the parents request extra homework as part of his punishment.

It is not surprising that Julio, in a separate interview, reports that he dreads home-school contacts and the subsequent extra homework. The complexity builds, however, when we consider that at least part of the problem for Julio is that his parents cannot help with homework but profoundly want to help. At home, Julio tries to avoid his mother's help "because I can hardly understand her . . . in English and in Spanish" and pointedly asked, "how would you [interviewer] say 'reciprocal fractions' in Spanish?" Julio prefers to confine his father's help to vocabulary words. He discusses his parents' limited educational opportunities as further reasons that he prefers help from friends over the phone to his parents' attempts. For Julio, it is important that he understand "how a problem works" before he leaves school. He readily asks teachers and peers for assistance.

Expectations and Management Style

Father worries that Julio will not use opportunities available to him. His primary goal for Julio is that he "go through school and maybe go to college." In either case the ultimate goal is a good job. Father does not further differentiate strategies nor the goal they serve. Good work is high paying and done in the daylight. Schooling (and homework) is how you get there.

Julio's father wants him to learn from father's failure to take advantage of educational opportunities. When Julio's behavior and/or achievement is less than desired, father compares himself to his son and says he doesn't want Julio to do things "like that" because "it is not good for your future." Father's reported modeling of and coping with personal mistakes is limited to the one historical mistake—and its major, distal, consequences. It is recounted whenever Julio's present behavior and/or achievement is found wanting. Distal consequences of considerable magnitude are believed to function as guidelines to get Julio "back on the right track" in the ever-present.

And father expects Julio to be on the right track. He demands respect; he expects the demand is necessary.

> I was raised that when an older person talked to you, you listen. You don't answer back to that person. And I want them [the children] to learn to be that way too.

Julio's father punishes him for rule infraction, especially lack of respect for elders. Punishment may "once in a while" include "a little smack on the back," but "mostly" involves "look[ing] for things that he really enjoys or likes and tak[ing] these privileges away. So far it has worked." "Worked" roughly translates into Julio "has basically been pretty good." Father reportedly does not like to punish Julio—"I hate to do things like that to him"—but believes that

> I'm doing it for his own good. If I let it go one time then he might say, "well I [sic] let it go when I did it before." He might be getting worse and worse, so I try to stop it right then and there when it happened so he won't do it a second time. You got to control this.

Father also exerts control over Julio through more positive channels. He reinforces behavior or achievement considered exceptional with a "positive comment." Good report cards can get you a dinner with Dad at McDonald's:

> We let them know that we appreciate what they are doing and give them some confidence about it so they know that we like and enjoy the work they're doing as much as they do.

An illustration of this policy in action is informative. Father describes an event where the teacher said something to Julio and "he answered back to her . . . in a way he shouldn't have . . . and we won't allow that." Even though this was the "first time we had any trouble all through school" Julio was still being punished four weeks after the event. Punishment consisted of "no more outside or TV for the rest of the school year [approximately two months], study for two hours each night, and we even asked for extra [home]work for him as part of his punishment." Julio was warned, "If the teacher call us again, then it's going to be for the whole summer" and additional restrictions would be added.

Father believes that soon Julio will be "back to his old self again," studying and respecting adults. Father's linkage of study and respect is initially puzzling, until a second interview with Julio is considered, one that took place within approximately a week of his father's. Julio was discussing the kinds of things he wished the researcher would learn about to make classrooms better places for students. First on his list was that teachers provide help when you needed it and not embarrass or make fun of you if you ask. Julio described an event concerning work on math seatwork problems. He was sufficiently concentrating on his work that he was not listening to classroom talk. He came to a problem he did not understand and asked the teacher for help. The teacher had apparently just answered a similar question and, according to Julio, she sometimes gets mad because you ask her a question that she just answered and you weren't really listening, you were doing your work. That's what, like, if you hear somebody ask a question and you don't really listen and then you're at that problem or something and you need to ask a question and she gets mad and she just embarrasses you sometimes.

On this occasion the teacher reportedly talked in a "baby voice" to Julio; peers laughed. Julio still felt the embarrassment.

When the interviewer suggested that this sounded like an important thing to talk about with teachers so classrooms could be better places for students, Julio cautioned not to say anything as the researcher might get herself (and him) in trouble. He had already told the teacher he didn't think it was "very funny" and he had been told he was "not supposed to be talking back to grown-ups." It is this event that resulted in the call home and the extended punishment described by father.

View of Children

In Julio's home, you are what you do. Children are judged by their actions; children's perceptions and intentions are not considered or explored when attempting to understand a given situation. One exception to this general noncognitive framework is that, when specifically asked, father did note that sometimes Julio

can get a little upset if [when he's doing his homework] it doesn't come the right way, right away. . . . [When this happens] we try to calm Julio down so he can get back on the track. We tell him, if you get mad, your mind ain't going to be on the problem, you got to relax, so you can get to the bottom of the problem . . . let it cool off a little so you can get your mind, concentrate. . . . Get control and get to work.

The more typical and general lack of consideration of a psychological context or of potential multiple causes of situational behavior at home is evident in the father's understanding of misbehavior in school. Father assumed discussion of his son's mistakes in school meant misbehavior. He believes that if you work you learn and equates lack of understanding with misbehavior. Thus, for father, good behavior in the classroom is the cause of good grades; reciprocally, good grades prove good behavior. Julio is not a good boy if his grades are not. If Julio needs to ask a question the teacher already answered, it is because he was not paying attention. Not paying attention is misbehaving and is the cause of not learning. If you misbehave, if you do not learn, you will not finish school.

Hence, at home there is no "instruction" following lack of learning in school, there is only behavioral control. The goal of control is to get the "old," perhaps younger, Julio back: back like he was when he didn't question authority. Back like he was when his first grade teacher communicated high achievement expectations to Julio's father, she

> asked me if I wanted to sell him to her . . . I told her that he was not a car or something that you buy and sell . . . she saw that he was going to be a pretty good student all through school and college and that. And we're hoping he won't let her down—and us too.

Father recalls first grade teacher expectations for his son that are quite variant with sixth grade teacher expectations at the time of the interview. Julio's sixth grade teacher described him as relatively low in ability and "mixed" in his motivation to learn: sometimes he seemed overwhelmed, sometimes he didn't care, sometimes he gave up, mostly he "endures." As we see shortly, teacher perception of Julio's motivational pattern is amply documented in his quarterly report cards; teacher perception of his ability to achieve, however, is not. Julio's father certainly understands Julio's school achievement differently from Julio's present teacher. As we will see, Julio's self-perceptions of ability form yet a third perspective and, of each of these—teacher, father, and son—Julio's self-perception is most congruent with actual "objective" performance data.

Such descrepancies in teacher expectations, however, underscore the potential harm of inappropriate teacher expectations, be they too high or too low, especially with children from families who rely so heavily on the school for information about their children's abilities and likelihood of success—both in the present and in the future. Parents like Julio's invest their hopes for their child in the school. And they contribute to this process as best they can. As Julio's father says:

> We try to get involved as much as we can . . . . and we told the teacher that anything that we can help to give us a call. If he starts misbehaving or something, whatever she needs to talk to us, whenever she needs to talk to us, give us a call and we'll be right there.

And they will be there, just as Julio's father was "there" for his son, taking time off the night shift to participate in this research because he was concerned for him. Julio's success in school is also father's success in the home. Unfortunately for Julio and his father, however, expectations in school do not remain static. Expectations for independent thinking and learning—for self-regulation—differ dramatically across the elementary school years.

School Learning

Achievement Profile

In general, report card grades address two domains of student learning: realized achievement and expended effort. Grades range from the usual A - D, but there is no "F," but rather an "N," for "no progress." Expended effort includes appropriate conduct, and is assessed numerically: 1 is "outstanding," 2 "satisfactory," and 3 "improvement needed." In addition to subject matter achievement and effort judgments, teachers also evaluate student "Personal Growth." Items in this category, each independently and numerically assessed, include: accepts responsibility for action, shows respect for others, uses time wisely, works well independently, works well in a group, completes assignments, observes class and school rules, and prepares neat work.

Julio's quarterly reports in math indicate that he was a consistent "B" student, at grade level, and with satisfactory effort. His performance was uneven in reading and language development. Julio was reading at grade level. His achievement and effort grades covaried so that "satisfactory" judgments in effort accompany a grade of "B." "Outstanding" effort accompanies an "A"; "Improvement needed" coincides with a "C." Julio began each semester with a "B"; he finished the year with a "C." Finally, language development was apparently the most difficult subject for Julio. His effort was consistently judged "satisfactory," but three of his four quarter grades were "C," the remaining a "B." In the three subjects, then, Julio received 1 A, 7 B's, and 4 C's. His effort was satisfactory. Julio's judged "personal growth" was not as consistently positive. His first two quarter ratings were "satisfactory"; his second two "improvement needed."

Julio's performance on the standardized achievement tests, taken at the beginning of April during sixth grade, measured achievement in reading (grade equivalent of 7.3, a national percentile of 60), math (grade equivalent of 8.4, a national percentile of 86), and "total" performance (grade equivalent of 7.4, a national percentile of 63). It would appear that Julio is neither the high ability student envisioned by his father and first grade teacher nor the low ability student described by his sixth grade teacher. However, in terms of *relative* ability in the classroom, Julio's standardized scores can be compared with those of participating classmates. Of the 15 participating students, Julio's standardized test scores ranked 13.5 in reading, 8 in math, and 14 in overall performance. Thus, his teacher's ranking is appropriate in a relative, if not absolute, sense. Julio appears to be a student of enabling ability who must commit himself if he is to achieve. The performance score that appears to cue achievement concern is his relative difficulty with language development.

Perception of School

Julio's discussion of school is two-fold: stay out of trouble and nonacademics. His advice to "the new student" consists of how to stay "off the wall" (a sort of time-out zone) during recess, which he considers "kind of rough" to accomplish. Advice is limited to proscriptives and when specifically probed what it means "to act right" as opposed to "not act right" in school, Julio elaborated upon the "shalt nots." Julio did not focus on the academic aspects of schooling, refering instead to "special classes, like gym," lunch, playground equipment, and recess games. He sees no need for the school to change, because "all what we, mostly, need is here."

Other Perception: Achievement

Julio's responses to each of the four vignettes portraying moderate ability learners who differ in effort and outcome on a specific task (described previously), indicate that he perceived each uniquely. Julio's interpretation of each, however, rested on attention to two cues, one essential to the vignette, the other constructed by Julio. Julio focused on (1) personal effort that was built into each vignette and that he transformed to the more behaviorally descriptive and visible, "work," and (2) use of social resources, which he constructed for each vignette, as the critical features of student performance.

For Julio, learning was not possible without sustained student work and enabling teacher instruction, or if the instruction was found wanting, additional help. From his perspective, help from others is an essential achievement ingredient, independent of level of effort or level of outcome: if you succeed you can thank earlier help; if you are having difficulty now, get help; if you are to continue to understand as you do now, continue to get help. Julio does not project "ability" into the equation, his conception corresponds to spending "time on task." Because if you work on it long enough, you'll start to understand—if effective teaching or extra help are available. Thus, students can "own" the disobedience of not working or not working long enough, but they can not lay claim to any potential understanding that may result.

And not working long enough has consequences. Julio understood the student who ultimately gives up in frustration, as "mad when he doesn't understand something" and claims:

> That he don't like this. He don't really want to do it. It's kind of, like, boring, and it's cheap and he hates school.

Julio portrays self-destructive consequences of anger in that, in his scenario, the student refuses to ask for help. Julio predicts the character (and only this character) will flunk the grade: extreme distal consequences of current task frustration. Julio has learned from his father's mistake.

General Self-Perception

Julio names Pete, the character who succeeds relatively effortlessly, as the character most like himself. He, like Pete, "does his work slowly and takes a while to understand it." Julio transformed what was intended to be a portrayal of low effort with successful task completion into a sort of task submersion not unlike Csikszentmihalyi's (Csikszentmihalyi & Larson, 1984) notion of the flow experience. For Julio, being done "before he knew it" was not a cue of speed, but rather, sustained, concentrated task engagement and, because of this sustained work and previous teacher explanation, successful learning occurs. Recall it was just such task immersion that led to the home-school punishment described earlier.

Julio continues that when he gets "mad I don't feel like doing the work but I keep doing it" and describes several alternative routes to getting the kind and quality of help he needs. He has some difficulty, for instance, with the nature of teacher help because "she talks a lot about the work and she usually get [sic] me mixed up . . . . [it is both] the words she uses and she uses pretty much words too." Thus, much of the time, at school and at home, Julio prefers the help of peers.

In short, Julios' general perception of himself as a student is that classroom learning in general goes pretty well. If he keeps at it he will learn, and he believes that he has learned to keep at it. But it doesn't come easily.

Contextual Self-Perception

Julio elaborates his general self-view to include anger when he faces difficult tasks. In this context he perceives himself as being like Matt, the boy who gives up in frustration (and whom Julio predicts will flunk). Julio gets frustrated and he leaves the problems "for to ask the teacher" because he doesn't know he doesn't understand something until he starts to do it. He wishes the teacher wouldn't have given the work and that "she would explain it more," including vocabulary, but he apparently does not know the instruction is not sufficient until he begins assigned work. By that time, Julio believes, the only hope of his coming to understand is reliance on the good help of others. Julio can only take control of his work, not his understanding.

When asked to consider himself in relation to work that was not difficult for him, that was relatively easy, Julio again identified with Pete (indicating that this is typical of his classroom experience) and again made the point that work is never quick, but it is engaging:

> He remembers . . . .he works on it . . . .he's understanding it and he works hard at it. He works and he keeps working . . . ."

Julio reports no inner speech when engaged in relatively easy tasks, "just work."

Finally, Julio discussed which character he would most like to be like. He wants to be like Pete. Julio believes that Pete likes math and that explains his correct answers:

> If you're really interested in your work you get, like, a lot of things right. Like, if you're not interested and you don't really like the subject, you don't do that good.

But it's even more than that:

> He works at his problems and he usually get them almost all right but he probably gets good grades in math and reading and all the different subjects.

Relation Between Other and Self-Perception

Julio's beliefs about others and himself, both in general and in specific types of learning difficulty, indicate that, for Julio, the dynamics of classroom learning function similarly for everyone: you work and, if the conditions are right, you learn. He does not spontaneously employ a construct of differential ability and compensatory effort. For Julio, tasks and teacher instruction and sources of help may vary, but work endures. Julio believes that he is a worker.

Reported Inner Speech During Actual Task Engagement

Julio's portrayal of his inner speech when working on more and less difficult tasks in general can be compared with his "think aloud" protocols when actually engaged in solving 14 problems identified by his teacher as being of low, moderate, or high difficulty for him and his recall of that task engagement.

Julio chose to work with an ink pen, proceeded through each problem in order, used none of the material resources available, and asked for interviewer clarification four times, all within the initial moments of the interview. His behavior indicated, and he recalled, one instance of problem reformulation, which he said was triggered by his watch. He was working a problem involving time to travel between cities and noticed his watch had "army time," which caused him to reconsider how he was going about it. Julio reported that he generally found the entire task "easy" and figured that, because it was easy, he would probably get a "little over half" right.

Julio did consider one problem difficult, however, recalling that it was because "I had to use fractions, because . . . dividing fractions is kind of hard because I forgot how to do that, and then I remembered." Julio found three problems interesting: the one that he could use "army time" to solve, one involving the "metric stuff," and the one that was difficult "because you . . . . you really have to think about it, and then when you think about it, you know it just gets all easy . . . . at first I thought it was really hard . . . and then I remembered that you had to flip the other one to a ratio . . . use the ratio and divide it, and then that's when it got easy."

Examination of Julio's process tracing protocol indicates that time allocated per problem varied from 0.05 minutes (spent on the "interesting metric stuff") to 3.11 minutes (spent on the "interesting hard problem"). Throughout, Julio's reported "inner" speech is task- rather than self-involved, and usually engaged in knowledge acquisition and knowledge "telling": reading or rereading the problem, appearing to "recite" the algorithm as much as "use" it. "Put down the zero and carry the one" computational procedures seemed to accompany action, not guide it. In one problem requiring a table as part of the solution, Julio reported a plan: "I'll make a table, like a square . . . two small tables (prior to actually drawing them) . . . I have to make this a little higher" (after initial drawing).

Self-involved speech only occurs in three problems (one of which had been identified as hard and interesting), which also are the only problems that Julio spent at least a minute working on (2.16, 2.10, and 3.11 minutes, respectively). Self-involved utterances in these problems, although infrequent, suggested a basic sense of numeracy as a standand against which computational results were compared. Julio's reported computation in each of these problems is more deliberate than in the others.

When at work, Julio's focus appears to be on the engagement of the task per se, not on clear understanding of task demands, their solution, or his predicted expectancy for success, which was "a little over half right" because it was easy. One week later, Julio described the problem solving/process tracing interview. He recalled feeling "okay," saying to himself that "this is pretty easy and these chairs are small" [the interview took place in the kindergarten room], and figured he got an "A." He liked it only "a little bit."

My Classroom Journal

Julio's class participated in the experiential sampling phase of the study. For three weeks, as described earlier, students periodically were asked to record their actions and thoughts in a journal. Focus here is on Julio's reported self- (metacognitive) and other (incidental observation) awareness.

Julio completed 31 entries, he was absent one day of this phase of the study. Julio reported he generally knew what was expected of him and how to go about task procedures. He figured he was mostly doing "ok" (89%). Julio described behavior that was off-task at the time of the journal entry 31% of the time; most of his off-task behavior was talking with peers. He reports generally feeling all right in class: of the codable 30 reports (noncodable = blank) 23% described positive affect, 46% feeling "ok," and 26% portrayed negative affect, most of which had to do with anxiety and stress.

Julio reports *thinking* about the task at hand, however, only 27% of the time. His descriptions indicate the he (like others in his class) is especially attentive in health class, which had been focusing extensively on illegal drugs, their appearance, use, dangers, and so on. The remaining 73% of Julio's reports of what he thought about during class include peers (27%), nonschool events (20%), the teacher or student teacher (whom he had a crush on) (17%), and affective reactions to the work (10%).

Fifty percent of Julio's reported inner speech while working consisted of task-involved speech; of these, approximately one half focused on his evaluation of the task. Most task evaluations were negative ("this is dumb"). Remaining task involved speech indicated reflection ("the Vietnam war wasn't necessary"), and some instances indicated attempted task direction ("how do you know what kind of compound is the word?").

Julio's inner speech reports were self-involved 23% of the time. One half of these were self-directive ("I have to straighten up my act"). Remaining reports were focused on instances of wishful thinking ("I hope I do good in gym"). Inner speech concerning others that Julio reportedly engaged (20%) was evaluative; positive if it was about the teacher ("Miss Teacher is an ok teacher") or the student teacher ("she is fine"), and essentially negative if about a classmate ("Tim is a jerk sometimes"; "he thinks he could beat me up").

Finally, Julio reported 28 instances of incidental observation, a clue to his awareness of the context of his learning. These observations were most apt to involve peers (43%): 28% were descriptive ("Tom got a haircut"); 15% were evaluative, primarily consisting of references to female classmates ("she has nice ankles"). Twenty-eight percent of Julio's incidental reports concerned task issues in school ("I didn't remember anything about the story"; "the words are hard to see from where I'm sitting at"). Fifteen percent of recorded incidental observations were self-referent ("my necklace was on wrong"); 15% about the teacher or student teacher ("teacher wore the same clothes last week"). Julio's incidental observations never left the classroom nor did they include references to time.

The multiple sources of information about what it is like for Julio to learn in the classroom indicate that he believes that learning takes time and work and help. And "keeping at work" is not easy for Julio. His sense of himself as a worker, a person who *does* what it takes to understand, is not congruent with his descriptions of himself in the classroom, where his reports indicate on-task behavior only 69% of the times sampled. It is the case, however, that Julio completed these journal entries from mid-March through the first week of April and that time of year may be a factor. One week of journal entries was completed during the annual standardized testing, however, and it seems likely that timing would inflate Julio's reported task-appropriate behavior and cognition.

More importantly, Julio's journal reports and his problem-solving protocols indicate that when he is "on task," that is, doing the work, his thoughts are on "automatic pilot" if they are on the task at all. Julio is "at work," but "at work" has not yet been defined as including thinking, as transforming the self or the task. Julio does not appear to have an enabling conception of learning nor a sense of his own self-regulation in that process. He is effortful, but he is not adaptive. He appears to have interiorized his father's beliefs, values, and goal for him, but Julio, like his father, does not possess the strategies to attain it. He does not understand that you can't work all the time and simply working is not enough. Expectations and criteria for learning progressively change across the grades. Julio's focus on obedience and reliance on others rather than on one's self are strategies with increasingly diminishing returns.

CASE TWO: NORA

Home Learning

Parent Values

Nora's family consists of several brothers and working parents. Each family member has assigned chores. Nora's include helping with dishes, keeping her room in order, and caring for two younger brothers after school a "couple of days a week" until her mother gets home from work.

Nora's mother, with whom the interview took place, juggles multiple roles. She, like her husband, works full time, has preschool children, and maintains a commitment to "be there" for each individual child. Nora's mother wants the children to see that she "plays" multiple roles, that she is "not just a mother," and that life is not always interesting or reinforcing. Mother is resigned to the role of boredom and evaluation in life, be it at home, work, or school. She states:

> So I just tell her, you know, we're all tired of certain things. I hate to go to work every day and I have to, I hate to deal with certain people every day, and I must, and that's that.

Mother also shares her work evaluations with her children so they can better learn how to respond to others' judgments.

> I tell them you are constantly being evaluated at home and at school, and people will always tend to look at you in another light that you never thought existed. And I tell them, "You ought to be aware of that."

Thus, mother describes taking on different roles and it's implication: "wherever we are, we adapt to wherever we are." You can't plan on other persons or other things to bring you satisfaction or worth. You must look to yourself.

Not surprisingly, mother values being responsible, setting priorities, and meeting commitments. These themes dominate all aspects of the interview. Mother enacts her values: she models and directly teaches her children what it means to be responsible and why setting priorities is a critical feature of responsible behavior. And she meets her commitments to "be there" for each child. Nora had asked her mother to participate in the study. The interview took place during afternoon school hours on mother's day off. Father comes home for lunch. Nora's mother had started dinner preparation at noon while she fixed her husband's meal and listened to some "of what he calls 'constructive criticism' about the house cleaning." She had a toddler with blanket and stuffed animals in tow. Nora was to come home after school with her other younger brother in case we weren't finished.

Expectations and Management Style

Nora's mother worries that Nora will not learn to set her priorities. She understands this as the prerequisite to responsibly meeting commitments. Setting priorities, from mother's perspective, is all about effort. Effort involves thinking through and following through. It is the first step in acting responsibly. This chain of reasoning is consistent with the norms by which we hold ourselves and one another accountable: competence obligates intentional enactment.

Nora can fall short on this obligation. Mother describes Nora-the-babysitter who:

> comes home and she gets involved with TV, spaces out, doesn't know that life is going on. And it kind of annoys me that, "Nora, are you really watching them? Do you know what's going on? Are you being a responsible babysitter?"

Nora-the-student can at times be galling as well. Mother recalls Nora getting an "F" on an incomplete assignment:

> that really blew her mind. And she was upset with it for awhile, and then she said, "I'm going to change that. I'm going to turn that around." And she did. . . . I knew that she wouldn't have gotten an F, and she knew that too. I think she had been sick a couple of days, and . . . she wasn't setting her priorities. You know, "it doesn't phase me anymore. I'm tired of the homework. I'm tired of the studying."

And then there was "the other day," the more typical case, where Nora-the-student-who-lives-in-my-home had a book report due:

> She stayed up till one o'clock. She had a whole month to do it. Okay? She's still a child. She definitely needs to set her priorities. And some of her attitudes . . . I'd like to cut right out.

The obligation of responsible behavior requires an understanding of those things for which we are not responsible. We are not always competent and our intentions are not always protected. This is part of Nora's home learning as well. Mother describes a kitchen incident in which Nora broke a dish and was cautiously awaiting the storm. Mother recalls:

> I said, "Well, come on, let's clean it up and throw it away." And she kept waiting to see the reaction. She thought I was really going to be angry. I said the dish could be replaced. I can't get angry over that. "It happened, it slipped out of your hand. You didn't take the dish and throw it across the room intentionally. This was a mistake, an accident, it happened." You try to keep it in perspective.

Mother's admonition to Nora-the-babysitter, her exasperation with Nora-the-student, and her explanation to Nora-the-dishwasher each contain instructive components. The series of questions in the first instance convey what it means to be a "responsible" babysitter. In the second, mother nixes any notion that one can choose not to be responsible. In the last example, she teaches what is not included in the concept "responsible." Mother's goal is that Nora learn what is meant by responsibility. She also wants Nora to learn how to organize herself in ways that afford responsible behavior:

> go back to setting her priorities, not realizing that when I tell you your bedtime is nine o'clock, I tell you this for a reason, okay? This almost sounds funny . . . "I tell you bedtime is at nine o'clock because you are a difficult person to wake up in the morning, and you need your rest."

Mother is teaching Nora intricate social-cognitive rules and self-regulatory processes that attend to motivation, competence, and enactment that likely empower Nora to "wherever we are, we adapt to wherever we are." Mother is also imparting a value structure to Nora that, at its core, defines integrity as responsibility for self and commitment to other. It is this more basic internalization for which mother listens to know she is successful as a parent:

> So I think she's taking it all in, and every now and then I hear what she's absorbed. You know, these things come out, and like, "in the last six months, you really did grow up."

Attention, then, is paid to indications that Nora has internalized and integrated mother's values, has the strategies (especially setting priorities) to realize them, and commits to their enactment.

Mother did not spontaneously discuss rewards and punishments in her dealings with Nora. When specifically asked, however, and only in the context of school, she described what she considered appropriate responses to Nora's classroom successes and failures: keep it informative and keep it private. Notably, in both instances, mother assumed the reference was to social, rather than academic, concerns. And in the social domain, Nora needs to know what is laudable in her behavior just as she needs to know what is problemmatic. Nora does not need humiliation. If she has done something wrong, mother believes it best to take her aside afterward and explain, on a "feeling level," be "adult" about it.

Mother believes that all kids need praise. A lot of praise; private praise. Public praise is just as embarrassing as public criticism:

> Any kind of public, you know, picking her out, I know that would embarrass me too. She doesn't like that. But she kind of likes to know that you're back there rooting for her.

And that's where her mother is:

> Like last year, she's on the softball team, and I got there just in time to see her up at bat. I didn't see the rest of the game. And she said, "Oh, Mom, you missed the whole game!" And I know I made the other mothers feel like this . . . well, I didn't mean to, but I just said, "I got here for the most important part of the whole thing. I saw you up at bat." And she just glowed.

View of Children

In Nora's home, you are your commitments. As previously noted, commitment, responsibility, and priority are intricately related to the enactment of valued behavior. In Nora's home, children are viewed as distinct individuals who are in the process of becoming: becoming more their own person, becoming more self-aware and capable of self-control, and becoming more integral parts of the family. In this family growing up means internalizing the values of home concommitant with increasing competence to enact them so that you can be counted on: external evaluation or remediation is not required.

Mother thinks of Nora as a relatively shy child who does not like to stand out, not even to have her birthday announced over the P.A. in school. Mother describes Nora:

> I see personality, I don't see an intellect. She's coming into her own groove.... She really sees right from wrong. . . . I can see her morals coming in here. . . . I think her strong points are knowing who she is now, who she really is. I can't help but repeating this, but her morals are really very strong now, and she doesn't care about the kids. She doesn't care to be trendy or anything. It doesn't bother her that she is not. You know she doesn't need to go along with the tide. She's a good kid, she's just a normal 12-year-old kid. Sometimes I think, "What's

> wrong . . . the other girls are looking at boys now, and . . . she's not. She's just enjoying life.

Mother feels good about her daughter. She is pleased that her teacher thinks of her similarly:

> You know, her teacher told me that, "She's an enjoyable child." It really made me feel good. It made me feel like I've done my job right, to have grown up this kid.

Mother does not volunteer comments about academic facets of Nora. When specifically asked, however, she mentioned that learning comes easily to her; perhaps too easily. Nora doesn't seem to "earn" her way:

> She learns easily. She doesn't need much study. Sometimes I see that as a problem. She doesn't have to work hard at it. Things just come to her. You show her, she deals with it, she does it.

And Nora doesn't need much study to succeed in the sixth grade. As we will see, with reasonable effort she is a quite successful student. Nora's teacher describes her as a moderate ability learner who is positively motivated and "enjoys" schoolwork. Nora's school records include redundant reports from school psychologists puzzled with testing results. Throughout elementary school, Nora's consistently high classroom grades led to staff expectations that she would place in the "gifted and talented" program, but her performance always fell short. Test results are accompanied with anecdotal reports of Nora-the-third-grader saying she doesn't want to leave her classroom; Nora-the-fifth-grader stating she likes things like they are.

There is no premium on innate ability at home; the premium is on the striving, the doing the best that one can. Achievement without effort is not especially valued. Nor is complacency. Mother describes the frustration that Nora's "coming into her own" can arouse:

> I think the fact now that she, in her class and in her [K-6] school, she's at the top now. She thinks that's great, she thinks she's king of the mountain. She feels like that at home, too. She feels like the know-it-all. You know, "I'm grown. Now I know right from wrong." She doesn't see any gray. And I tell her life is not like that. Sometimes there's a lot of gray. . . . I think that is her weakness.

And Nora is not always embarrassed by mistakes at home as she is in school. At home:

> She'll tell me it wasn't a mistake. At home it was meant to be. She won't admit to it, or she'll laugh it off . . . "I don't know why, I don't know what possessed me to."

And then there is Nora's flippant reply to mother's rationale for her nine o'clock bedtime:

> Whether I go to bed at nine o'clock or twelve o'clock, I just can't get up, so . . .

Mother laughs at the telling. "She's a smart kid!" Even so, in Nora's home, satisfaction with self has its limits.

Children-as-becoming require instruction. And children coming into their own certainly can be challenging. There is a wealth of teaching going on and patience in Nora's home. Sometimes, however, the learning is uneven and patience wears thin. When Nora falls short of mother's expectations, however, she is described as "still a child," implying that she has much yet to learn. Mother does not lose her process orientation. It is likely that, in this home, falling short of expectations followed by renewed efforts to meet them may well inform mother *and* daughter that "values are in the right place" and serve to reaffirm commitments to self and other.

Nora's mother strives to create a "good environment" in which children "feel at ease enough" to be themselves. For Nora's mother, home is an "arena of comfort" where one guides a child through the labrynth of coming into her own while responsibly meeting her commitments. No small task: not for mother; not for Nora. As we will see, book learning comes easily to Nora; being her own person does not.

School Learning

Achievement Profile

Nora is an "A" student. Her report card grades in math (on grade level), reading (above grade level), and language development consist of 11 "A's" and 1 "B." Nora received "outstanding" effort ratings in each subject, each marking period. Teacher assessments of her "personal growth" changed from a rating of "satisfactory" in the first quarter to "outstanding" for the rest of the year. Nora performed above grade level on each standardized achievement test in the spring, including reading (grade equivalent of 8.5, a national percentile of 81), math (grade equivalent of 9.0, a national pecentile of 93), and "total" performance (grade equivalent of 8.9, a national percentile of 90%). Nora is a student of considerable ability; her teacher's anomalous rating of her ability as "moderate" is likely influenced by her nonselection for the gifted program and what the teacher sees as her consistent and considerable effort.

Perception of School

Nora likes school. She describes a safe, small environment where you can "belong" if you try, even though some kids may call you names to start a fight.

Nora enjoys her classwork and teacher, but finds teacher explanations uneven, due in part to unknown vocabulary. Unclear directions and new work can be problematic, but Nora believes she usually knows when she doesn't understand, and will ask for an alternative explanation rather than a repetition of the previous one. One social advantage of understanding your work that Nora enjoys is the ability to help friends over the phone, where schoolwork reportedly gets done more efficiently than in class because "parents won't let you stay on the phone very long."

Nora's social-cognitive knowledge is strategic and evident in her ordering of classroom life. She exhibits what Corno (1989) terms "classroom literacy." She suggested, for instance, that the researcher expand the interview to allow students to discuss the tensions between sociability and self-reliance in small group work. She also suggested more careful distinction between task difficulty and task appeal: one can apparently not understand work but still find it enjoyable; easy work is not necessarily fun. In short, Nora is verbal, academically able, self-aware, "motivated," and, although relatively shy, her social-cognitive ability is notable.

Other Perception: Achievement

Nora was individually interviewed about her perceptions of four fictional classmates as described earlier. Nora perceived each of the four vignette characters uniquely. Her interpretation of each, however, rested on attention to a single cue: effort, which for Nora, encompasses thinking through and following through. Thus, the depicted outcome in each vignette (success or failure) derived value from her understanding of the character's expended effort; success and failure per se do not have inherent value. Nora also uniquely elaborated the vignettes by constructing interpersonal factors as important elements of each achievement situation. In three vignettes Nora predicted the response of the fictional character's mother, in one she envisioned peer relations. A brief synopsis of her discussion is informative.

In her discussion of Margaret, the effortful and ultimately successful character, Nora focused on Margaret's initial concern with her confusion, its effect ("She takes a long time to do her stuff"), and her concerns about a "bad" grade. In the process, Nora ultimately discounted the difficulty of the task, reconstructing a "hard won" learning event into a more modest one:

> Later, when she figured it out she would say that, "This wasn't very hard and I made it through."

Nora predicted that Margaret's

> Mom's going to be really proud of her, because her mom knows that she's not very good at math, and she tries her best.

Nora's discussion of Sue, the effortful, yet ultimately unsuccessful student, provides a telling contrast. Nora predicts that her mother will be angry, not because Sue did not ultimately understand, but because the vignette says that Sue, tired and defeated, finally "stopped even though she is not finished. All the ones she did are wrong." The story was meant to convey the limits of sheer effort and arguably *appropriate* withdrawal from a too-difficult task. Nora perceived that the task was too difficult but she didn't expect Sue's mother would. Even though Nora believed that,

> She's getting frustrated at herself because she's not doing them right. And she knows she's going to get a bad grade on it and she can't help it.

Nora assumed the mother would not be so sympathetic. Mother will not infer as Nora did that "she can't help it," an inference that, by the social-cognitive rules of home should result in parental concern and support. Instead Nora predicted:

> Her mom's going to get mad at her because she didn't even try . . . . Her mom'll probably give her a lecture [on trying to do your best] and then . . . .talk to her teacher about a class that she can put her in."

Quitting when you know you do not understand is costly. Not trying if you do not *realize* you should, however, is not. Especially if when you do realize you need to try harder, you follow through, you try again. Thus, Nora interprets Jill, a third vignette character whose effortless behavior is followed by failure, as *not knowing* that she did not understand and, once aware, as wanting to try again. Jill is therefore not accountable for her failure; her effortless behavior is not blameworthy. Nora predicts Jill's inner speech:

> This is not hard, but it's going to take me a little long to do. . . . I think I'd better take more time on this. Maybe take another test.

Hence, new work and rate of learning recast failure into a manageable task— if given enough time and another opportunity to perform. Commitment to try again places the failure mid-stream; it is only part of the process, it is not the outcome.

Nora predicts that Jill's mother will be concerned. Where Sue's behavior elicited anger, Jill's engages mother support:

> When she brings it home to her mom, her mom might suggest to take a little more time on it and she [both mother and daughter] might talk to her teacher about it.

In each of these three situations, Nora volunteers home involvement. There were no questions that sought home issues. Nora apparently considers home a part of schooling experience, at least in situations that she predicts will bring mother pride (effortful success), anger (knowingly unsustained effort and failure), or concern (lack of effort due to lack of awareness, failure, and renewed effort). Interestingly, Nora confines discussion of the next vignette, depicting Ann's effortless success, to school. Interpersonal factors in this scenario involve peers.

Nora described Ann as good at math (keeping the attribution task specific) and predicts inner speech that is similar to the type of cognitive engagement predicted for students in competitive goal structures (Ames, 1984):

> This is really easy and I could probably go ahead of the rest of the class. . . . I knew I would do this good.

Nora predicts a peer-competitive fall-out because she assumes conceit, although Ann, like the other vignette characters, is described as well-behaved and of moderate ability. In this particular task, however, Ann knows how to do the work and gets almost all of them right. Nora assumes she will brag about her performance and peers will retaliate. She elaborates upon the range and effects of bragging "styles."

Nora apparently does not assign effortless success a value in its own right. Instead, she assumes it co-occurs with inappropriate posturing: negative interpersonal behavior and intrapersonal characteristics. What is most interesting, however, is the *absence* of home involvement in Nora's discussion. Unlike the other situations, in the case of effortless success, Nora does not blend home and school, instead predictions are confined to peer competition and loss of friendship. In Nora's framework, Ann endures a double loss—she does not get to integrate home and school and she pays for her self-pride with damaged friendships.

Nora seemingly has constructed an approach to understanding achievement in the sixth grade that incorporates her mother's valuing of effort above all. Responsibility for trying is defined as awareness that one does not understand. Nora's social cognition is mediated by a value structure, described by her mother as "strong," yet too ready to dichotomize events into "black or white." Thus, Nora does not simply replay events, she attempts to assess culpability. Her apparent rules, based as they are in the "thinking through and following through" of responsible behavior, are not unlike the social-cognitive rules of home. One must make—and meet—one's commitments.

General Self-Perception

Nora was unable to make a general description of herself as a learner. She waffled between self-comparisons with Ann and Margaret (who both ultimately succeed) and then between Ann and Jill (who both engage in minimal effort). Nora's speech became atypically tentative, her language confused. She made several recall "errors," which do not occur elsewhere in the interview. Nora finally settled on a self-comparison with Jill, who did her assignment effortlessly and quickly, but got many problems wrong. Recall that Nora had reconstructed this vignette so that Jill was a victim of her lack of understanding and, failing the assignment, sought another opportunity to perform. She was responded to with maternal concern and helpfulness. Nora was unable to say that she generally is quite capable in school.

Contextual Self-Perception

Task-specific self-perception is much easier for Nora to engage. She readily named Margaret, the high effort and ultimately successful character, as the person she is most like when confronting difficult tasks. She focused upon their similarities in rate: "I try to get my work done. I don't usually finish when it's time."

Nora reportedly remains task-focused when she is coping with difficult tasks, rather than becoming undone by detrimental self-involved inner speech:

> [I think] just about the problems. I just think of what I'm going to do when they come up, how I'm going to figure them out.

Her account of how she is going to "figure them out" consists of task-involved strategies aimed at understanding the work and self-reliance:

> I go through the steps, step by step . . . [I know its hard] when I can't figure it out quickly, and I wait a little while, and I go on to different problems, and I come back to it, and I still can't figure it out . . . [So I] put it on scrap paper, and just leave it, and hand in the test, and when it comes back, and she [teacher] has the answer on the paper, I'll try to figure it out, and how she got the answer.

Nora equates difficult tasks with tests. What about the easier tasks? Nora compares herself with Ann, who effortlessly succeeds, "because when the stuff isn't that hard, and its real easy, I can get it done fast, and I get a good grade." And her reported inner speech: "None. I just go right through it."

Finally, Nora discussed which character she would want to be like. Nora thought Margaret liked math more than Ann, because "Ann, you know, she doesn't seem like she cares, because she seems to know math, and she doesn't think that she needs it." For Nora, effort indicates value, as it does for her mother. Of the four characters, Nora wanted to be like Margaret because:

> She seems to be a person who's into her own . . . she seems to be a person who's not into a group. A person who doesn't want to make up or doesn't hang around with a lot of people. She . . . she's not . . . very bright.

Nora is her mother's child. Being like Margaret, particularly as elaborated by Nora, has several benefits. First, she has "earned" her success; she is "coming into her own." Second, she stays with difficult tasks and ultimately gets most of the work correct; thus, she receives good grades and "outstanding" effort ratings. Third, Margaret takes a long time; she does not finish before her classmates and, hence, does not have to worry about competitive battles with peers. In her relations with home, with her teacher, and with her peers it is easier for Nora to be less capable and, thus, more effortful in school.

Relation Between Other and Self-Perception

Nora's beliefs about others and herself indicate that she has fused issues of learning and morality and modesty in her understanding of achievement. Learning in school is not just about the outcome. Although Nora was concerned about grades, her priorities for self and for others were in making a commitment to do one's best and following through responsibly. Nora manages task failure by recasting it as an opportunity for effortful behavior. She apparently believes that effortful behavior will ultimately be efficacious. Thus, quitting is not allowed. Failure is transitional, it is only part of the learning process, not the final word. Quitting makes failure final; the quitter culpable. And not having to try in the first place isn't much better. Achievement without striving has little to recommend it.

Reported Inner Speech During Actual Task Engagement

An extensive analysis of Nora's reported inner speech while actually engaged in solving problems of varying difficulty is available elsewhere (see McCaslin Rohrkemper, 1989b). Discussion here will simply highlight Nora's general hardiness when she engages tasks. As one might predict, she remains effortful and strategic if the task requires it. Easy tasks are simply and rotely completed. Tasks that are judged too difficult are beyond her expectations for understanding. After attempts to make them accessible, and thereby accountable, fail, Nora radically transforms the too-difficult problems. They take on qualities of puzzles. Goals change from correct solution to mere completion.

When Nora engages problems of moderate difficulty she exhibits sophisticated task-involved strategies that include problem organization, reformulation, "fresh starts" both figuratively and literally, and facility with heuristic procedures and specific algorithms. She also exhibits stress. Nora manages her frustration through self-involved inner speech aimed at keeping the specific problem in perspective: there are others to work on. Self-beration is limited to these problems, even so, Nora does not become undone by her chagrin. Within each problem she takes control and re-engages task-involved strategies. She continues to try—to a point. Nora eventually closes an unsolved problem with a guess, expecting to get it wrong, but noting that it is "finished."

Moderately difficult problems were the only problems to engage both task- and self-involved inner speech. And they were apt to be recalled as among the most difficult problems. It seems that one reason for this reconstruction is because Nora recognized them as something she had either done before, or as similar to it, and she was unable to complete them with certainty. Thus, her problem transformations were limited to plausibly correct transformations; such is the burden of experience. Familiarity can increase anxiety, especially for learners like Nora who distinguish between recognition and understanding (see also, Fields, 1990). Effortful cognition, the "thinking through and following through" maxim of home learning, does not always result in understanding; a reality Nora typically does not confront. Nonetheless, she remains effortfully task-involved. Nora's time per problem ranged from 8.36 minutes to 24 seconds. Of the 12 problem set, she engaged 3 problems for over 4 minutes, 3 problems for less than a minute.

When asked to assess her performance immediately after finishing the problems, Nora said that she "finished most of them" and expected to get 7 of the 12 correct, 1 partially correct. One week later, Nora recalled feeling "ok" during, and "tired and happy" after, the interview. She recalled saying to herself that "I can go on if it is too hard and some of them are really hard and some easy." She estimated that she got about "half right, half wrong," thought overall it was pretty hard, and only liked it "a little bit."

My Classroom Journal

Nora's conception of achievement, based in a sort of a "golden rule" of cognition, and her capacity to enact that conception, are evident in her self- and other- constructions and in her problem solving protocols. We have noted that moderate difficulty tasks afford the integration of the affective and the intellectual for Nora. We also have learned that Nora values her mother's regard and being her own person. We now turn to Nora in her classroom, describing her moment-to-moment experiences, to assess how these conceptions and opportunities permeate her classroom life.

Nora completed 27 journal entries, she was absent two days during the three week journal phase of the study. Nora reported that she always (100%) knew what was expected of her and that she usually knew how to go about task procedures (91%). Nora described her achievement expectations in relation to the construct "well." She predicted she was doing "well" or "very well" on 56% of the tasks, "well enough" on 33%, and "not well enough" on 11%. Nora described herself as "on task" at the time of the journal entry 85% of the time. When she reported off-task behavior (15%), although infrequent, it was as apt to involve peers ("talking to my friends") as not ("wasting time"). Nora's descriptions of how she feels in the classroom indicate that she generally is aware of her feelings (72%) and also seems preoccupied with concerns about school work and home (28%) ("how would my mom feel when I said to her I didn't have any math homework"). Evenso, Nora typically feels good (48%) ("great, up to it," "like singing") or "OK" (29%) in class. When she reports negative feelings (24%), however, they appear intense ("uneasy," "horrible").

Nora reports *thinking* during task engagement 81% of the time. Of these reported thoughts, only 32% concern the task and are either quite general ("my reports"), yet to be assigned ("homework"), or yet to be completed ("if I would get out of the math chapter, fractions"). Twenty-seven percent of Nora's reported thoughts while task engaged were self-involved ("how I would get through the day," "how well I did").

Nora's most typical reported thoughts during task engagement, however, were other-involved (41%). These included equivalent attention to (1) family and home events, which possibly was inflated as Nora's birthday occurred during this period, ("everything I would do when I got home," "taking the guinea pig home this weekend"); (2) after-school activities ("softball practice tonight"); and (3) peers. Thoughts about peers involved girls and ranged from apparent concern ("how she must feel when she gets her paper back because it was graded") to hostility ("how I would tell M. I hated her") to suspicion ("how J. is writing about me").

Nora reported inner speech while working 68% of the times sampled. Of these reports, the majority were self-involved (58%). Self-involved inner speech spanned self-description ("I want this to get done") (36%), self-direction ("hurry up you stupid brain and give me the answer!") (36%), and self-evaluation (27%), usually negative ("I did very bad on this"). Reported task-involved inner speech (32%) evenly encompassed task-description ("6 more! 6 more!"), task-direction ("should I put the line here or not?"), and negative task-evaluation ("this is stupid"). Only two reports (11%) concerned peers and were descriptive of girls and their achievement ("A. got a lot wrong").

Finally, Nora's incidental observation reports indicate that she typically is aware of the context of classroom learning (78%). What Nora notices is her peers (86%). Only 1 incidental report concerned the task at hand, 2 herself ("I was hungry"). All remaining reports concerned the ubiquitous "everyone" or specific girls. Reports about others include observations upon: (1) achievement ("B. didn't pass her lesson," "everyone else did better than me at my table"); (2) rate ("R. is almost done with her poster," "other people are ahead of her"); (3) norms ("everyone was really interested"); and (4) interpersonal relationships ("K. went and told M. that I hated her").

The multiple lenses on what it means to be Nora in the classroom indicate that Nora's home learning permeates her understanding and valuing of classroom striving and achievement. Responsibility, setting priorities, and meeting commitments are transformed by Nora-in-the-classroom to a code of effortful cognition fused with the golden rule. Nora is a quite capable learner who has difficulty conceptualizing herself as such. She prefers the modesty (and controllability) of sustained effort.

Nora's journal records indicate that she may well exaggerate the amount of effort she invests in school tasks. Although she reports "on task" behavior most of the times sampled, Nora's thoughts typically are elsewhere. She thinks about home but mostly she thinks about her classmates, namely the other girls. It is noteworthy that Nora reportedly is not overtly engaged with her classmates. Her journal entries indicate Nora was involved with peers only 7.5% of the times sampled. Nora's involvement is internal.

In short, Nora discounts her ability and inflates her self-reliance. Book learning comes readily; being her own person does not. Nora's reports indicate that she has internalized her mother's values. The enactment of those values, however, is a daily and challenging task.

CLOSING COMMENTS

In this paper we have attempted to make a case for the theoretical power and practical utility of the construct "emergent interaction" for understanding students' classroom behavior. We have illustrated the value of considering the developing child in emergent interaction with the multiple social/instructional environments of home and school. Second, we hypothesized that some home and school social/instructional environments require more adaptive learning of students than do others because some home environments are more synchronous with the contexts of school. We found that children, home, and schooling expectations are in emergent interaction: what is congruent between home and school in early grades may not be congruent in later grades. Third, we have attempted to portray one method that appears promising for research on emergent interaction as it informs analytical discussion even as it generates hypotheses for continued consideration. Finally, and throughout, we have called for the deliberate enhancement of "adaptive learning" as one outcome of schooling. We hypothesize that the presentation of tasks that allow the integration of the affective and the intellectual within a supportive "arena of comfort" will afford the enactment and, thus, enhancement of self-involved and task-involved inner speech and, hence, foster the potential for adaptive learning.

Julio and Nora, the two cases of emergent interaction of home and school in the development of adaptive learning, are especially informative when we compare them with the traditional constructs that typically are used to interpret students in classrooms. For example, research on factors "internal" to a student may well interpret the ego-ideals of Julio and Nora as a function of gender. That is, the male seeks effortless achievement in math that is construed as high ability and is generalized to other subjects. The female vision is more confining. She seeks effortful achievement in math. The interpretation of "classic" gender differences in perceptions of ability, particularly mathematics ability, is incomplete given what we know about the ongoing social/instructional influences of home and school that contribute to each student's ego-ideal.

Julio and Nora each have internalized the value of effort at home. Their respective ego-ideals emerge within these home constructions. In Julio's home effort is known *by* the outcome. His ego-ideal, as Julio has reconstructed him, succeeds through perpetual effort, and he subsequently achieves well everywhere. In Nora's home, effort *is* the essential outcome. Her ego-ideal succeeds, but more importantly, she exhibits sustained effort. And effort is understood uniquely by each student. For Julio, effort is endurance. For Nora, it includes the facility to monitor her learning and alter her "efforts" in line with task demands. Nora views herself as a source of effort and knowledge; Julio looks to self for effort and counts on the availability of others like Nora to supply the necessary knowledge when something is not immediately known.

Consideration of ego-ideal and the differential valuing and interpretation of effort and achievement at home, and by these students, also calls into question the utility of an "ability" construct in our understanding of students' classroom achievement. Recall that Julio's performance on the standardized mathematics test ranked in the 86th national percentile, Nora's in the 93rd. Furthermore, an ability interpretation of each student's understanding of what it means to be effortful and display of effortful problem solving behavior would likely conclude that Nora's more fluid problem solving strategies are a function of ability differences. Given what we know about the differences that underlie and continuously influence each student's expended "effort," however, ability conclusions are not particularly informative. The cases illustrate, instead, the power of the fusion of "will" and "skill." Both Julio and Nora have internalized the will to "achieve": their constructions of what it means to achieve differ as do the skills they bring to those unique constructions.

We also can consider the cases of emergent interaction in relation to theory and research on factors "external" to the student, for example, parent managerial styles. The homes differ in parental authority structure and, thus, predicted probability of successful internalization by children. Yet, in both homes, the children have internalized their parents' values and goals for them. It is apparent that the pursuit of these goals is a daily challenge for both Julio and Nora. It is not easy for either of them to meet parental expectations. Yet each tries. Thus, even though the homes differ in authority and management structures, they are both instilling their values in their children. The cases also illustrate the evolving congruence between home and school expectations: Julio's home learning is becoming less effective as an approach to learning in school. In contrast, as Nora progresses through school, her home learning will likely serve her even better than it did in earlier grades. The cases illustrate as well the inappropriateness of categorization of one type of parenting (assuming love for the child is a constant) as by definition "better" or "more successful" than another (cf. Epstein, 1989, see also Berliner, 1989).

It also is notable that "sociological" approaches to the study of home influence on school learning would likely not have "found" what appear to be important differences between these home social/instructional environments. Recall that in these two cases parental occupation, ultimate education, and place of residence are each located within the same socio-economic "category." Hence, their distinctiveness likely would not have been observed nor learned from.

In short, the utility of examining isolated concepts, or their discrete interaction, appears limited if we wish to understand students' emerging constructions of themselves as learners and their evolving strategies for learning in classrooms. Our specific goal is to better understand the development of adaptive learning. We include in this construct the internalizion of goals, the motivation to commit, challenge, or reform them, and the strategic competence to enact and evaluate those commitments. The construct of "emergent interaction" appears to be an enabling concept and the case method an informative tool to bring to this pursuit.

ACKNOWLEDGMENTS

The research reported in this paper was supported in part by the first author's participation in the Junior Leave Program of Bryn Mawr College and a Spencer Postdoctoral Fellowship. Interview transcription costs were undertaken by the Center for Effective Elementary and Middle Schools of Johns Hopkins University. Manuscript preparation was facilitated by the Center for Research in Social Behavior at the University of Missouri-Columbia. The authors wish to acknowledge and thank Tom Good, Lyn Corno, Abbie M. Segal-Andrews, and Phyllis Blumenfeld for their helpful comments.

REFERENCES

Ames, C. (1984). Competitive, cooperative, and individualistic goal structures: A cognitive-motivational analysis. In R. Ames & C. Ames (Eds.), *Research on motivation in education: Student motivation* (Vol. 1). Orlando, FL: Academic Press.

Astin, H. S. (1974). Sex differences in mathematical and scientific precocity. In J. Stanley, D. Keating, & L. Fox (Eds.), *Mathematical talent: Discovery, description, and development.* Baltimore, MD: The Johns Hopkins University Press.

Bandura, A. (1977). *Social learning theory.* Englewood Cliffs, NJ: Prentice Hall.

_____. (1981). Self-referent thought: The developmental analysis of self-efficacy. In J. H. Flavell & L. D. Ross (Eds.), *Development of social cognition.* New York: Cambridge University Press.

Baumrind, D. (1971). Current patterns of parental authority. *Developmental Psychology Monographs, 4* (No. 1, Part 2).

_____. (1987). A developmental perspective on adolescent risk taking in contemporary America. In C. Irwin, Jr. (Ed.), *Adolescent social behavior and health.* San Francisco: Jossey Bass.

Berliner, D. (1989). Furthering our understanding of motivation and environments. In C. Ames & R. Ames (Eds.), *Research on motivation in education: Goals and cognitions* (Vol. 3). San Diego, CA: Academic Press.

Blumenfeld, P., Pintrich, P., & Hamilton, L. (1986). Children's concepts of ability, effort, and conduct. *American Educational Research Journal, 23,* 95-104.

Blumenfeld, P., Pintrich, P., Meece, J., & Wessels, K. (1982). The formation and role of self-perceptions of ability in elementary classrooms. *Elementary School Journal, 82,* 401-420.

Brattesani, K., Weinstein, R., & Marshall, H. (1984). The formation and role of self perceptions of ability in elementary school classrooms. *Journal of Educational Psychology, 76,* 236-247.

Brophy, J. (1983). Research on the self-fulfilling prophecy and teacher expectations. *Journal of Educational Psychology, 75,* 631-661.

Corno, L. (1989a). Self-regulated learning: A volitional analysis. In B. Zimmerman & D. Schunk (Eds.), *Self-regulated learning and academic achievement: Theory, research, and practice.* New York: Springer-Verlag.

_____. (1989b). What it means to be literate about classrooms. In D. Bloome (Ed.), *Learning to use literacy in educational settings.* New York: Ablex.

_____. (1990, April). *The "best laid plans": Individual differences in modern conceptions of volition.* Paper presented at the meeting of the American Educational Research Association, Boston.

Csikszentmihalyi, M., & Larson, R. (1984). *Being adolescent.* New York: Basic Books.

Deaux, K. (1976). Sex: A perspective on the attribution process. In J. Harvey, W. Ickes, & R. Kidd (Eds.), *New directions in attribution research* (Vol.1). Hillsdale, NJ: Erlbaum.

DiMarino-Linnen, E. (1990). *Identity development from a dialectical perspective: Toward a richer understanding of the identity formation process.* Unpublished doctoral dissertation, Bryn Mawr College, Bryn Mawr, Pennslyvania.

Dweck, C., Goetz, T., & Strauss, N. (1980). Sex differences in learned helplessness, IV: An experimental and naturalistic study of failure generalization and its mediators. *Journal of Personality and Social Psychology, 38,* 441-452.

Eccles (Parsons), J. (1983). Expectancies, values, and achievement behaviors. In J. Spence (Ed.), *Achievement and achievement motives: Psychological and sociological approaches.* San Francisco: W. H. Freeman.

Engels, F. (1890/1972). Socialism: Utopian and scientific. Reprinted from the authorized English edition of 1892, in R. C. Tucker (Ed.), *The Marx-Engels reader.* New York: Norton.

Entwistle, D., & Hayduk, L. (1978). *Too great expectations: The academic outlook for young children.* Baltimore, MD: The Johns Hopkins University Press.

Epstein, J. (1989). Family structures and student motivation: A developmental perspective. In C. Ames & R. Ames (Eds.), *Research on motivation in education: Goals and cognitions* (Vol. 3). San Diego, CA: Academic Press.

Eshel, Y., & Klein, Z. (1981). Development of academic self-concept of lower-class and middle-class primary school children. *Journal of Educational Psychology, 73,* 287-293.

Fennema, E. (1974). Mathematics learning and the sexes: A review. *Journal for Research in Mathematics Education, 5,* 126-139.

Fetterman, N. (1990). *The meaning of success and failure: A look at the social instructional environments of four elementary classrooms.* Unpublished doctoral dissertation, Bryn Mawr College, Bryn Mawr, Pennsylvania.

Fields, R. D. (1990). *Classroom tasks, children's control perceptions, and their relation to inner speech.* Unpublished doctoral dissertation, Bryn Mawr College, Bryn Mawr, Pennsylvania.

Frey, K., & Ruble, D. (1987). What children say about classroom performance: Sex and grade differences in perceived competence. *Child Development, 58,* 1066-1078.

Frieze, I., & Snyder, H. (1980). Children's beliefs about the causes of success and failure in school settings. *Journal of Educational Psychology, 73,* 186-196.

Gigliotti, R., & Brookover, W. (1975). The learning environment: A comparison of high and low achieving elementary schools. *Urban Education, 10,* 245-261.

Glazier-Robinson, B. (1990). *Effects of a mediated learning parent training program on low SES pre-school children.* Unpublished doctoral dissertation, Bryn Mawr College, Bryn Mawr, Pennsylvania.

Good, T., & Brophy, J. (1987). *Looking in classrooms.* New York: Harper & Row.

Gordon, T. (1970). *Parent effectiveness training.* New York: Wyden.

Harris, M., & Rosenthal, R. (1985). Mediation of interpersonal expectancy effects: 31 meta-analyses. *Psychological Bulletin, 97,* 363-386.

Heath, S. B. (1982). Questioning at home and at school: A comparative study. In G. Spindler (Ed.), *Doing the ethnography of schooling.* New York: Holt, Rinehart, and Winston.

Hess, R. (1970). Social class and ethnic influences upon socialization. In P. Mussen (Ed.), *Carmichael's manual of child psychology* (3rd ed., Vol. 2). New York: Wiley.

Hoffman, M. L. (1983). Affective and cognitive processes in moral internalization. In E. T. Higgins, D. Ruble, & W. Hartup (Eds.), *Social cognition and social development: A sociocultural perspective.* New York: Cambridge University Press.

Kallman, J., & Stollak, G. (1974). *Maternal behavior toward children in need arousing situations.* Paper presented at the meeting of the the the Midwestern Psychological Association, Chicago.

Keeves, J. (1972). Educational environment and student achievement. *Stockholm Studies in Educational Psychology, 20,* 1-309.

Kohn, M. (1977). *Class and conformity* (2nd ed.). Chicago: University of Chicago Press.

Lepper, M. (1981). Intrinsic and extrinsic motivation in children: Detrimental effects of superfluous social controls. In W. A. Collins (Ed.), *Minnesota symposium on child psychology* (Vol. 14). Hillsdale, NJ: Erlbaum.

Luria, A. R. (1969). Speech development and the formation of mental processes. In M. Cole & I. Maltzman (Eds.), *A handbook of contemporary Soviet psychology.* New York: Basic Books.

————. (1979). *The making of mind: A personal account of Soviet psychology* (M. Cole & S. Cole, Eds.). Cambridge, MA: Harvard University Press.

Maccoby, E., & Martin, J. (1983). Socialization in the context of the family: Parent-child interaction. In P. Mussen (Ed.), *Handbook of child psychology* (Vol. 4). New York: Wiley.

Marcus, T., & Corsini, D. (1978). Parental expectations of preschool children as related to child gender and socioeconomic status. *Child Development, 49,* 243-246.

Marshall, H., & Weinstein, R. (1984). Classroom factors affecting students' self-evaluations: An interactional model. *Review of Educational Research, 54,* 301-325.

Marx, K. (1867/1972). *Capital.* Selections from Volume 1 from the English text of 1887 as edited by Engels, in R. C. Tucker (Ed.), *The Marx-Engels reader.* New York: Norton.

McCaslin, M. (1989). *The contexts of social comparison.* Unpublished manuscript.

————. (1990). Motivated literacy. In J. Zutell & S. McCormick (Eds.), *Literacy theory and research: Analyses from multiple perspectives.* Thirty-ninth Yearbook of the National Reading Conference (NRC). Chicago, IL: NRC.

————. (in progress). *Adaptive learning study.*

McCaslin Rohrkemper, M. (1989a, April). *Social cognition, interpersonal awareness, and the development of self-directive inner speech in elementary school students.* Paper presented at the meeting of the American Educational Research Association, San Francisco.

_____. (1989b). Development of self-regulated learning: A Vygotskian perspective. In B. Zimmerman & D. Schunk (Eds.), *Self-regulated learning and academic achievement: Theory, research, and practice.* New York: Springer-Verlag.

Midgley, C., Feldlaufer, H., & Eccles, J. (1989). Changes in teacher efficacy and student self- and task-related beliefs in mathematics during the transition to junior high school. *Journal of Educational Psychology, 81,* 247-258.

Newman, R. (1984). Children's achievement and self-evaluations in mathematics: A longitudinal study. *Journal of Educational Psychology, 76,* 857-873.

Nicholls, J. (1978). The development of the concepts of effort and ability, perceptions of academic attainment and the understanding that difficult tasks require more ability. *Child Development, 49,* 800-814.

_____. (1979). The development of the perception of own attainment and causal attributions for success and failure in reading. *Journal of Educational Psychology, 71,* 94-99.

Parsons, J., Adler, T., & Kaczala, C. (1982). Socialization of achievement attitudes and beliefs: Parental influences. *Child Development, 53,* 310-321.

Parsons, J., Frieze, I., & Ruble, D. (1976). Introduction. *Journal of Social Issues, 32,* 1-5.

Parsons, J., Kaczala, C., & Meece, J. (1982). Socialization of achievement attitudes and beliefs: classroom influences. *Child Development, 53,* 322-339.

Parsons, J., & Ruble, D. (1977). The development of achievement-related expectancies. *Child Development, 48,* 1075-1079.

Pavlov, I. (1927). *Conditional reflexes.* London: Oxford University Press.

Phillips, D. (1984). The illusion of incompetence among academically competent children. *Child Development, 55,* 2000-2016.

_____. (1987). Socialization of perceived academic competence among highly competent children. *Child Development, 58,* 1308-1320.

Phillips, D., & Ziegler, E. (1980). Children's self-image disparity: Effects of age, SES, ethnicity, and gender. *Journal of Personality and Social Psychology, 39,* 689-700.

Phillips, D., & Zimmerman, M. (1990). The developmental course of perceived competence and incompetence among competent children. In R. Sternberg & J. Kolingian (Eds.), *Competence considered.* New Haven, CT: Yale University Press.

Piaget, J. (1970). Piaget's theory. In P. Mussen (Ed.), *Carmichael's manual of child psychology* (3rd ed., Vol. 1). New York: Wiley.

Posner, M. (1979). *Cognition: An introduction.* Glenview, IL: Scott, Foresman.

Reuman, D. (1989). How social comparison mediates the relation between ability-grouping practices and students' achievement expectancies in mathematics. *Journal of Educational Psychology, 81,* 178-189.

Rohrkemper, M. (1984). The influence of teacher socialization style on students' social cognition and reported interpersonal classroom behavior. *Elementary School Journal, 85,* 245-275.

_____. (1986). The functions of inner speech in elementary students' problem solving behavior. *American Educational Research Journal, 23,* 303-313.

Rohrkemper, M., & Bershon, B. (1984). The quality of student task engagement: Elementary school students' reports of the causes and effects of problem difficulty. *Elementary School Journal, 85,* 127-147.

Rohrkemper, M., & Brophy, J. (1980, April). *Teachers' general strategies for dealing with problem students.* Paper presented at the meeting of the American Educational Research Association, Boston.

_____. (1983). Teachers' thinking about problem students. In J. Levine & M. Wang (Eds.), *Teacher-student perceptions: Implications for learning.* Hillsdale, NJ: Erlbaum.

Rohrkemper, M., & Corno, L. (1988). Success and failure on classroom tasks: Adaptive learning and classroom teaching. *Elementary School Journal, 88,* 299-312.

Rohrkemper, M., Slavin, R., & McCauley, K. (1983, April). *Investigating students' perceptions of cognitive strategies as learning tools.* Paper presented at the meeting of the American Educational Research Association.

Rosenholtz, S., & Simpson, C. (1984). Classroom organization and student stratification. *Elementary School Journal, 85,* 21-38.

Ruble, D. (1983). The development of social comparison processes and their role in achievement-related self-socialization. In E. T. Higgins, D. Ruble, & W. Hartup (Eds.), *Social cognition and social development: A sociocultural perspective.* New York: Cambridge University Press.

Scarr, S., Phillips, D., & McCartney, K. (1989). Working mothers and their families. *American Psychologist, 44,* 1402-1409.

Schaefer, E. (1959). A circumplex model for maternal behavior. *Journal of Abnormal and Social Psychology, 59,* 226-235.

Seigner, R. (1983). Parent's educational expectations and children's academic achievements: A literature review. *Merril-Palmer Quarterly, 29,* 1-23.

Simmons, R. (1987). Social transition and adolescent development. In C. Irwin Jr. (Ed.), *Adolescent social behavior and health.* San Francisco: Jossey Bass.

Simon, H. (1969). *The sciences of the artificial.* Cambridge, MA: MIT Press.

Stevenson, H., Chaunsheng, C., & Uttal, D. (1990). Beliefs and achievement: A study of black, white, and Hispanic children. *Child Development, 61,* 508-523.

Stipek, D. (1981). Children's perception of their own and their classmates' ability. *Journal of Educational Psychology, 73,* 404-410.

Stipek, D., & Daniels, D. (1988). Declining perceptions of competence: A consequence of changes in the child or changes in the educational environment? *Journal of Educational Psychology, 80,* 352-356.

Stipek, D., & Hoffman, J. (1980). Development of children's performance-related judgments. *Child Development, 51,* 912-914.

Stipek, D., & Tannatt, L. (1984). Children's judgments of their own and their peers' academic competence. *Journal of Educational Psychology, 76,* 75-84.

St. John, N. (1972). Mothers and children: Congruence and optimism of school-related attitudes. *Journal of Marriage and the Family, 32,* 422-430.

Surber, C. (1984). The development of achievement-related judgment processes. In J. Nicholls (Ed.), *Advances in achievement motivation: The development of achievement motivation* (Vol. 3). Greenwich, CT: JAI Press.

Vygotsky, L. (1962). *Thought and language.* Cambridge, MA: MIT Press.

———. (1978). *Mind in society: The development of higher psychological processes.* Cambridge, MA: Harvard University Press.

Weiner, B. (1985). *An attributional theory of motivation and emotion.* New York: Springer-Verlag.

Weinstein, R., Marshall, H., Brattesani, K., & Middlestadt, S. (1982). Student perceptions of differential treatment in open and traditional classrooms. *Journal of Educational Psychology, 74,* 287-312.

Weinstein, R., Marshall, H., Sharp, L, & Botkin, M. (1987). Pygmalion and the student: Age and classroom differences in children's awareness of teacher expectations. *Child Development, 58,* 1079-1093.

Weinstein, R., & Middlestadt, S. (1979). Student perceptions of teacher interactions with male high and low achievers. *Journal of Educational Psychology, 71,* 421-431.

Wertsch, J. (Ed.). (1985). *Culture, communication, and cognition: Vygotskian perspectives.* New York: Cambridge University Press.

———. (1985). *Vygotsky and the social formation of mind.* Cambridge, MA: Harvard University Press.

Wertsch, J., & Stone, C. (1985). The concept of internalization in Vygotsky's account of the genesis of higher mental functions. In J. Wertsch (Ed.), *Culture, communication, and cognition: Vygotskian perspectives*. New York: Cambridge University Press.

Zinchenko, V. P. (1985). Vygotsky's ideas about units for the analysis of mind. In J. Wertsch (Ed.), *Culture, communication, and cognition: Vygotskian perspectives*. New York: Cambridge University Press.

THE CLASSROOM CONTEXT AND STUDENTS' MOTIVATIONAL GOALS

Judith L. Meece

Schools provide an important context for both the development and the expression of children's achievement motivation. Yet only a handful of studies has examined the effects of the classroom context on children's motivation. Much of what is known about the factors that either sustain or inhibit the development of motivational processes comes from experimental studies outside the classroom. As several researchers (Brophy, 1983a; Corno & Rohrkemper, 1985; Lepper & Hodell, 1989; Ryan, Connell, & Deci, 1985) have noted, the special nature and complexity of the classroom environment limit the applications of this research.

This paper reports on a qualitative study of the classroom context and students' motivational goals. This research draws upon recent conceptions of motivation, which view children's and adults' achievement behavior as goal directed. Goal conceptions of motivation differ from traditional approaches that have focused on individual differences in internal states and traits, such as achievement needs, motives, and values. Achievement goal research has shown that although dispositional traits can influence the type of goals individuals pursue, aspects of the achievement setting itself can exert a powerful

Advances in Motivation and Achievement, Volume 7, pages 261-285.
ISBN: 1-55938-122-1

influence and, in some cases, override the effects of individual differences (Ames & Archer, 1988; Meece, Blumenfeld, & Hoyle, 1988). This body of research has further shown that the achievement goals individuals pursue can influence self-regulatory processes in learning situations.

The paper begins with a brief review of the research on goal conceptions of motivation and describes applications of this research to educational settings. In subsequent sections, I report findings from a study of the classroom context and elementary school students' goal orientations. The chapter concludes with a summary of classroom features that influence students' goal orientations.

GOAL CONCEPTIONS OF
ACHIEVEMENT MOTIVATION

Several motivation theorists (Dweck & Elliot, 1983; Maehr & Nicholls, 1980; Nicholls, 1984) have argued that in order to develop a better understanding of achievement behavior we need to consider the specific goals individuals pursue or value. Research has primarily focused on two types of achievement goal orientations. Some individuals pursue what are known as learning-oriented (Dweck & Elliot, 1983) or task-oriented (Nicholls, 1984) goals. They seek to master a skill, gain competence or to understand a problem. Learning is valued as an end in itself. Other individuals seek to demonstrate high ability or to gain favorable judgments of their abilities in relation to the efforts and performance of others. The terms performance-oriented (Dweck & Elliot, 1983) and ego-oriented (Nicholls, 1984) describe the goal states of these individuals.

Two field-based studies have examined sources of individual variation in students' goal orientations. Bandura and Dweck (cited in Dweck & Bempechat, 1983) established relations between children's ability conceptions and goal orientations. They found that children who have an incremental conception of ability and believe that their abilities can be increased through their own efforts, prefer learning tasks that are hard, new and challenging so "they could learn from them." When, on the other hand, children view ability as a fixed and stable trait (i.e., entity theorists), they prefer tasks that will show "how smart they are." Dweck and Bempechat (1983) maintain that by middle to late elementary school, most children have acquired both conceptions of ability (see also Nicholls & Miller, 1984), but tend to act more in accordance to one than the other. They also argue that characteristics of the learning situation may create strong tendencies to adopt one conception of ability over the other.

In another study, Nicholls, Patashnick, and Nolen (1985) examined relations between high school students' goal orientations and beliefs about the causes of success. Their results revealed that students with a task-oriented goal orientation view effort, interest, attempts to understand, and cooperative work as important causes of success in school. An ego-involved goal pattern corresponds to students' beliefs that success depends on impressing the teacher and attempting to do better than others. The responses of these students indicate a greater concern with measuring or demonstrating the adequacy of their ability in relation to others.

Several related studies have shown that learning situations can elicit different goal orientations by emphasizing either self- or norm-referenced standards of evaluation. Experimental conditions that emphasize interdependent reward structures (Ames & Felkner, 1979), self-improvement (Ames & Ames, 1981, 1984; Butler, 1987), discovery of new information or concepts (Jagacinski & Nicholls, 1984), and the usefulness of learning material (Elliot & Dweck, 1988) can induce task or learning goal states. Under these goal conditions, high effort attributions result in high perceived competence. By contrast, experimental conditions that raise concerns about one's ability, such as interpersonal competition (Ames, 1981, 1984), tests of intellectual skills (Jagacinski & Nicholls, 1984) or creativity (Ryan, 1982), and public learning situations that involve normative evaluation (Elliot & Dweck, 1988) can foster ego or performance goals. In these cases, low effort attributions increase perceptions of ability, particularly if the individual outperforms others who exhibit high effort.

In summary, recent research on motivation has focused on differences in the goals individuals pursue in achievement situations. While some individuals are interested in learning as much as possible, others show greater concern with how their performance or abilities will be evaluated by others. The goals individuals pursue in achievement situations appear to be related to their conceptions of ability and causal beliefs. Furthermore, experimental studies have shown that it is possible to modify or to induce certain goal orientations by introducing interpersonal competition or by manipulating the salience of normative evaluation.

ACHIEVEMENT GOALS AND SELF-REGULATORY PROCESSES

The goals individuals pursue in achievement situations result in different patterns of cognition, affect, and problem-solving behavior. In one study that examined these effects, Elliot and Dweck (1988) experimentally induced learning and performance goal orientations, by manipulating the salience of normative evaluation. They then compared the influence of different goal conditions on fifth-grade children who were led to believe they had either low or high ability on a problem-solving task. The findings indicate that the learned helpless and mastery-oriented achievement patterns identified in Dweck's early work (Dweck & Reppucci, 1973) occur under different goal conditions.

In the Elliot and Dweck (1988) study, low ability children oriented toward evaluation (performance goals) expressed negative affect toward their own abilities and the task, and they showed a marked deterioration in their persistence and problem-solving efforts on difficult tasks. This pattern did not appear in children with high ability in the performance condition, although they chose to avoid challenging tasks involving public errors. Children in the learning-oriented condition, regardless of ability level, displayed the mastery-oriented pattern in the face of difficulty. They maintained a task focus and persisted in finding better solutions to the problem.

Elliot and Dweck's findings are consistent with those reported by Ames (1984) who contrasted fifth- and sixth-grade children's achievement cognitions under individualistic versus competitive goal structures. Goal states were experimentally manipulated by varying the task conditions and instructions. In the individualistic condition, children worked alone, with instructions to solve as many puzzles as possible; children in competitive condition worked in pairs, with the instructions to compete with each other ("Let's see who is better at solving the puzzle"). The findings suggest that when children focus on improving their performance, rather than competing with others, they report more effort-related attributions, positive affect statements, and self-instructional statements, such as telling themselves to think harder or to work more carefully.

Both of the above studies indicate that the goals children pursue in achievement settings are critical mediators of self-regulatory processes. Performance or competitive goal conditions create a self-focus, which diverts attention away from the learning task. If the individual lacks confidence in his or her ability to perform the task, the negative affect and worry that ability concerns engender can also impede problem-solving efforts. It may be that in order to avoid negative evaluations by others, some individuals consciously give up or minimize their efforts so that lack of effort, and not ability, becomes the reason for poor performance or failure. Learning-oriented goals, on the other hand, create a task focus in which individuals attend primarily to the quality of their performance and the effort needed to succeed. The positive affect derived from mastering a skill or activity sustains problem-solving efforts.

APPLICATIONS OF ACHIEVEMENT GOAL RESEARCH TO EDUCATIONAL SETTINGS

Several researchers have examined relations between students' existing goal orientations and learning processes in the classroom. Nolen (1988) assessed students' goal orientations and study strategies in junior high school science classes. She found that students who indicated that their goals were to understand and to learn used a set of study strategies that can potentially enhance conceptual understanding, such as integrating information or monitoring comprehension. In contrast, students who were primarily concerned with doing better than others or impressing the teacher tended to use surface level processing skills, such as memorizing and rehearsing information.

Ames and Archer (1988) reported relations between junior high school students' perceptions of the classroom goal orientation and use of planning, self-monitoring, and comprehension checking strategies. The results indicate that a mastery-oriented classroom environment, in which self-improvement, developing new skills, learning from errors are the salient norms and expectations, can have a strong positive influence on students' preference for challenging tasks, causal beliefs, and reported use of learning strategies.

My colleagues and I (Meece, Blumenfeld, & Hoyle, 1988) have also examined relations between students' goal orientations and level of cognitive engagement in science lessons. In this classroom study, fifth- and sixth-grade students who indicated that their goals were to master or to learn show a high degree of cognitive engagement in learning activities, as indicated by their reported use of active learning strategies, such as regulating attention, integrating information, and monitoring comprehension. Students who indicated that their goals are to do better than others or to impress the teacher reported greater use of effort-minimizing strategies, such as eliciting help from others, guessing at answers, or skipping the hard parts.

The Meece et al. study also assessed the influence of work-avoidant goals on students' engagement patterns. Whereas mastery- and ego-oriented goals represent different forms of approach motivation, work-avoidant goals represent a form of avoidance motivation (Nicholls et al., 1985). Under this goal condition, students seek to complete their work with a minimum of effort. The Meece et al. results suggest that students with work-avoidant goals have the most negative attitudes toward learning and report the lowest level of cognitive engagement in classroom activities.

Current research is beginning to analyze the effects of the classroom environment on students' goal patterns. Several researchers (Ames & Archer, 1988; Meece, Blumenfeld, & Puro, 1989; Nicholls & Thorklidsen, 1987; Nolen & Haladyna, in press) have found significant classroom differences in students' goal orientations. This research indicates that the classroom as well as individual students can be characterized according to a specific goal orientation. Most studies to date, however, have used rating scales to characterize the classroom environment that focus on a single group of variables. These findings need to be further grounded in research on classroom processes and integrated with other aspects of the classroom environment that can potentially affect students' goal orientations.

A QUALITATIVE STUDY OF THE CLASSROOM CONTEXT AND ELEMENTARY STUDENTS' GOAL ORIENTATIONS

In the following section, I describe findings from a recent study of the classroom context and elementary students' goal orientations. The study is part of a larger investigation of students' motivational and cognitive engagement patterns in elementary science lessons (Blumenfeld & Meece, 1990). For the purposes of the present study, I analyze data from 10 classrooms to identify teacher differences in students' goal orientations. Next, using qualitative data analysis procedures, I analyze characteristics of the classroom environment that can potentially explain teacher differences in students' goal patterns. Below I summarize the various lines of research that guided my analysis of the classroom environment.

Background of Study

The middle childhood years are an important time for the development of children's school-related competence (Connell, in press). During this period, children become more knowledgeable of how to learn as they begin to use active strategies for integrating information, monitoring comprehension, and constructing meaning (Brown, Bransford, Ferrara, & Campione, 1983). Classroom environments that support and stimulate the development of these cognitive abilities can have a positive influence on students' motivation to learn by fostering an increased sense of competence (Eccles & Midgley, 1989).

There is some evidence to suggest, however, that students may not respond positively to challenging or cognitively demanding learning activities. Brophy (1983a) has argued that because performance in the classroom is public and subject to evaluation by others, few students are likely to be interested in tasks that involve errors, confusion, or a great deal of effort, unless they are certain they will succeed. According to Brophy, the level of mastery students derive from successful completion of learning activities in the classroom depend not only on the difficulty level of the task, but also on the teacher's ability to provide adequate instructional support and feedback, so that success appears attainable with reasonable effort. Similarly, Corno and Rohrkemper (1985) maintain that teacher judgments concerning the appropriate level of challenge and instructional support to provide are critical determinants of children's motivation to learn in the classroom.

Other field-based studies have focused on the control structure of learning activities. Using an ecological approach, Grannis (1978) and Stodolsky (1988) have shown that learning activities vary with regard to students' opportunities to exercise control over behavioral options, the pace of the activity, materials feedback, and peer relations. Whole class activities tend to be highly teacher structured and controlled; student participation is generally limited to answering teacher questions. In contrast, individual and small group activities generally allow children to exercise some limited control over behavioral options. Both Grannis and Stodolsky's research indicates that students exhibit more task involvement in student-controlled versus teacher-controlled learning activities.

Similarly, motivation theorists have shown that a high degree of teacher control can negatively influence students' self-ratings of academic competence and intrinsic motivation (Deci, Schwartz, Sheinman, & Ryan, 1981; Ryan & Grolnick, 1986). Ryan, Connell, and Deci (1985) propose that availability of choice and some degree of student control can foster an internal locus of control, whereby students believe they are engaging in learning activities by their own volition. In contrast, when teachers provide limited opportunties for students to direct and to assume responsibility for their own learning, children come to view their learning as controlled by others and extrinsically motivated.

Another set of studies suggests that the salience of ability-related information in the classroom can have a strong influence on children's motivational orientations. Numerous studies have examined the classroom processes by which teachers communicate ability-related information. Much of this research focuses on the differential treatment of low and high achieving students (for review, see Brophy, 1983b). According to recent research (Nicholls & Thorkildsen, 1987), the presence of an ability hierarchy in the classroom can influence students' goal orientations. Students report a task-oriented goal pattern when they perceive the teacher as encouraging and supporting the learning efforts of both low and high achieving students. Correspondingly, the perceived differential treatment of low and high achieving students can foster an ego-oriented goal pattern.

The salience of ability-related information appears to be influenced by the organizational structure and evaluation norms of the classroom. Research by Rosenholtz and Rosenholtz (1981) and by Stipek and Daniels (1988) characterized elementary classrooms according to four dimensions that influence the comparability of students' performances: (1) task differentiation, (2) grouping practices, (3) opportunities for student choice of learning options, and (4) social comparative forms of evaluation. Rosenholtz and Rosenholtz found a high degree of agreement on academic rankings among students and between students and teachers in fifth- and sixth-grade classrooms whose organizational features accentuate ability differences, produce comparable and public performance information, and thereby, increase the salience of social comparison information. Similarly, Stipek and Daniels found that classrooms of this type have a negative influence on young children's ability perceptions. Both studies show that students maintain positive ability perceptions in classrooms characterized by high differentiation and individualization of tasks, instruction, and evaluation.

The use of cooperative learning activities in the classroom can also have a positive influence on students' ability perceptions and motivational orientations (Ames, 1987; Nicholls, 1983). Activities with interdependent reward stuctures reduce students' concerns about failure and evaluation, because responsibility for learning is shared. Students focus their attention on helping others, and high effort attributions increase ability perceptions. In support of this suggestion, numerous studies have documented the positive effects of cooperative learning activities on students' subject matter interests, involvement in learning, and other motivation-related variables (for reviews, see Johnson & Johnson, 1985; Slavin, 1983).

A final set of studies indicate that the incentives teachers use to promote task engagement can influence the approach students adopt to learning. The frequent use of grades, time contraints and competition can undermine students' sense of control and interest in learning (Ryan et al., 1985). Such conditions also lead students to be concerned more about their productivity or their ability relative to others than about what they are learning (Ames & Archer, 1988; Marshall, 1988; Nicholls, 1983). In contrast, teachers can have a positive influence on students' motivation when they are enthusiastic and interested in the subject matter and when they emphasize the inherent importance and value of the learning material (Brophy, 1987; Brophy, Rohrkemper, Rashid, & Goldberger, 1983).

This brief review has identified several interactional and structural characteristics of the classroom that can affect students' motivation to learn. Classroom learning structures that enable students to develop an increased sense of competence and to assume increased responsibility for their learning are likely to promote a mastery-oriented goal orientation. It is also clear that the instructional and evaluation practices teachers use can moderate the effects of learning structures. If teachers do not provide adequate instruction or feedback, students, especially low achievers, are not likely to benefit from challenging or unstructured tasks. Grouping and evaluation practices that minimize social comparison information and emphasize the inherent value or benefits of the learning material help students to maintain a mastery focus while engaged in the activity.

Much of the research reviewed in the preceding section has focused on single elements of the classroom environment. In a recent study of students' ability perceptions, Marshall and Weinstein (1986) showed how various structural and interactional variables interact to negate or to compensate one another. Classroom structural variables, such as grouping practices and task different-iation, had less of an influence on students' ability perceptions than the attitudes and expectations teachers expressed within these structures. The evidence suggests further that teachers' attitudes and expectations can override the potentially negative effects of ability grouping practices and public evaluation. These findings are based on a small sample of classrooms and need to be replicated.

In summary, previous research has identified several different aspects of the classroom environment that can influence students' goal orienation. The study described below was designed to (1) ground findings based on rating scales in observations of ongoing classroom activities, (2) provide descriptive evidence of the relations suggested in previous research, and (3) examine how different aspects of the classroom environment combine to influence students' goal orientations.

The study uses a social-ecological perspective (Bronfenbrenner, 1976). Classrooms, like other social settings, are believed to have a fairly explicit set of social structures, norms, and expectations that govern and shape children's behavior. Although individual differences in children's needs, abilities, and values can influence how they interpret and react to different aspects of the learning environment, teachers play a crucial role in creating a classroom that encourages students with varying needs and abilities to become active self-motivated learners.

Data Sources

The study took place in one elementary and three middle schools during the 1985-86 school year. The schools were located in predominantly White suburban neighborhoods in southeastern Michigan. The sample consisted of 10 science classrooms taught by five teachers (three women and two men), with an average of 15 years of teaching experience. Science classrooms were selected because research comparing elementary subject areas (e.g., Goodlad, 1983) had suggested that science lessons vary the most in terms of instructional format and materials.

The research team collected data on 275 fifth- and sixth-grade students, with approximately the same number of boys and girls in each of the 10 classrooms. The average class size was 28 students. Students' standardized achievement test scores ranged from the 2nd to 99th percentile based on national norms, with the sample mean falling at the 60th percentile. The achievement level of students was comparable across classrooms.

We observed a total of 15 lessons in each science classroom. Teachers taught the same lesson to each of their two classes. The 15 lessons varied with regard to topic, format, length, and types of materials used. For most lessons, students completed some type of written product (e.g., worksheet, graph, chart, etc.). Students completed a group-administered questionnaire at the end of six different activities. The six activities varied in terms of instructional format (whole class, small group, etc.), cognitive difficulty, procedural complexity, and use of manipulative materials.

The questionnaire included 15 items to assess the strength of students' task mastery, ego-social, and work-avoidant goal orientations. Table 1 includes sample items from the goal scales. Information about scale construction and

Table 1.   Sample Items of Task Mastery, Ego-social, and
Work-avoidant Goal Scales

Task Mastery Orientation (alpha = 94)
1.   I wanted to find out something new.
2.   I wanted to learn as much as possible.
3.   The work made me want to find out more about the topic.
4.   I felt involved in my work.

Ego-Social Orientation (alpha = .85)
1.   I wanted others to think I was smart.
2.   It was important to me to do better than the other students.
3.   It was important to me that the teacher thought I was doing a good job.

Work-Avoidant Orientation (alpha = .77)
1.   I wanted to do things as easily as possible so I wouldn't have to work hard.
2.   I just wanted to do what I suppose to do and get it done.
3.   I wanted to do as little work as possible.

Note: Each item is rated on 4-point scale ranging from "Not very true" to "Very true." Maehr and Nicholls
(1980) categorized pleasing the teacher or gaining social approval as an extrinsic goal. These items
appeared to be highly correlated with ego-oriented items in the Meece, Blumenfeld, & Hoyle (1988)
study; therefore the two orientations were combined. Items in the ego-social scale represent a concern
with doing better than others or with teacher evaluation.

validation appears in Meece, Blumenfeld, and Hoyle (1988). Relations between
students' goal orientations and use of self-regulatory learning strategies are
reported in an earlier section of the paper.

For each of 15 lessons observed per classroom, trained observers collected
detailed observational records. Using fieldnotes and an audiotape of the lesson,
they prepared a written transcript of each lesson that described the (1)
instructional presentations, (2) teacher and student questioning patterns, (3)
feedback patterns, (4) grouping arrangements, (5) evaluation practices, and (6)
motivational strategies. The total time each class was observed ranged from
545 to 640 minutes.

Analysis of Observational Records

The analysis draws on several different data sources. First, as one indicator
of the cognitive level and complexity of learning activities, the research team
coded each written assignment for the number of questions or steps students
had to complete, the type of response required (short answer, visual
representation, written descriptions, etc.), and cognitive difficulty. We
categorized products that primarily involved knowledge or comprehension
skills as low difficulty. If one-third of the questions or procedures involved

skills above the comprehension level of Bloom's *Taxonomy of Educational Objectives* (Bloom, Englehart, Furst, Hill, & Krathwohl, 1956), we coded the assignment as high difficulty.

Second, we developed a simple coding scheme for categorizing teacher question and feedback patterns. We coded the frequency of low and high teacher questions using the same categorization used above to characterize the cognitive level of the written assignments. We also coded information on teacher feedback patterns. We assumed that teachers who frequently probed students' levels of understanding and asked for explanations, rather than simply affirming or negating answers, create a "press" for mastery in their classroom.

Last, we analyzed lesson transcripts for several additional features and patterns based on previous research. Two members of the research team read the lesson transcripts and prepared an initial summary of each case. Here, guided by previous research, we examined the types of instructional supports and incentives used to sustain students' involvement in learning activities, the salience of evaluation, and organizational features of the classroom. The transcripts were read again to confirm these analyses and to consciously seek out evidence that did not fit the described patterns.

Analysis of Student Goal Patterns

Scores on the goal measures were aggregated across the six questionnaire administrations in each class. Because different learning structures can influence students' scores on the goal measures (Meece & Blumenfeld, 1987; Meece, et al., 1988), aggregating scores across lessons provides a more reliable measure of students' goal tendencies than single assessments. Table 2 presents students' mean scores on the three goal measures used in this study.

To test for teacher differences, I collapsed data across classes taught by the same teacher and performed an one-way analysis of variance (ANOVA) on each goal scale.[1] As shown in Table 2, significant teacher differences appear in all three goal scales.

Post-hoc analysis using Tukey's test revealed that students in Cooper's and Dayton's classes have a stronger task mastery orientation than do students in Brown's and Eaton's classes.[2] The task mastery ratings of Allen's students fall between these two groups of teachers. Four tests reached significance for students' ego-oriented and work-avoidant goals. Dayton's students were less ego-oriented than were students in Allen's or Eaton's classes. Eaton's students were more work-avoidant than were Dayton's or Cooper's students.

For analysis purposes, I grouped teachers according to their students' task mastery scores. Fifth-grade teachers, Ms. Cooper and Mr. Dayton form the high mastery-oriented group, because their students have the highest average scores on the task mastery goal scale. Sixth-grade teachers, Mr. Brown and Ms. Eaton form the low mastery-oriented group, because of the relatively low

Table 2. Means, Standard Deviations, and *F*-tests on Goal Orientation Scales

Goal Scales	Allen (N = 56)		Brown (N = 56)		Cooper (N = 51)		Dayton (N = 45)		Eaton (N = 56)		MS_e	df	F
	M	SD	M	SD	M	SD	M	SD	M	SD			
Taks Mastery	3.25	.38	3.01	.51	3.50	.35	3.31	.45	2.98	.52	.20	4,263	12.52***
Ego-Social	2.70	.64	2.45	.74	2.49	.74	2.10	.75	2.65	.78	.53	4,263	5.13**
Work-Avoidant	1.39	.29	1.47	.36	1.37	.33	1.28	.24	1.45	.33	.09	4,263	2.94*

Notes: * $p < .05$
     ** $p < .01$
     *** $p < .001$

272

scores of their students on the task mastery scale. I also examined the distinguishing features of Ms. Allen's sixth-grade classes. Although students' task mastery scores in Ms. Allen's classes were slightly higher than the scores of students in the low teachers' classes, the difference was not statistically significant.

Summary of Findings

I describe below the patterns that differentiated the low and high mastery-oriented classes as well as variations between teachers. Five distinctive themes emerged from the analysis of the data, which I discuss in relation to previous research on students' motivation in the classroom.

Opportunities to Develop an Increased Sense of Competence

Previous research sugested that the cognitive complexity and difficulty of learning activities can influence children's motivational orientations. The teachers in this study were selected because they reportedly use a variety of learning activites. Given that the study involved a select group of teachers, there was very little variation in the difficulty level of learning assignments. One-third of the written assignments in four of the five teachers' classes involved application, analysis or evaluation processes. Eaton was the exception to this pattern, with only 1 of the 15 coded assignments requiring the use of higher-order thinking skills.

There was greater variability in the cognitive level of teacher questions during lessons. Here the analyses showed some variation between teachers, but no difference between high and low motivation teachers. Approximately 20% of the classroom interactions in Brown's and Cooper's classes per lesson included a high level teacher question requiring the use of application, analysis, or evaluation skills. Although Dayton, one of the high mastery motivation teachers, frequently asked comprehension questions, less than one-tenth of the classroom interactions per lesson included a teacher question above this level. Again, Eaton had the lowest frequency of high level questions per lesson. Only 2% of the interactions coded in these classes per lesson included a high level teacher question.

There was also some variation between teachers in how students could demonstrate their knowledge and understanding. This was limited to answering oral or written questions in the classes taught by Allen, Brown, and Eaton. In contrast, a few of Cooper's and Dayton's lessons involved visual representations, such as making a graph, chart, or diagram. Thus, in high mastery-oriented classes, students were provided opportunities to demonstrate their competence in ways that were not solely dependent on their reading and writing skills.

Another important feature that differentiated the teachers was the degree to which the learning material was adapted to the students' level of knowledge and understanding. Learning material that is unfamiliar, abstract or inaccessible to the students is not likely to foster an increased sense of mastery or competence. Both of the high mastery motivation teachers, Cooper and Dayton, presented concrete illustrations of scientific laws and principles such as speed and distance, and they related unfamiliar information to the students' personal knowledge. Cooper, for example, introduced the concept of interdependence among living things by having students describe who they depended on and who depended on them.

In contrast, the low motivation teachers, Brown and Eaton, used unfamiliar terms and concepts in their presentations. For example, Eaton expected students to learn scientific terms that were difficult for sixth-grade students to spell and pronounce such as *epiglottis, peristalsis, amylase,* and *phylorus.* Eaton rarely related learning material to the students' personal knowledge. Although Brown occasionally related activities to students' experiences, we observed several instances in which he missed opportunities to build on personal knowledge. In one lesson, for instance, he asked students for examples of saving natural resources. A student replied, "Saving money in a bank." Brown rejected the answer saying, "I want to limit the discussion to natural resources." In general, several of the practices we observed in the low motivation classes would not enable students to feel confident about their own reasoning abilities.

Opportunities for Self-directed Learning

Previous research suggested that students are likely to report a high level of mastery motivation when they are given opportunities to direct or to assume responsibility for their own learning. Table 3 shows the amount of time students spent in whole class, small group, and individual activity structures for the 15 lessons we observed in the five teachers' classes. As indicated here, students in the high mastery-oriented classes (Cooper's and Dayton's) did not spend a disproportionate amount of time in small group or individual activities that would allow them to assume more responsibility for their learning. Whereas Brown's classes spent proportionately more time than the mastery-oriented classes in whole class activities, students in the other low mastery-oriented classes (Eaton's) spent a greater amount of time in both small group and individual activities.

In all classes, students exercised limited control over the pace of the lessons, the materials used, how they carried out the work, and when they completed their activities. However, students exercised slightly more control over learning options in the high than low motivation classes. On a few occasions, Cooper and Dayton allowed students to choose materials and to decide how they

Table 3. Time Spent in Different Activity Structures

Teacher	Whole Class (WC)		Small Group (SMG)		Individual (IND)		Total Time	
	Class 1	Class 2	Class 1	Class 2	Class 1	Class 2	Class 1	Class 2
Allen	400 (.73)	420 (.72)	110 (.20)	130 (.22)	35 (.06)	30 (.05)	545	580
Brown	420 (.69)	460 (.74)	85 (.14)	75 (.12)	100 (.16)	90 (.14)	605	625
Cooper	325 (.59)	385 (.68)	140 (.25)	95 (.17)	85 (.15)	85 (.15)	550	565
Dayton	340 (.67)	375 (.68)	110 (.22)	115 (.21)	60 (.12)	60 (.11)	510	550
Eaton	260 (.41)	310 (.48)	220 (.31)	150 (.23)	175 (.28)	180 (.28)	635	640

Note: Values in parentheses represent proportion of total time observed.

wanted to do their assignments. In 2 of the 15 lessons observed in these classes, students planned and designed an entire experiment.

The pattern was not as consistent for the low mastery-oriented classes. Compared with Eaton, Brown more often encouraged students to use different materials and to experiment, but because the freedom to explore was inconsistent with Brown's emphasis on task completion, he would sometimes criticize students who were "experimenting" rather than completing their worksheets. Although Eaton's classes appeared to have greater opportunities than the other classes to direct their own learning, she determined most of the tasks and procedures. Due to the amount of work assigned, time pressures were inherent in most of the small group and individual activities observed in Eaton's classes.

There were also important differences in the types of instructional supports that were available to help students successfully complete small and individual activities on their own. Allen, Cooper, and Dayton did not assign individual or small group activities that were either too procedurally or cognitively complex for the students. Dayton would often do the more difficult activities as a whole class, whereas Allen and Cooper tended to highlight and demonstrate complex procedures before letting students complete the activity on their own. All three teachers tended to problem-solve with students when they had difficulty. In addition, students in Cooper's and Dayton's classes did not have to rely on the teacher for feedback about their work because it was inherent in the activity, either there were no right or wrong answers or a source was available for checking the work. Allen also encouraged the development of self-reliance by helping students to evaluate their own work when they sought teacher feedback.

We did not observe these patterns in low motivation classes. Most of the individual or small group activities in Eaton's classes required extensive teacher assistance, because they were too difficult for students to do on their own. Although the student-directed activities in Brown's classes were less complex, the students sometimes lacked the skills and knowledge to complete the activities. As a result, we often observed students in the low motivation classes asking for teacher assistance.

Brown and Eaton, however, were less likely than the other teachers to provide the type of assistance students need to become independent learners. They rarely helped students to work through the problem. Students were either referred back to the directions or given direct assistance.

Salience of Ability-related Information and Evaluation

Previous research had suggested that certain organizational features of the classroom can increase the salience of ability-related information and lead students to engage in social comparison processes. All the teachers in this study used heterogeneous grouping practices and whole class lessons as a primary mode of instruction. There was very little task differentiation within the different classes.

However, given that students in Cooper's and Dayton's classes could choose how to do some assignments, these learning structures may reduce the comparability of performance in the high motivation classes. Also, as we described earlier, Brown and Eaton, the low motivation teachers, tended to probe or rephrase questions when students answered incorrectly, which could draw attention to their abilities, especially if these feedback episodes occurred primarily in whole class situations. In addition, "slower" students in Eaton's classes were sometimes asked to finish their work in an adjoining room while the teacher went over the answers with the other students. This practice may increase the students' awareness of ability differences.

The salience of grades and evaluation can also raise students' concerns about their abilities. Tests and grades were fairly salient features of the low mastery-oriented classes. Although we observed several references to tests and quizzes in both teachers' classes, this occurred more frequently in Eaton's classes. In one-third of the lessons, Eaton mentioned an upcoming test or quiz. Test grades counted the most in the low mastery-oriented classes and poor work was not redone. Eaton's grading scale was the most demanding of all the teachers, and evaluation was fairly public in this classroom. Students called out scores on their homework, and the teacher posted grades on the bulletin board.

Tests were also a salient feature of Allen's lessons. Students were routinely reminded that they would need to know the learning material for an upcoming test, and on a few occasions, Allen threatened to give students a quiz when they were unable to recall or remember information. As observed in the low mastery-oriented classes, students' grades were largely determined by their test performance.

In contrast, grades and evaluation were not salient features of the high mastery-oriented classes. Cooper, for example, wrote comments on daily assignments but did not grade them. Quizzes were for review, and they generally included one question that asked students to either draw or describe what they had learned about a particular topic. When Cooper's students did poorly on a test, they could take the test again using their books, and they would receive the average of their two grades. We did not observe any formal evaluation in Dayton's classes. This teacher stated that he favored competency-based forms of evaluation, and he based students' grades on their daily assignments and class participation.

Emphasis Placed on Peer Cooperation and Collaboration

As described earlier, numerous studies have documented the positive effects of collaborative and cooperative learning activities on students' interests and ability perceptions. All teachers in this study used small group activities in which students worked together or shared materials, but they differed in terms of the emphasis placed on cooperation and collaboration. Several of the activities in the high mastery-oriented classes (Cooper's and Dayton's) required a group product, like a rocket design or visual display on the origin of the moon. In presenting these lessons, both teachers stressed the importance of teamwork and provided some guidance in how students could work together.

Cooper was more consistent than Dayton in reminding students of how they could use each other as resources for help and information. Also, Cooper was particularly skilled at teaching through peer consensus in whole class activities. She would pose questions, ask students to share opinions, seek out opposing points of view, and then help students to agree on an answer or solution.

Peer cooperation and collaboration were not as strongly emphasized by the other teachers, although Allen occasionally praised students for working well together. Small group activities in Allen's, Brown's, and Eaton's classes seemed to have the purpose of helping students to complete experiments or manipulative activities more efficiently. Many of the activities involved sharing materials, but the students completed an individual worksheet or product. Although the teachers expected students to help one another, they made very little effort to develop group relations in these classes. Eaton's students had the most negative reactions to working in small groups.

Emphasis on the Intrinsic Value of Learning

The incentives teachers use to promote task engagement can also influence the approach students adopt to learning. Both the high mastery-oriented teachers, Cooper and Dayton, stressed the value of what students were learning in science, and they related the learning material to students' personal interests and expereinces. Dayton was particularly skilled at pointing out the value of science for the students' lives outside of school and the challenges science presents:

> I don't expect you to grow up to be Robert Goddards, but I do want you to think about science, since science is all around you (Lesson 13).

> Do you realize how hard this is? Do you see the problems we have when aiming for the moon? It's not easy. It took six top mathematicians in the world, putting them in a closed room for two days straight, doing math calculations to figure out the exact window—meaning the moment you can blast off and where you can land (Lesson 15).

Cooper was equally skilled at communicating the value of science, but she did so by posing questions and problems in which students applied information from previous lessons. Students in her classes were able to experience firsthand the value of what they were learning. For example, in one lesson, she asked students to pretend their spaceship had crashed on the dark side of the moon and to use what they had learned about gravity to find their way back to the "mothership."

In contrast, many of the activities in the low motivation classes were disjointed and not well integrated with the overall objectives of the lesson or unit. It is unlikely that Brown's and Eaton's students perceived the value of what they were learning for other science activities. Although both Dayton and Eaton were knowledgeable science teachers, they rarely connected the learning material to the students' personal experiences or to what scientists do. In addition, the low motivation teachers made little effort to adapt learning activities to students' interests. We observed students complaining about assignments in both teachers' classes. Students were slow to begin assignments and, in Eaton's classes, students actually refused to do some of the activities, even though they would lose points or have to stay after school.

SUMMARY AND CONCLUSIONS

In this paper, I have reviewed recent research on children's goal orientations. Previous research has shown that the goals students pursue in achievement settings are strongly linked to self-regulatory processes. The evidence clearly indicates that children benefit the most from learning situations when they are oriented toward task mastery goals. My primary purpose was to identify features of the classroom that enhance children's mastery-oriented goal patterns. Under what conditions do students perceive learning and mastery as valued goals? Whereas previous research has focused on single features of the classroom, such as evaluation or grouping practices, this study described how various classroom dimensions can combine to shape students' goal orientations.

Consistent with the research of Marshall and Weinstein (1986), the findings indicate that structural variables alone cannot adequately explain variations in motivational variables. There was very little variation in the cognitive level of learning activities and teacher questioning patterns in four of the five teachers' classes. Also, in all classes, the learning activities afforded students opportunities to work independently, to exercise some degree of control, and to assume responsibility for their own learning. The results emphasize the need to examine the types of interactions that occur within various learning structures.

Teachers in the present study differed primarily in their instructional approaches and evaluation practices. Specifically, teachers of low versus high mastery-oriented classes differed in the degree to which they (1) promoted meaningful learning, (2) adapted instruction to the developmental levels and personal interests of their students, (3) established learning structures supportive of student autonomy and peer collaboration, and (4) emphasized the intrinsic value of learning.

In the high mastery-oriented classes, teachers Dayton and Cooper used an instructional approach that promoted meaningful learning. The interaction patterns observed in these classes suggested that teachers expected students to understand, to apply, and to make sense of what they were learning. Although students in the high mastery classes spent a significant amount of time in whole class activities, Cooper and Dayton posed questions and problems that elicited students' active participation in the learning process. To facilitate students' involvement in learning activities, Dayton and Cooper adapted lessons to the students' level of understanding and knowledge, modified lessons to increase their personal relevance, and supported students' independent learning. Grades and other extrinsic incentives were not used to motivate students in these classes. Instead, Cooper and Dayton motivated students by posing meaningful problems and questions and by making science personally relevant.

The preceding patterns sharply contrast with those observed in the low mastery-oriented classes. Learning activities in these classes emphasized the transmission and recall of simple facts and information. Brown's and Eaton's students had limited opportunities to actively construct meaning, to view themselves as a source of knowledge, and to apply what they were learning. Teachers Brown and Eaton made little effort to adapt lessons to the developmental levels and interests of their students. Compared with the high mastery-oriented classes, the activity structures observed in Brown's and Eaton's classes were less supportive of peer collaboration and independent problem-solving. In addition, both teachers emphasized learning for grades and evaluation was a salient feature of their classes.

In both the high and low mastery-oriented classes, the evaluation practices reflected the teacher's instructional goals. For example, Cooper's lessons emphasized conceptual understanding, and she used tests to diagnose students' level of understanding, rather than to keep students focused and working. There were some interesting discrepancies between the instructional and evaluation features of Allen's sixth-grade classes. Some of Allen's teaching practices resembled those of teachers Dayton and Cooper who taught the high mastery-oriented classes. However, in Allen's classes, concerns about getting through the material seemed to take precedence over modifying lessons to make them more appealing or to allow students to have a more active role in the learning process. In addition, evaluation was an implicit feature of Allen's lessons and she sometimes used tests to control students' productivity. These factors militate against a strong mastery-oriented goal orientation.

The results of this qualitative study make several important contributions to the research on student motivation in the classroom. First, many descriptions of student motivation in the classroom have overlooked the important influence of the teacher's instructional approach. The present study suggests that the nature of the instruction itself can have a significant influence on students' motivational patterns. Specifically, classroom environments in which students are passive recipients of knowledge are not conducive to the development of mastery-oriented goal patterns. These goal patterns are more likely to be observed in classrooms where students are given opportunities to actively create meaning out of their own experiences and interactions with peers and adults. Similar findings are emerging in a study of a problem-centered mathematics program for second grade students (Nicholls, Cobb, Yackel, Wood, Whetley, in press).

Second, it is generally assumed that cognitively complex learning activities will have a positive influence on students' motivation to learn because they are challenging, inherently interesting, and more demanding of mental effort (Stodolsky, 1988). Similarly, previous research suggests that students respond favorably to classroom structures in which they can exercise some control (Ryan, Connell, & Deci, 1985) or collaborate with their peers (Ames, 1987; Nicholls, 1983). Few studies, however, have examined the patterning of these task conditions in classroom lessons. Many of the small group activities in this study involved complex procedures and required students to work together. The results show that elementary school students need a considerable degree of instructional support to successfully complete challenging, cooperative, or independent learning activities, especially if two or more of these conditions should occur simultaneously in the same activity.

Recent research based on a Vygotskian perspective has used the "scaffolding" metaphor to describe the process by which more capable adults and peers support children's mastery of learning activities that are slightly above their current level of functioning (Corno & Rohrkemper, 1985). There was less evidence of this scaffolding process in the low mastery-oriented classes than in the classes of Allen, Cooper, and Dayton. These three teachers modelled difficult procedures, helped students break complex tasks into smaller units, monitored students' level of comprehension, developed group relations, and guided students' independent problem-solving efforts.

Students in the low mastery-oriented classes often lacked the prerequisite skills and knowledge they needed to successfully complete difficult small group or independent learning activities on their own. Teachers Brown and Eaton tended to provide direct assistance when students had difficulty, rather than provide the type of support students need to become independent learners. As others have noted (Corno & Rohrkemper, 1985; deCharms, 1976; Marshall, in press; Ryan et al., 1985), the problem for teachers is one of establishing a supportive environment that allows students to gradually assume responsibility for their learning.

Last, previous research has primarily focused on the negative influence of grades and other external incentives on students' motivation to learn. Extending the work of other researchers (Brophy, 1987; Brophy, Rohrkemper, Rashid, & Goldberger, 1983), the findings reported here identified some instructional practices that can promote task involvement without the use of grades and rewards as the major incentives. In the high mastery-oriented classes, teachers Dayton and Cooper emphasized the intrinsic value of learning. These teachers adapted lessons to students' interests and pointed out the importance of science for their lives outside school. They went beyond merely stating the purpose or goal of an activity to pose interesting questions and problems, so that students could experience firsthand the value of what they were learning.

The qualitative study described in this chapter has several limitations that need to be examined in subsequent studies. First, the teachers who participated in this study were highly experienced and used a variety of instructional materials. There was more variety in the types of activities observed in these classes than would be found in most elementary classrooms (Goodlad, 1983). Therefore, differences in students' goal patterns are relative. Students in the low motivation classes are probably more mastery-oriented than students taught by less experienced teachers.

Another issue concerns the influence of grade level differences and the larger school environment. In this study, fifth-grade students were more mastery-oriented than their sixth-grade peers. Although the fifth- and sixth-grade classes had several distinguishing features that may explain these findings, the influence of grade level differences in the content of the learning material cannot be ruled out at this point. In addition, the high mastery-oriented classes were located in an elementary setting, whereas the low mastery-oriented classes were located in middle schools. Research suggests that children show significant declines in their ability perceptions and intrinsic motivation to learn as they enter a new educational environment (Eccles & Midgley, 1989). Grade level differences in students' goal orientations may reflect aspects of the larger school environment.

This study did not formally test the effects of classroom variables on students' motivation patterns. Additional research is thus needed to confirm the pattern of relations suggested in this descriptive study. Taken together, the findings emphasize the importance of conceptualizing classrooms as complex environments with distinctive opportunities and expectations for learning, support structures, and evaluation norms. Focusing on single dimensions of the learning environment may limit our understanding of students' motivation in the classroom.

ACKNOWLEDGMENTS

This study is part of a larger investigation supported by a grant (MDR-8550437) from the National Science Foundation to Phyllis Blumenfeld and Judith Meece. I am grateful to Phyllis Blumenfeld and Pam Puro for their assistance with data collection and analysis, to Blanche Arons for her assistance with the preparation of this manuscript, and to Phyllis Blumenfeld, Jane Kahle, Sam Miller, and Ken Tobin for their helpful comments on earlier drafts. The generous support and contribution of the teachers and students who participated in this study are gratefully acknowledged. A special thanks is also extended to Susan Griffith. Analysis of the classroom observation records was facilitated by a research leave from the University of North Carolina at Chapel Hill.

NOTES

1. Before testing for teacher effects, I examined differences between classes taught by the same teacher. A significant class difference was found for only one teacher. One of Eaton's classes scored significantly higher on the task mastery goal scale than the other. Eaton's score on the task mastery scale was mainly due to the low ratings of this class.

2. All names are pseudonyms.

REFERENCES

Ames, C. (1984) Achievement attributions and self-instructions under competitive and individualistic goal structures. *Journal of Educational Psychology, 76*, 478-487.

————. (1987). The enhancement of student motivation. In M. Maehr & D. Kleiber (Eds.), *Advances in motivation and achievement* (Vol. 5, pp. 123-148). Greenwich, CT: JAI Press.

Ames, C., & Ames, R. (1981). Competitive and individualistic goal structures: The salience of past performance information for causal attributions and affect. *Journal of Educational Psychology, 73*, 411-418.

————. (1984) Systems of student and teacher motivation: Toward a qualitative definition. *Journal of Educational Psychology, 76*, 535-556.

Ames, C., & Archer, J. (1988). Achievement goals in the classroom: Student learning strategies and motivation processes. *Journal of Educational Psychology, 80*, 260-267.

Ames, C., & Felker, D.W. (1979). An examination of children's attributions and achievement-related evaluations in competitive, cooperative, and individualistic reward structures. *Journal of Educational Psychology, 71*, 413-420.

Bloom, B.S., Englehart, M.C., Furst, E.S., Hill, W.H., & Kratwohl, D.R. (1956). *Taxonomy of educational objectives: The classification of educational goals.* New York: Longman.

Blumenfeld, P.C., & Meece, J. (1990). *Promoting a mastery orientation toward science learning.* Unpublished manuscript.

Bronfenbrenner, U. (1976). The experimental ecology of education. *Educational Researcher, 5*, 5-15.

Brophy, J. (1983a). Fostering student learning and motivation in the elementary school classroom. In S. Paris, G. Olson, & H. Stevenson (Eds.), *Learning and motivation in the classroom* (pp. 283-305). Hillsdale, NJ: Lawrence Erlbaum.

Brophy, J. (1983b). Research on the self-fulfilling prophecy and teacher expectations. *Journal of Educational Psychology, 5*, 631-661.

————. (1987). Synthesis of research on strategies for motivating students to learn. *Educational Leadership*, 40-48.

Brophy, J., Rohrkemper, M., Rashid, H., & Goldberger, M. (1983). Relationship between teachers' presentations of classroom tasks and students' engagement in those activities. *Journal of Educational Psychology, 75*, 544-552.

Brown, A., Bransford, L., Ferrara, R., & Campione, L. (1983). Learning, remembering and understanding. In J. Flavell & E. Markman (Eds.), *Handbook of child psychology. Vol. 3: Cognitive development* (pp. 77-166). New York: Wiley.

Butler, R. (1987). Task-involving and ego-involving properties of evaluation. Effects of different feedback conditions on motivational perceptions, interest and performance. *Journal of Educational Psychology, 79*, 474-482.

Connell, J.P. (in press). Context, self, and action: A motivational analysis of the self-system process across the lifespan. In D. Cicchetti (Ed.), *The self in transition: Infancy to childhood.* Chicago: University of Chicago Press.

Corno, L., & Rohrkemper, M. (1985). The intrinsic motivation to learn in classrooms. In C. Ames & R. Ames (Eds.), *Research on motivation in education: The classroom milieu* (Vol. 2, pp. 53-84). New York: Academic Press.

deCharms, R. (1976). *Enhancing motivation: Change in the classroom.* New York: Irvington.

Deci, E.L., Schwartz, A.J., Sheinman, L., & Ryan, R.M. (1981). An instrument to assess adults' orientations toward control versus autonomy with children: Reflections on intrinsic motivation and perceived competence. *Journal of Educational Psychology, 73*, 642-650.

Dweck, C.S., & Bempechat, J. (1983). Children's theories of intelligence: Consequences for learning. In S. Paris, G. Olson, & H. Stevenson (Eds.), *Learning and motivation in the classroom* (pp. 239-258). Hillsdale, NJ: Lawrence Erlbaum.

Dweck, C.S., & Elliot, E.S. (1983). Achievement motivation. In E.M. Hetherington (Ed.), *Handbook of child psychology. Vol. 4: Socialization, personality, and social development* (pp. 643-691). New York: Wiley.

Dweck, C.S., & Reppucci, N.D. (1973). Learned helplessness and reinforcement responsbility in children. *Journal of Personality and Social Psychology, 25*, 109-116.

Eccles, J., & Midgley, C. (1989). Stage/environment fit: Developmentally appropriate classrooms for early adolescents. In R. Ames & C. Ames (Eds.), *Research on motivation in education: Goals and cognition* (Vol. 3, pp. 283-331). New York: Academic Press.

Elliot, E., & Dweck, C. (1988). Goals: An approach to motivation and achievement. *Journal of Personality and Social Psychology, 54*, 5-12.

Goodlad, J. (1983). *A place called school.* New York: McGraw-Hill.

Grannis, J.C. (1978). Task engagement and the consistency of pedagogical controls: An ecological study of differently structured classroom settings. *Curriculum Inquiry, 8*, 3-37.

Jagacinski, C.M., & Nicholls, J.G. (1984). Conceptions of ability and related affects in task involvement and ego involvement. *Journal of Educational Psychology, 76*, 909-919.

Johnson, D., & Johnson, R. (1985). Motivational processes in cooperative, competitive, and individualistic learning situations. In C. Ames & R. Ames (Eds.), *Research on motivation in education: The classroom milieu* (Vol. 2, pp. 249-286). New York: Academic Press.

Lepper, M., & Hodell, M. (1989). Intrinsic motivation in the classroom. In R. Ames, & C. Ames (Eds.) *Research on motivation in education: Goals and cognition* (Vol. 3, pp. 73-103), New York: Academic Press.

Maehr, M., & Nicholls, J.G. (1980). Culture and achievement motivation: A second look. In W. Warren (Eds.), *Studies in cross-cultural psychology* (Vol. 3, pp. 221-267). New York: Academic Press.

Marshall, H. (1988). Work or learning: Implications of classroom metaphors. *Educational Researcher, 17*, 9-16.

Marshall, H. (in press). Beyond the workplace metaphor: Toward conceptualizing the classroom as a learning setting. *Theory into Practice.*

Marshall, H., & Weinstein, R. (1986). Classroom context of student-perceived differential teacher treatment. *Journal of Educational Psychology, 78*, 441-453.

Meece, J., & Blumenfeld, P.C. (1987, April). *Elementary school children's motivational orientation and patterns of engagement in classroom activities.* Paper presented at the annual meeting of the American Educational Research Association, Washington, DC.

Meece, J., Blumenfeld, P.C., & Hoyle, R. (1988). Students' goal orientations and cognitive engagement in classroom activities. *Journal of Educational Psychology, 80,* 514-523.

Meece, J., Blumenfeld, P.C., & Puro, P. (1989). A motivational analysis of elementary science learning environments. In M. Matyas, K. Tobin, & B. Fraser (Eds.), *Looking into windows: Qualitative research in science education.* Washington, DC: American Association for the Advancement of Science.

Nicholls, J. (1983). Conceptions of ability and achievement motivation: A theory and its implications for education. In S. Paris, G. Olson, & H. Stevenson (Eds.), *Learning and motivation in the classroom* (pp. 211-238). Hillsdale, NJ: Lawrence Erlbaum.

Nicholls, J.G. (1984). Achievement motivation: Conception of ability, subjective experience, task choice, and performance. *Psychological Review, 91,* 328-346.

Nicholls, J.G., Cobb, P., Yackel, E., Wood, T., Wheatley, G. (in press). Students' theories about mathematics and their mathematical knowledge: Multiple dimensions of assessment. In G. Kulm (Ed.), *Assessing higher order thinking in mathematics.* Washington, DC: American Association for the Advancement of Science.

Nicholls, J.G., Miller, A. (1984). Development and its discontents: The differentiation of the concept of ability. In J.G. Nicholls (Eds.), *Advances in motivation and achievement: The development of achievement motivation* (Vol. 3, pp. 185-218). Greenwich, CT: JAI Press.

Nicholls, J.G., Patashnick, M., Nolen, S. (1985). Adolescents' theories of education. *Journal of Educational Psychology, 77,* 683-692.

Nicholls, J.G., & Thorklidsen, T.A. (1987, October). *Achievement goals and beliefs: Individual and classroom differences.* Paper presented at the meeting of the Society for Experimental Social Psychology, Charlottesville, Virginia.

Nolen, S.B. (1988). Reasons for studying: Motivational orientations and study strategies. *Cognition and Instruction, 5,* 269-287.

Nolen, S.B., & Haladyna, T. (in press). Personal and environmental influences on students' beliefs about effective study strategies, *Contemporary Educational Psychology.*

Rosenholtz, S., & Rosenholtz, S. (1981). Classroom organization and the perception of ability. *Sociology of Education, 54,* 132-140.

Ryan, R.M. (1982). Control and information in the interpersonal sphere: An extension of cognitive evaluation theory. *Journal of Personality and Social Psychology, 43,* 450-461.

Ryan, R., Connell, J.P., Deci, E. (1985). A motivational anaysis of self-determination and self-regulation in education. In C. Ames & R. Ames (Eds.), *Research on motivation in education: The classroom milieu* (Vol. 2, pp. 1-51). New York: Academic Press.

Ryan, R.M., & Grolnick, W. (1986). Origins and pawns in the classroom: Self-report and projective assessments of individual differences in children's perceptions. *Journal of Personality and Social Psychology, 50,* 550-558.

Stipek, D., & Daniels, D. (1988). Declining perceptions of competence: A consequence of changes in the child or the educational environment? *Journal of Educational Psychology, 80,* 352-256.

Slavin, R. (1983). *Cooperative Learning.* New York: Longman.

Stodolsky, S. (1988). *The subject matters.* Chicago: University of Chicago Press.

GOALS AND SELF-REGULATION:
APPLICATIONS OF THEORY TO WORK SETTINGS

Ruth Kanfer and Frederick H. Kanfer

During the last decade, concepts of self-regulation, such as goals, self-monitoring, and commitment, have come to occupy center stage in the study of motivation. Although interest in self-regulation has appeared periodically throughout the history of psychology (e.g., James, 1890; Woodworth, 1929), systematic empirical research on the topic began in earnest during the early 1960s with the application of social learning and information-processing perspectives to problems in adult self-control (see, e.g., F. Kanfer & Phillips, 1970), investigations of delay of gratification in children (see, e.g., Mischel, 1974), and the study of vicarious learning processes (see, e.g., Bandura, 1971). Developments in the broader field of psychology have combined with such efforts to result in a marked increase in self-regulation theorizing across a wide variety of psychological subdisciplines. In the past ten years, major motivation theories have been proposed in clinical, experimental, developmental, personality-social, educational, and industrial-organizational psychology. Theories that pertain to self-regulation have been proposed by Bandura (1977a, 1986), Carver and Scheier (1981), Ford (1987), Heckhausen (1977; Heckhausen & Kuhl, 1985), F. Kanfer (1970; F. Kanfer & Hagerman, 1981), R. Kanfer

Advances in Motivation and Achievement, Volume 7, pages 287-326.
Copyright © 1991 by JAI Press Inc.

and Ackerman (1989), Klinger (1975, 1987), Kuhl (1984, 1985), Naylor, Pritchard, and Ilgen (1980), Nicholls (1978, 1984), Nuttin (1984), and Weiner (1985, 1986). Summaries of these theories from several different perspectives have appeared in R. Kanfer (in press b) and in edited volumes by Frese and Sabini (1985), Halisch and Kuhl (1987), Kuhl and Beckmann (1985), Pervin (1989), and Sorrentino and Higgins (1986), respectively. The abundance of theoretical activity during this decade is further reflected in work that elaborates upon the major theories of self-regulation, for example, by Dweck (1986; Dweck & Leggett, 1988), Hollenbeck and Klein (1987), Humphreys and Revelle (1984), Hyland (1988), Locke and Latham (1990), Lord and Hanges (1987), Naylor and Ilgen (1984), and Pervin (1983). Theoretical writings by Emmons (1986) and Cantor and Kihlstrom (1987) further advocate the importance of self-regulatory processes within a broader personality perspective.

The steady stream of theoretical writing in motivation, and in particular with respect to goals and self-regulation, has been accompanied by a considerable amount of empirical research in the basic and applied research domains. Most of this research has focused on testing specific theoretical predictions rather than testing theoretical models in their entirety. Although the paradigms associated with various models differ substantially, empirical research on all models typically involves experimental examination of the joint effects of person and situation characteristics on cognitive, information-processing and behavioral activities associated with performance on some target task. As might be expected, empirical research stemming from models that emphasize individual differences characteristics has tended to concentrate on construct validation using correlational methods.

The heavy reliance on observable indices of cognitive and behavioral change as a consequence of goals and self-regulatory activities has led to more careful attention to the criterion variables used to test various theoretical predictions. In the laboratory, many researchers have moved toward use of longitudinal and repeated-measure designs in attempts to capture the dynamic and cumulative effects of self-regulatory activities on behaviors that contribute to task performance. A growing number of laboratory researchers have also used advances in computer technologies to create complex and multimodal tasks that simulate real-world conditions. These developments in methodology have substantially lessened concerns about the distinction between laboratory and field research (see, e.g., Campbell, 1986).

Theoretical developments in motivation and self-regulation have been complemented by applied research on the influence of these processes on behavior and their relation to learning and performance in work settings. Evidence from several subdisciplines of psychology indicates that individual differences in cognitive abilities alone are often insufficient for predicting an individual's performance (cf. Snow, 1986). In the educational domain, interest in motivation and self-regulation has focused on questions such as why learners of higher ability levels sometimes demonstrate poor performance, and how and which educational interventions may be used to promote intrinsic task motivation. Among clinical psychologists, interest has continued to concentrate on delineation of the specific self-regulation components and processes that influence depression and the frequency of specific dysfunctional behavior patterns, such as smoking and substance abuse.

In the industrial and organizational psychology domain, workplace performance has long been viewed as influenced by the interaction of two major determinants: individual differences in abilities and motivation (Vroom, 1964). The centrality of cognitive determinants of performance has led motivation researchers in this field to pay particular attention to the criterion constructs, and to the validity and reliability of job performance measures used in motivation research (see, e.g., J. Campbell & R. Campbell, 1988). Practical issues in this domain can be organized into three distinct, yet related areas: (1) the identification of stable, noncognitive individual differences that affect long-term task and job performance; (2) the development of managerial techniques that promote work motivation; and (3) the clarification of self-regulatory processes that sustain persistence in the face of difficulties.

The purpose of this paper is to coordinate recent developments in the broader self-regulation research literatures with theoretical issues, practical problems, and abiding issues pertaining to adult behavior and performance in the workplace. The paper is organized into four sections. The first section presents a general framework for integrating key features of various theoretical approaches to choice, goals, and self-regulation. The second section focuses more narrowly on the influence of goal-directed, self-regulation processes during learning and performance. A resource allocation model is described and empirical results derived from this framework are discussed. The third section discusses specific issues pertaining to the coordination of goal and self-regulation theories with work settings and organizational research. This section begins with mapping goal and self-regulation constructs to the work setting. Next, selected empirical evidence from the organizational domain is reviewed. The fourth, final section discusses promising areas of research that emerge from consideration of goals and self-regulation processes in organizational contexts.

THEORETICAL OVERVIEW

Choice and Volition

Most motivation researchers currently view the domain of motivation as comprised of two interrelated systems: goal choice and self-regulation (e.g., Ajzen, 1985; Bandura, 1986; Gollwitzer & Kinney, 1989; Heckhausen & Kuhl, 1985; Heckhausen, Schmalt, & Schneider, 1985; F. Kanfer & Hagerman, 1981;

R. Kanfer, in press b; R. Kanfer & Ackerman, 1989; Klinger, 1987; Kuhl, 1982, 1984). In this perspective, goals take on crucial importance as the key construct linking choice and volitional aspects of the domain. Given the fundamental importance of goals for both choice and volition, the conceptual arguments for making this linkage are described briefly below.

In an integrative conceptualization, the products of cognitive choice processes are frequently termed intentions. Intentions and goals share the characteristic of providing individuals with a cognitive representation of a future situation that signifies a desired state. However, goals define more specific end-states (F. Kanfer, 1987; Klinger, 1987). Intentions and goals may relate to one's own behavior (e.g., I intend to work overtime for three hours) or to an outcome the individual seeks to attain (e.g., I intend to obtain a promotion). The precise product of choice processes depends upon two key determinants: (1) the individual's expectations, and (2) the individual's subjective valuation of expected consequences stemming from various alternative actions. Person and situation characteristics influence expectations and valences, as well as the level of specificity at which intentions are developed.

The exact process by which intentions become goals imbued with self-regulatory potency remains poorly understood. Several researchers have proposed that intentions (or specific elements of an intention) gain currency as self-regulatory goals only when the strength of the intention passes one or more critical thresholds (e.g., Carver & Scheier, 1981, 1985; F. Kanfer & Hagerman, 1981; Kuhl, 1985). Again, both person and situation factors have been suggested as moderating the conversion of intentions into goals. Heckhausen and Kuhl (1985), for example, view the conversion of intentions into goals as a two-stage process. In the first stage, individuals become committed to the product of choice processes following the successful passing of the intention through a mental check of various anticipated future conditions (e.g., opportunity for action, time for accomplishment of the intention, fit of intention with other salient concerns, etc.). In Heckhausen and Kuhl's (1985) model, a choice product that passes this mental filter is termed an intention. Although intentions of this type *may* serve as goals for further cognized representation of desired outcomes, they do not activate or guide self-regulatory activities until they have passed a second mental filter (Heckhausen & Kuhl, 1985). Cognitive activities at this point are aimed toward assessment of the feasibility of acting on the intention at the present. Positive assessments typically yield commitment to action (F. Kanfer, 1987).

In summary, theorizing about the intention-goal relation suggests that further processing of an intention is required before it assumes a role in the self-regulation system. In Kanfer and Ackerman's (1989) resource allocation model, the endpoint of this transition is indicated by the deliberate allocation of some portion of one's total available attentional resources (i.e., cognitive effort) toward accomplishment of a cognized goal. That is, when an individual establishes a goal, he/she devotes a portion of his or her total available attentional resources to goal accomplishment. Dedication of a substantial portion of one's total attentional resources differentiates goals from intentions. For example, an individual's intention to achieve a high score on a test remains a weak influence on action until the individual commits attentional effort to the desired outcome.

Self-regulation

Goals influence the initiation and focus of self-regulatory activities. Self-regulatory activities are triggered when (a) a routinized activity is interrupted or not available, (b) the perceived difficulty of achieving the goal is high, and (c) the individual maintains (at least initially) a minimal degree of confidence that he or she has the capability to achieve the goal (Bandura, 1977a, 1986; Carver & Scheier, 1981, 1985; Hyland, 1988; F. Kanfer, 1977; R. Kanfer, 1987; R. Kanfer & Ackerman, 1989). The second of these conditions (confidence) appears to be a major determinant of the process of commitment that transforms an intention into a goal.

Self-regulation refers to the intrapersonal processes by which an individual exercises control over the direction, persistence, and intensity of thinking, affect, and behavior for the purpose of goal attainment. Self-regulation is typically viewed as comprised of three related sets of activities: (a) self-monitoring, (b) self-evaluation, and (c) self-reactions (Bandura, 1982; F. Kanfer, 1970). Self-monitoring typically refers to attention given to specific aspects of one's own behavior or goal-related environmental events. Individuals cannot continuously attend to all aspects of their behavior; persons must selectively attend to particular dimensions of behavior and events. This selective attention depends, for example, on which features of activity have functional significance for goal attainment, the individual's emotional state, and the importance of behavioral outcomes.

Self-monitoring provides the individual with information necessary to enable effective operation of self evaluation and self-reaction components of the system. Through self-monitoring individuals gain knowledge about person and situational factors. Although self-monitoring is viewed as necessary for effective self-regulation, it is important to note that successful self-monitoring requires that the individual attend to activities corresponding to the goal. For example, self-monitoring of one's affective reactions to a task provides little information for self-evaluation of one's progress toward accomplishing a difficult task, and may even induce self-reactions that debilitate task performance.

In organizational settings, individuals obtain information about their behavior and performance from several sources. Direct methods include attention to task-generated feedback or explicit performance feedback provided by others. Indirect methods for obtaining information include learning about one's actions through observation of similar others and asking others for information. Investigations of feedback-seeking in work contexts suggest that methods of feedback seeking relate to the individual's experience with the job (Ashford, 1986). Ashford (1986) found that, compared to new employees, persons with longer job tenure tended to avoid use of public inquiry methods of monitoring. Ashford's findings suggest that deficits in self-monitoring may occur as a consequence of the perceived social costs of obtaining goal relevant information from others.

Self-observation can also occur in response to external prompts and negative or positive outcomes. Employees can be instructed, for example, to observe specific critical features of their performance. Individual differences in self-focused attention may also affect the extent to which self-monitoring of thoughts and behaviors occurs following a negative outcome.

Self-evaluation refers to the comparison of the goal with the current state of affairs. Failures in self-monitoring, due to either the absence of monitoring, or the monitoring of activities that do not correspond to the goal preclude efficient self-evaluation.

The motivational importance of self-evaluation lies with the effects that this procedure has on affective self-reactions. Bandura's (1986, 1988) social cognitive theory posits two distinct types of self-reactions: (a) self-satisfaction/ dissatisfaction, and (b) self-efficacy expectations. Satisfaction/dissatisfaction refers to an affective reaction about *past actions*. Self-evaluation indicating a current state below the goal state is likely to yield dissatisfaction; self-evaluation indicating activity or performance that meets or exceeds one's goals should yield satisfaction. In contrast, self-efficacy expectations refer to complex cognitive judgments about one's *future capabilities* to organize and execute activities requisite for goal attainment (Bandura, 1977b). Task-specific self-efficacy expectations develop from a variety of sources, including performance feedback, vicarious experiences, previous performance history, and social influence (see Bandura, 1986, for a review). Through self-evaluation, persons gain further knowledge about the effectiveness of goal-relevant skills and abilities. Such knowledge may substantially alter self-efficacy judgments about goal attainment.

Ideally, self-regulation processes enable persons to modify their goals and performance strategies in concert with task demands. For example, a clerk-typist with the goal of typing 50 letters in a three-hour period might become fatigued after an hour, resulting in a gradual reduction of on-task attentional effort and diminished performance. Through self-monitoring of task performance, the clerk-typist would obtain information indicating a slowdown in rate of progress. Self-evaluation of current performance level with the desired goal state would indicate a discrepancy and trigger self-reactive processes. Through self-reactions, the clerk-typist might alter both goals and self-regulatory strategies to sustain performance in the face of difficulties associated with a change in internal state. For example, the clerk might attempt to offset the detrimental effect of fatigue on performance by devoting more effort to the task or changing the focus of self-regulatory activity (e.g., more attention to task details). Without self-regulation, persons would be expected to continue to devote the same amount of effort and use the same strategies they originally committed to the task (R. Kanfer & Ackerman, 1989).

Goals and Self-regulation

Research in several domains suggests that both type and attributes of the goal influence self-regulation processes. Locke, Shaw, Saari, and Latham (1981) proposed that goals influence task behavior through four mechanisms: (1) directing attention, (2) mobilizing on-task effort, (3) encouraging task persistence, and (4) facilitating strategy development. Locke et al. (1981) also specified intensity and content as two relevant attributes of goals that affect behavior. Intensity refers to the strength of the goal and is influenced by factors such as perceived goal importance and goal commitment (Lee, Locke, & Latham, 1989). Goal content encompasses features such as difficulty, specificity, complexity, and multiplicity of goals. Evidence for the influence of various goal attributes of explicit goals on task and job performance is reviewed in a later section.

In contrast to the attribute perspective, motivational orientation theories (e.g., Dweck & Leggett, 1988; Nicholls, 1978, 1984) suggest that the type of goal adopted by the individual affects the character of information-processing and self-regulatory activities during task engagement. For example, Nicholls and his colleagues (Nicholls, 1978, 1984; Nicholls & Miller, 1984; Nolen, 1988) distinguish two forms of goal orientation in achievement settings, ego orientation and task orientation. Persons who seek to demonstrate their ability (i.e., capacity at a fixed or maximum level of effort) via superior task performance relative to others are held to maintain an ego orientation. Persons with a task orientation are proposed to maintain self-referenced conceptions of ability (i.e., how much has been learned). Dweck and Leggett (1988) proposed a similar goal typology in which they distinguish between performance and learning goals. In this formulation, persons are posited to adopt performance goals when the purpose of task engagement is perceived to be for demonstrating one's ability (relative to others). Persons who adopt performance goals are proposed to view task performance as a means to an end, that is, in service of proving of one's superior ability. In contrast, persons are posited to adopt learning goals when they perceive the purpose of task engagement to be for increasing one's competence via task mastery. Evidence for the influence of such motivational orientations is provided by Elliott and Dweck (1988), Nicholls (1978), Nolen (1988), and Wood and Bandura (1989).

A fundamental difference between attribute- and typology-based formulations of goal influences on learning and performance lies in the level of analysis. Attribute-based research typically focuses on the effects of specific goal attributes (e.g., goal difficulty) on task effort (as indexed by level of performance). In the typology perspective, the aim of research is to identify motivational patterns associated with particular types of goals. Task performance (indexing on-task effort) represents only one element of the constellation of responses examined. For example, Elliott and Dweck (1988) found that children who adopted a performance goal orientation during a discrimination task exhibited a pattern of cognition, affect, and behavior consistent with learned helplessness. However, children who adopted a learning goal orientation showed a more adaptive pattern of responses over the course of task performance. In contrast to attribute research, typology research tends to employ persistence measures of task effort.

The difference in scope between attribute and typology perspectives also has implications for understanding how performance problems associated with the self-regulation portion of motivation may be remediated. For example, in the attribute perspective, difficult and specific goals are posited to enhance performance by increasing task-relevant self-monitoring and promoting the likelihood that the product of self-evaluation will yield self-reactions that, in turn, increase task effort. In contrast, easy and specific goals are posited to exert negligible effects on performance due to the failure of easy goals to elicit self-reactions that increase effort. These results suggest that interventions to enhance effort and task performance should highlight the adoption of difficult goals.

In contrast, typology research suggests that the type of goal adopted affects task performance through its influence on the integrated pattern of cognitive, effective, and behavioral activities instigated by the individual's purpose for task engagement. Although there appears to be no fundamental disagreement between typology and attribute researchers as to the importance of self-regulation components, the typology approach implies that goal orientation affects goal attributes rather than the reverse relation (R. Kanfer, in press a). Initial support for this notion is provided by Wood and Bandura (1989) in a study of goal orientation effects on self-regulatory components during a organizational decision-making task. Wood and Bandura (1989) found that subjects with a learning-goal orientation reported higher self-set performance goals and self-efficacy expectations over trials compared with subjects with a performance-goal orientation.

The typology perspective implies that interventions aimed at alteration of the individual's motivational or goal orientation toward task engagement may provide more cost-effective and long-term benefits than interventions aimed at modifying specific goal attributes. Clinical research on the effectiveness of self-control therapies provides further support for this notion (see, e.g., Karoly

& Kanfer, 1982). As many researchers have noted, adoption of a mastery-goal orientation toward behavior change appears to be critical for long-term treatment gains.

SELF-REGULATION IN THE CONTEXT OF GOAL-DIRECTED LEARNING AND PERFORMANCE

Advances in cognitive, information-processing psychology have had a profound impact on how self-regulation is conceptualized. For example, several recent theories of the self and self-regulation draw heavily from the application of Shiffrin and Schneider's (1977) seminal work on automatic and controlled-information processing to the noncognitive arena (e.g., Cantor & Kihlstrom, 1987; Higgins, 1987; F. Kanfer & Busemeyer, 1982; Lord & Hanges, 1987). The thrust of these recent developments has been largely in terms of applying information-processing principles to motivational processes.

However, recent progress in cognitive psychology may also be used to provide a unified foundation through which to examine the joint influence of cognitive abilities, task demands, and motivation on performance in the workplace. Although numerous studies demonstrate the role of one or another basic determinant, relatively little attention has been given to understanding the role of motivational processes *in the context of abilities and task characteristics*. Unified conceptualizations are particularly useful for identifying the potential costs and benefits of various self-regulation processes on performance, across a variety of work contexts and among persons who differ in level of cognitive abilities. For example, most motivational theorists assume that individual differences in cognitive abilities exert their effects on performance through their influence on the type or attributes of individuals' goals (e.g., Bandura, 1986; Carver & Scheier, 1981; F. Kanfer & Hagerman, 1981). However, it is quite likely that individual differences in cognitive abilities also affect the direction and efficiency of self-regulation processing.

One approach to a unified framework stems from recent theorizing by Kanfer and Ackerman (1989; R. Kanfer, in press b). In Kanfer and Ackerman's resource allocation framework, the construct of attentional resources is used to provide a common metric for the joint analysis of the effects of abilities, motivation/self-regulation, and task demands on task performance.

Figure 1 illustrates the Kanfer-Ackerman framework. Building upon Kahneman's (1973) model of attentional capacity, attentional effort is viewed as cognitive resources of limited availability. Individual differences in general intellectual abilities are mapped to cognitive resource capacity based upon Ackerman's theory of ability determinants of individual differences in skill acquisition (Ackerman, 1988). Motivation and self-regulation processes provide the basis for allocation of one's attentional resources across different

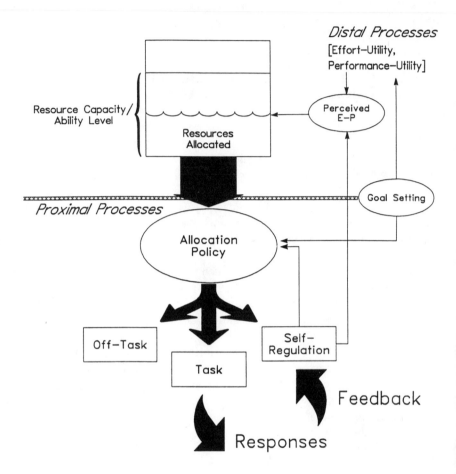

Source: R. Kanfer and Ackerman (1989).

Figure 1.   Kanfer and Ackerman's Integrative Resource Allocation Model
of Learning and Task Performance

activities. Distal motivational processes refer to choice processes that engage
some proportion of an individual's total attentional effort toward a task-related
goal. These motivational processes place a volitional limit on total resource
availability. Proximal resource allocation processes occur in the context of
goal-directed action. These processes govern the allocation of attentional
resources across on-task, off-task, and self-regulatory processes. As such, these
processes reflect information-processing strategies used to build and sustain
goal-directed behavior. Feedback loops are posited for adjustment of

allocations, proportion of total capacity allocated, and for external influences at the level of allocation of capacity and allocation policy.

A basic assumption underlying the model is that changes in the amount of capacity utilized and policies for the allocation of attention are accomplished through motivational and self-regulatory processes.

The resource allocation framework also provides a means of conceptualizing dynamic changes in performance as a function of abilities, motivation, and task characteristics. Over time, distal and proximal motivational processes influence the re-allocation and/or mobilization of additional portions of capacity to various activities. When task resource demands are high, the individual may allocate more available attention to the task, or adjust the proportion of capacity engaged. Conversely, when task demands are reduced, the individual may attend to off-task activities and/or may reduce the proportion of capacity engaged. This reduction in attentional demands associated with task practice involving consistent components provides an explanation of the common observation that performance of skilled, well-practiced tasks often requires less attention than performance of novel, complex tasks (see, e.g., Fisk, Ackerman, & Schneider, 1987 for a review).

In the Kanfer and Ackerman framework, self-regulation is an essential mechanism for bringing about changes in allocation policy toward a task or total proportion of resource capacity actually engaged. Without activation of self-regulatory processes, an individual would be expected to continue to devote the same amount of resources originally committed to a task via the initial distal decision processes.

The Kanfer and Ackerman model also indicates that self-regulation processes *during* task engagement demand a cognitive resource overhead. As such, engagement of self-regulation processes differentially affects performance of novel and well-learned tasks. When a task is well-learned, self-regulation enhances performance by strengthening goal commitment and increasing on-task attentional effort. Activation of self-regulation processes in these instances may be particularly useful when individuals perceive their performance to be satisfactory; at that point, individuals may be inclined to disengage self-regulatory activities as the result of small goal-performance discrepancies.

On the other hand, when performing a difficult and novel, or complex task, attentional demands imposed by the task itself mediate (or obviate) the beneficial influence of self-regulatory activity. Self-regulatory activities that prompt greater allocation of attentional effort (a distal effect) are limited because there is little additional effort available. Furthermore, attentional effort is required to develop new declarative knowledge for task performance. Attentional demands associated with proximal self-regulation must compete with attentional demands of the task (cf. F. Kanfer & Stevenson, 1985). Therefore, the beneficial consequences of self-regulation can only be obtained when there are sufficient cognitive resources available for engaging in self-regulatory activity itself. When the self-regulatory activities demand a resource overhead that can only be provided through a reduction in resources allocated to the task, self-regulation impairs learning and performance.

Empirical support for the integrated resource allocation framework was obtained in a series of studies investigating the impact of difficult and specific goal assignments on performance of a complex, computerized air traffic controller simulation task (R. Kanfer & Ackerman, 1989). Results of three studies, involving over 1,000 trainees showed that the imposition of performance goals during the early phase of skill acquisition hampered performance, particularly among lower-ability persons. In contrast, performance goals assigned during later phases of skill acquisition enhanced task performance among lower-ability persons. Consistent with performance findings, frequency of reported self-regulatory processes was lower during the initial phase of skill acquisition compared to later phases of skill acquisition.

It is important to note that the Kanfer and Ackerman model posits that availability of attentional resources represents the critical determinant of whether self-regulation aids performance. Analysis of performance in the larger training context, involving both on-task and rest periods, provides a paradigm for further investigation of the resource availability explanation. This paradigm also can be used for potential clarification of the processes through which goal setting may affect complex task learning and performance.

Most goal setting studies have examined goal effects in the context of a massed practice paradigm. In this procedure, persons perform a series of task trials with little or no break between trials. In the Kanfer and Ackerman (1989) studies, for example, subjects performed consecutive trials of a real-time simulation task. However, in many real-world contexts, complex task performance is carried out over an extended period of time. For example, air traffic controller trainees may perform the task for a thirty minute period once each day. In experimental terms, tasks that involve spaced or distributed performance provide for distinct rest intervals between performances. In spaced performance, the rest interval provides a release of attentional resources that may be unavailable during task performance. During a rest interval, now available cognitive resources can potentially be used for self-regulation. In the absence of other strong demands on cognitive resources, motivational interventions that engage self-regulatory processes during the rest interval are expected to promote subsequent on-task performance.

In contrast, goal assignments in massed practice procedures should exacerbate the conflict between the demands on attentional effort imposed by the task and the attentional demands imposed by self-regulation processes (stimulated by goal assignments). In these instances, goal assignments divert cognitive resources away from on-task processing and should result in lower levels of performance.

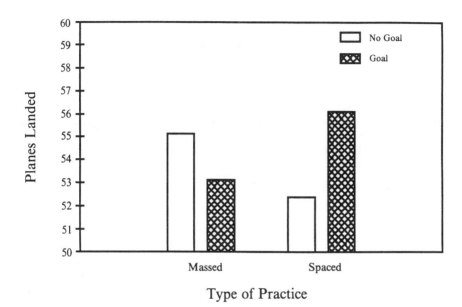

Type of Practice

Source: Kanfer et al. (1988).

Figure 2. Planes Landed in the ATC Task at 140 Minutes of Total Training
Time (ATC task trial 14 in the Massed Practice condition;
ATC task trial 10 in the Spaced Practice condition)

To test this hypothesis, R. Kanfer, Dugdale, Nelson, and Ackerman (1990)
examined the effects of difficult and specific goal assignments and structure
of task practice on performance in an air traffic controller simulation task.
Subjects were randomly assigned to one of four conditions: (1) Goal, Massed
practice, (2) No-goal, Massed practice, (3) Goal, Spaced practice, or (4) No-
goal, Spaced practice. As shown in Figure 2, the results obtained indicated
a significant interaction between Goal and Practice on performance. Consistent
with the R. Kanfer and Ackerman (1989) findings, subjects in the Goal, Massed
practice condition performed significantly more poorly than subjects in the No-
goal, Massed practice condition. In the spaced conditions, however, subjects
in the Goal condition performed significantly better than No-goal subjects.
Self-report measures of cognitive activities during rest intervals for subjects
in the spaced practice conditions showed that subjects in the Goal condition
engaged in significantly more on-task processing during the breaks compared
with subjects in the No-goal condition.

The Kanfer et al. (1990) findings provide further support for the resource availability explanation, and suggest several issues for understanding the influence of goals on engagement of self-regulation processes. The impact of goals on cognitive processes during rest intervals is consistent with Klinger's (1975, 1987) view on the potency of current concerns (in this instance the individual's performance goal) across behavioral contexts. According to Klinger (1987), activation of a current concern causes a fundamental shift in attention and information processing. From this perspective, the imposition of the first performance goal assignment in the Kanfer et al. (1990) study may be viewed as instantiating a current concern about performance. On-task processing during the rest interval is consistent with the view that performance goals had gained the status of a current concern.

The results obtained in the Kanfer et al. (1990) study also indicate that the detrimental influence of goals in the Massed practice condition was immediate, and was followed by a learning curve similar to that shown by subjects in the Massed, No-goal condition. These results suggest that the goal assignment in the massed condition simply disadvantaged subjects early on, rather than impede the learning process.

Alternatively, it may be that subjects in the Massed-Goal condition actively prevented *further* impediments to learning by reducing attentional effort to self-regulatory processes during task engagement despite the goal assignment. Indirect evidence for this notion stems comparison of the groups on self-report measures of attention during task trials. Although Massed- and Spaced-Goal subjects reported similar levels of goal commitment at the onset of performance, Massed-Goal subjects reported significantly lower levels of goal commitment as the number of trials increased. These findings suggest the possibility of some sort of internal mechanism that evaluates the cost and benefits of self-regulatory processing and suspends or terminates such processing if the costs outweigh the benefits. Such a mechanism might be related to noncognitive individual differences, such as knowing how and when to reduce attentional demand conflicts. Suspension or disengagement of self-regulation processes may be particularly useful when the product of self-regulatory activity results in hopelessness or helplessness. In a skill acquisition context, however, the suspension of self-regulatory activities is preferred to disengagement since the declining demands on attention imposed by the task provide persons with later opportunities to realize the benefits of self-regulatory activities. In contrast, disengagement is more likely to preclude the opportunity for later use of self-regulatory activities to sustain high levels of performance once attentional demands have diminished.

The integrated resource allocation framework suggests that the performance benefits of mobilizing self-regulatory processes depends upon the action context and individual differences in abilities. When performance goals are used to activate self-regulatory processes during the performance of cognitively-demanding actions, the associated cognitive requirements may hinder, rather than help learning and performance. This negative consequence is most likely to occur in settings where persons must engage in novel and complex performances for some lengthy period of time (e.g., initial on-the-job training for fast-food workers).

When attentional demands imposed by the task are diminished, or the performance context is punctuated by periods of lessened attentional demands, the provision of performance goals and activation of self-regulatory processes may aid performance. In educational and clinical settings, the most powerful benefit of performance goals may lie in their ability to stimulate self-regulatory processing in the form of mental rehearsal during off-task periods. In clinical settings, guided covert rehearsal of anticipated problem situations is regularly advocated as a method for maximizing behavioral success in problem situations (see, e.g., F. Kanfer & Goldstein, 1986). Similarly, Taylor and Schneider (1989) propose that mental simulations of difficult situations provide a useful opportunity for developing coping strategies and emotional control over stressful events.

Additional research is needed, however, to delineate the joint situational and personal factors that activate various kinds of self-regulatory strategies. For example, Kuhl (1985) has proposed that individual differences in action orientation affect the operation of self-regulatory activities during task performance. Research by Kuhl and his colleagues (e.g., Beckmann & Kuhl, 1984; Kuhl & Koch, 1984; Kuhl & Wassiljew, 1985; Kuhl & Weiss, 1985) indicates that persons high in action orientation engage in less disruptive emotional self-regulatory processing during task engagement than persons low in action orientation.

TOWARD A COORDINATED PERSPECTIVE ON SELF-REGULATION IN THE WORKPLACE

Before mapping self-regulation theories to the adult work setting it is first necessary to consider motivation in the organizational context. Broad theories of human motivation differ from work motivation theories in several ways. First, broad theories tend to promote investigation of psychological processes across life domains. Social-cognitive and control theories of motivation, for example, may be employed to understand a variety of clinical disorders as well as problems in the educational domain (e.g., see Bandura, 1986; Dweck & Leggett, 1988; Kuhl & Kraska, 1989). In contrast, modern motivation theories in the industrial-organizational literature have focused specifically on understanding the causes of poor job performance. The emphasis on performance, rather than learning, in organizational psychology had prompted far greater attention to contextual factors, such as conditions of work and pay equity, than self-regulation processes per se.

However, several features of the adult workplace provide an excellent context for the study of self-regulation. To maintain employment, persons must regulate their nonwork activities to avoid unexcused absenteeism and tardiness. During work, persons must allocate their time and cognitive effort across a variety of work and nonwork goals. Poor performance ratings may thus occur as the consequence of deficits in self-regulation at multiple levels.

In self-regulation research, the term "performance" generally refers to behavior that can be reliably aggregated into a single performance score. For example, numerous studies of self-regulation operationalize performance in terms of the number of problems correct, or behavioral persistence on a target task. In organizational psychology, however, the term "performance" refers to an *evaluation* of the individual's actions or behaviors (Naylor, Pritchard, & Ilgen, 1980). That is, in contrast to the notion of performance as a pre-defined criterion, performance in the work setting is subject to an evaluator's judgments and biases. For example, a slow-typing secretary in a busy office may successfully employ self-regulation strategies to reduce tardiness but still receive a poor performance evaluation by a supervisor who places greatest weight on typing speed. In other words, performance in work settings critically depends on both what features of action are taken into consideration, as well as other factors, such as individual differences variables (e.g., abilities) and environmental factors (e.g., situational constraints). As a consequence, the identification of appropriate and unbiased criterion variables (rather than aggregated measures of performance) is an essential prerequisite for the investigation of self-regulation effects on workplace performance.

Theories of job performance have historically placed strong emphasis on abilities as determinants of performance. Recently, however, there has been increasing attention to the role and function of organizational citizenship behaviors (e.g., Organ & Konovsky, 1989; Smith, Organ, & Near, 1983; Staw, 1984). Organizational citizenship behaviors refer to prosocial, cooperative behaviors that are not mandated by formal role requirements nor directly compensated by the organization. Organizational citizenship behaviors, such as staying late to help others, or volunteering to take on unexpected work, are posited to contribute to organizational effectiveness (Organ & Konovsky, 1989). The conceptualization of organizational citizenship behaviors as volitional behaviors suggests that these behaviors also serve as appropriate criteria for the investigation of self-regulation in the workplace.

Another concern in the application of self-regulation to the organizational context pertains to the definition of goals. Most basic research on self-regulation has focused on the influence of self-regulatory activities in conjunction with commitment to a personally salient goal, such as getting a promotion or losing weight. From an organizational perspective, however, goals typically refer to salient objectives *as defined by the organization.* To gain potency as personal goals, organizations and individuals must translate organizational objectives into personally important goals. The process of transforming organizationally-valued performance goals into salient personal goals that promote self-regulatory activities represents a major difficulty for most organizations.

A related problem in the application of self-regulation theory to the work context pertains to the notion of feedback. As discussed previously, performance feedback represents a critical element for effective self-regulation. In self-regulation theories, performance feedback related to one's goals is essential for self-evaluation. In the work context, however, task generated feedback provides only one of several important types of feedback that may be required for assessment of goal progress (see, e.g., Greller & Herold, 1975; Herold & Parsons, 1985; Ilgen, Fisher, & Taylor, 1979; Taylor, Fisher, & Ilgen, 1984). Self-evaluation of one's progress in obtaining a promotion, for example, may require performance information that cannot be readily obtained from self-monitoring of one's work progress. Furthermore, in the workplace, the costs of accurate performance monitoring may prohibit effective self-regulation.

A final issue for consideration pertains to how principles of self-regulation may be used by organizational personnel to improve training methods. Anticipated changes in the composition of the available workforce and the rapid pace of technological changes in work have generated interest in the development of effective training methods to promote asymptotic levels of learning and enhance intrinsic task motivation. Recent research in this area suggests that self-regulatory processes play an important role in this area of organizational functioning (see, R. Kanfer, in press a).

With these points in mind, the next section provides a selective overview of recent organizational research pertaining to the influence of goals and self-regulation in the workplace. Discussion is organized around three prominent issues in the organizational literature: (1) the effects of individual differences in motivation-related tendencies on performance; (2) the influence of goal attributes and contextual factors on components of self-regulation and performance; and (3) self-regulation training and workplace performance.

Individual Differences, Goals, and Self-regulation

Task Performance

Most investigations of individual differences determinants of motivation have focused on how these factors affect goal choice and self-regulation when performing a specific task, such as an academic course or an anagram task. This research concentrates on two individual differences constructs: (a) motive for success (and failure), and (b) self-focused attention. In the expectancy-value paradigm, substantial evidence has accumulated indicating the influence of noncognitive individual differences on goal choice and preferred level of task difficulty. Recent studies using control and action theory conceptualizations provides empirical support for the influence of individual differences in attentional tendencies on the efficiency of self-regulation in achievement contexts (see, e.g., Carver & Scheier, 1981; Kuhl & Beckmann, 1985).

A common feature of many expectancy-value theories of motivation is the emphasis given to individual differences in motive to achieve success (M_s) relative to the motive to avoid failure (M_f). Atkinson's (1957) original theory of achievement motivation, for example, proposed that individuals' choices among tasks and task persistence is determined by stable individual differences in success/failure motives, expectations of task success, and the perceived valence of task success. Extensions and elaborations of Atkinson's theory (e.g., Atkinson & Birch, 1970; Atkinson & Feather, 1966; Heckhausen, 1977; Raynor, 1969; Vroom, 1964; for reviews see Feather, 1982; Heckhausen, Schmalt, & Schneider, 1985) retain these fundamental individual difference variables.

Raynor's (1969, 1978) expansion of Atkinson's original theory has particular import for work motivation. Raynor (1969) proposed that motivation for an immediate activity is partly determined by the individual's perception of how immediate task success will affect his/her opportunity to attain related future goals. According to Raynor (1978; Raynor & Entin, 1982), many personal goals, such as career advancement, require that persons perform a hierarchical series of tasks. In these "contingent-path" situations, success at each task serves as a prerequisite for the opportunity to proceed to the next task. Preferred task difficulty in these paths depends not only on motives and incentives for the immediate task, but also on the number of steps and the position of the task in the goal path. In contrast, "non-contingent" paths refer to situations in which persons perceive that performance on each of a series of tasks is unrelated to the opportunity to proceed to the next task in the series.

Raynor's theory of future orientation and achievement motivation leads to several interesting hypotheses (see Raynor & Entin, 1982, for discussion of implications of the theory). Empirical evidence (see, e.g., Raynor & Entin, 1982; Raynor & Roeder, 1987) provides support for the following predictions: (a) motivation for first-step, immediate task performance in contingent paths is higher than motivation in noncontingent paths, (b) individuals labeled as success-oriented prefer easier tasks in contingent path situations, but moderately difficult tasks in laboratory settings where task performance is typically unrelated to the opportunity to proceed to the next task, and (c) as the number of steps in a path increase, individual differences in achievement motives exert stronger effects on task performance; achievement-oriented persons demonstrate higher levels of motivation than failure-oriented persons on the first step in longer contingent paths.

The cumulative findings in research on future orientation indicate that motive effects can be attenuated or accentuated depending on environmental and cognitive structuring of tasks requisite for attainment of personal goals. In the organizational context, individual differences in achievement motives are likely to be more pronounced when personal and work goals are characterized by a series of contingent work task performances. Raynor's theory and associated research suggests that employee commitment to external goal assignments (e.g., by a supervisor) will depend in part on the individual's perception of how the assigned goal relates to other salient work and nonwork goals.

Another important individual differences variable pertains to direction of one's attentional focus. Carver and Scheier (1981), for example, propose that individual differences in self-focus affect the activation and operation of self-regulation processes. According to their theory, self-regulation processes are activated only when individuals are high in self-focus (i.e., attention focused on the self). Individual differences in self-focus are typically assessed using the Fenigstein, Scheier, and Buss (1975) Public and Private Self-Consciousness Scale. Although the factor structure of the Fenigstein et al. (1975) scale remains unclear, several laboratory studies on the effects of dispositional tendencies in self-focus have provided support for predictions derived from the Carver and Scheier (1981) model (e.g., Carver & Scheier, 1981 for a review). In the organizational domain, Hollenbeck and his colleagues (Hollenbeck, 1989; Hollenbeck & Williams, 1987) found further field support for the influence of self-focus on self-regulation components. Hollenbeck and Williams (1987) examined the impact of self-set goals, goal importance, and self-focus on sales volume performance among salespersons. Results obtained indicated that self-set goals were highest among high self-focus salespersons who viewed the goal as important. Further support for the role of self-focus was obtained by Hollenbeck (1989) in a study of the influence of self-focus on job satisfaction, organizational commitment, and future outcome expectations among salespersons. Among other things, Hollenbeck (1989) found that outcome expectations and organizational commitment were more closely related among persons high in self-focus compared to persons low in self-focus.

A related individual differences construct that has received considerable research attention pertains to action control. Based on theorizing by Kuhl (1984), individual differences in action control influence the efficiency of self-regulation processes. Individuals high in action control are posited to be task-focused and to concentrate on developing strategies for resolving goal-performance discrepancies. In contrast, persons low in action control, or state-oriented, are posited to focus attention on internal emotional states or external conditions. Action control orientation is typically assessed using a self-report measure developed by Kuhl (see R. Kanfer, Dugdale, & McDonald, in press; Kuhl, 1984, in press). Studies by Kuhl and his colleagues provide empirical support for the influence of action control on performance of difficult and complex tasks.

Summary

Evidence demonstrating the influence of specific noncognitive individual differences on task performance is generally consistent with previous notions of motivation. What differentiates recent studies in this area from previous research is the attention given to identifying the intermediate mechanisms by which these dispositional tendencies exert their effects. Research stemming from Raynor's theory suggests that individual differences in motivational orientation must be considered in light of the array of an individual's goals. Consistent with research on the determinants and consequences of goal commitment, Raynor's theory implies that motivational orientation interacts with goal attributes to affect the activation and focus of self-regulation processes.

Research on self-focus and action control has concentrated on the effects of these dispositions on self-regulation components and patterns of self-regulatory activity. Results obtained in the organizational domain are consistent with clinical research on the role of similar individual difference constructs in depression and learned helplessness (e.g., see Dweck & Leggett, 1988; Hyland, 1987; Kuhl, 1984). High self-focus, or low action control, appears to debilitate performance through effects on components of self-regulation. For such persons, deficits in task performance relate to misdirection of cognitive effort during task performance and excessive negative self-reactions that promote task withdrawal. Consistent with findings obtained by Kanfer and Ackerman (1989), misregulation of attentional effort exerts more negative effects on complex task performance and among persons of lower ability than during performance of well-learned tasks and among persons of higher ability.

Job Performance

In most organizations, an employee's cumulative work accomplishments and citizenship behaviors are more highly valued than one-time performance accomplishments. Superior employees are often described as persons who consistently meet challenging performance goals, persist in the face of difficulties, come to work regularly and on time, stay late if needed, and help coworkers when necessary. From a motivational perspective, those individual differences in dispositional tendencies related to goal striving and self-regulatory tendencies may importantly account for individual differences in workplace behavior and job performance.

Several recent organizational studies provide support for an individual differences conceptualization of self-regulation in the work context. The assumption underlying this line of research is that individual differences in dispositional tendencies with motivational properties may influence variability in job performances where persistence is an important component of successful performance. Helmreich, Sawin, and Carsud (1986), for example, examined the influence of individual differences in three forms of achievement motivation on training and job performance of airline reservation agents. In their study, two dependent measures of performance, percentage of time spent on the telephone with customers and percentage of time agents were available to receive calls (i.e., time that agents were not on break or otherwise engaged in off-task activity) were obtained at 1-3 months, 4-6 months, and 7-8 months following hire. Helmreich et al. (1986) found that motive orientation, assessed by the Work and Family Orientation Questionnaire (WOFO; Helmreich & Spence, 1978) was unrelated to job performance measures at 1-3 months following hire. However, at later periods of job tenure, work and mastery achievement motives were significantly and positively related to job performance.

Similar results were obtained in a field investigation by Day and Silverman (1989). In that study, measures constructed from the Jackson Personality Research Form (PRF; Jackson, 1974) were used to assess the extent to which dispositional tendencies predicted dimensions of job performance among accountants (beyond that predicted by cognitive ability measures alone). Day and Silverman (1989) found that work orientation, ascendancy, and interpersonal orientation scales added significantly to the prediction of component job performance ratings. Of particular note is the finding that work orientation ratings demonstrated incremental validity for client relation performance ratings.

Results of the U.S. Army Selection and Classification Project (Project A; see Campbell, 1990) provide further evidence for the predictive validity of dispositional tendencies on long-term, volitional facets of job performance. As described by Peterson, Hough, Dunnette, Rosse, Houston, Toquam, and Wing (1990), Project A researchers identified six personality constructs from the personality literature that were related to non-cognitive job-related criteria. Preliminary testing of construct-related items taken from a variety of personality and biodata instruments resulted in the development of a non-cognitive paper-pencil inventory, called the Assessment of Background and Life Experiences (ABLE; Peterson et al., 1990). Empirical evidence for the predictive validity of the ABLE was obtained in concurrent and longitudinal field studies involving several thousand military personnel. In the longitudinal portion of this project, four composite scores, assessing achievement orientation, dependability, adjustment, and physical condition, were computed from the ABLE for use in predicting five job performance factors. Analyses of the incremental validity of ABLE composites (above that obtained when using general cognitive ability composites alone) indicated significant and substantial improvement in the predictive validities for three job performance factors: (a) effort and leadership, (b) personal discipline, and (c) physical fitness and military bearing (McHenry, Hough, Toquam, Hanson, & Ashworth, 1990).

Summary

After years of neglecting dispositional tendencies, organizational researchers have begun to reexamine the role of noncognitive individual differences in prediction of long-term job performance. Recent findings indicate that noncognitive individual differences with motivational components do predict critical features of long-term job performance, at least in some types of jobs. A key difference between recent and earlier research pertains to how the criterion measure of performance is conceptualized. Results of the Helmreich et al. (1986) study, for example, indicate that form of achievement motivation exerts a specific effect on one component of well-learned performance—time-on-task. Results of the Project A investigation indicate that noncognitive factors more highly predict volitional elements of job performance than they predict skill-based elements. Attempts to predict job performance based largely on ratings of skill are likely to yield low predictive validity for noncognitive measures. In most jobs, however, skill is likely to represent only part of overall job performance.

A central problem in organizational research of this type concerns the paucity of well-validated measures of individual differences in self-regulatory tendencies. Although theories of personality provide evidence for broad factors related to personal control and achievement orientation, it is not clear how and whether stable individual differences in the use and focus of self-regulatory activities can be identified. It may be, for example, that broad dispositional tendencies, such as achievement motivation, influence the adoption of goals and use of self-regulation strategies, which in turn affect job performance. As such, further attention to differential patterns of self-regulation associated with particular dispositional tendencies appears warranted. Such research may provide knowledge about the extent to which organizations may remediate or train self-regulation patterns associated with optimal job functioning.

Components of Self-regulation and Work Performance

The majority of work motivation studies during the past decade have focused on the effects of assigned goal attributes (difficulty and specificity) on work, rather than job, performance; namely, performance on a single work task, such as number of sales. In goal setting research, the effects of goal difficulty and specificity are often studied by contrasting performance in a nonspecific goal assignment condition (e.g., "Do your best" goal instructions) with performance obtained in a specific and difficult assigned goal condition (e.g., "Sell 10 insurance policies this month"). Goal difficulty level is typically manipulated through assignment of performance goals associated with different objective probabilities of attainment, where the probability of attainment is based on mean performance levels obtained by some reference sample. Thus, difficult goal assignments refer to performance levels attained by relatively few persons, and easy performance goals refer to performance standards attained by most persons. Goal specificity is typically operationalized as the extent to which the goal assignment is made explicit with respect to the target of action (Locke et al., 1981). Few researchers have manipulated goal specificity independently of goal difficulty.

Results of recent metaanalyses of goal setting research results indicate support for the thesis that persons assigned (and who adopt) difficult and specific goals outperform persons provided "do your best" goal assignments (Latham & Lee, 1986; Mento, Steel, & Karren, 1987; Tubbs, 1986; Wood, Mento, & Locke, 1987). The accumulated evidence demonstrating the beneficial effects of difficult and specific goal assignments on work performance has prompted widespread use of goal setting techniques in industry (see Locke & Latham, 1990).

Empirical demonstrations of goal setting effects on task performance led to several studies directed specifically toward understanding the processes, mechanisms, and moderator variables involved in the goal-performance relationship (see, Austin & Bobko, 1985; Kanfer, in press b). Using social learning and control theory conceptualizations, goal setting research has focused on two topics: (a) the relative influence of goals and feedback, and (b) the effects of the goal setting process on acceptance and commitment to assigned goals.

Goals and Performance Feedback—are Both Necessary?

Early investigations in the goal setting literature showed that goals mediated the effect of feedback on performance (e.g., Locke, Cartledge, & Koeppel, 1968). Self-regulation models, however, imply that although performance feedback is not sufficient for behavior change, it is necessary for effective behavior change. Research investigating the independent and interactive influence of goals and performance feedback provides support for the self-regulation perspective. Erez (1977) found that the goal-performance relationship was stronger when feedback was provided. Further investigation of the independent and interactive effects of goals and feedback by Bandura and Cervone (1983, 1986) indicated that performance on an ergometer task was maximized when both components (specific and difficult goal assignments and performance feedback) were present.

It should be noted, however, that persons who do not receive a specific goal assignment may still establish difficult and specific personal goals following performance feedback (cf. Mitchell, Rothman, & Liden, 1985). When persons engage in repeated task trials, individual differences in achievement orientation as well as task experience may affect self-regulation through their influence on spontaneous goal setting following performance feedback. In assembly-line work, for example, the provision of weekly performance feedback may prompt the establishment of difficult and specific goals among new employees who maintain a high achievement orientation, but not among longer-tenured, and low achievement-oriented employees. In the work setting, individual differences in achievement orientation, job characteristics and characteristics of performance feedback (e.g., salience, frequency) may, at times, compensate for the absence of explicit goal assignments.

Self-observation in the Workplace

Effective self-regulation requires self-observation on dimensions corresponding to the individual's goals. In the workplace, goals may necessitate more than self-monitoring of one's task performance. A computer programmer, for example, might monitor his/her performance with respect to whether the newly written program code works (in isolation), but might not be able to independently evaluate how efficiently the code was written or whether the code worked when combined with code written by other programmers. Practical difficulties in the monitoring component of self-regulation processes may seriously impair self-regulatory efficiency.

Working from a control theory framework, Ashford and Cummings (1983) suggested that employees seek and obtain critical feedback about goal progress in several ways. They proposed a fundamental distinction between the use of "monitoring" and "direct inquiry" strategies. Monitoring strategies involve passive receipt of performance feedback, such as might be obtained when employee productivity records are posted on a bulletin board. In contrast, direct inquiry strategies require the individual to actively request feedback from either a peer or supervisor. According to Ashford and Cummings (1983), direct inquiry strategies for obtaining feedback involve a "face cost" and potential threat to self-esteem. Partial confirmation of this notion was obtained by Ashford (1986) in a study of feedback-seeking strategies among job incumbents. Consistent with her hypotheses, Ashford (1986) found that longer-tenured and poor-performing employees tended to use direct inquiry strategies less frequently than newer employees and high performing employees. Her results imply that failure to use more informative feedback seeking strategies may hinder self-regulatory efficiency among those employees who are most likely to benefit from self-regulation.

Participative Versus Assigned Goal Setting and Goal Commitment

Locke's (1968) original goal setting model focused on the goal-performance relation; the model did not address the process or factors that influence acceptance and commitment to externally-imposed goals (see Locke, 1968). In early tests of goal setting hypotheses, variance in the acceptance of external goal assignments was minimal (cf. Erez, Earley, & Hulin, 1985). However, as goal setting researchers examined the generalizability of the goal-performance effect, concern grew about how the process of goal assignment might affect commitment and task performance. As Erez and Kanfer (1983) noted, the goals that influence self-regulation are the *individual's goals*. Although an individual's goal may be influenced by a goal assignment made by a supervisor, it is not uncommon for employees to privately reject organizational goal assignments or to set different personal goals. Growing recognition of the potential importance of goal commitment for activation of self-regulation processes led to extensive investigation of the process factors and individual differences characteristics that might influence employee acceptance and commitment to externally-imposed goals (e.g., Hollenbeck & Brief, 1987; Hollenbeck, Williams, & Klein, 1989).

The approach taken to resolving this issue was to compare the effects of participatively-set versus assigned goals. Participatively-set goals refer to goals that the individual helps to establish. In contrast, assigned goals typically refer to goals that the individual does not help to establish. Participatively-set and assigned goals are typically conceptualized as opposing ends of a personal influence continuum. At one end (participatively-set), individuals exert maximum and often sole control over the goal level that is established. At the other end (assigned goals), individuals exert minimum and often no control over the goal level.

According to Locke's goal setting model, participatively-set goals should enhance performance expressly through their effects on the difficulty level of the goal the individual adopts. That is, according to this model, method of goal setting is not expected to affect performance *as long as the procedures result in goal acceptance and commitment to similar goals*. Empirical support for this view was obtained in a series of studies by Latham and his colleagues (e.g., Latham & Saari, 1979a, 1979b). In these studies, method of goal setting had no effect on goal commitment or performance when level of goal difficulty was held constant.

However, a number of other goal setting studies provided discordant results (Austin, 1989; Campbell & Gingrich, 1987; Earley & Kanfer, 1985; Erez & Arad, 1986; Erez, Earley & Hulin, 1985; Hollenbeck & Brief, 1987; Hollenbeck, Williams, & Klein, 1989). Erez and her colleagues found that method of goal setting did affect goal commitment, which in turn affected performance. These researchers argued that involvement in the goal setting process, provision of an opportunity to express one's opinions, and enhanced sense of personal control achieved through participatively-set goal procedures in turn enhance employee commitment and thereby enhance performance.

Latham, Erez, and Locke (1988) suggested five possible methodological explanations for the conflicting findings, including, for example, differences in perceived task importance, and opportunities provided for group discussion. Three experiments were designed to test these hypotheses. The results obtained suggested that the critical difference between self-set and participatively-set goal procedures was associated with the instructions and rationale provided to subjects during the goal setting procedure. Latham et al. (1988) refer to this distinction as the difference between "tell" and "tell and sell" approaches. In participatively-set procedures, individuals are typically given a rationale for the goal assignment ("tell and sell"); in assigned goal procedures, individuals may be given brief instructions and no rationale ("tell"). Use of a "tell and sell" procedure in the assigned goal condition resulted in similar levels of goal commitment and performance compared with subjects in the participatively-set goal condition. These results complement research by Sansone (1986) and Wood and Bandura (1989) indicating that the purpose of task engagement influences goal commitment as well as affects the character of self-regulatory processing.

The results of goal setting research on participative versus assigned goals indicates that either procedure may be effective in enhancing performance as long as the procedure generates a threshold level of commitment to the goal. Consistent with these findings, Hollenbeck and Klein (1987) proposed a model that delineates the relationship between goal commitment and goal setting processes. Working from an expectancy-value framework, they suggested that expectancy of goal attainment and valence of goal attainment interact to determine goal commitment. Goal commitment was, in turn, posited to moderate the goal assignment-performance relation.

Hollenbeck and Klein (1987) also suggested contextual and individual difference variables that may influence expectancy and valence factors. Situational variables include publicness of the goal assignment, social influence, supervisor supportiveness, reward structures, and competition. Personal determinants include need for achievement, endurance, Type A personality, organizational commitment, job involvement, locus of control, and ability.

Evidence that supports part of Hollenbeck and Klein's model was provided by Hollenbeck, Williams, and Klein (1989) in a study of the effects of individual differences in need for achievement and goal publicness on goal commitment. Hollenbeck et al. (1989) found that both need for achievement and goal publicness exerted independent and interactive effects on goal commitment. For example, students high in need for achievement who were assigned a public goal demonstrated higher levels of goal commitment and subsequent task performance than subjects high in need for achievement who were assigned a privately-held goal.

Summary

Locke and Latham (1990) have argued that the strong influence of assigned goals on personal goals and subsequent performance stems from several features of the goal setting context. Typically, employees receive goal assignments from a superior who is perceived to have legitimate authority to establish such goals. Locke and Latham further suggested that the assignment of the performance goal enhances employee confidence in goal attainment. Goal assignments are also posited to challenge the individual to demonstrate their competence and to more fully define the standard to be used in self-evaluation.

The Locke and Latham analysis of factors that enhance adoption of external goals, enhance commitment, and improve task performance may be compared to clinical analyses of the conditions that facilitate self-management skill development in a therapeutic context. With respect to the supervisor-employee relationship, perceptions of the therapist as an "expert" appears to be a critical ingredient in therapeutic behavior change (see, e.g., Goldstein & Myers, 1986). However, as Karoly (1982) has suggested, initial perceptions of the helping agent as a legitimate authority may be a necessary but insufficient condition for long-term behavior change. In the work domain, the supervisor's authority may be undermined when he/she assigns the employee goals that far exceed the individual's capabilities. Unless supplemented by the linking of assigned goal accomplishments to tangible extrinsic outcomes, we expect that employee commitment to externally-imposed goals would become increasingly weaker as supervisors repeatedly make goal assignments that fall far above or below the individual's previous record of performance (ceteris paribus). Consistent with the notion of challenge, the analysis of facilitative conditions in the clinical context indicates that goal assignments must be perceived by employees as within their reach.

Locke and Latham also note that goal assignments promote self-confidence. They suggest that the mere assignment of the goal is interpreted by the employee as information that the assigned level of performance is possible. Similarly, Kanfer and Karoly (1982) note that "communicating confidence and esteem for the client's capacity for self-direction all serve to activate 'latent' self-regulatory functions" (p. 593). Nonetheless, other methods (e.g., modeling) may provide even more powerful means of strengthening self-confidence for goal attainment.

Activation of Self-regulation Processes and Job Performance

Goal setting research aims at understanding the self-regulatory mechanisms guiding behavior in a single-task context. However, as noted previously, job performance involves multiple tasks and goals. Theorizing about the psychological processes governing allocation of time and attention at this level derives principally from cybernetic control perspectives. Expanding on Carver and Scheier's (1981) theory, Lord and his colleagues (Campion & Lord, 1982; Klein, 1989; Lord & Hanges, 1987; Lord & Kernan, 1989) have proposed cognitive, information-processing models of work motivation that emphasize the role of cognitive scripts and different types of decision processes. In the Klein (1989) model, for example, cognitive scripts represent organized goal structures that permit smooth transitions across goal levels. When performing complex tasks, previously learned scripts are posited to reduce attentional effort demands by providing persons with a cognitive guide for executing various activities necessary for task success. Lord and Hanges (1987) further proposed that speed of environmental feedback affects which type of decision mechanism will be used to deal with a perceived discrepancy. When environmental feedback is slow and initial decisions cannot be quickly modified, persons are posited to use rational choice or avoidance choice processes. In contrast, when environmental feedback is rapid and initial decisions can be quickly modified, persons are expected to use routinized choice or action-first decision processes. Routinized choice processes are proposed to be used more frequently when the situation is familiar; in such situations routinized choice processes may resemble automatic or mindless processing. In contrast, when confronted with unfamiliar situations involving rapid environmental feedback, Lord and Hanges (1987) suggest that persons may use action first processes, such as trial-and-error.

The elaborated control theory perspectives advanced by Lord and his colleagues addresses several of the most difficult issues faced when coordinating self-regulation theories with work settings. First, the control perspective provides a theoretical basis for understanding the influence of task complexity on goal-performance relations. According to Lord and Kernan (1989), performance problems in simple tasks are often readily dealt with using previously learned cognitive scripts and routinized choice processes. In contrast, performance problems in complex tasks require greater attentional effort. In some such tasks, cognitive scripts are often unavailable and environmental feedback is likely to be slower, resulting in greater use of rational choice processes.

From a goal and self-regulation perspective, the emphasis on routinization of cognitive processes provides another attractive explanation for understanding the complex, and sometimes inconsistent effects of goal assignments on performance. On the one hand, the provision of a goal assignment in the context of a practiced task can be hypothesized to disrupt partially routinized processes and initiate controlled processing for the purpose of improving performance. A variety of clinical methods emphasize this strategy (e.g., see F. Kanfer & Schefft, 1988). In cognitive behavioral approaches to depression, for example, guided rehearsal of problem behaviors is often used for this purpose. In the work domain, the imposition of performance goal assignments among expert performers may be hypothesized to facilitate performance by disrupting routinized processing and encouraging further development of component performance skills.

On the other hand, the specifics of a goal assignment may disrupt partially routinized processing and divert needed attention *away* from further task improvement. Goal assignments that promote concerns about performance competency, for example, may further hinder skill development. Instructional manipulations that stress task mastery and proximal goal assignments that focus on behavior are likely to reduce the likelihood of a shift in goal orientation and attentional effort. Research by Bandura and Schunk (1981) on the beneficial effects of proximal compared with distal goal assignments, as well as recent findings by Wood and Bandura (1989) on the influence of instructional set, indicate potential benefits of carefully structured goal assignments in enhancing task performance during learning. In contrast, goal assignments that allude to competency appear to debilitate learning (R. Kanfer & Ackerman, 1989).

The control theory perspective also suggests that self-regulatory processes may be suspended when performing well-practiced tasks and in the absence of environmental cues signalling difficulty in execution of the goal. This conceptualization suggests, however, that performance feedback plays a major role in the resumption of self-regulatory processing. Given the difficulties of obtaining feedback in the work setting, it may be that the practical advantage of goal setting procedures in organizational settings lies with the corresponding increase in the frequency and type of feedback provided to individuals about their performance. In other words, provision of feedback indicating performance inadequacies may facilitate resumption of the self-regulation process, including specification of the performance standard to be achieved. Research investigating the effects of feedback availability on self-regulatory processing is needed to test this hypothesis.

Self-regulation Training and Job Performance

Substantial attention has been given to self-regulation training in the clinical literature. Surprisingly, however, only two studies have been conducted on the use of this procedure in the work context. Frayne and Latham (1987) examined the impact of self-management training on attendance rates among unionized government employees. Employees with a history of organizational sanctions for absenteeism were randomly assigned to one of two conditions: (1) control group, or (2) experimental group. Employees in the experimental group received self-management training, including instruction on self-monitoring, goal setting, and self-evaluation during eight, 1-hour training sessions over the course of eight weeks. Analysis of job attendance measures over a period of three months following training showed significantly higher rates of attendance compared to employees in the control condition. A follow-up study (Latham & Frayne, 1989) found that employees who had received self-management training maintained a higher rate of attendance compared to the control condition at nine months.

SUMMARY AND IMPLICATIONS

The attempt to coordinate theories of goal-directed action with workplace behavior and performance underscores the complex interplay of theory and practice in advancing the field. A substantial number of theories have been recently proposed. A central theme characterizing these theories is their emphasis on the critical role of goal commitment and self-regulation processes. The fundamental difference between these theories pertains to which aspects of the goal and self-regulatory process are emphasized. Cybernetic control approaches, for example, highlight the structure of goals and the conditions that facilitate activation of self-regulation processes. Social learning and social cognitive theories emphasize the influence of goal properties and environmental conditions on self-regulatory components and patterns of self-regulatory function. Although interest in identifying the role of stable individual differences on goals and self-regulation has grown over the past decade, this perspective remains relatively unexplored.

Not surprisingly, organizational research on work motivation has also focused increasingly on goal and self-regulation constructs. In contrast to theoretical developments in other fields, however, the impetus for this interest stems largely from attempts to understand inconsistent findings from the perspective of Locke's (1968) goal setting model. Major issues that have emerged from this literature focus on the process underlying acceptance and commitment of assigned goals and the role of goal assignments in tasks varying in complexity. Applications of social learning and control theory conceptualizations to these topics has resulted in a broadening of the theoretical frameworks used to understand motivation in the workplace.

The major themes that emerge from this coordination are organized into two areas: (a) implications of theory for work settings, and (b) implications of applied research for theory.

Implications of Theory for Work Settings

Several prominent goal and self-regulation theories have been used by applied researchers to understand the intermediate mechanisms by which goal assignments affect task performance. Drawing from social learning and social cognitive theories, several studies have examined the role of the self-efficacy construct in work behavior and performance (e.g., Earley, Wojnaroski, & Prest, 1987; R. Kanfer & Hulin, 1985; Latham & Frayne, 1989; Locke, Frederick, Lee, & Bobko, 1984; Locke, Motowidlo, & Bobko, 1986). Kanfer and Hulin (1985), for example, found that, after controlling for search behavior and attitudinal variables, self-efficacy expectations for job search immediately following a job lay-off among nurses were significantly associated with later reemployment success. Research on the differential effects of goal assignments on performance in simple and complex tasks stems from the integration of cognitive, information-processing and social learning conceptualizations. The Kanfer and Ackerman (1989) resource allocation framework outlines the dynamic context in which self-regulation may aid or hinder performance during complex skill acquisition. Results obtained in studies testing this model provide further support for the notion that goals influence performance through their effects on self-regulation. The model also provides a conceptual explanation for why weaker goal setting effects have been occasionally obtained in studies involving complex, cognitively demanding tasks. Expectancy-value conceptualizations have also been used to identify the conditions that may promote or hinder employee acceptance or commitment to goal assignments (e.g., Hollenbeck & Klein, 1987). Recent studies by Wood and his colleagues (Wood & Bandura, 1989; Wood, Bandura, & Bailey, 1990) document the potential of motivational orientation perspectives.

Nonetheless, recent theorizing suggests further investigation in several areas. During the past decade, theories of intrinsic motivation have undergone substantial change (R. Kanfer, in press b). Work by Csikszentmihayli and LeFevre (1989), Sansone (1986), Harackiewicz and Larson (1986) for example, suggests that intrinsic motivation effects may be developed through structuring of the environment and more careful attention to the individual's purpose for task engagement. In the workplace, one might investigate the efficacy of a variety of procedures for enhancing intrinsic motivation among employees at different stages of employment. Cellar and Wade (1988), for example, have recently shown that modeling procedures may be used to enhance initial intrinsic task interest. The new emphasis on the development of intrinsic task interest has implications for both training to optimal levels of performance as well as sustaining work motivation in routine jobs.

Another promising area of research pertains to identification of the various self-regulatory strategies persons use when facing obstacles to goal accomplishment. Kuhl (1985), for example, suggested several distinct self-regulatory strategies that may be deployed under different circumstances. Investigation of the task characteristics and individual differences associated with use of these strategies may ultimately permit development of training programs to enhance goal persistence.

Implications of Applied Research for Theory

The diversity of theoretical approaches taken to understanding workplace motivation underscores many of the advantages associated with research in this context. The attempt to map goal and self-regulation theories to this setting suggests that personality-based and control theories may be best suited to understanding self-regulation in long-term analyses of job performance. In contrast, social learning and social cognitive theories appear ideally suited for investigation of understanding deficits in specific task performances. To date, there has been relatively little integration of these approaches. In the workplace, however, supervisor judgments of an employee's performance must take into account both the historical pattern of performance as well as behavior directed toward the accomplishment of specific goals. Development of a common framework linking dispositional influences and specific environmental conditions as they affect self-regulation processes would be both theoretically and practically useful.

Organizational researchers are keenly aware of the role that individual differences in cognitive abilities play in job performance. Until recently, however, little attention has been given to examining the influence of these individual differences on goals and self-regulatory processes. Although motivational orientation theories have begun to incorporate notions of perceived abilities, it is critical that these perceptions be linked to objective estimates of cognitive abilities. By coordinating perceived and objective abilities indices, researchers may disentangle the source of deficits in maladaptive patterns of self-regulation. Kanfer and Ackerman (1989), for example, found that monitoring of one's goal was more frequent among lower-ability persons than higher-ability persons, regardless of when during skill acquisition the goal was assigned. These results raise the possibility that deficits in self-regulation may also stem from cognitive and metacognitive sources.

Finally, organizational researchers have long been interested in the relationship among motivation, performance, and job satisfaction (see, e.g., Locke, 1976). Although it is often held that satisfaction is positively associated with performance, the results of many studies suggest that the direct relation between overall job satisfaction and performance is relatively small (see Iaffaldano & Muchinsky, 1985). Contemporary theories of motivation and self-regulation suggest an alternative perspective for study of the affect-motivation-performance relation. For example, affect may influence performance through its effects on self-regulation processes that are requisite for performance attainments (e.g., Kavanagh & Bower, 1985; Wright & Mischel, 1982). Specific affective states, such as anger, may short-circuit or impair self-regulatory activities. Deficits in this system, would in turn, be expected to affect job performance.

In summary, organizational research on goal setting provides strong evidence attesting to the impact of goals and self-regulation processes on behavior and performance. Several recent theories have been used to investigate the determinants of performance in the workplace. The products of this research indicate that further theoretical developments are needed to: (1) delineate the role of individual differences in self-regulation, and (2) clarify the mechanisms underlying different patterns of self-regulatory activity. Current theorizing also suggests that organizational researchers should widen their scope of investigation to consider the impact of goals and self-regulation in the context of employee training, organizational socialization, and long-term job performance. Investigations of this type will provide unique opportunities for advancing both theory and practice.

ACKNOWLEDGMENTS

Preparation of this paper was supported by National Science Foundation grant (SES-8910748) to Ruth Kanfer. We would like to thank Phillip L. Ackerman for his very helpful comments on this work.

REFERENCES

Ackerman, P. L. (1988). Determinants of individual differences during skill acquisition: Cognitive abilities and information processing. *Journal of Experimental Psychology: General, 117*, 288-318.

Ajzen, I. (1985). From intentions to actions: A theory of planned behavior. In J. Kuhl & J. Beckmann (Eds.), *Action control. From cognition to behavior* (pp. 11-39). New York: Springer-Verlag.

Ashford, S. J. (1986). Feedback-seeking in individual adaptation: A resource perspective. *Academy of Management Journal, 29*, 465-487.

Ashford, S. J., & Cummings, L. L. (1983). Feedback as an individual resource: Personal strategies of creating information. *Organizational Behavior and Human Performance, 32*, 370-398.

Atkinson, J. W. (1957). Motivational determinants of risk-taking behavior. *Psychological Review, 64*, 359-372.

Atkinson, J. W., & Birch, D. (1970). *The dynamics of action.* New York: Wiley.

Atkinson, J. W., & Feather, N. T. (Eds.). (1966). *A theory of achievement motivation.* New York: Wiley.

Austin, J. T. (1989). Effects of shifts in goal origin on goal acceptance and attainment. *Organizational Behavior and Human Decision Processes, 44*, 415-435.

Austin, J. T., & Bobko, P. (1985). Goal setting theory: Unexplored areas and future research needs. *Journal of Occupational Psychology, 58*, 289-308.

Bandura, A. (1971). Analysis of modeling processes. In A. Bandura (Ed.), *Psychological modeling: Conflicting theories* (pp. 1-62). New York: Aldine-Atherton.

————. (1977a). *Social learning theory.* Englewood Cliffs, NJ: Prentice Hall.

————. (1977b). Self-efficacy: Toward a unifying theory of behavioral change. *Psychological Review, 84*, 191-215.

————. (1982). The self and mechanisms of agency. In J. Suls (Ed.), *Psychological perspectives on the self* (Vol. 1, pp. 3 - 40). Hillsdale, NJ: Erlbaum.

————. (1986). *Social Foundations of thought and action: A social cognitive theory.* Englewood Cliffs, NJ: Prentice Hall.

————. (1988). Self-regulation of motivation and action through goal systems. In V. Hamilton, G. H. Bower, & N. H. Fryda (Eds.), *Cognition, motivation, and affect: A cognitive science view* (pp. 37-61). Dordrecht, Holland: Martinus Nijholl.

Bandura, A., & Cervone, D. (1983). Self-evaluative and self-efficacy mechanisms governing the motivational effects of goal systems. *Journal of Personality and Social Psychology, 45,* 1017-1028.

————. (1986). Differential engagement of self-reactive influences in cognitive motivation. *Organizational Behavior and Human Decision Processes, 38,* 92-113.

Bandura, A., & Schunk, D. (1981). Cultivating competence, self-efficacy, and intrinsic interest through proximal self-motivation. *Journal of Personality and Social Psychology, 41,* 586-598.

Beckmann, J., & Kuhl, J. (1984). Altering information to gain action control: Functional aspects of human information processing in decision-making. *Journal of Research in Personality, 18,* 223-237.

Campbell, D. J., & Gingrich, K. (1987). The interactive effects of task complexity and participation on task performance: A field experiment. *Organizational Behavior and Human Decision Processes, 38,* 162-180.

Campbell, J. P. (1986). Labs, fields, and straw issues. In E. A. Locke (Ed.), *Generalizing from laboratory to field settings* (pp. 269-279). Lexington, MA: Lexington Books.

————. (1990). An overview of The Army Selection and Classification Project (Project A). *Personnel Psychology, 43,* 231-240.

Campbell, J. P., Campbell, R. J., & Associates. (Eds.). (1988). *Productivity in organizations.* San Francisco: Jossey-Bass.

Campion, M. A., & Lord, R. G. (1982). A control systems conceptualization of the goal setting and changing process. *Organizational Behavior and Human Performance, 30,* 265-287.

Cantor, N., & Kihlstrom, J. F. (1987). *Personality and social intelligence.* Englewood Cliffs, NJ: Prentice Hall.

Carver, C. S., & Scheier, M. F. (1981). *Attention and self-regulation: A control theory approach to human behavior.* New York: Springer-Verlag.

————. (1985). A control-systems approach to the self-regulation of action. In J. Kuhl and J. Beckmann (Eds.), *Action control: From cognition to behavior* (pp. 237-266). New York: Springer-Verlag.

Cellar, D. F., & Wade, K. (1988). Effect of behavioral modeling on intrinsic motivation and script-related recognition. *Journal of Applied Psychology, 73,* 181-192.

Csikszentmihayli, M., & LeFevre, J. (1989). Optimal experience in work and leisure. *Journal of Personality and Social Psychology, 56,* 815-822.

Day, D. V., & Silverman, S. B. (1989). Personality and job performance: Evidence of incremental validity. *Personnel Psychology, 42,* 25-36.

Dweck, C. S. (1986). Motivational processes affecting learning. *American Psychologist, 41,* 1040-1048.

Dweck, C. S., & Leggett, E. L. (1988). A social-cognitive approach to motivation and personality. *Psychological Review, 95,* 256-273.

Earley, P. C. (1985). Influence of information, choice and task complexity upon goal acceptance, performance, and personal goals. *Journal of Applied Psychology, 70,* 481-491.

Earley, P. C., & Kanfer, R. (1985). The influence of component participation and role models on goal acceptance, goal satisfaction, and performance. *Organizational Behavior and Human Decision Processes, 36,* 378-390.

Earley, P. C., Wojnaroski, P., & Prest, W. (1987). Task planning and energy expended: Exploration of how goals influence performance. *Journal of Applied Psychology, 72*, 107-114.

Elliott, E. S., & Dweck, C. S. (1988). Goals: An approach to motivation and achievement. *Journal of Personality and Social Psychology, 54* 5-12.

Emmons, R. A. (1986). Personal strivings: An approach to personality and subjective well-being. *Journal of Personality and Social Psychology, 51*, 1058-1068.

Erez, M. (1977). Feedback: A necessary condition for the goal setting-performance relationship. *Journal of Applied Psychology, 62*, 624-627.

Erez, M., & Arad, R. (1986). Participative goal setting: Social, motivational and cognitive factors. *Journal of Applied Psychology, 71*, 591-597.

Erez, M., Earley, P. C., & Hulin, C. L. (1985). The impact of participation on goal acceptance and performance: A two step model. *Academy of Management Journal, 28*, 50-66.

Erez, M., & Kanfer, F. H. (1983). The role of goal acceptance in goal setting and task performance. *Academy of Management Review, 8*, 454-463.

Feather, N. T. (Ed.). (1982). *Expectations and actions: Expectancy–value models in psychology.* Hillsdale, NJ: Erlbaum.

Fenigstein, A., Scheier, M. F., & Buss, A. H. (1975). Public and private self-consciousness: Assessment and theory. *Journal of Consulting and Clinical Psychology, 43*, 522-527.

Fisk, A. D., Ackerman, P. L., & Schneider, W. (1987). Automatic and controlled processing theory and its applications to human factors problems. In P. A. Hancock (Ed.), *Human factors psychology* (pp. 159-197). Holland: Elsevier.

Ford, D. H. (1987). *Humans as self-constructing living systems: A developmental perspective on behavior and personality.* Hillsdale, NJ: Erlbaum.

Frayne, C. A., & Latham, G. P. (1987). The application of social learning theory to employee self-management of attendance. *Journal of Applied Psychology, 72*, 387-392.

Frese, M., & Sabini, J. (Eds.). (1985). *Goal directed behavior: The concept of action in psychology.* Hillsdale, NJ: Erlbaum.

Goldstein, A. P., & Myers, C. R. (1986). Relationship-enhancement methods. In F. H. Kanfer & A. P. Goldstein (Eds.), *Helping people change* (3rd ed.). New York: Pergamon Press.

Gollwitzer, P. M., & Kinney, R. F. (1989). Effects of deliberative and implemental mind-sets on illusion of control. *Journal of Personality and Social Psychology, 56*, 531-542.

Greller, M. M., & Herold, D. M. (1975). Sources of feedback: A preliminary investigation. *Organizational Behavior and Human Performance, 13*, 244-256.

Halisch, F., & Kuhl, J. (1987). *Motivation, intention, and volition.* New York: Springer-Verlag.

Harackiewicz, J. M., & Larson, J. R. (1986). Managing motivation: The impact of supervisor feedback on subordinate task interest. *Journal of Personality and Social Psychology, 51*, 547-556.

Heckhausen, H. (1977). Achievement motivation and its constructs: A cognitive model. *Motivation and Emotion, 1*, 283-329.

Heckhausen, H., & Kuhl, J. (1985). From wishes to action: The dead ends and short cuts on the long way to action. In M. Frese & J. Sabini (Eds.), *Goal directed behavior: The concept of action in psychology* (pp. 134-160). Hillsdale, NJ: Erlbaum.

Heckhausen, H., Schmalt, H. D., & Schneider, K. (1985). *Achievement motivation in perspective.* New York: Academic Press.

Herold, D. M., & Parsons, C. K. (1985). Assessing the feedback environment in work organizations: Development of the job feedback survey. *Journal of Applied Psychology, 70*, 290-305.

Helmreich, R. L., & Spence, J. T. (1978). The Work and Family Orientation Questionnaire: An objective instrument to assess components of achievement motivation and attitudes toward family and career. *JSAS Catalog of Selected Documents in Psychology, 8*, 1-35.

Helmreich, R. L., Sawin, L. L., & Carsrud, A. L. (1986). The honeymoon effect in job performance: Temporal increases in the predictive power of achievement motivation. *Journal of Applied Psychology, 71*, 185-188.

Higgins, E. T. (1987). Self-discrepancy: A theory relating self and affect. *Psychological Review, 94*, 319-340.

Hollenbeck, J. R. (1989). Control theory and the perception of work environments: The effects of focus of attention on affective and behavioral reactions to work. *Organizational Behavior and Human Decision Processes, 43*, 406-430.

Hollenbeck, J. R., & Brief, A. P. (1987). The effects of individual differences and goal origin on the goal setting process. *Organizational Behavior and Human Decision Processes, 40*, 392-414.

Hollenbeck, J. R., & Klein, H. J. (1987). Goal commitment and the goal-setting process: Problems, prospects, and proposals for future research. *Journal of Applied Psychology, 72*, 212-220.

Hollenbeck, J. R., & Williams, C. R. (1987). Goal importance, self-focus, and the goal setting process. *Journal of Applied Psychology, 72*, 204-211.

Hollenbeck, J. R., Williams, C. R., & Klein, H. J. (1989). An empirical examination of the antecedents of commitment to difficult goals. *Journal of Applied Psychology, 74*, 18-23.

Humphreys, M. S., & Revelle, W. (1984). Personality, motivation, and performance: A theory of the relationship between individual differences and information processing. *Psychological Review, 91*, 153-184.

Hyland, M. E. (1987). Control theory interpretation of psychological mechanisms of depression: Comparison and integration of several theories. *Psychological Bulletin, 102*, 109-121.

_____. (1988). Motivational control theory: An integrative perspective. *Journal of Personality and Social Psychology, 55*, 642-651.

Iaffaldano, M. T., & Muchinsky, P.M. (1985). Job satisfaction and job performance: A meta-analysis. *Psychological Bulletin, 97*, 251-273.

Ilgen, D. R., Fisher, C. D., & Taylor, M. S. (1979). Consequences of individual feedback on behavior in organizations. *Journal of Applied Psychology, 64*, 349-371.

Jackson, D. N. (1974). *Personality research form manual* (2nd ed.). Port Huron, MI: Research Psychologists Press.

James, W. (1890). *Principles of psychology*. New York: Holt.

Kahneman, D. (1973). *Attention and effort*. Englewood Cliffs, NJ: Prentice Hall.

Kanfer, F. H. (1970). Self-regulation: Research, issues and speculations. In C. Neuringer & L. Michael (Eds.), *Behavior modification in clinical psychology*. New York: Appleton-Century-Crofts.

_____. (1977). The many faces of self-control, or behavior modification changes its focus. In R. B. Stuart (Ed.), *Behavioral self-management*. New York: Brunner/ Mazel.

_____. (1987). Selbstregulation und Verhalten (Self-regulation and behavior). In H. H. Heckhausen, P. M. Gollwitzer, & F. E. Weinert (Eds.), *Jenseits des Rubikon: Der Wille in den Humanwissenschaften (On the other side of the Rubicon: Volition in Human Sciences)* (pp. 286-299). Berlin: Springer-Verlag.

Kanfer, F. H., & Busemeyer, J. P. (1982). The use of problem-solving and decision-making in behavior therapy. *Clinical Psychology Review, 2*, 239-266.

Kanfer, F. H., & Goldstein, A. P. (1986). *Helping people change*. (3rd ed.). New York: Pergamon Press.

Kanfer, F. H., & Hagerman, S. M. (1981). The role of self-regulation. In L. P. Rehm (Ed.), *Behavior therapy for depression* (pp. 143-179). New York: Academic Press.

Kanfer, F. H., & Karoly, P. (1982). The psychology of self-management: Abiding issues and tentative directions. In P. Karoly & F. H. Kanfer (Eds.), *Self-management and behavior change: From theory to practice* (pp. 561-600). New York: Pergamon Press.

Kanfer, F. H., & Phillips, J. S. (1970). *Learning foundations of behavior therapy*. New York: Wiley.

Kanfer, F. H., & Schefft, B. K. (1988). *Guiding the process of therapeutic change*. Champaign, IL: Research Press.

Kanfer, F. H., & Stevenson, M. K. (1985). The effects of self-regulation on concurrent cognitive processing. *Cognitive Therapy and Research, 9*, 667-684.

Kanfer, R. (1987). Task-specific motivation: An integrative approach to issues of measurement, mechanisms, processes, and determinants. *Journal of Social and Clinical Psychology, 5*, 237-264.

————. (In press a). Motivation and individual differences in learning: An integration of developmental, differential, and cognitive perspectives. To appear in *Learning and Individual Differences*.

————. (In press b). Motivation theory and industrial-organizational psychology. In M. D. Dunnette & L. Hough (Eds.), *Handbook of industrial and organizational psychology. Volume 1: Theory in industrial and organizational psychology*. Palo Alto, CA: Consulting Psychologists Press.

Kanfer, R., & Ackerman, P. L. (1989). Motivation and cognitive abilities: An integrative/aptitude-treatment interaction approach to skill acquisition. *Journal of Applied Psychology-Monograph, 74*, 657-690.

Kanfer, R., Dugdale, B., & McDonald, B. (in press). Empirical findings on the Action Control Scale in the context of complex skill acquisition. To appear in J. Kuhl & J. Beckmann (Eds.), *Volition and personality: Action- and state-oriented modes of control*. Göttingen, West Germany: Hogrefe.

Kanfer, R., Dugdale, B., Nelson, L., & Ackerman, P. L. (1990). *Goal setting and complex task performance: A resource allocation perspective*. Presented at the annual meeting of the Society of Industrial and Organizational Psychology, Miami Beach, FL.

Kanfer, R., & Hulin, C. L. (1985). Individual differences in successful job searches following lay-off. *Personnel Psychology, 38*, 835-848.

Karoly, P. (1982). Perspectives on self-management and behavior change. In P. Karoly & F. H. Kanfer (Eds.), *Self management and behavior change: From theory to practice* (pp. 3-31). New York: Pergamon Press.

Karoly, P., & Kanfer, F. H. (Eds.). (1982). *Self management and behavior change: From theory to practice*. New York: Pergamon Press.

Kavanagh, D. J., & Bower, G. H. (1985). Mood and self-efficacy: Impact of joy and sadness on perceived capabilities. *Cognitive Therapy and Research, 9*, 507-525.

Klein, H. (1989). An integrated control theory model of work motivation. *Academy of Management, 14*, 150-172.

Klinger, E. (1975). Consequences of commitment to and disengagement from incentives. *Psychological Review, 82*, 1-25.

————. (1987). Current concerns and disengagement from incentives. In F. Halisch & J. Kuhl (Eds.), *Motivation, intention, and volition* (pp. 337-347). New York: Springer-Verlag.

Kuhl, J. (1982). The expectancy-value approach within the theory of social motivation: Elaborations, extensions, and critique. In N. T. Feather (Ed.), *Expectations and actions: Expectancy-value models in psychology* (pp. 125-160). Hillsdale, NJ: Erlbaum.

————. (1984). Volitional aspects of achievement motivation and learned helplessness: Toward a comprehensive theory of action control. In B. A. Maher (Ed.), *Progress in experimental personality research* (Vol. 13, pp. 99-171). New York: Academic Press.

————. (1985). Volitional mediators of cognition-behavior consistency: Self-regulatory processes and action vs. state orientation. In J. Kuhl & J. Beckmann (Eds.), *Action control: From cognition to behavior* (pp. 101-128). New York: Springer-Verlag.

_____. (in press). Properties of the Action Control Scale. To appear in J. Kuhl & J. Beckmann (Eds.), *Volition and personality: Action- and state-oriented modes of control*. Göttingen, West Germany: Hogrefe.

Kuhl, J., & Beckmann, J. (Eds.). (1985). *Action Control. From cognition to behavior*. New York: Springer-Verlag.

Kuhl, J., & Koch, B. (1984). Motivational determinants of motor performance: The hidden second task. *Psychological Research, 46*, 143-153.

Kuhl, J., & Kraska, K. (1989). Self-regulation and metamotivation: Computational mechanisms, development, and assessment. In R. Kanfer, P. L. Ackerman, & R. Cudeck (Eds.), *Abilities, motivation, and methodology: The Minnesota symposium on learning and individual differences* (pp. 343-374). Hillsdale, NJ: Erlbaum.

Kuhl, J., & Wassiljew, I. (1985). An information-processing perspective on intrinsic task-involvement problem-solving and the complexity of action plans. In G. d'Ydewalle (Ed.), *Cognition, information processing, and motivation* (pp. 505-522). Amsterdam: North-Holland.

Kuhl, J., & Weiss, M. (1985). *Performance deficits following uncontrollable failure: Impaired action control or generalized expectancy deficits?* (Paper No. 5/84). Munich: Max-Planck Institute for Psychological Research.

Latham, G. P., Erez, M., & Locke, E. A. (1988). Resolving scientific disputes by the joint design of crucial experiments by the antagonists: Application to the Erez-Latham dispute regarding participation in goal setting. *Journal of Applied Psychology–Monograph, 73*, 753-772.

Latham, G. P., & Frayne, C. A. (1989). Self-management training for increasing job attendance: A follow-up and a replication. *Journal of Applied Psychology, 74*, 411-416.

Latham, G. P., & Lee, T. W. (1986). Goal setting. In E. A. Locke (Ed.), *Generalizing from laboratory to field settings* (pp. 101-118). Lexington, MA: Lexington Books.

Latham, G. P., & Saari, L. M. (1979a). The effects of holding goal difficulty constant on assigned and participatively set goals. *Academy of Management Journal, 22*, 163-168.

_____. (1979b). Importance of supportive relationships in goal setting. *Journal of Applied Psychology, 64*, 151-156.

Lee, T. W., Locke, E. A., & Latham, G. P. (1989). Goal setting theory and job performance. In L. A. Pervin (Ed.), *Goal concepts in personality and social psychology*. Hillsdale, NJ: Erlbaum.

Locke, E. A. (1968). Toward a theory of task motivation and incentives. *Organizational Behavior and Human Performance, 3*, 157-189.

_____. (1976). The nature and causes of job satisfaction. In M. D. Dunnette (Ed.), *Handbook of industrial and organizational psychology* (pp. 1297-1349). Chicago: Rand McNally.

Locke, E. A., Cartledge, N., & Koeppel, J. (1968). Motivational effects of knowledge of results: A goal setting phenomenon? *Psychological Bulletin, 70*, 474-485.

Locke, E. A., Frederick, E., Lee, C., & Bobko, P. (1984). Effect of self-efficacy, goals, and task strategies on task performance. *Journal of Applied Psychology, 69*, 241-251.

Locke, E. A., & Latham, G. P. (1990). Work motivation and satisfaction: Light at the end of the tunnel. *Psychological Science, 1*, 240-246.

Locke, E. A., Motowidlo, S. J., & Bobko, P. (1986). Using self-efficacy theory to resolve the conflict between goal-setting theory and expectancy theory in industrial/organizational psychology. *Journal of Social and Clinical Psychology, 4*, 328-338.

Locke, E. A., Shaw, K. N., Saari, L. M., & Latham, G. P. (1981). Goal setting and task performance: 1969-1980. *Psychological Bulletin, 90*, 125-152.

Lord, R. G., & Hanges, P. J. (1987). A control systems model of organizational motivation: Theoretical development and applied implications. *Behavioral Science, 32*, 161-178.

Lord, R. G., & Kernan, M. C. (1989). Application of control theory to work settings. In W. A. Herschberger (Ed.), *Volitional action* (pp. 493-514). Amsterdam: Elsevier.

McHenry, J. J., Hough, L. M., Toquam, J. L., Hanson, M. A., & Ashworth, S. (1990). Project A validity results: The relationship between predictor and criterion domains. *Personnel Psychology, 43*, 335-366.

Mento, A. J., Steel, R. P., & Karren, R. J. (1987). A meta-analytic study of the effects of goal setting on task performance: 1966-1984. *Organizational Behavior and Human Decision Processes, 39*, 52-83.

Mischel, W. (1974). Processes in delay of gratification. In L. Berkowitz (Ed.), *Advances in experimental social psychology* (Vol. 7, pp. 249-292). New York: Academic Press.

Mitchell, T. R., Rothman, M., & Liden, R. C. (1985). Effects of normative information on task performance. *Journal of Applied Psychology, 70*, 48-55.

Naylor, J. C., & Ilgen, D. R. (1984). Goal setting: A theoretical analysis of a motivational technology. In B. M. Staw and L. L. Cummings (Eds.), *Research in organizational behavior* (Vol. 6, pp. 95-140). Greenwich, CT: JAI Press.

Naylor, J. C., Pritchard, R. D., & Ilgen, D. R. (1980). *A theory of behavior in organizations.* New York: Academic Press.

Nicholls, J. G. (1978). The development of the concepts of effort and ability, perception of academic attainment, and the understanding that difficult tasks require more ability. *Child Development, 49*, 800-814.

————. (1984). Achievement motivation: Conceptions of ability, subjective experience, task choice, and performance. *Psychological Review, 91*, 328-346.

Nicholls, J. G., & Miller, A. T. (1984). Development and its discontents: The differentiation of the concept of ability. In J. G. Nicholls (Eds.), *Advances in motivation and achievement* (Vol. 3, pp. 185-218). Greenwich, CT: JAI Press.

Nolen, S. B. (1988). Reasons for studying: Motivational orientations and study strategies. *Cognition and Instruction, 5*, 269-287.

Nuttin, J. (1984). *Motivation, planning, and action.* Hillsdale, NJ: Erlbaum and Leuven University Press.

Organ, D. W., & Konovsky, M. (1989). Cognitive versus affective determinants of organizational citizenship behavior. *Journal of Applied Psychology, 74*, 157-164.

Pervin, L. (1983). The statis and flow of behavior: Toward a theory of goals. In M. M. Page (Ed.), *Personality: Current theory and research.* 1982 Nebraska symposium on motivation (Vol. 30, pp. 1-53). Lincoln, NE: University of Nebraska Press.

Pervin, L. A. (1989). *Goal concepts in personality and social psychology.* Hillsdale, NJ: Erlbaum.

Peterson, N. G., Hough, L. M., Dunnette, M. D., Rosse, R. L., Houston, J. S., Toquam, J. L., & Wing, H. (1990). Project A: Specification of the predictor domain and development of new selection/classification tests. *Personnel Psychology, 43*, 247-276.

Raynor, J. O. (1969). Future orientation and motivation of immediate activity: An elaboration of the theory of achievement motivation. *Psychological Review, 76*, 606-610.

————. (1978). Future orientation in achievement motivation: A more general theory of achievement motivation. In J. W. Atkinson & J. O. Raynor (Eds.), *Personality, motivation, and achievement* (pp. 121-154). New York: Hemisphere.

Raynor, J. O., & Entin, E. E. (1982). Achievement motivation as a determinant of persistence in contingent and noncontingent paths. In J. O. Raynor & E. Entin (Eds.), *Motivation, career striving, and aging* (pp. 83-92). Washington, DC: Hemisphere.

Raynor, J. O., & Roeder, G. P. (1987). Motivation and future orientation: Task and time effects for achievement motivation. In F. Halisch & J. Kuhl (Eds.), *Motivation, intention, and volition* (pp. 61-71). New York: Springer-Verlag.

Sansone, C. (1986). A question of competence: The effects of competence and task feedback on intrinsic interest. *Journal of Personality and Social Psychology, 51*, 918-931.

Shiffrin, R. M., & Schneider, W. (1977). Controlled and automatic human information processing: II. Perceptual learning, automatic attending, and a general theory. *Psychological Review, 84*, 127-190.

Smith, C. A., Organ, D. W., & Near, J. P. (1983). Organizational citizenship behavior: Its nature and antecedents. *Journal of Applied Psychology, 68*, 653-663.

Snow, R. E. (1986). Individual differences and the design of educational programs. *American Psychologist, 41*, 1029-1039.

————. (1989). Cognitive-conative aptitude interactions in learning. In R. Kanfer, P. L. Ackerman, & R. Cudeck (Eds.), *Abilities, motivation, and methodology: The Minnesota symposium on learning and individual differences.* Hillsdale, NJ: Erlbaum.

Sorrentino, R. M., & Higgins, E. T. (Eds.). (1986). *Handbook of motivation and cognition. Foundations of social behavior.* New York: Guilford Press.

Staw, B. M. (1984). Organizational behavior: A review and reformulation of the field's outcome variables. *Annual Review of Psychology, 35*, 627-666.

Taylor, S. E., & Schneider, S. K. (1989). Coping and the simulation of events. *Social Cognition, 7*, 176-194.

Taylor, S. M., Fisher, C. D., & Ilgen, D. R. (1984). Individuals' reaction to performance feedback in organizations: A control theory perspective. In G. Ferris and K. Rowland (Eds.), *Research in personnel and human resources management* (Vol. 2, pp. 81-124). Greenwich, CT: JAI Press.

Tubbs, M. E. (1986). Goal setting: A meta-analytic examination of the empirical evidence. *Journal of Applied Psychology, 71*, 474-483.

Vroom, V. H. (1964). *Work and motivation.* New York: Wiley.

Weiner, B. (1985). An attributional theory of achievement motivation and emotion. *Psychological Review, 92*, 548-573.

————. (1986). *An attributional theory of achievement motivation and emotion.* New York: Springer-Verlag.

Wood, R. E., & Bandura, A. (1989). Impact of conceptions of ability on self-regulatory mechanisms and complex decision-making. *Journal of Personality and Social Psychology, 56*, 407-415.

Wood, R. E., Bandura, A., & Bailey, T. (1990). Mechanisms governing organizational productivity in complex decision-making environments. *Organizational Behavior and Human Decision Processes, 46*, 181-201.

Wood, R. E., Mento, A. J., & Locke, E. A. (1987). Task complexity as a moderator of goal effects: A meta-analysis. *Journal of Applied Psychology, 72*, 416-425.

Woodworth, R. S. (1929). *Psychology: Revised edition.* New York: Henry Holt & Co.

Wright, J., & Mischel, W. (1982). Influence of affect on cognitive social learning person variables. *Journal of Personality and Social Psychology, 43*, 901-914.

LIFE TASKS AND SELF-REGULATORY PROCESSES

Nancy Cantor and William Fleeson

Accomplishing personal goals is fundamental to an adaptive life. Much of life is directed toward satisfying some interest or other. Some interests that people pursue are quite important to life, such as career, intimacy and companionship, and good health. Considerable resources are devoted toward attaining those goals, and people meet with varying degrees of success. Regardless of outcomes, many have argued that simply setting out to accomplish goals provides meaning and structure to life (Klinger, 1975; Ryff, 1989).

Purposive behavior has a direction that is responsive to many forces, both internal and external to the individual. There are at least three types of forces directing behavior. Each type has a set of standards, guidelines, demands, and expectations about how to direct one's activity. The *cultural context* sets age-graded tasks and opportunities, the *immediate context* of situations, people, and time inhibits some activities and facilitates others, and the *person's* set of abilities, expectancies, and motives make some pursuits more preferable than others. In Figure 1 we depict the goal, in the form of a life task, as emerging out of these forces. Each of these types of forces is pushing and pulling the person in various directions, often contradicting each other. The most obvious

Advances in Motivation and Achievement, Volume 7, pages 327-369.
Copyright © 1991 by JAI Press Inc.
All rights of reproduction in any form reserved.
ISBN: 1-55938-122-1

are the contradictions between forces internal to the person with those in the context of the person. The context often wants the person to do something different than the person wants to do. This kind of conflict has been documented since at least Freud (1930/1961). Conflict also exists within the person, as when two desires are mutually exclusive, and within the context, as when two aspects of the context push the person in different directions. Besides conflicting with each other, the forces often change over time. Sometimes the change is rapid, other times it is slow. Either way, a force can give way to a different force, or simply fade out. Finally, these forces operate at many levels. Often the forces suggest broad and unspecified ends: motives can be to affiliate, or to achieve, for example; cultural tasks can be to have an identity, or to raise a family, and so forth. There is little specification about how to accomplish these ends, but the person must endeavor to translate them into specific acts, thoughts, and feelings. On the other hand, the forces can be quite specific, as when a person doesn't like wearing suits, or prefers an early schedule. Contextual forces can also be specific, urging a person to have the wedding on a weekend, or to reciprocate dinner invitations.

Contradictory, changing, and multilevel forces make any accomplishment-oriented behavior difficult. With contradictory forces, the person is left in sort of a limbo. With changing forces, the end sought yesterday may not be attractive today. With multilevel forces, behavior may seem appropriate at one level, but not at another. To avoid behavioral chaos, and to instead maintain a thread of progress towards an accomplishment, requires effort in the face of these forces. The fundamental assumption of this paper is that people struggle to regulate a path through these demands and guidelines, attempting to take into account all of them, in an effort toward accomplishment. In this paper, we propose that, in order to do this, people form representations of goals, defining *what* the goal is and *how* to pursue it, in a way that is sensitive to internal and to contextual forces. Much interesting research in the self-regulation literature has explicated processes of goal maintenance and persistence—that is, the conditions that enable individuals to stay on a path once it is chosen and defined. However, relatively less work has focused on the nature of that definitional process—that is, on the ways in which individuals define what they will work on and when and how they will do it in their current life context. After discussing briefly self-regulation as a definitional process and the forces that contribute to goal definition, we will present the *life task* as a goal unit that might be sensitive to such forces and some research showing the integration of internal and contextual forces in the definition of individuals' life tasks.

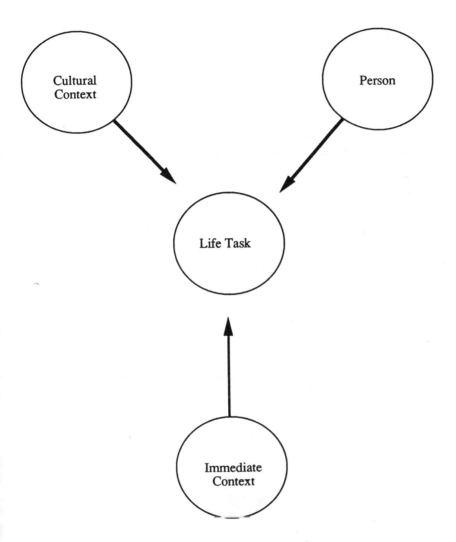

Figure 1.   Life Task Definition in Context

THE WHAT AND HOW OF GOAL DEFINITION

Defining, both what the goal is and how to pursue it, is a fundamental part of self-regulation. Defining is used here in the sense of creating and choosing specifics out of a number of alternatives. The goal-pursuer must choose what goals, and what aspects of those goals, interest her. After choosing which goals to pursue, she must choose a way of pursuing those goals. In both cases she is creating (or at least becoming cognizant of) alternatives and choosing from amongst them. Defining is also meant to suggest a (partly) cognitive activity, in that the choosing process is based on information, and the information is organized in the person's head. The resulting definition is unitary, yet is composed of many bits of information and choices. The definition is unitary so that it can direct action, but it is flexible so that it can evolve as parts of it change. Although the cognitive activity involved in defining the *what* and *how* of goals is interesting (Kluwe & Friedrichson, 1985), we will not address that specifically here.

Figure 2 pictorially represents the definitional process in four steps. The top panel represents the problem. The person is confronted with a number of forces pushing in a number of directions. In addition, several forces from within him are acting on his direction. Nothing is being done; nothing is being accomplished. The bottom (fourth) panel of the figure shows a person attempting to follow a path toward a goal. Traditionally, self-regulation research has focused on the problem of how people manage to accomplish anything in the midst of changing intentions. *Akrasia*, or weakness of the will, is a theoretical problem reaching back at least as far as the Greek philosophers. It refers to the condition people find themselves in too much, in which they intend to do something, but they just can't seem to do it. President Bush told us to read his lips when he said he wouldn't raise taxes, but try as he might, he just couldn't hold himself back. Many of the problem-solving and cybernetic self-regulatory models (e.g., Carver & Scheier, 1981; Kuhl, 1985; Miller, Galanter, & Pribram, 1960) present solutions to the problem of Akrasia, and in so doing they describe this panel, namely the efforts of the person to stay on the path. In this paper, we are primarily concerned with the intermediate steps illustrated in this figure. These panels describe two other steps that we see as crucial in allowing a person to exhibit goal-directed behavior in the face of conflicting and changing forces: they get the person from the top panel to the bottom panel. In fact, we see all three panels as inter-connected parts of the single enterprise of defining goals in the midst of varying forces.

The panel third from the top shows a step just previous to following a path, and that is defining *how* to pursue the goal. In order to follow a path, one must have a path. In research on self-regulation, the path is often straightforward, so that the processes of staying on that path can be isolated and studied. Self-regulation systems like Kuhl's (1985) or Carver & Scheier's (1981) work best with relatively specified goals. The problem is keeping oneself pursuing the goal. How to pursue the goal is not an issue, but rather whether to pursue the goal. For example, Kuhl (1985) describes six mechanisms of self-regulation (e.g., attentional selectivity, motivational control, environmental control) that serve to keep an individual on target toward a specified goal. However, in daily life, people must make behavioral choices in order to pursue the goal. People must define how they will achieve the goal, and they must do this in the face of many conflicting and changing forces. Very rarely do goals come with instructions. Although self-regulation keeps the light burning so that one can keep on track towards the light, the ground in between oneself and the light can be quite treacherous. Thus, in order to have progress towards a goal, one must make choices about how to get to the goal.

Not only must one create a definition of how to achieve the goal, but one must often make these decisions in social contexts in which there are strong prescriptions for goal pursuit. Situations permit only certain behaviors, other people are full of advice about how to achieve goals, and even the day of the week makes certain activities appropriate and others not so appropriate. Figure 2 represents the various forces operating as arrows, and the path as a dotted line. The path is designed in a way sensitive to contextual and internal forces, but not beholden to either.

This process of defining how to pursue one's goals is an important step that is not entirely separable from other self-regulation processes. Some behaviors are easier to maintain than others (Kuhl, 1985). A definition of how (and when and where) to achieve a goal that has behaviors that are hard to maintain will have little chance of succeeding. The best definitions will consist of behaviors that are easy to maintain in a current life context (Vallacher & Wegner, 1987). For this reason, we imagine that when defining how to pursue a task, people take into account the ease with which they will be able to regulate the behaviors (Bandura, 1986). Thus, people's self-regulatory efforts begin at the definitional stage. A complete study of self-regulation will include the ways in which people define how to pursue the goal. When intentions are unspecified (as with many goals), the process of buttressing an intention against competing intentions includes the process of defining the plan to complete that intention.

The second panel from the top shows another step just previous to the definition of how to achieve the goal. In theories of self-regulation, the nature of the pursued intention is rarely discussed. Indeed, the self-regulation processes are proffered as goal-independent general purpose modules. Whatever the goal, the self-regulation processes act to maintain persistence at that goal. In that set-up, the goal (intention) is provided by another module, and the self-regulation module initiates its own work. In experimental simulations of this problem-solving process, the intentions supplied in laboratories are relatively nondescript. For example, people are often presented with anagrams to solve, or puzzles to complete.

However, the goals that people pursue in daily life are often different from these goals pursued in self-regulation experiments. Namely, the goals are often much less well-specified and less end-state oriented. With end-state oriented and well-specified goals, people know when they have accomplished *the* goal. Yet many of life's most central goals are not so easily defined, nor are they quickly accomplished at one sitting. To the extent that goals are less well-specified, it becomes less clear what behaviors count as directed at the goal.

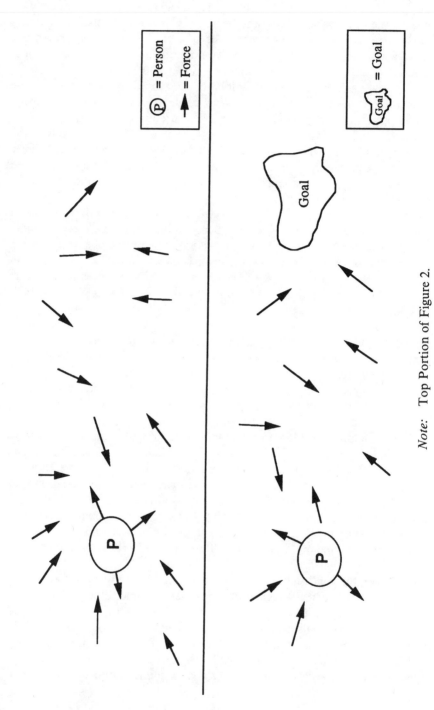

Note: Top Portion of Figure 2.

332

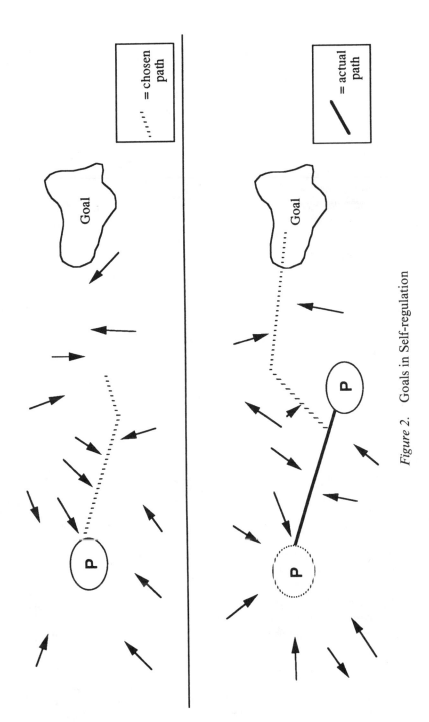

Figure 2. Goals in Self-regulation

It is unclear, for example, how much talking with people at a party in a different city counts as part of the goal of making friends. The question is no longer "Has the present state become the desired state," but rather "Am I doing something that counts as part of progress in this goal?" Thus, in daily life, a significant portion of the self-regulatory process, broadly-defined, is centered around the actual definition of the goal itself. This process of defining *what* a goal is, is represented in the second panel of Figure 2, with the various forces shaping the choice of goal, and the definition of the goal, from among the many possibilities.

Finally, this stage, defining *what* the goal is, also is not completely separable from the other two stages. Because the goals are ongoing, self-regulation processes will have to operate over time, and wane in strength at times and increase in strength at other times. Because goals are ill-defined, self-regulation processes will have to be attuned to which behaviors count as part of the goal and which do not. Self-regulation processes will need to be in concert with definitions of the goals. Self-regulators must make these macro-level decisions about what the goal is, and the way in which they do so will have implications for the effectiveness of their self-regulatory efforts.

The first two steps are also intricately linked. Defining what a goal is and defining how to pursue it are quite similar things. Decisions about what a goal is constrain how it can be pursued, and decisions about how to pursue it constrain what it is. In fact, defining what a goal is and defining how to pursue it may be the same thing, yet seen from different sides. In defining how to do well in school, someone might decide to do well in physics. Doing well in physics can now be seen as a (slightly smaller) goal. Powers (1973) devised a hierarchical system in which defining how to pursue a goal is accomplished by setting subgoals, which are then the goals to be defined. Again, defining what and defining how are interdependent.

Together, the links of defining what a goal is, how to pursue it, and how to maintain that pursuit, represent the three stages of exhibiting goal directed behavior in the midst of a sea of forces impinging on that direction. Defining what the goal is allows people to know which behaviors count as part of it. Defining how to pursue a goal allows concerted effort to it, effort that can accommodate a variety of forces. The final stage allows one to maintain effort towards a goal despite unexpected changes in circumstances. As we have seen, these stages are intricately linked: decisions in one affect decisions in the others. The problem of self-regulation encompasses the entire three-stage sequence, and because the three stages are interdependent, and goals are critical in all three stages, the definition of personal goals is central to self-regulation.

SOURCES OF INFORMATION IN GOAL DEFINITION

Conceiving of self-regulation as a definitional problem changes the role that internal and contextual forces play. Rather than being forces pushing and

Table 1. Forces in Life Task Definition

Definition	Source	
	Self	*Context*
What	Motives and needs	Age-graded tasks
How to	Abilities, expectancies	Immediate contexts

pulling the person, they become sources of information available in creating the definition. Each source of information provides a piece of information about what a person should be pursuing and about where and how to make progress on that goal. Forming a definition is a process of sifting through the information and coming to some sort of relatively consistent interpretation of it. How consistent it is varies, of course, with the particular task, the person, and the context. Table 1 visually represents different forces that might influence the definition of a goal—both in terms of *what* a person works on and *how* they do it. Each force can be seen as one type of informational source (self or context) affecting one aspect of the definition (what or how). Of course, this is a simplification because most sources provide some information about both aspects of the definitional problem, and most sources consist somewhat of both self and contextual information.

The top left cell represents traditional research on motivation, consisting of people's more or less enduring, and fairly abstract, motives, needs, or values. These motives can be seen as sources of information in that a person reacts to possible goals with personal preferences about *what* to pursue. As McClelland (1975) described, people see situations as presenting opportunities for goals that express their motives. People also react to possible goals with acceptance or rejection, depending on how they fit in with their motives. Motives and needs determine what specific goals are imagined and embraced in a daily life context. In practice, much of the research addresses very specific points in motivation, thereby defining "how to" as well as "what," but the thrust is on the content of social motives of power, affiliation, achievement, or intimacy, and on individual differences in the strength of these motives.

The bottom left cell represents the person's set of abilities, capacities, and expectancies. These are sources of information typically about *how* to pursue a goal after it has been specified, and they describe the person's beliefs about how he or she can go about attaining that goal. For example, one's sense of self-efficacy at a task (Bandura, 1986), or of internal locus of an control (Rotter, 1966), provides critical information about how to expend effort at the task in striving to fulfill a goal.

The top right cell represents the influence of culture on the definition of what to pursue in daily life. For example, Veroff (1983) delineated five aspects of the cultural context, including historical norms, organizational norms, and developmental tasks, that influence the meaning that social motives of achievement and affiliation took on in the lives of Americans between the 1950s and 1970s. Lifespan theorists have outlined progressive age-graded tasks that serve as informational input to individuals' choices of what goals to pursue (Erikson, 1950; Havighurst, 1953). The culture of schools and of the media present individuals with fairly clearly-delineated tasks to accomplish at each new stage of development (Higgins & Parsons, 1983). Although these messages may describe how one goes about the task as well, the focus is usually on defining what task is appropriate.

Finally, the bottom right cell describes the ways in which social life contexts and rituals are organized to help a person know how to work on those normatively-appropriate tasks (Goffman, 1974). In this cell go the immediate contextual forces that regulate time and place of behavior according to social norms—that is, the "rules of the game" for social life (Argyle, 1981). They can be seen as providing information about when and where to pursue particular goals. Other people in similar situations will draw people into their tasks, situations will suggest certain tasks and inhibit others, and even the day of the week is socially-regulated in terms of appropriate goals to pursue (e.g., you are a workaholic if you work constantly on weekends).

In this paper we wish to illustrate the ways in which individuals integrate both contextual and internal forces in their choice of goals and their goal-directed activity. The primary claim of this paper is that people go from being the recipient of a diverse set of forces to forming and acting upon a relatively unitary definition of a goal. In order to get from the uncoordinated forces to a unitary goal requires that the forces be integrated in some way. The most simple integration would be to choose one of the forces, and ignore the others (in actuality, this is no integration at all). For example, in defining his personal goals, a young adolescent could simply ignore the social, age-graded pressure for achievement, and pursue only his other interests. Of course, this alternative would lead to friction in people's lives, for the ignored forces would work against the person. Another possibility is more complex and more integrative: When forming a definition, the person incorporates both the contextual and personal forces. In order to come to a definition of a task, the person adds the forces from the context to the forces from the person, and follows the result. In this case, both contextual and personal forces contribute to the resulting definition, but the contributions are *independent*. In other words, each force contributes to the same degree independently of the particular contribution of the other force. Thus, the adolescent described above would work on achievement tasks a bit more than he might otherwise in recognition of those social prescriptions. The third possibility goes one more step, and removes the independence of the above possibility. In this third integration, once again both contextual and personal factors contribute to the definitions of what and how of the life task, but their contributions are not independent. Instead, how much one force contributes will depend on how much another force contributes. For example, the "nonachiever" adolescent might bow to social pressure to achieve, but only in selected school contexts; in other contexts he won't do any achievement activity. These alternatives will be discussed more concretely in the data sections of this paper. Each of these alternative scenarios for goal definition confronts an individual as he or she, more or less concertedly and decisively, frames the *what* and *how* of goal-directed activity in daily life.

LIFE TASKS AS AN INTEGRATIVE GOAL UNIT

Thus far we have made two basic suggestions about self-regulation and personal goals. First, we suggested that the self-regulatory process can be conceived in broad terms as a goal definition project, including three interweaving subprojects: defining *what* to pursue, defining *how* to pursue it, and defining *whether* to maintain the pursuit. Much concern has been accorded in the self-regulation literature to the latter question of the strategies by which individuals maintain or abandon goal pursuit. However, relatively less attention has been directed at explicating the basis for people's choices of what goals to pursue and when and where to work on them in a daily life context. In this regard, our second suggestion was that the project of goal definition, especially with regard to these questions of what to pursue and of how to do it, involves a fairly complex and continuously evolving process of integrating information about personal needs and expectancies with cultural and contextual messages about the appropriate form and forum for goal pursuit. As is frequently the case, these goal definitions represent dynamic interactions of persons and situations.

In order to study this goal definition process, it is necessary to begin with a unit of analysis of personal goals that can encompass both individuals' central motives and their more concrete expression in daily life. Middle-level goal units have been attracting research attention recently (Buss & Cantor, 1989; Pervin, 1989). Whether the units are personal projects (Little, 1983), current concerns (Klinger, 1977), personal strivings (Emmons, 1986), or life tasks (Cantor & Kihlstrom, 1987), the interest has been in the personal goals that people set out to accomplish. The ends vary, from monumental programs, to incidental tangents; from long-term projects, to quick marks; from end-states, to tasks in which the person continuously engages. Each research program has established a slightly different version of these goals, but they all are more specified than broad motives, and less concrete than behavioral intentions. For instance, Emmons (1989) described his units as halfway between motives and specific intentions.

In this paper, we concentrate on one such goal unit, the life task, as a representation of the individual's version of culturally-prescribed, age-graded tasks (e.g., Havighurst, 1953). Life tasks (Cantor & Kihlstrom, 1985) are the tasks that people see themselves as working on and devoting energy to in a particular life period. They take place in a daily life context, sometimes encompass many projects or activities, and typically unfold over substantial periods of time. They include a variety of tasks from "finding intimacy" to "being better organized about my chores." Life tasks vary with age and socio-cultural context, and we study them in those contexts. Life tasks are intended as sensitive to both personal needs and to contextual demands and opportunities, and to be adaptive to changes in these forces (Cantor, 1990).

The life task unit has heuristic value in the study of the goal definition process precisely because it encompasses relatively abstract cultural prescriptions and internal motives for task pursuit and yet it takes place in the specific and rather concrete contexts of everyday life. The individuals' sensitivity to cultural prescriptions can be seen in the consensuality of life tasks in particular social groups. The creativity of the task definition, however, can also be seen in the ways that individuals experiment with *what* normative tasks they pursue (Stewart, 1989). As people work on their tasks of "improving my marriage" or "getting tenure," they define those tasks in highly personal ways in their choices of *when* and how to pursue those ends. We see the interactive influence of personal investment and of social structure as individuals find their own schedule and means of task pursuit.

Moreover, it is easy to see in the analysis of strategies for life task pursuit that *whether* a person maintains that task depends upon his or her definition of *what* the task is and of *how* to pursue it (Norem, 1989). If "getting tenure" is defined as an all-encompassing, do or die project that is played out in every arena of life, then it is highly likely that the on-line motivation to persist will degenerate and the actor will succumb to helplessness (Kuhl, 1985). Therefore, the interdependence of the three aspects of life task definition—the process of choosing what tasks to work on, when and how to do it, and strategies for maintaining the task—are revealed in the analysis of individuals' efforts at life task pursuit.

Method Implications of a Task Approach

As a unit of analysis of self-regulation the life task is useful because it includes the current context of behavior, cultural as well as daily life context, and the actions that constitute the task (versus the outcome). It is a unit that simultaneously focuses upon *what* a person is working on and *how* they go about doing it.

Accordingly, the methods of analysis of life task pursuit address not only how a person feels about a task, but also what working on the task includes for the person (i.e., where, when, and how the person typically pursues the task). That is, we focus on the individual's definition of the task via the situations, activities, plans, and actions seen as relevant to the task in his or her current daily life context. Life tasks, such as those of building intimacy in a relationship or achieving career security, depend importantly for their meaning on the life context of the individual (e.g., intimacy for a college student differs totally from intimacy for a married couple). Of course, it could always be said that the motive or striving for intimacy (or achievement) is similar even across these different life contexts; but when the focus is on the task not the endstate goal, then those contextually-shaped meanings constitute critical differences (Veroff, 1983). The life task analysis is about *what* a person thinks he or she is pursuing when striving for intimacy, *when* he or she "works" on intimacy in daily life, and *how* the task is pursued. Thus, the *definition* of the task by the individual occurs in context and constitutes the self-regulatory process, and this is also a process that changes as the task is pursued from day to day, week to week, and year to year.

Our analysis usually begins with a free-listing of the person's current life tasks and the kinds of situations and activities that each task encompasses. In these lists it is easy to see both the consensual age-graded basis of life task definition (e.g., most college students list tasks related to being on their own away from family), and the individualized nature of task definition (e.g., the independence task can encompass agentic concerns of establishing a career direction and/or communal concerns of finding social support). Zirkel & Cantor (1990), for example, found that students who interpreted the independence task in broad, sweeping terms were more likely both to pursue it in daily life and to suffer through it, whereas those students who kept the meaning of independence confined to daily life chores also kept down the stress associated with this life transition—at least for the time being.

Much of the meaning of a task is uncovered through individuals' plans for how and when to pursue it (Cantor, Norem, Niedenthal, Langston, & Brower, 1987). In fact, for some individuals that planning process is a critical part of their constructive efforts to harness anxiety about the task (Norem, 1989). Defensive pessimists, for example, spend considerable time and energy preparing for tasks, thinking through the ins and outs of the task before, rather than during the relevant events (Norem & Cantor, 1986). We have found it quite useful to ask subjects to provide plans for handling task-relevant situations, and to code the complexity of those plans as an indication of how reflective the person is about the life task (Cantor et al., 1987; Spivak, Platt, & Shure, 1976). Although there are certainly tasks that require spontaneity, in many instances the more a person has mentally "walked through" task-relevant situations, the better able he or she is to cope with them.

As part of consideration of *what* the task is and of *how* to perform it, individuals define their life tasks via the choice of times and places in which to pursue the task (i.e., consideration of *when* and *how much* to work on a task). As we noted earlier, there are environmental pressures and/or norms for pursuing tasks in specific places and at certain times (e.g., it is more appropriate to pursue an intimate relationship than a career promotion at a party, even one hosted by one's boss) (Argyle, 1981; Jones & Pittman, 1982). Nonetheless, individuals differ considerably in the frequency and pattern of task efforts that they allocate in different daily life contexts. Experience-sampling methods (Hormuth, 1986) can be very instructive for investigating this patterning of life task efforts. For example, Cantor, Norem, Langston, Zirkel, Fleeson, & Cook-Flannagan (in press) studied the life task efforts of women living together in a sorority house on campus. We used a mixture of experience-sampling and diary methods, with the women reporting on five randomly sampled events per day for fifteen consecutive days. Each night they also completed a nightly diary in which they rated the relevance of each of the day's five events to each of seven central life tasks (e.g., how relevant was that lunch at the Union to "making friends," to "getting good grades," to "being on your own"). Together, these data provided a portrait for each person of the frequency and pattern of their life task efforts over this two-week period. We found, for example, that for each person the average daily life relevance of a task was associated with how important they believed the task to be in general (with task importance based on task appraisals gathered at an earlier point in time). The women were also more emotionally involved in daily life events that they viewed as highly relevant to at least one of their life tasks than in less task-relevant events.

These kinds of life task measures follow naturally from the focus on the task in context (i.e., as it unfolds in a daily life context in the shadows of broader sociocultural and age-graded norms). They complement questions about personal efficacy and task commitment and mastery that follow from a focus on the end-state or goal of a task process (e.g., Bandura, 1989; Markus & Ruvolo, 1989). For example, Langston & Cantor (1989) found that the negative effects of social anxiety about interpersonal tasks were substantially exacerbated by a "social constraint" strategy for pursuing social tasks (e.g., a strategy that encouraged the anxious person to follow the lead of others and to hold back in interactions). Over time, what individuals think about their tasks and their selves can be greatly altered by how and when they typically pursue those tasks. Therefore, methods of study should include, if at all possible, assessments of the What and the How and the When of life tasks, as well as those aimed at uncovering how subjects feel about mastering the task and achieving their goals. In the next sections of this paper, therefore, we turn to illustrative data on the *what* and the *how* of life task pursuits.

LIFE TASK DEFINITION: WHAT TO WORK ON

One of the most obvious but important questions about the ways in which individuals define their tasks is that of "what" they commit to as current life tasks. Whereas this is certainly a very personal part of the definition-regulation process, and individuals make their choices of goals for a variety of personal reasons, there is also considerable social input to the task commitment process. For example, most socio-cultural contexts present their participants with age-graded tasks throughout the lifespan (Havighurst, 1953). These "normative tasks" presumably help an individual to navigate his or her culture in appropriate, though not always personally gratifying ways. Thus the tasks of establishing an intimate relationship and of forging a satisfying career were presented, both explicitly in families and implicitly in the media, as gender-differentiated options for the young adult female and male American of the 1950s. These may not have been optimal choices for all women or all men, but they served as guidelines for navigating that culture at that point in history (Block, 1973).

According to this view, as is often pointed out in the lifespan development and anthropological literatures, a central meta-task of human adjustment is represented in the task commitment process: individuals need to choose their tasks so as to address these socio-cultural agendas in their own ways. Of course, there are several forms that this aspect of person-culture interaction might take in the task commitment process.

Individuals might enter particular periods of life relatively open to social agendas, poised to hear and to listen to the guidance of "experts." As "novices" in a new setting, it would be only reasonable to work on what everyone else is working on—that is, to figure out what you are "supposed" to do and to do it. Stewart's (1982) model of emotional stances suggests that individuals enter new situations in a *receptive* stance, and that over time they become more attentive to personal desires and somewhat less socially-attuned. Therefore, one plausible pattern of life task commitment might be that early on in an environment—for example, at the beginning of college; after a divorce—individuals would gravitate toward shared and appropriate life tasks (e.g., "getting good grades," "pursuing casual relationships"). Moreover, there might be some adaptive value in experimenting with a variety of these normative tasks, prolonging more intensive or focused task commitment until one is more thoroughly experienced in the environment.

Experts in a life setting and life period might be distinguishable from novices not so much in their independence from normative task concerns, but rather in the intensive or narrowed focus of their concerns. In the language presented earlier, we would say that the experts' definitions of what tasks to work on reflect not just the independent contributions of their knowledge of the tasks and the normative prescriptions, but also an interaction between their personal preferences and those social prescriptions (i.e., they pick and choose more carefully than do the novices). An alternative, and also plausible, account of shifting task commitments with experience would be one in which the experts relinquish the normative tasks of this period, either in favor of other age-graded tasks (e.g., ones more typical of the next life period) or because they have fine-tuned their tasks so uniquely that they are no longer representative of the normative task categories (e.g., highly idiosyncratic tasks). These models present somewhat different solutions to the "what" of life task definition and are thus worthy of investigation.

Examining the Task Commitment Process

In considering the task commitment process, we begin with several assumptions that are reflected in our methods: First, we do assume that individuals can talk about some of the tasks that they work on, although it is always useful to verify their reports with data about their daily life events (e.g., gathered in nightly diaries or in daily experience-sampling). We also assume that environments, such as colleges or sororities or families, present sets of "normative tasks" for their participants, and that individuals share a common language about these social agendas (e.g., sorority sisters talk about building social support). We ask individuals first to simply list their current life tasks, in any order as they come to mind, and then to categorize their own tasks, whenever reasonable, as representative of one or more normative tasks (i.e., tasks typically generated by their age and social life peers). It is important in this process that the participants first engage in their own listing of tasks, and that even when they do see the list of normative tasks, they feel free to categorize only those tasks that they see as easily representative of one or more normative tasks. These self-coded lists provide an initial, but actually quite useful view of what the individual is working on vis a vis the normative tasks of their life period and life setting.

Table 2 provides illustrative life task protocols gathered from participants in a five year longitudinal study of the transition through college (see Cantor et al., 1987 for method details). In this study, after listing their personal life tasks, the subjects were asked to code any of their tasks that fit one (or more) of six normative task categories that had been frequently generated by pretest subjects from several college populations (doing well academically, establishing future goals, managing time, making friends, being on one's own, and establishing an identity). This life task listing and self-coding procedure was repeated several times during their college years, and then again by telephone in the year after graduation. For our analysis of the life task commitment process, we have concentrated on the task listing protocols of ninety-three participants with data in the first and last years of college.

Openness to Normative Tasks

Perhaps the clearest way to characterize the first year students' openness to normative demands is in terms of two dimensions—prototypicality of task

Table 2. From Openness to Commitment in Life Tasks

Illustrative Life Task Protocols

ss # 481 —

First Year: Motivating myself to do homework ("grades")
Regulating social and academic activities ("time")
Making new friends and relationships ("friends")
Living away from home ("independence")
Doing laundry
Eating cafeteria food
Balancing a check book
Paying bills
Getting to classes
Picking a major ("future")

Senior Year: Finding a fulfilling summer job ("future")
Doing well in classes ("grades")
Leading the student group I'm the president of ("time")
Planning a high school UN conference for next year ("future")
Getting money for the conference ("future")
Keeping in touch with people I have been friends with here ("friends")
Breaking away from the people I can no longer keep in touch with ("friends")
Choosing between the people of 6 and 7 ("friends")
Getting into grad school ("grades")
Deciding what to do after school ("future")

ss # 84 —

First Year: Studying more ("time")
Thinking about family and friends at home less as one adjusts to new friends ("independence")
Succeeding at the goals I set for myself ("grades" and "future")
Meeting new people ("friends")
Enjoying new experiences ("identity")
Having fun without feeling guilty that I'm not studying ("time")

Senior Year: Choosing grad school or work after graduation ("future")
Choosing whether to work or travel this summer ("future")
Working on relationship with my boyfriend—i.e., improve ("future" and "friends" and "identity")
Working on relationships with friends—i.e., improve ("friends")
Getting along with one of my roommates ("friends")
Doing well in school this term ("grades")
Improving my self-esteem ("identity")
Getting to know myself better ("identity")
Letting others get to know me better ("friends")
Improving relationships with family ("independence" and "identity")

content and spread of personal tasks across several normative task categories.
As illustrated in the students' lists in Table 2, in their first year students often
described their tasks in very "classic" terms (e.g., "enjoying new experiences")

NUMBER OF CATEGORIES IN FIRST FIVE LISTED TASKS

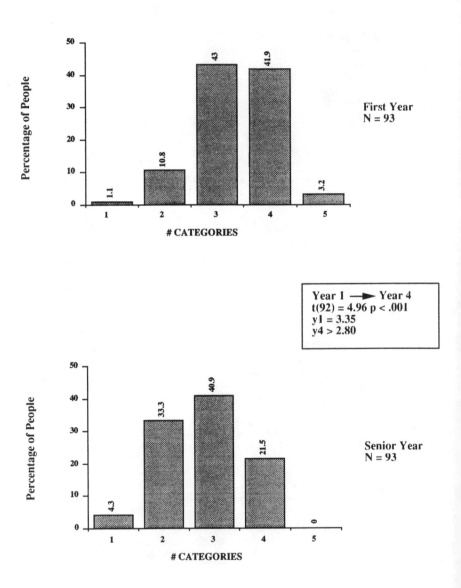

Figure 3.   From Experimentation to Commitment

and with an eye to particulars of the new environment that they felt a need to master (e.g., "balancing my check book"). The students made their own choices of tasks that did or did not fit these normative tasks, and frequently, as in the case of ss #481, they chose not to assign a normative label. In fact, their decisions to use or not to use the normative task labels in coding their personal tasks provide information about their unique definitions of these tasks (e.g., one student will see "working on a relationship" as part of being independent, whereas for another student it is just part of "making friends" and for yet another student it does not fit in any of these normative categories). As a group they categorized 75% of their tasks as representative of at least one of the six normative tasks; and they typically spread their task focus across these normative categories (e.g., one or two tasks in each category). As the top panel of Figure 3 shows, most students had at least three categories represented in their first five life tasks.[1]

Commitment to Normative Tasks

With the passage of time and the accrual of experience, students in this sample did not abandon these normative task categories (e.g., they still categorized approximately 75% of their tasks in these categories). Instead, they showed both a deepening of commitment to these tasks and a more articulated self-definition of their task focus. Their commitment took the form of a narrowed life task focus, with most students zeroing in on the "future goals" task and on one or two other task categories (e.g., "grades" and "independence" or "time management"). As the bottom panel of Figure 3 shows, their task listings in their senior year were significantly less spread across the normative categories, although each category still commanded a focus from many individuals. Moreover, as Table 2 again illustrates, by senior year these students often found a personal "voice" in which to define their tasks, even as they stayed comfortably within the (self-defined) limits of the normative categories (e.g., "Breaking away from the people I can no longer keep in touch with"). This personal voice is often apparent in their particular choice of normative tasks to assign to particular personal exemplars (e.g., "Leading the student group that I'm the president of" is an issue of time management for ss #481). Their task listings now had frequent, varied, and articulated exemplars of these categories, with fewer references than in earlier years to the prototypical exemplar of a task category (e.g., year 1: "meeting new people," year 4: "letting others get to know me better").

Alternative Patterns of Commitment

From our perspective, the key feature of these protocols of life tasks over time, is that they illustrate the multiple ways in which individuals "play" (or "work") with normative task systems as they navigate a path through a life period and setting. Even with these relatively simple task-listing and task-coding procedures, substantial evidence of alternative construals and alternative patterns of commitment emerged. For example, we submitted the task coding data (number of tasks in each category) from these students' first and last year protocols to a cluster analysis in order to see if different patterns of task focus across the six normative categories over time existed. In this sample, the cluster analysis revealed three coherent patterns, represented in Table 3. The largest ("normative") group followed the pattern, described above, of spread to focus, over the four year period. In their first year they were experimenting with all of the age-appropriate tasks, whereas by senior year they were committing to two task categories, typically the "future goals" and either the "grades" or "friends" task. An alternative pattern that emerged, labeled here as "accelerated," included students who demonstrated a task focus on a few of the normative task categories from the beginning. Typically, they focused on "identity" at the start and then shifted focus to the "future" and one other category in senior year. As the example in Table 3 suggests, these students often focused explicitly from the beginning on self-discovery in their tasks, though they did so in a rather open and general way that is reminiscent of the more normative first year pattern of experimentation. Frequently, they changed their focus by senior year, although the emphasis on self-discovery sometimes returned in their protocols from the first year after college. In other words, their particular transition through college is represented in a "focused openness"—they are almost explicit in their commitment to the "identity quest" and yet open to new experiences in the form of normative tasks. In contrast, the third group, labeled here as "lagging," ends college where the others began— working hard on a variety of normative tasks, with, understandably, a strong emphasis on time management and markedly less directedness toward the future than is apparent in the other groups.

This qualitative look at the process of life task commitment in a normative context is intended to suggest that individuals are constantly in the midst of a life task definition project—that is, what they work on is always evolving against the broad context of sociocultural agendas and the more specific and personal context of life experience. The normative tasks leave room for alternative construal in several ways. As described above, students in this sample traversed the path of task commitment in different patterns. Within each pattern there was considerable range in how happy and/or stressed the students felt about their tasks. Students within each group were able to find daily life activities to suit their particular task focus and definitions; in fact, part of the latitude that normative tasks represent is evident in the alternative outlets for task-consistent activities that individuals who ostensibly share the same environments create and take advantage of in their daily lives. In prior work, for example, Zirkel & Cantor (1990) have shown this alternative

Table 3. Patterns of Life Task Focus Over Time
(By Cluster Groups)

Normative—From Spread to Focus Across Years
($N = 63$)

ss # 143

First Year: Learning to look at things open-mindedly
Concentrating on getting all I can out of my years here ("grades")
Exploring many fields of interest
Exploring job opportunities ("future")
Seeking out opportunities which are not obvious
Developing your own interests outside of academics (e.g., politics, volunteer work, etc.) ("identity")
Finding friends among students at the university ("friends")
Figuring out the order of my priorities ("time")

Senior Year: Graduating ("grades")
Finding a full-time job ("future" and "independence")
Performing my two current jobs ("identity")
Keeping in contact with friends now and in the future ("friends" and "future")
Working on my relationship with boyfriend ("friends")
Applying to graduate schools ("future")
Finding a summer sublet
Thinking about having a family ("future")
Meeting new people ("friends")
Getting more organized ("identity")

Accelerated—Focused From the Start
($N = 22$)

ss # 178

First Year: Learning a lot in my classes ("grades")
Getting good grades ("grades")
Making friends ("friends")
Getting a direction for my future ("identity")
Keeping in touch with family and old friends
Doing fun things
Getting involved in activities ("identity")
Coping with my emotions ("identity")
Finding the purpose in life ("identity")
Spending time with people I like ("friends")

Senior Year: {this subject had graduated in Fall term}
Finding a job till the fall ("independence")
Investigating graduate schools ("future")
Enjoying my leisure time ("time")
Keeping in touch with far away friends ("friends")
Keeping myself in shape
Getting along with my friends ("friends")
Making new friends ("friends")
Figuring out what I want to do with my life ("future")
Improving family relationships
Getting used to my new car

continued

Table 3.   Continued

Lagging—Increased Spread and Less Future-Oriented
($N = 8$)

ss # 204

First Year: Living with roommates
Organizing time efficiently ("time")
Developing a nice balance between work and relaxation ("time")
Finding new friends ("friends")
Getting involved with friends and activities
Keeping in touch with old friends

Senior Year: Figuring out what I want to do in life ("identity" and "future")
Not giving in to the status quo ("identity")
Staying honest to myself
Caring for my parents
Making sure that I maintain my friendships ("friends")
Completing this school year ("grades")
Confirming my summer job ("future")
Continue to exercise and remain physically healthy ("time")
Remain emotionally healthy under stress ("time")
Continue to enjoy and value daily life events

---

construal of normative tasks in the daily life activities of students pursuing the "independence" life task. In that work, the creativity of task construal was demonstrated in *what* individuals viewed independence as being comprised of in terms of their daily life activities and events. Another, related aspect of the task definition process is the slightly more specific question of *how*—that is, when and how often in daily life—individuals pursue common life tasks. Here, too, the latitude for individualized definitions within the broader normative context is possible, and we turn now to consideration of that facet of life task definition.

LIFE TASK DEFINITION:
HOW TO WORK IN A DAILY LIFE CONTEXT

Another important way in which individuals make their mark on consensual life tasks is revealed by *how* they work on the task in daily life. Again, this aspect of the definitional process occurs within a highly structured normative context—a context that provides information about *when* and *where* and in *what ways* to perform the task. When college students, for example, work on "making friends" or "finding intimacy," they are well aware of the norms for which situations or daily life events are appropriate for such strivings to take place (e.g., "making friends" in the library is all right, but having an intimate moment in the library can be tricky). Moreover, there are shared beliefs about the appropriate scripts or strategies to use in enacting such tasks (e.g., hugging a stranger won't work but a brief touch for a new friend can be very effective). Whereas the contextual influences of cultural norms on the definition of *what* tasks to work on are relatively abstract, these situational and behavioral "rules of the game" are much more concrete and openly discussed (Abelson, 1981; Argyle, 1981; Price & Bouffard, 1974). There are many such concrete prescriptions to aid a person in defining *how* to work on a life task (Athay & Darley, 1981; Forgas, 1982; Goffman, 1974).

Although there has been considerable work, both within the self-regulation literature and in the personality literature more broadly, on the ways in which individuals choose situations and define behavioral plans, less attention has been given to the ways in which people manage their behavior in a *temporal* context (cf. Larsen, 1989). The temporal aspects of self-regulation become particularly important when we consider life tasks. Few such tasks are completed instantaneously; most require some time and effort towards their accomplishment. However, time is not abundantly available. Other tasks demand time, and people get tired of concentrating on one task for too long of a time. Moreover, the immediate context for task-directed activity is often highly structured with regard to time (e.g., how much free time does one have for pursuing intimacy in the face of daily life chores, career pressures, and the care of children?). As such, the temporal regulation of task pursuits becomes a central part of the definition process, and individuals do their own juggling to manage their tasks over time.

The temporal regulation of life tasks provides a particularly clear illustration of the interactionist nature of such goals: life tasks are typically nonspecific and continuous projects, such as forming new friends or being independent from family, yet they unfold in a very specific and concrete immediate daily life context (e.g., Cantor et al., in press). People give their own personal meaning to consensual life tasks in part by their choice of how to work on the task, and a major element of that choice involves temporal self-regulation—that is, the *when* of life task pursuit.

Defining a task in terms of its temporal features involves a decision—however implicit and automatic it may be—about the frequency and spacing of life task efforts. Such decisions are regulated in large part by the opportunity structure of the immediate daily life context (e.g., college students go to class regularly and thus have the opportunity to work on "grades" quite frequently). However, even highly structured daily life situations or events typically provide opportunities for a rather wide variety of life task pursuits, and individuals can bring to bear their most central tasks even in the most unusual of places (e.g., college students work quite frequently on social tasks even in the library or in class). Therefore, we suspect that individuals overcome situational constraints and give their personal mark to consensual life tasks by regulating the frequency and spacing of their task pursuits, even in highly structured life contexts.

There are several ways that individuals with particularly strong task investments might regulate the frequency and spacing of their task pursuits so as to reflect their special commitment to the task. First, we assume that there is a normative structure to life task pursuit, such that most tasks are systematically embedded within daily life routines. One example of this normative structure is the association of work with weekdays and recreation with weekends. Certainly this is a widely held norm, though many of us with particular task commitments violate the typical day of the week pattern (e.g., working on weekends or playing golf during the weekdays). Day of the week is thus an interesting parameter of task pursuit. Second, individuals might vary their task pursuits across days of the week in several systematic ways. In a purely *additive* way, personal investment in a task might be reflected by more effort at the task across all days of the week, with the absolute amount of task effort adjusted to fit the day of the week norms for that task and environment. For example, even workaholics pursue their careers slightly less often on weekends than during the weekdays, although they always do more than the average person does on any given day. A more *interactive* pattern of day of the week task regulation might reflect a person's attention to the normative cues in a complex way: for example, the highly invested person might work on the task especially vigorously on those days when it is most appropriate to do so, and do other tasks on the less appropriate days. An individual invested in finding "the right life partner," might frequent parties and other social events *very regularly* on weekends, even though he pursued his career interests during the week.

Regardless of the particular pattern by which personal investment and day of the week norms are combined, all of these examples reveal an active process of task regulation that is linked to the unfolding of task pursuits in time. In each example, the individual defines his or her life task by regulating how to work on the task—how often and on which days—in a daily life context. Of course, the particular pattern of day of the week task pursuit will be influenced by aspects of the task itself, in addition to the existence of day of the week norms and of personal investment. For example, some tasks, like finding an intimate partner, nearly require that an invested person work hard on it when others also do so, whereas other tasks, such as "getting tenure" can demand that extra effort precisely when others don't typically give it. The content of the life task, or at least the way it is construed by the particular person, may also influence the clarity of the contextual norms for task pursuit. When people construe their tasks in very abstract and "existentially meaningful" ways, such as "finding myself in midlife," then even the existence of day of the week norms may be less obvious—in fact, part of the stress associated with such tasks is that people have difficulty translating these abstract strivings into specific projects in a daily life context (Little, 1989; Zirkel & Cantor, 1990).

In order to discover the principles of how a person regulates the time spent on each of his or her tasks, it is helpful to take the perspective that self-regulation is a definitional problem. Then the day of the week, or other relevant contexts, can be seen as sources of information. As a result, the research agenda becomes discovering how people incorporate this information into their definitions and how they modify it for their own particular purposes. With daily diary and experience-sampling data, we were able to consider the problem of time-management from this task perspective.

Experience-Sampling of Life Tasks in a Daily Life Context

Consideration of the temporal regulation of life task pursuits requires a careful look at people's daily life activities. Such processes are bound to be complex and thus we also assume that it is useful to start with a life environment that is fairly regularly and openly structured itself. For this purpose we chose to study the life task pursuits of a group of college women living together in an on-campus sorority house. The presence of both shared life tasks, such as "getting good grades" and "finding intimacy," and of shared daily life activities (e.g., sorority meetings; study hours)' provided a normative context for this in-vivo analysis that was similar to the laboratory contexts in which more fine-grained self-regulatory processes typically are mapped.

In order to see this kind of creative management of life task efforts in daily life, we turned to an experience-sampling methodology in which individuals report on a regular basis on their activities (e.g., Hormuth, 1986). The experience-sampling or "beeper" methodology is ideal for charting the ups and downs of task-relevant activity in a rather unobtrusive manner. In most cases, subjects respond to alarm watches that are programmed to beep at random intervals across the day, and for a week or more at a time. In this study, 54 sorority women took part in the experience-sampling phase of the study. They responded with activity reports (and other profiles) to alarm watches preprogrammed to go off five times a day for fifteen consecutive days (see Cantor et al. [in press] for details of the method and response rate).

The experience-sampling method provides an excellent avenue for an on-the-spot view of life task pursuits in daily life contexts. It allows us to see when and how they work on their tasks without much disruption of those efforts. However, since people bring to bear many life tasks in single events or situations, it is also vital to extend this method beyond the single event report. For example, when a sorority sister in our study reports that she is working in the library, although it is most likely that she is pursuing her "grades" task, she may also be working with an eye towards "making friends." Therefore, in the service of capturing this aspect of life task relevance in daily life events, we asked these women to report each night on the relevance of each of seven consensual life tasks to each of the day's beeper events (e.g., they rated the relevance of "grades" "friends" and "intimacy" to the five specific events that had been beeped that day). (Thus, for any given subject, an event from the day could be seen as relevant to anywhere from zero to seven of these consensual life tasks.) In this way, by combining experience-sampling and nightly diary ratings of task relevance, we were able to get a two-week sample of the average relevance of each life task for each person on each day. The relevance ratings provide a measure of the frequency with which each subject brought each life task to bear in her daily life activities.

Our objective here is to highlight the rather subtle ways in which these women's own personal investment in a life task interacted with the normative structure of their daily lives to produce systematic patterns of task relevance across the days of the week. Therefore, we restrict attention here to three particularly central life tasks for this group—"getting good grades" "making friends" and "finding intimacy." There were clear day of the week norms for these tasks and the women also differed considerably in personal investment in each of these tasks. The "grades" and "friends" tasks were the most frequently relevant tasks across days in this study, and the "intimacy" task, though relatively infrequently a part of daily life for these women, pulled a great deal of emotional weight in their lives (Cantor et al., in press).

Once again, our model predicts that the day of the week will have effects in two ways. First, there should be an overall effect of the day of the week on which tasks are worked on. Namely, the day of the week provides a consistent piece of information about which tasks to be pursuing on that given day. Second, there should be individual differences in how people respond to that overall effect. This would show up in consistent differences between people across days.

Day of the Week Norms

The average daily life relevance for these three tasks across a two-week experience-sampling period are illustrated in Figure 4 (relevance could range from 0 to 2). Clearly, the day of the week was important to what task people were working on. (ANOVAs revealed a significant effect of day for each task.) Furthermore, the pattern is rather what one would expect for these tasks. The grades task, for example, was worked on most heavily on Tuesday and Wednesday. It dropped a bit on Thursday, more so on Friday, was almost nonexistent on Saturday, and then began a climb back up to Tuesday. The data revealed that day of the week was an important element in the structure of activity directed toward a task. Each day had a "standard" level for task activity, and the level differed with day.

The shape of the patterns gives us three pieces of information. One is that an important part of regulating one's work on tasks, and thus one's representation of how to do so, is being sensitive to the individual day. A second piece of information is that the pattern is cyclic. Each week shows one high point and one low point. In this way, the pattern of grade relevance also has

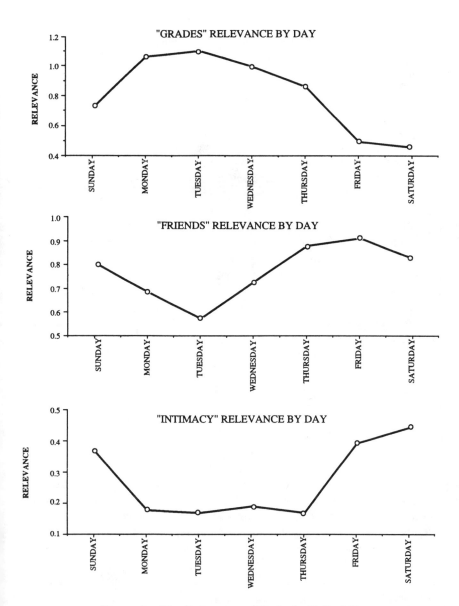

Figure 4.   The Relevance of Tasks in Daily Life

the repetitive feature of cycles. The third piece of information is a more fine-grained feature. The transitions along days of the week are smooth. It is not as though each day of the week independently sets its own "standard" level, but rather each day has a level that is not too different from the level of the days before and after it. Each day acts as a midpoint between the two surrounding days. So the self-regulation of task-pursuit seems to work across days, in which people gear up over a couple of days for the focused one or two days at the height of the cycle. After these one or two days, the relevance slowly slips off until it reaches the low point.

Personal Investment

According to our model, life tasks integrate contextual forces such as day of the week with personal factors. So, although the information provided by the day of the week is powerful in determining how relevant a task is on that day of the week, different people may pay attention to that information differently. One broad and central personality feature that may influence this aspect of task regulation is simply the investment into the task. Some tasks are more central than are others, and consume more energies and efforts. This section of the paper serves to explore the importance of an individual's investment in a task to predicting her behavior concerning that task. In other words, this section describes the personalization of the contextual definition of how to work on the task.

People make choices, as part of *defining how* to pursue a task, of how much time and energy to invest in a task. These choices are often made on the spot, in the midst of daily activity, and are in the form of behavior actually directed towards the task. The choices about *how much* time and energy to expend on the task make up the subject's *investment* in the task. In keeping with this definition, we operationalized investment as the average relevance of a task to a subject's daily events. Not only does this capture the notion of investment as behavioral choices about how much effort and time to spend, but earlier reports (Cantor et al., in press) indicated that the order in which each subject ranked the importance (in the abstract) of her tasks was correlated with how invested she was in the tasks in a daily event context.

The investment measure was computed from the daily diary ratings of task relevance. During the course of the day, the alarms of watches worn by the subjects went off five different randomly determined times, which will be referred to as "events." Each subject had different times from other subjects, but the same times on each day. After one week, subjects were given a new set of five randomly determined times. Each time the alarm sounded, the subject described what she was doing and how she felt. At the end of the day, subjects retrospectively rated the relevance of each of the events to each of the seven consensual life tasks. Subjects could rate a given event as a 0: "Not at all relevant" to the task; as a 1: "Somewhat relevant" to the task; or as a 2: "Highly relevant" to the task. Perusal of these data showed that, on occasion, subjects found an event to be relevant to none of the tasks, and that some events were relevant to as many as all seven tasks for some subjects. In the stream of daily life, however, subjects generally found two or three tasks highly relevant to a given event. In order to obtain the relevance of a task for a subject on a given day of the week, the relevance of each of the events of that day were averaged (because the study lasted two weeks, there were two occasions of each day of the week). To compute a subject's investment in a task, the subject's day-of-the-week averages for that task were averaged.

In the current model, definitions of what is and how to pursue a life task are the results of integrations of both contextual and personal factors. This model suggests two hypotheses about the relation of investment in a task with the relevance of that task on any given day. The first hypothesis is that level of investment predicts level of relevance on any given day (i.e., there exists a main effect of investment on daily relevance).[2] This hypothesis follows from the model's contention that the person has an effect on the plan of how to pursue a task. The second hypothesis is that investment matters to daily relevance to different degrees on different days (i.e., there exists an interaction between investment and day on daily relevance). The model does not demand this hypothesis, but rather allows for it. The contributions of day of the week and personal investment are not necessarily independent. The subject makes choices in the context of the day of the week. Some days, her choices may make a great deal of difference in how much she finds the task relevant; other days, she may make fewer choices, or the choices may be less important. For example, personal investment in "getting good grades" might strongly predict how much one studies on weekends, and so have a large effect on the relevance of "getting good grades" on the weekends, but only weakly predict how much one studies on Wednesday, and so have a smaller effect on the relevance of "getting good grades" on Wednesday.

Regression Analyses

For each task, seven regressions were performed. Each regression predicted the relevance of the task on a given day from the investment in that task (computed from the other six days). Three tasks were chosen for the analyses, as they represented important tasks in these subjects' lives. The resulting non-standardized betas represented the expected change in relevance on the predicted day for each change in investment. Using an ANOVA analogy, the beta represents the effect size of investment on relevance for that day. If the beta is significantly different from zero, then investment predicts relevance on that day. Testing the difference between two betas tests the interaction: if the betas on two days are significantly different from each other, than investment has a stronger effect on one day than on the other day. Unfortunately, there is presently no satisfactory method for testing the difference between two nonindependent betas (Howell, 1987), but if there is little or no overlap between the confidence intervals of two betas, they are most probably significantly different from each other.

Figures 5 through 7 show the regressions for each task. The horizontal axis represents the seven days of the week. The vertical axis represents the size of

PANEL A

Notes: Average relevance of the "getting good grades" task on each day. Relevance ranged from 0 to 2. *N* varied with each day, ranging from 46 to 51.

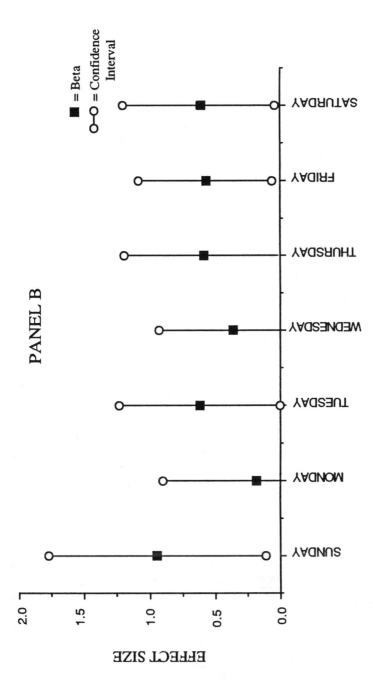

PANEL B

Figure 5. Getting Good Grades

Notes: The effect of personal investment in "getting good grades" on the relevance of "getting good grades" for each day. Betas indicate the expected change in relevance on that day for each unit change in investment. Confidence intervals are each at the 99.3% level. *N* varied with day, ranging from 46 to 51.

PANEL A

Notes: Average relevance of the "making friends" task on each day. Relevance ranged from 0 to 2. *N* varied with each day, ranging from 46 to 51.

358

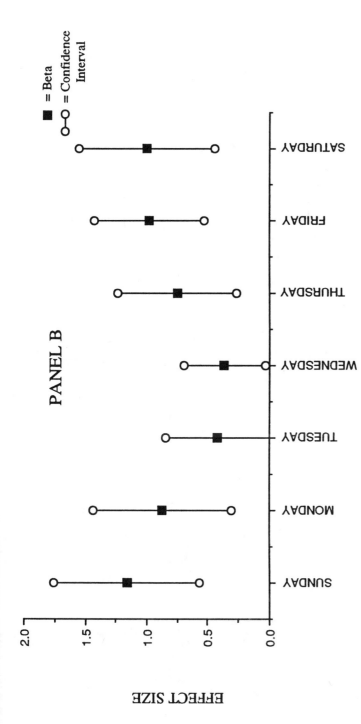

Notes: The effect of personal investment in "making friends" on the relevance of "making friends" for each day. Betas indicate the expected change in relevance on that day for each unit change in investment. Confidence intervals are each at the 99.3% level. *N* varied with day, ranging from 46 to 51.

Figure 6. Making Friends

PANEL A

Notes: Average relevance of the "finding intimacy" task on each day. Relevance ranged from 0 to 2. N varied with each day, ranging from 46 to 51.

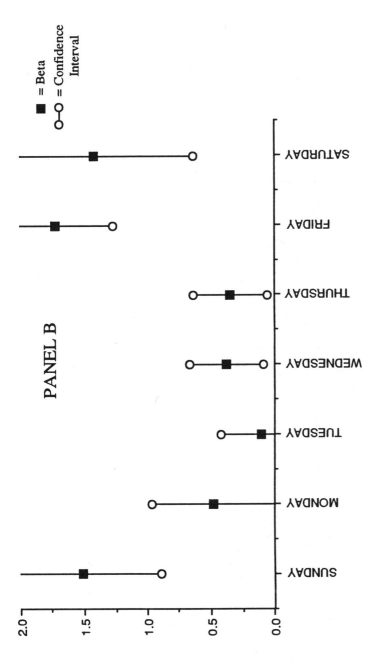

Notes: The effect of personal investment in "finding intimacy" on the relevance of "finding intimacy" for each day. Betas indicate the expected change in relevance on that day for each unit change in investment. Confidence intervals are each at the 99.3% level. N varied with day, ranging from 46 to 51.

Figure 7. Finding Intimacy

the beta (the expected change in relevance of a task on the predicted day of the week for each change in personal investment in that task). The betas are represented by black squares. Confidence intervals have also been placed around each of these betas, and are represented by lines ending in open circles. The confidence intervals have been adjusted for multiple tests, and so represent a 99.3% confidence that the population beta falls within the interval. Taken together, all the population betas for a given task will fall within their confidence intervals 95% of the time. If a confidence interval does not contain zero, then the beta is significantly different from zero.

Getting Good Grades

One important task for these subjects was doing well in school. It is the manifest reason for being in college, and was significantly more relevant in daily life than all other tasks save "making friends" (Cantor et al., in press). As Figure 5 indicates, four of the seven regressions for the "getting good grades" task produced significant betas. On Sunday, Tuesday, Friday, and Saturday, investment significantly predicted the relevance on those days. In other words, if a particular subject was more invested in "getting good grades" than her peers were, she was also likely to find "getting good grades" more relevant than her peers did on Sunday, Tuesday, Friday, and Saturday. In contrast, although a particular subject was more invested in "getting good grades" than her peers were, she was no more likely to find "getting good grades" more relevant than her peers did on Monday, Wednesday, or Thursday, in the middle of the week. The second hypothesis concerned the interaction between the day of the week and personal investment. From Figure 5, it is clear that none of the betas for the "getting good grades" task were significantly different from each other. This indicates that there was no interaction between day of the week and personal investment for the task of "getting good grades": the effect of personal investment on daily relevance was the same across all days. For the task of "getting good grades," the contributions of personal investment and day of the week to daily relevance were independent.

Making Friends

Another important task for these subjects was "making friends—getting along with others." This task was significantly more relevant to daily life than all other tasks (save "getting good grades"). This task represented much of the social activity of college for these subjects, although other tasks represented specific aspects of social activity (e.g., "intimacy," "sorority"). Figure 6 shows that for the task of "making friends," the relevance of the task on almost every day was predicted by the relevance of the task on the other six days. Only Tuesday failed to show a significant relationship, indicating that personal investment contributed to the daily relevance on nearly every day of the week. None of the betas were significantly different from each other, indicating that the contributions of investment and day of the week were independent. However, Sunday, Friday, and Saturday were close to significantly different from Tuesday and Wednesday. Furthermore, Sunday, Friday, and Saturday represented the days on which "making friends" was most relevant, and Tuesday and Wednesday represented the days on which "making friends" was least relevant. This suggests that for the task of "making friends," the contributions of investment and day of the week may be non-independent. Investment seemed to have a larger effect on some days than others, and those were specifically the days on which the context was most strongly suggesting that the task be relevant.

Finding Intimacy

Finding intimacy was an important task in an unusual way. Its average daily life relevance was not high; in fact, it showed one of the lowest levels of average relevance. However, it was significant in these subjects' lives in other ways. For example, these subjects' most extreme moments of happiness occurred in intimacy-relevant events (Cantor et al., in press). Panel A of Figure 7 highlights the lack of total relevance of the "intimacy" task, but also shows that it was most relevant when expected, on Friday, Saturday, and Sunday. These days provided the most cues to work on the task of "intimacy." Panel B of Figure 7 shows that for the task of "finding intimacy," only Monday and Tuesday failed to show a significant relationship between investment in "intimacy" and relevance on that day. So, again for the task of "intimacy," personal investment had an effect on daily relevance of the task. The most striking feature of the figure is the difference in predictability from the weekend to the middle of the week. Friday, Saturday, and Sunday showed a significantly stronger effect of investment on relevance than did the other days. Thus, the contributions of personal investment and day of the week were not independent: personal investment had a stronger effect on the days on which "finding intimacy" was relevant for everyone.

In sum, the results indicated that in each task both day of the week (context) and investment (person) contributed to daily relevance. For the task of "getting good grades," these contributions were independent; for the task of "making friends," these contributions were independent, but with a trend towards interaction; for the task of "finding intimacy," these contributions interacted with each other. The difference between the three tasks highlights the importance of the content of the tasks. Something about the content of these tasks resulted in them being described in different ways.

One possibility has to do with the interdependence of the task. Tasks which require others for activity on them are interdependent. The interdependence is only an issue to the extent that others are unavailable. If others are easily available, then the interdependence will not affect the activity on the task. But if the others are difficult to find, then activity on the task will vary with the event of the availability of others. No matter how much a person is invested in a romantic dinner, without another the dinner cannot take place. When others are available, then the personal investment into the task can make a difference in how much activity on the task occurs. So, for interdependent tasks, personal investment can only matter when others are available as well. The availability of others depends partly on whether they are willing to engage in the task. Since the willingness of others to engage in the task is a function of the day of the week, then the availability of others will increase when the contextual forces suggest that task as the appropriate activity. So, personal investment can make more difference on days on which the cues strongly suggest activity on that task, which leads to the availability of others. "Getting good grades" is mainly a non-interdependent task: one can work on it by oneself. Thus, an interaction between day of the week and investment would not be predicted. However, if in another culture, "getting good grades" was an interdependent task, say if people mainly studied with others, then one would expect an interaction for the task of "getting good grades" in that culture (Markus & Kitayama, in press). "Making friends, getting along with others" is a task that is interdependent. One must have friends with which to get along. However, it is only moderately so. Primarily, the task is so generally relevant, and people are relatively abundant, that there is often someone with which to engage in the task. Even with the general availability of others, there are still some restrictions on the days on which the task is somewhat lower in relevance. Because of this, the task should show a mild interaction, in which investment has an effect more so on those days on which everyone finds the task relevant. "Finding intimacy," however, is highly interdependent. There is a shortage of available partners, and once a suitable one is found, activity in the task can only occur with that one person. With this highly interdependent task, activity on it will depend on the other also seeing it as an appropriate day. Thus, we saw the pattern of high predictability on those days on which the task had the highest mean levels of relevance.

Person-Situation Interactions in Life Tasks

The above data provided a window on the process of forming a behavioral plan covering how to work on the three tasks. In so doing, they showed how the unit of life task leads to a new way of conceiving of self-regulation. The problem in self-regulation is getting oneself to actually follow through on one's intentions. The traditional way of investigating people's efforts at this problem has been to give them a relatively specified, small, and end-state oriented goal. The unit of life tasks represents goals that are relatively unspecified, large, and continuous. As a result, self-regulation looks different. The essence of the difference concerns the need to structure behavior as part of the self-regulation process. When the goals are unspecified, plans need to be made as to how to carry out the goal. The goals we studied, "grades," "friends," and "intimacy," are all somewhat unspecified as to how to complete them. Furthermore, these goals are large, encompassing many behaviors and large stretches of time. Because of this, the plans need to be organized to be effective. In all, this leads to studying the behavioral plans that people structure in their efforts to achieve these tasks.

The data showed that indeed a plan existed for each subject representing how they were going to work on these three tasks. This plan specifically concerned how much effort to exert towards each of the three tasks on each day. The plan was organized around a cyclic theme, with each week making up one cycle. The cycle had smooth transitions between consecutive days, demonstrating the continuity of the plan, and was repetitive, demonstrating that the work on the task continued even through temporary declines in the level of activity relevant to the task. As continuous tasks will be present through a large period of time, a period during which other tasks will engage the person as well, a cycle allows efficient organization of time spent on a given task, while also allowing other tasks to be pursued. These data also demonstrated the behavioral nature of the plan, as it consisted of choices about investment made "on line," as the behavior was happening.

The integrative nature of the plan was demonstrated in the data. Both contextual factors and personal factors had an influence on the resulting structure of the plan. The present contextual factor was the immediate context of day of the week, and the present person factor was investment in the task. The result that both contextual factors and personal factors had an effect on behavior indicated that the plan was an integration of both factors. However, the method allowed exploration into the type of integration present. Namely, the integration could have been additive, in which the contributions of day of the week (the context) and investment (the personal factor) were independent, on the other hand, the contributions may not have been independent, so that the effect of investment may have been larger on some days than on others. It was offered that a possible interpretation of why some tasks showed the interaction and others did not revolved around the interpersonal interdependence of the tasks, with those tasks involving joint participation showing the interaction.

LIFE TASKS AND SELF-REGULATORY PROCESSES

In concluding, we return to the question of *Akrasia*, and ask whether weakness of will is indeed the most difficult part of self-regulation. Certainly it is often tiring and frustrating to try to persist towards goals in the face of setbacks, changing circumstances, newly emerging interests, and so forth. As Kuhl (1985) noted, frequently we enlist social support just to keep on track with personal goals. Nonetheless, there is more to goal-directed behavior than persistence— more obstacles stand in the way of accomplishment than *Akrasia*. In particular, as Nuttin (1984) also suggested, there is the prior need for goal definition. Individuals constantly are faced with choices of *what* to work on and of *how* to do it, and this definitional work is quite a complex feat.

The definitional process involves an intricate interweaving of decisions about what to work on, how and when to pursue it, and whether to persist in these efforts. For example, relatively abstract choices about what normative tasks to pursue have implications for the concrete texture of daily life activities. The college student who is invested in "finding an intimate partner" will persist long and hard on the task, on weekends, even as she invests in achievement during the week. Her choices, both at the abstract level of a normative task commitment and at the concrete level of day of the week task regulation, will make it easier to persist and maintain this task pursuit—that is, to avoid the pitfalls of *Akrasia*. The intertwining of self-interest and normative structure provides avenues of social support for personal goal strivings.

Of course, individuals work on many life tasks at one time, and they undoubtedly achieve this balance between self-interest and normative demands more successfully in some than in other task domains. Brian Little (1989) has spoken of the "manageability" of personal projects, pointing out the tendency for people to invest too much meaning in a single project, thereby making it almost impossible to accomplish. One aspect of the tradeoff between meaning and manageability in life task definition has to do with the level of abstraction at which the task is conceived (Vallacher & Wegner, 1987). Some tasks simply get too abstract, too big to work on in our everyday lives. In those instances, it often seems as if there are no normative cues to *how* (when and where) to pursue the task (e.g., how exactly do I find myself?). In other cases, the choice of *what* task has been defined in a counter-normative way that isolates the individual from social support in his or her goal pursuit. For example, some people choose to work on a normative task at the wrong time in life and risk embarrassment (e.g., in the midlife crisis, adults are working on identity too late in life). Whether the problem resides in the definition of what task to pursue or of how to do it, the maintenance of task pursuit is difficult when personal and normative forces are at odds.

Fortunately, however, the life task perspective suggests that people create definitions differently in different domains of life and so the potential for success in at least some facets of goal-directed activity is increased. For example, Wright and Mischel (1987) have shown how rigid individuals can get in their behavioral pursuits when the demands of the task overwhelm their competencies. Yet those same children in their study that became rigidly aggressive when provoked too much by peers, could handle the demands of other social life tasks with more flexibility and ease (e.g., they can meet strangers and interact with adults). Therefore, in charting the successes and the failures at task definition and self-regulation, we need always be attuned to the complexities of individuals' task systems. The interaction of individuals in a normatively regulated environment works more smoothly sometimes than at others, and in some life tasks than in others. The reality of life task pursuit is, perhaps inevitably, a mixture of ups and downs.

ACKNOWLEDGMENTS

We are pleased to acknowledge the technical assistance of Nancy Exelby, and the comments on this work by Michele Acker, Carol Cook-Flannagan, Robert Harlow, Susan Jenkins, Christopher Langston, Eric Stone, and Sabrina Zirkel. This research was supported in part by Grant BNS #87-18467 (Cantor & Norem) from the National Science Foundation, as well as a National Science Foundation Graduate Fellowship (Fleeson).

NOTES

1. We analyzed the content of the first five tasks because nearly all students listed at least five tasks and we could then consider the pattern of task-listing across people and over time.

2. This hypothesis will be trivially true on at least some days as the investment measure now stands. This is because investment will certainly predict the relevance on a given day if investment is computed, in part, from the relevance on that given day. However, if the day of interest is taken out of the computation of investment, then the hypothesis is no longer trivially true. It is quite imaginable that relevance averaged across six days (i.e., investment) is not related to relevance on the seventh day: transient, contextual, or random forces could instead determine relevance on the seventh day. Thus our analyses do constitute tests of the hypothesis that investment predicts relevance on any given day.

REFERENCES

Abelson, R. (1981). Psychological status of the script concept. *American Psychologist, 36*, 715-729.

Argyle, M. (1981). The experimental study of the basic features of situations. In D. Magnusson (Ed.), *Toward a psychology of situations: An interactional perspective* (pp. 63-83). Hillsdale, NJ: Erlbaum.

Athay, M., & Darley, J. (1981). Toward an interpersonal action-centered theory of personality. In N. Cantor & J. F. Kihlstrom (Eds.), *Personality, cognition, and social interaction.* Hillsdale, NJ: Erlbaum.

Bandura, A. (1986). *Social foundations of thought and action: A social cognitive theory.* Englewood Cliffs, NJ: Prentice Hall.

_____. (1989). Self-regulation of motivation and action through internal standards and goal systems. In L. A. Pervin (Ed.), *Goal concepts in personality and social psychology* (pp. 19-86). Hillsdale, NJ: Erlbaum.

Block, J. H. (1973). Conceptions of sex role: Some cross-cultural and longitudinal perspectives. *American Psychologist, 28*(6), 512-526.

Buss, D. M., & Cantor, N. (Eds.). (1989). *Personality psychology: Recent trends and emerging directions.* New York: Springer-Verlag.

Cantor, N. (1990). From thought to behavior: "Having" and "doing" in the study of personality and cognition. *American Psychologist, 45*(6), 735-750.

Cantor, N., & Kihlstrom, J. F. (1985). Social intelligence: The cognitive basis of personality. In P. Shaver (Ed.), *Review of personality and social psychology* (Vol. 6, pp. 15-33). Beverly Hills, CA: Sage.

————. (1987). *Personality and social intelligence.* Englewood Cliffs, NJ: Prentice Hall.

Cantor, N., Norem, J., Langston, C., Zirkel, S., Fleeson, W., & Cook-Flannagan, C. (in press). Life tasks and daily life experience. *Journal of Personality*, Special issue on daily events and personality.

Cantor, N., Norem, J. K., Niedenthal, P. M., Langston, C. A., & Brower, A. M. (1987). Life tasks, self-concept ideals, and cognitive strategies in a life transition. *Journal of Personality and Social Psychology, 53*(6), 1178-1191.

Carver, C. S., & Scheier, M. F. (1981). *Attention and self-regulation: A control-theory approach to human behavior.* New York: Springer-Verlag.

Emmons, R. A. (1986). Personal strivings: An approach to personality and subjective well-being. *Journal of Personality and Social Psychology, 51*(5), 1058-1068.

————. (1989). The personal striving approach to personality. In L. A. Pervin (Ed.), *Goal concepts in personality and social psychology* (pp. 87-126). Hillsdale, NJ: Erlbaum.

Erikson, E. H. (1950). *Childhood and society.* New York: Norton.

Forgas, J. (1982). Episode cognition: Internal representations of interaction routines. *Advances in Experimental Social Psychology, 15*, 59-101.

Freud, S. (1930/1961). *Civilization and its discontent* (Vol. 21 of The Standard ed.). London: Hogarth.

Goffman, E. (1974). *Frame analysis.* New York: Harper & Row.

Havighurst, R. J. (1953). *Human development and education.* New York: Longmans, Green.

Higgins, E. T., & Parsons, J. C. (1983). Social cognitions and the social life of the child: Stages as subcultures. In E. T. Higgins, D. N. Ruble, & W. W. Hartup (Eds.), *Social cognition and social development: A socio-cultural perspective* (pp. 15-62). New York: Cambridge University Press.

Hormuth, S. (1986). The random sampling of experiences in situ. *Journal of Personality, 54*, 262-293.

Howell, J. (1987). *Statistical methods for Psychology.* Boston: Duxbury Press.

Jones, E. E., & Pittman, T. S. (1982). Toward a general theory of strategic self-presentation. In J. Suls (Ed.), *Psychological perspectives on the self* (Vol. 1, pp. 231-262). Hillsdale, NJ: Erlbaum.

Klinger, E. (1975). Consequences of commitment to and disengagement from incentives. *Psychology Review, 82*, 1-25.

————. (1977). *Meaning and void: Inner experience and the incentives in people's lives.* Minneapolis: University of Minnesota Press.

Kluwe, R. H., & Friedrichsen, G. (1985). Mechanisms of control and regulation in problem solving. In J. Kuhl & J. Beckmann (Eds.), *Action control: From cognition to behavior* (pp. 183-218). New York: Springer-Verlag.

Kuhl, J. (1985). From cognition to behavior: Perspectives for future research on action control. In J. Kuhl & J. Beckmann (Eds.), *Action control: From cognition to behavior* (pp. 267-275). New York: Springer-Verlag.

Langston, C. A., & Cantor, N. (1989). Social anxiety and social constraint: When "making friends" is hard. *Journal of Personality and Social Psychology, 56*(4), 649-661.

Larsen, R. J. (1989). A process approach to personality psychology: Utilizing time as a facet of data. In D. M. Buss & N. Cantor (Eds.), *Personality psychology: Recent trends and emerging directions* (pp. 177-193). New York: Springer-Verlag.

Little, B. (1983). Personal projects: A rationale and methods for investigation. *Environment and Behavior, 15*, 273-309.

_____. (1989). Personal projects analysis: Trivial pursuits, magnificent obsessions and the search for coherence. In D. M. Buss & N. Cantor (Eds.), *Personality psychology: Recent trends and emerging directions* (pp. 15-31). New York: Springer Verlag.

Markus, H., & Kitayama, S. (in press). Culture and the self: Implications for cognition, emotion, and motivation. *Psychological Review.*

Markus, H., & Ruvolo, A. (1989). Possible selves: Personalized representations of goals. In L. A. Pervin (Ed.), *Goal concepts in personality and social psychology* (pp. 211-241). Hillsdale, NJ: Erlbaum.

McClelland, D. C. (1975). *Power: The inner experience.* New York: Irvington.

Miller, G. A., Galanter, E., & Pribram, K. H. (1960). *Plans and the structure of behavior.* New York: Holt, Rinehart, & Winston.

Norem, J. K., & Cantor, N. (1986). Defensive pessimism: "Harnessing" anxiety as motivation. *Journal of Personality and Social Psychology, 51*(6), 1208-1217.

Norem, J. K. (1989). Cognitive strategies as personality: Effectiveness, specificity, flexibility, and change. In D. M. Buss & N. Cantor (Eds.), *Personality psychology: Recent trends and emerging directions* (pp. 45-60). New York: Springer-Verlag.

Nuttin, J. (1984). *Motivation, planning, and action: A relational theory of behavior dynamics.* Hillsdale, NJ: Erlbaum.

Pervin, L. (Ed.). (1989). *Goal concepts in personality and social psychology.* Hillsdale, NJ: Erlbaum.

Powers, W. T. (1973). *Behavior: The control of perception.* Chicago: Aldine.

Price, R., & Bouffard, D. L. (1974). Behavioral appropriateness and situational constraint as dimensions of social behavior. *Journal of Personality and Social Psychology, 30*, 579-586.

Rotter, J. B. (1966). Generalized expectancies for internal versus external control of reinforcement. *Psychological Monographs, 81*(1, Whole No. 609).

Ryff, C. D. (1989). Happiness is everything, or is it? Explorations on the meaning of psychological well-being. *Journal of Personality and Social Psychology, 57*(6), 1069-1081.

Spivak, G., Platt, J., & Shure, M. (1976). *The problem-solving approach to adjustment.* San Francisco: Jossey-Bass.

Stewart, A. J. (1982). The course of individual adaptation to life changes. *Journal of Personality and Social Psychology, 42*, 1100-1113.

_____. (1989). Social intelligence and adaptation to life changes. In R. S. Wyer & T. K. Srull (Eds.), *Advances in social cognition* (Vol. 2, pp. 187-196). Hillsdale, NJ: Erlbaum.

Vallacher, R. R., & Wegner, D. M. (1987). What do people think they're doing? Action identification and human behavior. *Psychological Review, 94*, 3-15.

Veroff, J. (1983). Contextual determinants of personality. *Personality and Social Psychology Bulletin, 9*, 331-344.

Wright, J. C., & Mischel, W. (1987). A conditional approach to dispositional constructs: The local predictability of social behavior. *Journal of Personality and Social Psychology, 53*(6), 1159-1177.

Zirkel, S., & Cantor, N. (1990). Personal construal of life tasks: Those who struggle for independence. *Journal of Personality and Social Psychology, 58*(1), 172-185.

STUDENT GOAL ORIENTATION AND SELF-REGULATION IN THE COLLEGE CLASSROOM

Paul R. Pintrich and Teresa Garcia

Almost all motivational theories posit some type of goal, purpose, or intentionality to human behavior, although, as Zukier (1986) points out, these goals may be relatively accessible and cognitive as in current cognitive theories of motivation (e.g., Dweck & Leggett, 1988: Little, 1989; Nuttin, 1984; Veroff & Veroff, 1980; Weiner, 1986) or less cognitive as in Murray's (1938) classic needs theory or unconscious as in psychodynamic models (e.g., Freud, 1914/ 1957). These goals are assumed to provide direction for behavior, especially in terms of choice and persistence behavior. However, having a goal and choosing one activity over another does not necessarily mean that individuals know how to accomplish the activity in the most adaptive, effective, or efficient manner or how to persist appropriately at the activity in the face of difficulty (e.g., there may be times when persistence is not useful or helpful). More recent conceptions of goals have tried to address this "know how" problem by integrating motivational conceptions of goals with constructs such as cognitive strategies and prior knowledge (in the form of declarative and procedural

Advances in Motivation and Achievement, Volume 7, pages 371-402.
Copyright © 1991 by JAI Press Inc.
All rights of reproduction in any form reserved.
ISBN: 1-55938-122-1

knowledge) from cognitive psychology (e.g., Cantor & Kihlstrom, 1987). At the same time, the addition of constructs like goals and purpose to strictly cognitive models of learning promise to provide a more realistic and "warmer" description of the individual learner in contrast to "colder" models of cognition based on the person-as-a-computer metaphor. As Pintrich, Cross, Kozma, and McKeachie (1986) have pointed out, the current interest in integrating motivational constructs like attributions, goals, and self-efficacy with cognitive constructs such as declarative and procedural knowledge, learning strategies, and metacognition represents an important new direction in psychology.

There are a variety of models that are exemplars of this renewed interest in both motivation and cognition. For example, Dweck and Leggett (1988) propose that student goal orientation leads to different adaptive or maladaptive patterns of affect, cognition, and behavior. They propose that adopting a learning goal, where the focus is on seeking challenge and mastery of a task, leads to an adaptive pattern of cognition in terms of seeing the outcome (success or failure) in a positive light (e.g., making ability attributions for success and effort or strategy attributions for failure). In addition, students with a learning goal are assumed to interpret their effort as positively related to their ability to accomplish the task. In contrast, students with a performance goal, where the focus is on the demonstration of high ability and avoidance of judgments of low ability, are more likely to believe that effort and ability are inversely related with the subsequent inference that high effort signifies low ability. A performance goal orientation also seems to lead to more concern about the outcome with failure leading to attributions regarding the lack of ability.

Besides these cognitions, Dweck and Leggett (1988) propose that learning and performance goals lead to different affective reactions and behavior. In terms of affect, students operating under performance goals are assumed to be more likely to experience anxiety about their success and failure and suffer loss of self-esteem if they fail. In contrast, students with a learning goal should strive to improve their performance, resulting in an increase in mastery feelings and intrinsic motivation (Dweck & Leggett, 1988). Finally, these two types of goals are assumed to influence behavior in terms of task choice, persistence, and involvement in the task, with learning goals leading to the choice of more difficult and challenging tasks and higher levels of involvement and persistence. This formulation of learning versus performance goals parallels Nicholls' (1984) distinction between ego versus task involvement. In addition, the distinction between learning and performance goals can be seen as a more cognitive extension of intrinsic motivation theory (e.g., Deci & Ryan, 1985; Harter, 1981), which emphasizes the basic need for mastery of the environment, following White's (1959) lead. However, an explicit emphasis on social cognitive goals, in contrast to needs, implies that individuals can be more cognizant of their goals and adopt different goals depending on the situation.

Elliott and Dweck (1988), in an experimental study where they manipulated students' goals, found support for the proposed pattern of cognition in terms of students' attributions for their performance and in the pattern of their affective reactions as a function of goal adoption. They also found that high and low ability students' strategies for solving the task varied under different goal conditions. There were no differences between high and low ability students' strategies in the learning goal condition, but in the performance goal condition low ability students showed a deterioration in the use of appropriate strategies. However, the discrimination task used in this study has low ecological validity and limits generalization to the types of academic tasks found in most classrooms. Consequently, there is a need for studies that examine the relationship between students' goals and their actual learning strategies for classroom academic tasks.

Cantor and her colleagues (e.g., Cantor & Fleeson, this volume; Cantor & Kihlstrom, 1987; Cantor & Langston, 1989) also have developed a model that links students' beliefs about the "life tasks" they are working on in college, in effect their goals for themselves, to their strategies for accomplishing these goals. Other work by Emmons (1989) on individuals' personal strivings and Little (1989) on the personal projects individuals choose to pursue present similar ideas. This work begins with some of the insights from life-span developmental theories about the normative developmental issues that individuals confront in the course of their everyday life (e.g., issues of identity, intimacy), but assumes that people will have different personal construals of these issues. This constructivist view proposes that individuals' life tasks don't necessarily follow a prescribed, universal pattern of development and that individuals can have a number of goals or life tasks that serve to guide their behavior. For example, Cantor and her colleagues have found that students can identify academic goals (i.e., doing well and getting organized) as well as social and personal goals (making friends, being on one's own, establishing an identity) that are salient to them as they cope with the demands of college life. Obviously, these goals reflect normative life tasks (e.g., achievement, intimacy, identity) that would be predicted by life-span approaches (i.e., Erikson, 1963; Veroff & Veroff, 1980), but the important difference is that this model proposes that students will define these issues somewhat differently, and given these different conceptions, seek out and use different strategies to accomplish the life task. For example, in their research they found that some students defined independence in terms of coping without parental support, whereas others concentrated on more practical and mundane matters such as money management. These different conceptions of the life task lead to different problem solving strategies for coping with the task (Cantor & Kihlstrom, 1987).

This model provides a powerful way of thinking about individuals in terms of their personal constructions of life tasks which allows for the integration of both individual (self-beliefs and interests) and situational or contextual factors (normative developmental issues, situational and contextual demands and constraints of the specific college setting) which helps resolve the person-situation conundrum and issues of ecological validity. In addition, the model borrows concepts from cognitive psychology (e.g., declarative and procedural knowledge) and applies them to social and personal development, reflecting the emphasis on the integration of both cognitive and motivational constructs. For the most part, however, the empirical work on this model has focused on social and personal issues that college students confront. Yet, college students are confronted with a variety of academic tasks as they enroll in different courses over their years in postsecondary institutions. For example, the academic tasks they must complete in a required English composition course (i.e., essays and papers) may be very different in both form and content in comparison to the exams they may take in an elective psychology course or a lab report they must prepare for a biology course in their major. Although the nature of these academic tasks can influence how students approach the task (Blumenfeld, Mergendoller, & Swarthout, 1987, Doyle, 1983; Pintrich, 1989; Ramsden, 1984), students also bring with them a repertoire of goals and strategies for accomplishing these academic tasks (Pintrich, 1988a, 1988b; Pintrich & De Groot, 1990a, 1990b).

In our own research program, we have been integrating motivational constructs such as goals and self-efficacy beliefs with the cognitive and self-regulatory strategies that students may use to complete these academic tasks. Our model parallels the two models just discussed in its focus on motivational beliefs such as goals and cognitive strategies, but it takes a more detailed look at the actual cognitive strategies that college students may use as they confront different academic tasks. In addition, our work reflects a concern for ecologically valid tasks and students' motivation and cognition in the actual college classroom, obviously sacrificing some internal validity for external validity. The general purpose of this paper is to describe the nature of the relationships between students' goals, other motivational beliefs, and the cognitive and self-regulatory strategies they may use to accomplish academic tasks in the college classroom.

A SOCIAL COGNITIVE MODEL OF STUDENT GOALS AND SELF-REGULATION

In our research program on student learning in the classroom, we have developed a general social cognitive model that incorporates both motivational and cognitive variables. We briefly describe the components of the model here to set the context, for more detail on the model see McKeachie, Pintrich, Lin, & Smith (1986), Pintrich, (1988a, 1988b, 1989), Pintrich and De Groot (1990a, 1990b). In our model, cognition is defined by two general components-knowledge and learning and thinking strategies, paralleling current distinctions between declarative knowledge (knowing "that") and procedural knowledge (knowing how to do or perform some task). Accordingly, the knowledge component includes students' declarative knowledge of the content of the course (e.g., amount of knowledge they have and how it is organized), while the learning and thinking strategies consist of students' tactics for learning, remembering, and understanding the course content. Our model represents student motivation in terms of three general components-value, expectancy, and affect. We assume that all three components play an important role in students' motivation. The affect component in our model includes test anxiety and other emotional reactions students may have to a task (e.g., pride, shame, guilt, self-worth). The expectancy component concerns students beliefs about their self-efficacy for the coursework in a given class as well as their beliefs about how much control they have over their own learning. The value component includes students' general goal orientation to the course as well as their perceptions of the value (task value) of the course material for them in terms of its importance and interest. Given that the focus of this paper is on the role of student goals and self-regulation, we will limit most of our discussion to the value component of student goal orientation and the various learning strategies that comprise the different methods college students use to regulate their learning for college courses.

Student Goal Orientation

In our model, the general value component concerns students' reasons for engaging in an academic task, that is, we assume students ask themselves the question: Why am I doing this task? We have divided their reasons into two value components: (1) their goals for the course and (2) their beliefs about how interesting, important, or useful the course material is for them (task value). We assume that students can have different beliefs about the nature of the course material in terms of how important and interesting it is to them that may differ from their general goal orientation to the course. The goal component is further broken down into intrinsic and extrinsic orientations. Following the lead of other motivational researchers (e.g., Dweck & Elliott, 1983; Harter, 1981; Nicholls, 1984), we assume that students can have intrinsic reasons for performing in a classroom setting which include rationales such as wanting to learn more, being challenged, being curious, and trying to understand the material in depth. At the same time, students may have extrinsic reasons for attempting classwork including getting good grades, proving they are smarter than others, and seeking approval from others such as family or friends. These two goal orientations, intrinsic and extrinsic, will be the focus of this paper.

Our distinction between intrinsic and extrinsic goal orientation parallels Harter's (1981) intrinsic-extrinsic dichotomy, Dweck & Elliott's (1983) distinction between learning and performance goals, and Nicholls' (1984) task-involved versus ego-involved orientations. However, in contrast to most of the these researchers, we assume that adults, including college students, can have multiple goals for a course, reflecting both intrinsic and extrinsic orientations for the same task. For example, an assistant professor could be involved in a research project because she is intrinsically challenged by the problem, but also be involved because of the publications that will result, reflecting a simultaneous concern for extrinsic goals such as obtaining tenure. In a similar fashion, a college student may strive to really understand the course material due to an intrinsic rationale, but, at the same time, be concerned about her grade in the class because of its implications for graduate school admission or career prospects.

In fact, we assume that in many situations both intrinsic and extrinsic rationales may be operating at the same time for an individual, and, moreover, that having both types of goals may be very adaptive. Certainly, in the case of the assistant professor, a total lack of concern about publications can lead to failure in terms of not attaining tenure and reduce the possibility of continuing to do research on the intrinsically challenging research problem. For college students, a lack of concern about the external constraints of grades and course requirements can lead to academic problems, prohibiting the pursuit of the intrinsic learning and mastery goals. Given the assumption of multiple goals and the potential benefits of having both intrinsic and extrinsic goals, we expected that students who endorsed both intrinsic and extrinsic goals might have different affective reactions (e.g., the anxiety component in our model) as well as different perceptions of the the the value of the task for them (the task value component in our model) and beliefs about their self-efficacy for the task (cf. Dweck & Leggett, 1988). In addition, given that students may be more or less involved in an activity depending on their goal orientation, we wanted to examine students' use of different types of learning strategies as a function of both their relative intrinsic and extrinsic orientation. The nature of these different learning strategies and their relation to goal orientation are described in the next section.

Strategies for Learning and Self-regulation

In our model of student cognition, we have concentrated on the role of students' declarative knowledge and its structure (e.g., Naveh-Benjamin, Lin, & McKeachie, Lin, 1989; Naveh-Benjamin, McKeachie, & Lin, 1989; Naveh-Benjamin, McKeachie, Lin, & Tucker, 1986) and the role of learning and thinking strategies (e.g., Pintrich, 1989). In this paper, we focus on the different learning strategies that college students have available to them and the links between these strategies and students' intrinsic and extrinsic goal orientations. In our research program we have divided learning strategies into three general categories: cognitive, metacognitive, and resource management strategies.

Cognitive strategies refer to the general methods students use to comprehend the course material, including material presented in both lectures and text. Researchers in Great Britain and Sweden have documented two general information-processing patterns that college students use to learn academic material—surface and deep processing (e.g., Marton, Hounsell, & Entwistle, 1984; Marton & Saljo, 1976a, 1976b). Surface processors seem to concentrate on finishing the reading and focus on facts and details in the text by using simple cognitive strategies such as rehearsal. In contrast, deep processors attempt to discover the goals of the author and focus on the meaning and organization of the text and tend to use more elaborative cognitive strategies such as paraphrasing or summarizing. This distinction parallels other work on rote versus meaningful learning (Ausubel, 1963), identifying, reproducing, and understanding types of learning (Entwistle, Hanley, & Hounsell, 1979), serial-operation versus wholist-comprehension learning (Pask, 1976), factual versus conceptual learning (Siegel & Siegel, 1965), and shallow-reiterative versus deep-elaborative learning (Schmeck, 1983). Many of these descriptions of learning assume that these patterns of information processing are rather stable individual differences between students that cut across different academic tasks or domains.

In contrast, recent research on the surface and deep processing styles (e.g., Entwistle & Marton, 1984; Marton, Hounsell, & Entwistle, 1984) suggests that these two general information-processing patterns represent individuals' goals and intentions for learning as well as their actual learning and study strategies. In addition, this research seems to support the view that these two orientations to learning are sensitive to differences in course content and context (Ramsden, 1984; Saljo, 1984). As Pintrich (1990) notes, this conceptualization of learning styles proposes a more constructivist view of the learner in which individuals attempt to derive meaning from the course material in line with their goals and intentions, their actual use of different cognitive strategies, and the nature of the academic task and context (cf. Entwistle, 1984). This current view of surface and deep processing seems to include two basic components: motivational (the students' goals for the task) and cognitive (the strategy used to accomplish the academic task). These two components appear to work together to determine the students' information-processing pattern. The surface processors seem to have a completion, learn-just-the-facts goal that leads them to use rote rehearsal strategies. This pattern appears to be more extrinsically oriented, with the students concentrating on small details of the material in order to do well on the exams or assignments without regard for deep understanding. In contrast, the deep processors seem to have a much more intrinsic orientation to learning, actually seeking to understand the course material, and, in service of this goal, evoking more elaborative and metacognitive learning strategies.

Although the surface-deep processing pattern is a useful heuristic for describing students, it seems likely that students can adopt different motivational goals and different cognitive learning strategies for different academic tasks. In addition, it appears that there may be individuals who endorse more intrinsic goals for learning, yet lack the actual cognitive and metacognitive strategies that can really help the student obtain their goal of deep understanding (e.g., Pintrich & De Groot, 1990b). Consequently, it seems useful to unpack the motivational goals and cognitive strategies components in our descriptions of college student learning. This unpacking will allow for more dynamic, sophisticated, and multivariate analyses of the links between students' motivation and cognition in the college classroom. Rather than two types of learners, it is possible to hypothesize that there will be students who have different patterns of goals and use a variety of different cognitive and metacognitive strategies and that these patterns may vary by the academic task or course context.

In line with this general assumption of unpacking motivational goals and learning strategies, we have attempted to examine three types of general cognitive strategies in our research program. Following the work of Weinstein and Mayer (1986), we have identified rehearsal, elaboration, and organizational strategies as important cognitive strategies that are related to academic performance in the classroom (McKeachie et al., 1986; Pintrich, 1989). Rehearsal strategies involve the reciting of items to be learned or the saying of words aloud as one reads a piece of text. Highlighting or underlining text in a rather passive and unreflective manner also can be more like a rehearsal strategy than an elaborative strategy. These rehearsal strategies are assumed to help the student attend to and select important information from lists or texts and keep this information active in workng memory.

However, rehearsal strategies do not seem to be very effective in helping the student incorporate the new information into existing schemas in long-term memory (McKeachie et al., 1986; Weinstein & Mayer, 1986). Cognitive strategies such as elaboration and organization seem to be much more useful for integrating and connecting new information with previous knowledge. Elaborative strategies include paraphrasing or summarizing the material to be learned, creating analogies, generative note-taking (where the student actually reorganizes and connects ideas in their notes in contrast to passive, linear note-taking), explaining the ideas in the material to be learned to someone else, and question asking and answering (Weinstein & Mayer, 1986). The other general type of deeper processing strategy, organizational, includes behaviors such as selecting the main idea from text, outlining the text or material to be learned, and the use of a variety of specific techniques for selecting and organizing the ideas in the material (e.g., sketching a network or map of the important ideas, identifying the prose or expository structures of texts, see Weinstein & Mayer, 1986). All these strategies have been shown to result in a deeper understanding of the material to be learned in contrast to rehearsal strategies. In terms of their links to students' goals, we assume that students high in intrinsic orientation, given their interest in really learning the material, will be more likely to use these elaborative and organizational strategies in contrast to those students low in intrinsic orientation. At the same time, it is not clear if students high in extrinsic orientation will use these more sophisticated strategies, although given their similarity to the goal orientation of surface processors, they may be more likely to use rehearsal strategies.

Besides these cognitive strategies, students' use of metacognitive strategies to regulate their learning can have an important influence upon their achievement. There are two general aspects of metacognition, knowledge about cognition and self-regulation of cognition (Brown, Bransford, Ferrara, & Campione, 1983; Flavell, 1979). In this paper, we concentrate on the self-regulatory functions of metacognitive strategies for learning. Most models of metacognitive control strategies include planning, monitoring, and regulating behaviors. Although these three types of strategies are highly related and, at least in our data (e.g., Pintrich, 1989), seem to be highly correlated empirically, they can be discussed separately. Planning activities that have been investigated in various studies of students' learning include setting goals for studying, skimming a text before reading, generating questions before reading a text, and doing a task analysis of the problem. These activities seem to help the learner plan their use of cognitive strategies and also seem to activate or prime relevant aspects of prior knowledge, making the organization and comprehension of the material much easier. Learners that report using these types of planning activities seem to perform better on a variety of academic tasks in comparison to students who do not use these strategies (McKeachie et al., 1986; Pressley, 1986).

Monitoring of one's thinking and academic behavior seems to be an essential aspect of metacognition. Weinstein and Mayer (1986) see all metacognitive activities as partly the monitoring of comprehension. Monitoring activities include tracking of attention while reading a text or listening to a lecture, self-testing through the use of questions about the text material to check for understanding, monitoring comprehension of a lecture, and the use of test-taking strategies (i.e., monitoring speed and adjusting to time available) in an exam situation. These various monitoring strategies alert the learner to breakdowns in attention or comprehension that can then be subjected to repair through the use of regulating strategies.

Regulation strategies are closely tied to monitoring strategies. For example, as learners ask themselves questions as they read in order to monitor their comprehension, and then go back and reread a portion of the text, this rereading is a regulatory strategy. Another type of self-regulatory strategy for reading occurs when a student slows the pace of their reading when confronted with more difficult or less familiar text. Of course, reviewing any aspect of course material (e.g., lecture notes, texts, lab material, previous exams and papers, etc.) that one does not remember or understand that well while studying for an exam reflects a general self-regulatory strategy. During a test, skipping questions and returning to them later is another strategy that students can use to regulate their behavior during an exam. All these strategies are assumed to improve learning by helping students correct their studying behavior and repair deficits in their understanding. We assume that students who endorse an intrinsic orientation goal of learning would be more likely to use these metacognitive strategies in comparison to students who do not focus on learning goals.

The third and final aspect in our model of learning and self-regulatory strategies, resource management strategies, concerns strategies that students use to manage their environment (their time, their study envrionment, and others including teachers and peers) and themselves (their own effort) as they attempt different academic tasks. In line with a general adaptive approach to learning, we assume that these resource management strategies help students adapt to their environment as well as change the environment to fit their goals and needs (cf. Sternberg, 1985). The resource management strategies that we have focused on in our model include time and study environment, effort management, and help-seeking.

Students' management of their time and the actual place they choose to study are not cognitive or metacognitive strategies that may have a direct influence on eventual learning, but they are general strategies that can help or hinder the students' efforts at completing the academic task. Effort management seems to be an important aspect of self-control in terms of persisting in the face of difficult or boring tasks (cf. Corno, 1986; Kuhl, 1987). Students that are able to protect their intention to study in terms of arranging their time, their study place, and their actual behavior while studying to facilitate concentrated and deeper processing of the material should perform better than those students who are not able to manage their resources as effectively. In the same fashion, students that know when, how, and from whom to seek help (see Newman, this volume) should be more likely to be successful than those students who do not seek help appropriately. The empirical relations between these resource management strategies and students' goal orientation also will be examined in this paper.

In summary, our social cognitive model proposes that both motivational and cognitive components play an important role in student learning in the college classroom. We assume that students can have both intrinsic and extrinsic goal orientations and that these different orientations may be linked in different ways to students' cognitive strategies for learning as well as their self-regulatory strategies such as metacognitive strategies, resource management strategies, and help-seeking. In addition, we assume that these cognitive and self-regulatory strategies will be more closely tied to actual academic performance than students' motivational beliefs, but that the strength of these relationships may vary as a function of students' goals. We now turn to a description of some results from our program of research that provide empirical support for our model and some of our ideas about the relationships between students' goal orientation and their self-regulation in the college classroom.

EMPIRICAL FINDINGS

Subjects

Subjects were 263 college students in six classes: three biology courses ($N = 163$) and three social science courses ($N = 97$). These classrooms were sampled from three midwestern institutions: a community college, a small private four-year college, and a large public four-year university. The gender breakdown was 108 men and 155 women; no differences in gender distribution were found between the six classes. The majority of subjects were in either their first or second year at college ($N = 216$). One of the biology courses was an upper-level elective; accordingly, the students in this classroom were in their third or fourth years of college. The remaining five classrooms were similar with respect to the distribution of freshmen and upperclassmen.

The data were collected on a volunteer basis during the winter 1987 term. Subjects received no monetary compensation for their participation. The classes were visited twice, once at the onset of the semester (Time 1) and again at the end of the semester (Time 2). The Motivated Strategies for Learning Questionnaire (MSLQ) was administered at each visit.

Measures

The Motivated Strategies for Learning Questionnaire (Pintrich, McKeachie, Smith, Doljanac, Lin, Naveh-Benjamin, Crooks, & Karabenick, 1987) is a self-report, Likert-scaled (1 = not true of me, to 7 = very true of me) instrument designed to measure student motivational beliefs and learning strategy use. The 1987 version of the MSLQ consisted of 55 motivation and 55 cognitive strategy items. The 110 items comprise 16 scales, ten of which were examined in this study. The ten MSLQ scales used were: intrinsic goal orientation; extrinsic goal orientation; task value; self-efficacy; test anxiety; rehearsal; elaboration/organization; metacognition; resource management; and help seeking. Subjects' mean scores on these scales were computed and used for the following analyses. The internal reliability coefficients from time 2 and sample items for the scales used are provided in Table 1. Time 1 alphas did not differ significantly from those reported in Table 1 and the only MSLQ scales used from time 1 were intrinsic orientation (time 1 alpha = .60) and extrinsic orienation (time 1 alpha = .64).

Table 1.   Scales and Sample Items from the 1987 Version of the
Motivated Strategies for Learning Questionnaire

Scale	Sample Item	Posttest Alpha
Intrinsic Goal Orientation (4 items)	Even when I do poorly on an exam I try to learn from my mistakes.	.68
Extrinsic Goal Orientation (2 items)	I like to work on difficult problems and tasks to show how smart I am.	.69
Task Value (9 items)	Understanding the subject matter of this course is important to me.	.94
Self-Efficacy (5 items)	I'm certain I can understand the ideas and concepts taught in this course.	.84
Test Anxiety (8 items)	I worry a great deal about tests.	.94
Rehearrsal (6 items)	When I study I practice saying the material to myself over and over.	.54
Elaboration/Organization (16 items)	I try to apply ideas from course readings in other class activities (lecture, discussion).	.81
Metacognition (13 times)	I try to think through a topic and decide what I'm supposed to learn from it rather than just read it over when studying.	.80
Resource Management (9 items)	I work hard to get a good grade even when I don't like a course.	.82
Help-Seeking (5 items)	I try to get help with my study skills when I'm having difficulty in my courses.	.75

Correlational Relations Between MSLQ Scales

Simple zero-order correlations between intrinsic and extrinsic goal orientation at time 1 and time 2 and the motivational and cognitive strategy scales were calculated and are presented in Table 2. Although not presented in the table, it is important to note that intrinsic goal orientation and extrinsic goal orientation were correlated .11 at time 1 and .04 at time 2, suggesting that they are different orientations, not just two endpoints on one continuum.

Relations Between Goal Orientation and Motivational Beliefs

As expected, task value was much more strongly correlated with intrinsic goal orientation than extrinsic goal orientation both at the beginning and end of the course (.28 vs. .00 at time 1; .47 vs. .10 at time 2, see Table 2). Students who adopted an intrinsic orientation to the course were more likely to think the course material was interesting and important to them in comparison to students who did not endorse an intrinsic goal, while task value was not related to endorsement of an extrinsic goal. A similar, but not as marked a difference was found in self-efficacy (.22 vs. .13 at time 1; .36 vs. .30 at time 2). Students high in intrinsic orientation were more likely to feel efficacious than those students low in intrinsic orientation. At the same time, students high in extrinsic

Table 2. Zero-Order Correlation Between Goal Orientation
(Time 1 and Time 2) and Motivational and Cognitive Scales

Motivational/Cognitive Scales at Time 2	*Intrinsic Goal Orientation*		*Extrinsic Goal Orientation*	
	Time 1	*Time 2*	*Time 1*	*Time 2*
Task Value	.28	.47	.00	.10
Self-Efficacy	.22	.36	.13	.30
Test Anxiety	−.05	−.06	.07	.08
Rehearsal	.06	.13	−.03	−.04
Elaboration/Organization	.32	.39	.03	.11
Metacognition	.36	.40	.00	.06
Resource Management	.20	.25	−.03	.02
Help-Seeking	.14	.27	.10	.19

orientation at the end of the term were more likely to feel efficacious than those students low in extrinsic orientation. Given that our efficacy scale included items about confidence in getting a good grade, and this finding occurred at the end of the term when students have some idea about what their final grade will be, this relation is not that surprising. The correlations between goal orientation and test anxiety were weak, countering expectations about goals and anxiety (cf. Dweck & Leggett, 1988). Note, however, that test anxiety correlated with intrinsic goal orientation negatively (−.05 and −.06), and with extrinsic goal orientation positively (.07 and .08) as would be expected from previous research.

Goal Orientation and Cognitive and Self-regulatory Strategy Use

Rehearsal strategies were weakly related to goal orientation; the correlations between intrinsic goal orientation and rehearsal were weakly positive (.06 and .13 for time 1 and time 2 intrinsic goal orientation, respectively) while those between extrinsic goal orientation and rehearsal were weakly negative (−.03 and −.04, see Table 2). This disconfirms one of our expectations about students high in extrinsic orientation being more likely to use rehearsal strategies as suggested by the surface-deep processing literature (cf. Marton et al., 1984). Elaboration/organization, metacognition, and resource management were much more strongly related to intrinsic rather than extrinsic goal orientation (see Table 2). As expected, and consonant with the surface-deep processing research, students who were high in intrinsic orientation were more likely to use deeper, more elaborative strategies, be more metacognitve, and more likely to regulate their resources well in contrast to those students low in intrinsic orienation. In contrast, the correlations of these scales with extrinsic goal orientation averaged close to zero (*r*s ranged from −.03 to .11). It appears that extrinsic goal orientation is not related to students' use of cognitive, metacognitive, or resource management strategies. Help-seeking was slightly more positively correlated with intrinsic goal orientation than with extrinsic goal orientation (see Table 2), however, both students high in intrinsic orientation and those high in extrinsic orientation were more likely to seek help at least at time 2 at the end of the course.

Interactions Between Intrinsic Goal and Extrinsic Goal Orientation

We hypothesized that there may be some interactions between different levels of intrinsic and extrinsic goal orientation. For example, it may be that having both a high intrinsic and high extrinsic orientation may be the most adaptive pattern for college students in comparison to students who are low in both, in effect those students who do not care about learning or grades. Time 1 and time 2 scores on intrinsic and extrinsic goal orientation were trichotomized in order to examine possible non-linear effects of goal orientation upon motivation and strategy use. Intrinsic and extrinsic goal orientation were split into the lowest quartile, middle 50%, and highest quartile. Intrinsic goal orientation was negatively skewed: the means for this variable were 5.52 for time 1 and 5.57 for time 2. The distribution of extrinsic goal orientation approximated the normal curve much more closely; the means for this variable were 3.19 for time 1 and 3.32 for time 2. The formation of these two three-level categorical variables resulted in the classification of students along both intrinsic and extrinsic dimensions. The cell sizes for the nine cells that were generated by crossing intrinsic by extrinsic orientation were reasonable. The smallest cell had 17 individuals in it and the largest cell had 52 people in it. Two-way ANOVAs were performed using these three-level goal orientation variables to stratify mean scores on measures of: task value, test anxiety, self-efficacy, and use of rehearsal, elaboration/organization, metacognition, resource management, and help seeking strategies. The results of these ANOVAs for intrinsic and extrinsic orientation at time 1 and time 2 can be found in Tables 3 and 4.

Main Effects of Intrinsic Goal Orientation

The main effects of both time 1 and time 2 intrinsic goal orientation (with F-values calculated upon (2,262) degrees of freedom) were significant for scores of task value ($F = 8.48, p < .001$ at time 1 and $F = 24.83, p < .0001$ at time 2), self-efficacy ($F = 4.07, p < .02$ and $F = 11.26, p < .0001$), elaboration/organization ($F = 11.23, p < .0001$ and $F = 12.47, p < .0001$), metacognition ($F = 13.56, p < .0001$, and $F = 15.94, p < .0001$), and resource management ($F = 3.88, p < .02$ and $F = 8.23, p < .001$). As levels of intrinsic goal orientation increased, levels of task value, self-efficacy, use of elaboration/organization, metacognition, and resource management strategies increased as well (see Tables 3 and 4), paralleling the results of the zero-order correlations. Although

Table 3. Mean Differences in Motivational and Cognitive Scales by Intrinsic and Extrinsic Goal Orientation at Time 1

Motivational/Cognitive Scales at Time 2	Intrinsic Goal Orientation (time 1)			Extrinsic Goal Orientation (time 1)		
	low (N = 74)	middle (N = 122)	high (N = 67)	low (N = 70)	middle (N = 104)	high (N = 89)
Task Value	5.39a	5.66a	6.12b	5.86a	5.47b	5.86
Self-Efficacy	4.68a	4.92	5.21b	4.81	4.85	5.11
Test Anxiety	3.84	3.62	3.74	3.64	3.67	3.82
Rehearsal	4.40	4.61	4.58	4.55	4.54	4.53
Elaboration/Organization	4.33a	4.68b	4.92c	4.73	4.50	4.74
Metacognition	4.46a	4.88b	5.11c	4.94	4.67	4.90
Resource Management	4.31a	4.63b	4.83b	4.72	4.48	4.62
Help-Seeking	4.20	4.49	4.51	4.37	4.34	4.52

Note: Means with different letters indicate groups that are significantly different at the .05 level (Student-Neuman-Keuls procedure).

Table 4. Mean Differences in Motivational and Cognitive Scales by Intrinsic and Extrinsic Goal Orientation at Time 2

Motivational/Cognitive Scales at Time 2	Intrinsic Goal Orientation (time 2)			Extrinsic Goal Orientation (time 2)		
	low (N = 81)	middle (N = 95)	high (N = 81)	low (N = 100)	middle (N = 90)	high (N = 73)
Task Value	5.13a	5.76b	6.24c	5.65a	5.55a	5.99b
Self-Efficacy	4.46a	5.09b	5.21b	4.60a	4.95b	5.36c
Test Anxiety	3.74	3.69	3.64	3.65	3.59	3.87
Rehearsal	4.48	4.53	4.65	4.54	4.62	4.49
Elaboration/Organization	4.34a	4.66b	4.91c	4.53	4.70	4.71
Metacognition	4.47a	4.84b	5.13c	4.71	4.91	4.83
Resource Management	4.31a	4.51a	4.97b	4.53	4.70	4.54
Help-Seeking	4.03a	4.46b	4.68b	4.20a	4.37	4.69b

Note: Means with different letters indicate groups that are significantly different at the .05 level (Student-Neuman-Keuls procedure).

these results arestill correlational, the fact that differences in intrinsic orientation at the beginning of the term were significantly related to students use of cognitive and self-regulatory strategies at the end of the term suggest that students' general goal orientation can influence the level of their cognitive engagement throughout a course. No significant differences between levels of intrinsic goal orientation (at either time) were found in mean levels of test anxiety or use of rehearsal strategies. Time 2, but not time 1, level of intrinsic goal orientation, had a significant main effect ($F(2,262) = 5.93, p < .003$) on help seeking. The more intrinsically motivated a student was at the end of the course, the greater the reported level of help seeking.

Main Effects of Extrinsic Goal Orientation

In contrast, levels of extrinsic goal orientation showed few significant main effects. Time 1 extrinsic goal orientation was significant for task value ($F(2,262)$ = 4.16, $p < .02$), and approached significance for metacognition ($F(2,262)$ = 2.40, $p < .09$). In both cases, students high in extrinsic orientation at the beginning of the term had higher levels of task value and metacognition at the end of the term (see Table 3). Time 2 levels of extrinsic goal orientation had significant main effects on task value ($F(2,262)=3.09, p<.05$), self-efficacy ($F(2,262) = 9.96, p < .001$), and help seeking ($F(2,262) = 2.90, p < .05$). As levels of extrinsic goal orientation at the end of the term increased, self-efficacy and help seeking increased (see Table 4). However, a different trend was seen in task value and time 2 extrinsic goal orientation: the middle group showed *lower* task value than the low or high extrinsic groups at the end of the course.

Interactions Between Levels of Intrinsic and Extrinsic Goal Orientation

Three significant interaction terms emerged from these ANOVA analyses. The first was in metacognition by time 1 intrinsic and extrinsic goal orientation ($F(4,262) = 2.95, p < .02$). The second was in elaboration/organization by time 1 intrinsic and extrinsic goal orientation ($F(4,262) = 2.35, p < .05$). The third was in self-efficacy by time 2 intrinsic and extrinsic goal orientation ($F(4,262) = 2.93, p < .02$). Post-hoc paired contrasts were performed to distinguish groups that were significantly different (Student-Neuman-Keuls procedure, with alpha fixed at .05) from one another. These results are detailed below.

The interaction for metacognition showed that at the end of the term, the highest mean level of use of metacognitive strategies was reported by students who were classified as high intrinsic, low extrinsic at the beginning of the course (5.59, see Figure 1). The lowest average level of metacognition was reported by students classified as low in intrinsic goal orientation, regardless of their level of extrinsic goal orientation. Intrinsic goal orientation showed its greatest effects on metacognition at the lowest level of extrinsic goal orientation. For students classified as low in extrinsic goal orientation at the start of the course, their metacognition means by pretest intrinsic goal orientation were 4.37, 4.91, and 5.59 for the low, middle, and high intrinsic students respectively (see Figure 1). Post hoc contrasts showed that all three groups differed significantly from one another at $p < .05$.

The interaction for the use of elaboration/organizational strategies showed the same pattern of means by intrinsic/extrinsic combination as the metacognition interaction above. The highest mean level of use of elaboration/ organization strategies was reported by students who were assessed as low extrinsic, high intrinsic at the start of the semester (5.36). The lowest average level of elaboration/organization was in the low intrinsic group: this held true

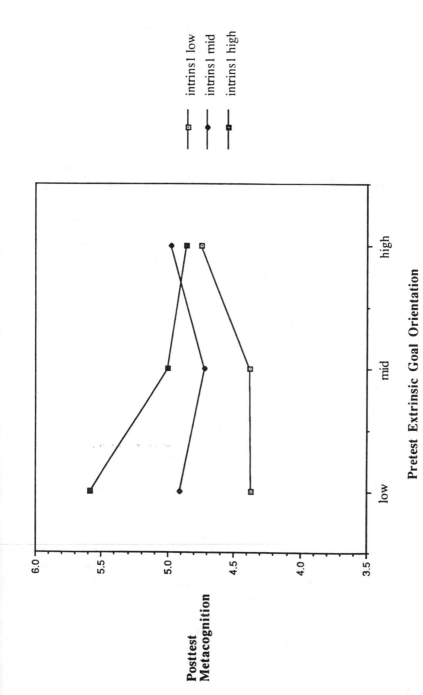

Figure 1. Mean Posttest Metacognition Scores by Pretest Student Goal Orientation

387

across the three levels of extrinsic goal orientation. Similar to the first interaction reported, intrinsic goal orientation showed its greatest effects at low levels of extrinsic goal orientation. For students who were low extrinsic at beginning of the course, their elaboration/organization means by intrinsic goal orientation were 4.24, 4.67, and 5.36 for the low, middle, and high intrinsic students respectively (see Figure 2). Post hoc contrasts showed that the high intrinsic, low extrinsic group of students differed significantly ($p < .05$) from the other two groups.

The self-efficacy interaction showed that students' goal orientation at the end of the course, whether it be intrinsic or extrinsic, had an impact on students' reported levels of self-efficacy. The lowest level of self-efficacy was reported by students who were low intrinsic, low extrinsic at the end of the course (3.87). Students who were high intrinsic, high extrinsic had the highest level of efficacy (5.59). Again, intrinsic goal orientation had its greatest effects when extrinsic goal orientation was low. For students classified as low in extrinsic goal orientation at the end of the course, self-efficacy means by intrinsic goal orientation were 3.87, 5.04, and 4.97 for the low, middle, and high intrinsic students respectively (see Figure 3). Post hoc contrasts showed that low extrinsic, low intrinsic students at the end of the course differed significantly ($p < .05$) from the low extrinsic, mid intrinsic and low extrinsic, high intrinsic students in mean level of efficacy.

Two additional relationships were examined. While the main effects of intrinsic and extrinsic goal orientation were not significant, we were intrigued by the fact that the interaction terms themselves approached significance. Student levels of intrinsic and extrinsic goal orientation at the start of the course tended to have nonlinear effects upon the levels of use of rehearsal strategies and test anxiety at the end of the semester (see Figures 4 and 5).

The rehearsal interaction ($F(4,262) = 1.98, p < .09$) showed that the lowest mean level of rehearsal strategies was in the group of students who were high on both intrinsic and extrinsic goal orientation at the start of the term (4.19, see Figure 4). The interactive effect of intrinsic goal orientation here was found at the highest level of extrinsic goal orientation (see Figure 4). For students who were classified as high in extrinsic goal orientation, use of rehearsal strategies decreased as levels of intrinsic goal orientation increased (4.72, 4.62, 4.19 were the rehearsal means for the low, mid and high intrinsic students).

The test anxiety interaction ($F(4,262) = 2.18, p < .07$) indicated that test anxiety was lowest in students who were low extrinsic and high intrinsic at the beginning of the course (Mean = 3.05). As found earlier, intrinsic goal orientation seemed to have its most positive effects when extrinsic goal orientation was low: at low and middle levels of extrinsic goal orientation, the higher one's intrinsic goal orientation, the lower the test anxiety. However, the highest mean was reported by students who were classified as high on both intrinsic and extrinsic goal orientation (4.56). At the highest level of intrinsic goal orientation, anxiety increased as extrinsic goal orientation increased (see Figure 5).

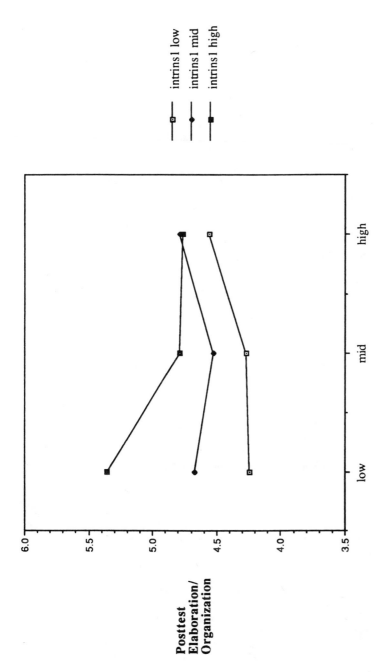

Figure 2. Mean Posttest Elaboration/Organization Scores by Pretest Student Goal Orientation

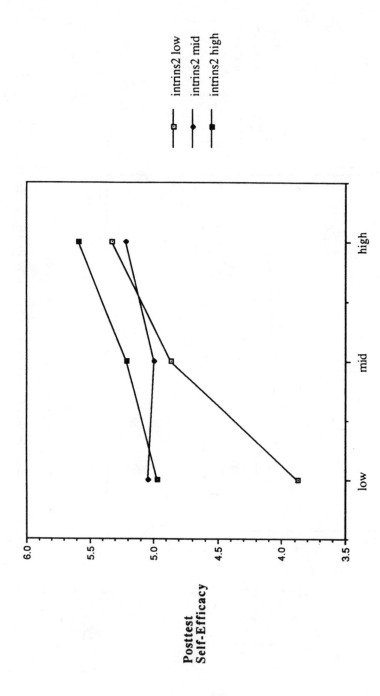

Posttest Extrinsic Goal Orientation

intrins2 low
intrins2 mid
intrins2 high

Figure 3. Mean Posttest Self-efficacy Scores by Posttest Student Goal Orientation

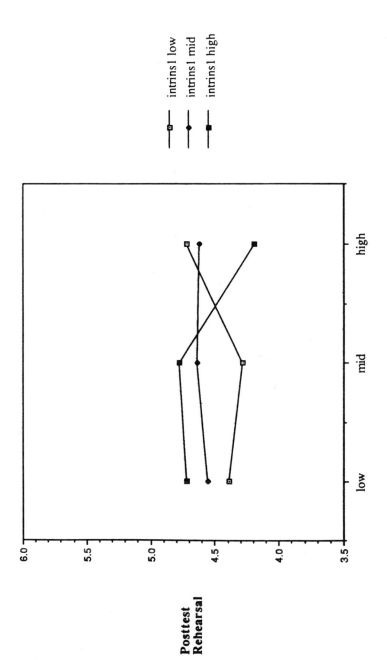

Figure 4. Mean Posttest Rehearsal Scores by Pretest Student Goal Orientation

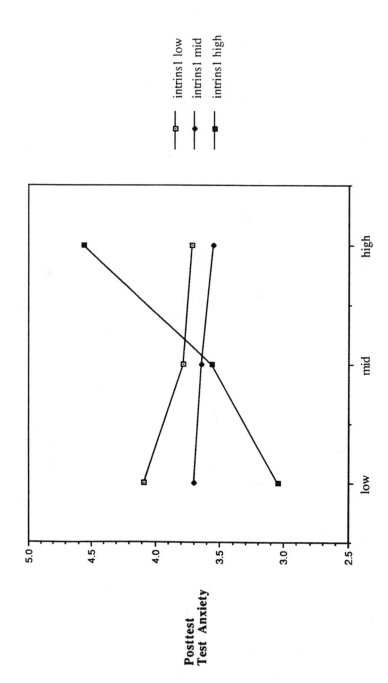

Figure 5. Mean Posttest Test Anxiety Scores by Pretest Student Goal Orientation

Correlations Between MSLQ Scales and Final Grade

Simple zero-order correlations were calculated between final course grade and the eight motivational and cognitive strategy scales (see Table 5). Course grade was standardized within each of the six courses to control for grading differences between instructors. Test anxiety was negatively related to final grade ($r = -.32$). Task value, self-efficacy, rehearsal, elaboration/organization, metacognition, and resource management were all positively correlated with final grade (r ranged from .21 to .58). Help-seeking was not related to final grade. Although not reported in the table, intrinsic and extrinsic orientation were not that strongly correlated with final grade. Intrinsic orientation at time 1 was correlated .16 with grade and .21 at the the end of the term. Extrinsic orientation was even less strongly related to final grade, .09 at time 1 and .08 at time 2.

Since the analyses of variance discussed previously indicated that different levels of goal orientation influenced motivational beliefs and cognitive strategy use, we also examined the magnitude of the correlations between the MSLQ scales and final grade *within* the different levels of intrinsic and extrinsic goal orientation (time 1 and time 2). We expected that the relations between the motivational and cognitive variables and final grade would vary as a function of the level of goal orientation. Simple tests for the differences between correlations were used to examine the differences by levels of goal orientation.

Final Grade-MSLQ Scale Correlations by Intrinsic Goal Orientation

As was expected, the correlations differed between levels of intrinsic goal orientation (at both time 1 and time 2 levels). Task value, elaboration/organization, metacognition, and resource management were more strongly correlated with final grade for students who were classified as low rather than middle or high in intrinsic goal orientation at the beginning of the course (see Table 5).

The final grades of students who were classified as low in intrinsic goal orientation at the the end of the course were more strongly related to task value, self-efficacy, elaboration/organization, and metacognition than those of students who were middle or high intrinsic. The correlations between test anxiety and final grade showed the same pattern for time 1 and time 2 levels of intrinsic goal orientation. Students who were in the mid-range of intrinsic goal orientation had the highest negative correlation between final grade and test anxiety ($r = -.40$ for mid-intrinsic at time 1, and $r = -.55$ for mid-intrinsic at time 2). As might be expected, students who were more concerned with learning (high in intrinsic motivation at the end of the semester) had the weakest correlation between final grade and test anxiety ($r = -.05$). Accordingly, for these students who really care about mastery and learning, anxiety does not interfere with their performance.

Table 5. Correlations Between Motivational and Cognitive Scales with Final Grade, by Level of Intrinsic Goal Orientation (Time 1 and Time 2)

Motivational/ Cognitive Scales at Time 2	Overall Correlation	Intrinsic Goal Orientation					
		Time 1			Time 1		
		low (N = 74)	middle (N = 122)	high (N = 67)	low (N = 81)	middle (N = 95)	high (N = 81)
Task Value	.30	.45a	.22b	.19b	**.47a**	**.09b**	**.18b**
Self-Efficacy	.58	.62	.59	.47	**.71a**	.53b	**.46b**
Test Anxiety	−.32	−.24	−.40	−.26	**−.24a**	**−.55b**	**−.05a**
Rehearsal	.31	.38	.24	.35	.28	.40	.21
Elaboration/ Organization	.30	**.49a**	**.13b**	.28	**.47a**	**.12b**	.26
Metacognition	.27	**.44a**	**.11b**	.22	**.48a**	**.00b**	.27a
Resource Management	.21	**.43a**	**.07b**	**.16b**	.22	.05a	.29b
Help-Seeking	.00	.03	.02	−.15	.07	−.05	−.08

Note: Correlations with different letters indicate pairs significantly different from one another at $p = 10$. Correlations in boldface indicate pairs that are significantly different at $p = .05$.

Final Grade-MSLQ Scale Correlations by Extrinsic Goal Orientation

As above, correlations between final grade and the MSLQ scales differed within levels of time 1 and time 2 extrinsic goal orientation (see Table 6). The detrimental effects of test anxiety were most strongly demonstrated in students who were classified as high extrinsic at the beginning of the term. The correlation between test anxiety and final grade for these students was −.50 (compared to −.21 for low extrinsic and −.26 for middle extrinsic students). Use of rehearsal strategies was also most strongly correlated with final grade for these high extrinsic students (.20, .29, and .45 were the correlations for low, mid and high extrinsic respectively).

The students who fell into the middle extrinsic group at the start of the class had lower correlations between final grade and task value, and final grade and elaboration/organization than the low or high extrinsic groups. The correlations between final grade and self-efficacy, and final grade and resource management were stronger for students who were low, rather than middle or high extrinsic at the end of the term. The unusual finding here was that help seeking was negatively related to final grade for students who were classified as mid-extrinsic at the end of the class ($r = -.26$), while the corresponding values for the low and high extrinsic students were positive.

CONCLUSIONS

The results have a number of implications for research on students' goals and self-regulation of learning. First, it appears that college students can have both

Table 6. Correlations Between Motivational and Cognitive Scales with Final Grade, by Level of Extrinsic Goal Orientation (Time 1 and Time 2)

Motivational/ Cognitive Scales at Time 2	Overall Correlation	Extrinsic Goal Orientation					
		Time 1			*Time 1*		
		low (N = 70)	*middle* (N = 104)	*high* (N = 89)	*low* (N = 100)	*middle* (N = 90)	*high* (N = 73)
Task Value	.30	.40	.18	.39	.32	.23	.34
Self-Efficacy	.58	.63	.51	.60	.65a	.57	.47b
Test Anxiety	−.32	−**.21a**	−.26a	−**.50b**	−.31	−.31	−.38
Rehearsal	.31	.20a	.29	.45b	.29	.36	.32
Elaboration/ Organization	.30	**.46a**	**.12b**	.36a	.31	.27	.31
Metacognition	.27	.35	.23	.24	.33	.14	.30
Resource Management	.21	.27	.21	.16	.33a	.11b	.13
Help-Seeking	.00	.15	−.09	−.07	**.12a**	**−.26a**	**.08a**

Note: Correlations with different letters indicate pairs significantly different from one another at $p = 10$. Correlations in boldface indicate pairs that are significantly different at $p = .05$.

intrinsic and extrinsic orientations at the same time and that endorsement of a high level on one dimension can be orthogonal to the endorsement of a high level on the other dimension. Accordingly, we had college students in our sample who were high in their intrinsic orientation but were either high or low in their extrinsic orientation and the same pattern held for students low in intrinsic orientation. This suggests that students can have multiple goals (cf. Wentzel, this volume) and that a simple intrinsic-extrinsic continuum (e.g., Harter, 1981) may not adequately characterize college students' perceptions of the reasons they engage in academic tasks in the college classroom.

At the same time, however, intrinsic orientation was linked more closely to students' motivational beliefs and self-regulatory strategies than students' extrinsic orientation. Students who were concerned about learning at the start of the course were more likely to report that they valued the course material and thought it was important to learn. This relationship remained the same at the end of the course for students who endorsed an intrinsic orientation. In support of Dweck and Leggett's (1988) model of goals, students who endorsed an intrinisc orientation to learning at both the beginning and at the end of the course did feel more efficacious about their ability to master the course material. In contrast to Dweck & Leggett's predictions, however, test anxiety did not vary significantly as a function of either an intrinsic or extrinsic orientation, albeit the signs of the correlations were in the expected directions (i.e., negative relationship between anxiety and intrinsic orientation and positive relationship between anxiety and extrinsic orientation). In summary, as would be expected from intrinsic motivation theory (e.g. Deci & Ryan, 1985) as well as goal theory (e.g., Dweck & Leggett, 1988), a general orientation to learning and mastery goals at the beginning of a course helps students maintain positive motivational beliefs about their capabilities and their interest in the course.

In terms of students' use of cognitive and self-regulatory strategies, the results suggest that an intrinsic orientation to learning is clearly linked to the use of cognitive strategies like elaboration and organization that result in a deeper processing of the course material (cf. Marton et al., 1984; Pintrich & De Groot, 1990a, 1990b). Students who want to learn the material are more likely to paraphrase the course material or use examples to improve their understanding in contrast to students who do not approach the task with a learning goal. In addition, students who approach their college courses with an orientation to learning and mastery are more likely to be planful as they prepare to study, to monitor their comprehension of what they are learning, and to repair any deficits in their understanding by rereading or reveiwing material that is difficult to comprehend. These students also are more likely to manage their time, their study environment, and their own effort well. They also are more likely to seek help from peers or teachers than students who do not endorse a learning goal.

In addition, it appears that the nature of the relations between students' motivational beliefs and their use of different self-regulatory strategies and their actual course performance varies as a function of students' goal orientation. The motivational and cognitive strategy variables were more strongly related to student performance for students who were low in intrinsic orientation. It appears that if students do not adopt a mastery or learning orientation, then their use of more complex cognitive strategies, their use of metacognitive strategies, and appropriate management of their resources becomes more important for their performance in contrast to those students who are more intrinsically oriented in the course. In addition, for those students lower in intrinsic orientation, test anxiety seems to interfere more with their performance and self-efficacy is more strongly tied to performance. It seems that if students do not see learning or mastery as important goals, then they must be able to mobilize effective motivational and self-regulatory strategies in order to perform well. In contrast, an intrinsic orientation seems to operate as a "buffer" for those students who really want to learn the course material, making the use of self-regulatory strategies and positive motivational beliefs (i.e., high self-efficacy, low anxiety) less important for academic performance. It is not clear from our data why this might be the case, it may be a function of just more time put towards studying for academic tasks for students high in intrinsic orientation, making the use of positive motivational beliefs and appropriate self-regulatory strategies less important. It may be that these high mastery students are more effective in using appropriate self-regulatory strategies. Future research is needed to clarify these issues.

Given the fact that intrinsic orientation was not directly related to actual performance, but was strongly related to students' motivational beliefs and self-regulatory strategies, it appears that raising the level of students' endorsement of mastery goals will not lead directly to improved performance (cf. Deci & Ryan, 1985). Rather, by increasing students' orientation to mastery and learning, it will increase the probability that they will become more cognitively engaged through the use of appropriate cognitive and self-regulatory strategies. The use of these cognitive and self-regulatory strategies will then lead to improved performance (Pintrich & De Groot, 1990a). Accordingly, changing the classroom environment to facilitate the adoption of mastery goals will not necessarily result in better achievement if the students are not able to use the relevant cognitive and self-regulatory strategies.

Extrinsic goal orientation did not have a strong direct link to students' motivational beliefs or self-regulation as expected, nor did high levels of extrinsic orientation have a positive multiplicative effect on students' cognitive engagement when combined with high levels of intrinsic orientation. Nevertheless, different levels of extrinsic orientation did condition or moderate the relationship between students' intrinsic orienation and their self-efficacy beliefs, their use of elaboration/organizational strategies, and their use of metacognitive strategies. The positive effects of an intrinsic orientation were most noticeable for students who also were lowest in extrinsic orientation. Students who did not care about grades were more likely to believe they were not able to accomplish the course work and less likely to use deeper processing and metacognitive strategies when they also did not care about learning or mastery. In contrast, for students who did not care about grades, but did care about learning and mastery, their levels of cognitive and metacognitive strategy use were at the highest levels of our sample as would be predicted by intrinsic motivation theorists (e.g., Deci & Ryan, 1985). Having an intrinsic orientation to learning and mastery seems to help students stay involved in learning and lead to beliefs they are capable even when these students are not concerned with grades (cf. Dweck & Leggett, 1988).

Another way to describe these interactions is that at high levels of extrinsic orientation, students began to look more similar to one another, regardless of their intrinsic goals for mastery or learning. Students who were concerned about grades showed higher levels of cognitive and metacognitive strategy use and higher confidence in their abilities, regardless of their intrinsic goals, than students who were low in both extrinsic and intrinsic orientations. The two trends for interactions for rehearsal and test anxiety are exceptions to this general conclusion, although they were not significant at the conventional level of significance. Here, it is clear that a high intrinsic orientation for mastery when combined with a high orientation to grades can lead to more anxiety over grades, although these same students are less likely to use simple rehearsal strategies. Accordingly, while having a higher concern for grades may reduce the positive effects of mastery or learning goals, a higher level of concern for grades still leads to better cognitive engagement and positive self-efficacy judgments than being relatively unconcerned about grades and learning.

Contrary to our predictions, it appears that the endorsement of extrinsic goals does not seem to have an adaptive function when intrinsic goals are high, but does have a facilitative influence when intrinsic goals are not seen as important. This suggests that if students are not committed to intrinsic goals, then it is still better for them to be committed to extrinsic goals like obtaining good grades rather than be "alienated" from school work in terms of not endorsing either intrinsic or extrinsic goals. At the college level, this finding seems very important because of the increased freedom of choice and control students have over what, when, and how they will pursue their academic studies. If they are not motivated by intrinsic goals, but by extrinsic goals, our results imply that they will be at least more cognitively engaged and more likely to manage their time and effort well than students who do not endorse intrinsic or extrinsic goals.

At the elementary and secondary school levels, this finding about extrinsic goals suggests a mediating mechansim to help explain the positive effects of good classroom managers on student achievement. It appears that the willingness of students to endorse classroom norms about achievement in terms of grades can be a function of how effective the teacher is as a classroom manager and socializes students to accept the classroom norms (see Blumenfeld, Hamilton, Bossert, Wessels, & Meece, 1983; Blumenfeld, Pintrich, & Hamilton, 1987). Our results then provide evidence for the next link in the chain of student mediating perceptions. In the absence of intrinsic goals, students who endorse extrinsic goals, as fostered by good classroom managers, are more likely to be cognitively engaged in terms of using appropriate strategies. Accordingly, if teachers cannot foster the adoption of intrinsic goals which can lead to high levels of cognitive engagement and self-regulation, then being a good classroom manager and facilitating the adoption of extrinsic goals can at least lead to moderate levels of cognitive engagement and self-regulation with the concomitant positive effects on academic performance. This interpretation is in line with the classroom research which suggests that being a good classroom manager is a necessary, but not sufficient, aspect of good instruction (e.g., Brophy & Good, 1986) as well as the research on the importance of teachers facilitating students' intrinsic motivation (e.g., Deci & Ryan, 1985). In fact, this interpretation provides a way to view the classroom management research and intrinsic motivation research as complementary, rather than antagonistic, due to their differential influence on students' extrinsic and intrinsic goals, respectively. Of course, research at the elementary and secondary levels needs to be done to examine the validity of the proposed relationships between teachers' managerial skill and their induction of intrinsic goals and students' endorsement of extrinsic and intrinsic goals, their use of cognitive and self-regulatory strategies, and actual achievement.

In summary, these findings, along with others in our research program (e.g., Pintrich, 1989; Pintrich & De Groot, 1990a, 1990b), provide ecologically valid data in support of the argument proposed by Dweck and Leggett (1988) and Nicholls (1984) that having a learning or mastery goal has a general facilitative effect on students' motivational beliefs, their use of cognitive strategies, and self-regulation of their learning. At the same time, this general positive effect may be moderated depending on the students' extrinsic goals for engaging in the academic tasks. These intrinsic and extrinsic goals, in turn, seem to influence the relationships between students' motivational beliefs and their self-regulatory strategies and their actual performance. In particular, lack of an intrinsic orientation to learning makes the use of self-regulatory strategies and positive motivational beliefs more important for performance. In effect, then, it may be most propaedeutic for learning and motivation to have an intrinsic orientation for learning and mastery (cf. Deci & Ryan, 1985; Ryan, this volume), but lacking that, a commitment to the norms of schools in terms of obtaining good grades can be helpful in maintaining cognitive engagement and motivational beliefs about efficacy. These beliefs about efficacy and actual cognitive engagement, in turn, are more closely tied to actual academic performance than students' goals. Accordingly, having appropriate goals is just one aspect of successful performance, students must also be equipped with appropriate cognitive and self-regulatory strategies for accomplishing the academic tasks in college classrooms.

This conclusion highlights the importance of considering not just students' goals for their academic work, but also their strategies for doing the work. The problem of procedural knowledge, of "knowing how" to do an academic task, is as important to consider as the problem of "what motivates" students. Students may have intrinsic mastery goals for their course work, but if they do not also have appropriate cognitive and self-regulatory strategies, they may not be as successful. In the same fashion, students may have the appropriate strategies, but if they are operating under goals that do not facilitate the activation and use of them, they will be less likely to do so. The implications for future research are clear; we need models and theories that integrate the varying motivational and cognitive components and that describe the relations between the different components (Pintrich, 1989; Pintrich et al., 1986). Our models of motivation must move beyond cognitively "empty" concepts such as "higher levels of effort" to include descriptions of how that effort is employed in terms of the activation and use of appropriate knowledge and strategies. At the same time, our relatively "cold" models of the student as a learner must be imbued with motivational "warmth," recognizing that students do pursue different goals and with different levels of intensity that influence their cognition. The implications for instruction that can be derived from this conclusion suggest that it may be important to design classroom tasks and environments that increase the probablity that students will adopt intrinsic, or at the least, extrinsic goals, but it is just as important that instructors also provide students with the cognitive "tools" that allow them to master the academic tasks.

ACKNOWLEDGMENTS

Data collection and preparation for this paper was made possible through funding to the National Center for Research to Improve Postsecondary Teaching and Learning (NCRIPTAL) at the School of Education at the University of Michigan. NCRIPTAL is funded by grant number OERI-86-0010 from the Office of Educational Research and Improvement (OERI), Department of Education. The ideas expressed in this papaer are not the positions or policies of NCRIPTAL, OERI, or the Department of Education. Thanks to Marty Maehr and Bill McKeachie for helpful comments on an earlier version.

REFERENCES

Ausubel, D. P. (1963). *The psychology of meaningful verbal learning.* New York: Grune & Stratton.

Blumenfeld, P.C., Hamilton, V.L., Bossert, S., Wessels, K., & Meece, J.L. (1983). Teacher talk and student thought: Socialization into the student role. In J. Levine & M. Wang (Eds.), *Teacher and student perceptions: Implications for learning* (pp. 143-192). Hillsdale, NJ: Erlbaum.

Blumenfeld, P.C., Mergendoller, J.R., & Swartout, D.W. (1987). Task as a heuristic for understanding student learning and motivation. *Journal of Curriculum Studies, 19*, 135-148.

Blumenfeld, P.C., Pintrich, P.R., & Hamilton, V.L. (1987). Teacher talk and students' reasoning about morals, conventions, and achievement. *Child Development, 58*, 1389-1401.

Brophy, J., & Good, T. (1986). Teacher behavior and student achievement. In M.Wittrock (Ed.), *Handbook of Research on Teaching and Learning* (pp. 328-375). New York: Macmillan.

Brown, A. L., Bransford, J. D., Ferrara, R. A., & Campione, J. C. (1983). Learning, remembering, and understanding. In J. H. Flavell & E. M. Markman (Eds.), *Handbook of child psychology: Cognitive development* (Vol. 3, pp. 77-166). New York: Wiley.

Cantor, N., & Kihlstrom, J.F. (1987). *Personality and Social Intelligence.* Englewood Cliffs, NJ: Prentice-Hall.

Cantor, N., & Langston, C.A. (1989). Ups and downs of life tasks in a life transition. In L.A. Pervin (Ed.), *Goal concepts in personality and social psychology* (pp. 127-167). Hillsdale, NJ: Erlbaum.

Corno, L. (1986). The metacognitive control components of self-regulated learning. *Contemporary Educational Psychology, 11*, 333-346.

Deci, E. (1975). *Intrinsic motivation.* New York: Plenum.

Deci, E., & Ryan, R.M. (1985). *Intrinsic motivation and self-determination in human behavior.* New York: Plenum.

Doyle, W. (1983). Academic work. *Review of Educational Research, 53*, 159-199.

Dweck, C.S., & Elliott, E.S. (1983). Achievement motivation. In E.M. Hetherington (Ed.), *Handbook of child psychology: socialization, personality, and social development* (Vol. 4, pp. 643-691). New York: Wiley.

Dweck, C.S., & Leggett, E.L. (1988). A social-cognitive approach to motivation and personality. *Psychological Review, 95,* 256-273.

Elliott, E.S., & Dweck, C.S. (1988). Goals: an approach to motivation and achievement. *Journal of Personality and Social Psychology, 54,* 5-12.

Emmons, R.A. (1989). The personal strivings approach to personality. In L.A. Pervin (Ed.), *Goal concepts in personality and social psychology* (pp. 87-126). Hillsdale, NJ: Erlbaum.

Entwistle, N. (1984). Contrasting perspectives on learning. In F. Marton, D. Hounsell, & N. Entwistle (Eds.), *The experience of learning* (pp. 1-18). Edinburgh, Scotland: Scottish Academic Press.

Entwistle, N., Hanley, M., & Hounsell, D. (1979). Identifying distinctive approaches to studying. *Higher Education, 8,* 3655-3680.

Entwistle, N., & Marton, F. (1984). Changing conceptions of learning and research. In F. Marton, D. Hounsell, & N. Entwistle (Eds.), *The experience of learning* (pp. 211-236). Edinburgh, Scotland: Scottish Academic Press.

Erikson, E.H. (1963). *Childhood and society* (2nd ed.). New York: W.W. Norton.

Flavell, J. H. (1979). Metacognition and cognitive monitoring: a new area of cognitive-developmental inquiry. *American Psychologist, 34,* 906-911.

Freud, S. (1957). Instincts and their vicissitudes. In J. Rickman (Ed.) *A general selection from the works of Sigmund Freud* (pp.70-86). Garden City, NY: Doubleday (original work published in 1914).

Harter, S. (1981). A new self-report scale of intrinsic versus extrinsic orientation in the classroom: motivational and informational components. *Developmental Psychology, 17,* 302-312.

Kuhl, J. (1987). Feeling versus being helpless: Metacognitive mediators of failure-induced performance deficits. In F. E. Weinert & R. H. Kluwe (Eds.), *Metacognition, motivation, and understanding* (pp. 217-235). Hillsdale, NJ: Erlbaum.

Little, B.R. (1989). Personal projects analysis: Trivial pursuits, magnificent obsessions, and the search for coherence. In D.M. Buss & N. Cantor (Eds.), *Personality psychology: Recent trends and emerging directions* (pp. 15-31). New York: Springer-Verlag.

Marton, F., Hounsell, D., & Entwistle, N. (1984). *The experience of learning.* Edinburgh, Scotland: Scottish Academic Press.

Marton, F., & Saljo, R. (1976a). On qualitative differences in learning: I. Outcomes and process. *British Journal of Educational Psychology, 46,* 4-11.

_____. (1976b). On qualitative differences in learning: II. Outcome as a function of the learner's conceptions of the task. *British Journal of Educational Psychology, 46,* 115-127.

McKeachie, W.J., Pintrich, P.R., Lin, Y.G., & Smith, D. (1986). *Teaching and learning in the college classroom: a review of the research literature.* Ann Arbor, MI: University of Michigan, National Center for Research to Improve Postsecondary Teaching and Learning.

Murray, H.A. (1938). *Explorations in Personality.* New York: Oxford University Press.

Naveh-Benjamin, M., Lin, Y. G., & McKeachie, W.J. (1989). Development of cognitive structures in three academic disciplines and their relations to students' study skills, anxiety, and motivation: further use of the ordered tree technique. *Journal of Higher Education Studies, 4,* 10-15.

Naveh-Benjamin, M., McKeachie, W.J., & Lin, Y. G. (1989). Use of the ordered tree technique to assess students' initial knowledge and conceptual learning. *Teaching of Psychology, 16,* 182-187.

Naveh-Benjamin, M., McKeachie, W.J., Lin, Y. G., & Tucker, D. G. (1986). Inferring students' cognitive structures and their development using the "ordered tree" technique. *Journal of Educational Psychology, 78,* 130-140.

Nicholls, J. (1984). Achievement motivation: Conceptions of ability, subjective experience, task choice, and performance. *Psychological Review, 91*, 328-346.

Nuttin, J. (1984). *Motivation, planning, and action: A relational theory of behavior dynamics.* Hillsdale, NJ: Erlbaum.

Pask, G. (1976). Styles and strategies of learning. *British Journal of Educational Psychology, 46*, 128-148.

Pintrich, P.R. (1988a). A process-oriented view of student motivation and cognition. In J. Stark & L. Mets (Eds.), *Improving teaching and learning through research: New directions for institutional research* (Vol. 57, pp. 65-79). San Francisco: Jossey-Bass.

_____. (1988b). Student learning and college teaching. In R. E. Young & K. E. Eble (Eds.), *College teaching and learning: Preparing for new commitments. New directions for teaching and learning* (Vol. 33, pp. 71-86). San Francisco: Jossey-Bass.

_____. (1989). The dynamic interplay of student motivation and cognition in the college classroom. In M. Maehr and C. Ames (Eds.), *Advances in motivation and achievement: motivation-enhancing environments* (Vol. 6, pp. 117-160). Greenwich, CT: JAI Press.

_____. (1990). Implications of psychological research on student learning and college teaching for teacher education. In W. R. Houston (Ed.), *Handbook of research on teacher education* (pp. 826-857). New York: Macmillan.

Pintrich, P.R., Cross, D., Kozma, R., & McKeachie, W.J. (1986). Instructional psychology. *Annual Review of Psychology, 37*, 611-651.

Pintrich, P. R., & DeGroot, E. (1990a). Motivational and self-regulated learning components of classroom academic performance. *Journal of Educational Psychology, 82*, 33-40.

_____. (1990b, April). *Quantitative and qualitative views of student motivation and self-regulated learning.* Paper presented at the annual meeting of the American Educational Research Association, Boston MA.

Pintrich, P.R., McKeachie, W.J., Smith, D.A., Doljanac, R., Lin, Y.G., Naveh-Benjamin, M., Crooks, T., & Karabenick, S. (1987). *The motivated strategies for learning questionnaire (MSLQ).* Ann Arbor, MI: NCRIPTAL, The University of Michigan.

Pressley, M. (1986). The relevance of the good strategy user model to the teaching of mathematics. *Educational Psychologist, 21*, 139-161.

Ramsden, P. (1984). The context of learning. In F. Marton, D. Hounsell, & N. Entwistle (Eds.), *The experience of learning* (pp. 144-164). Edinburgh, Scotland: Scottish Academic Press.

Saljo, R. (1984). Learning from readings. In F. Marton, D. Hounsell, & N. Entwistle (Eds.), *The experience of learning* (pp. 71-89). Edinburgh, Scotland: Scottish Academic Press.

Schmeck, R. R. (1983). Learning styles of college students. In R. F. Dillon & R. R. Schmeck, (Eds.), *Individual differences in cognition* (pp. 233-279). New York: Academic Press.

Siegel, L., & Siegel, L. C. (1965). Educational set: A determinant of acquisition. *Journal of Educational Psychology, 56*, 1-12.

Sternberg, R. J. (1985). *Beyond IQ: A triarchic theory of human intelligence.* New York: Cambridge University Press.

Veroff, J., & Veroff, J.B. (1980). *Social incentives: A life-span developmental approach.* New York: Academic Press.

Weiner, B. (1986). *An attributional theory of motivation and emotion.* New York: Springer-Verlag.

Weinstein, C., & Mayer, R. (1986). The teaching of learning strategies. In M. C. Wittrock (Ed.), *Handbook of research on teaching, 3rd edition* (pp. 315-327). New York: Macmillan.

White, R.H. (1959). Motivation reconsidered: The concept of competence. *Psychological Review, 66*, 297-333.

Zukier, H. (1986). The paradigmatic and narrative modes in goal-guided inference. In R.M. Sorrentino & E.T. Higgins (Eds.), *Handbook of motivation and cognition: Foundations of social behavior* (pp. 465-502). New York: Guilford Press.

AUTHOR INDEX

SUBJECT INDEX

415

Advances in Motivation and Achievement

Edited by **Martin L. Maehr,** *School of Education, University of Michigan*

The purpose of this series is to reflect current research and theory concerned with motivation and achievement in work, school and play. Each volume will focus on a particular issue or theme. While the discussions will be based on and fully reflect current developments in the field, a special goal of the series is to bring the best in social science to bear on socially significant problems.

Volume 6, Motivation Enhancing Environments
1989, 293 pp. $63.50
ISBN 0-89232-889-4

Edited by **Martin L. Maehr,** *University of Michigan, Ann Arbor* and **Carole Ames,** *University of Illinois at Urbana-Champaign*

CONTENTS: Preface, *Martin L. Maehr, University of Michigan and Carole Ames, University of Illinois at Urbana-Champaign.* **Probing the Psychological Environment: Children's Cognitions, Perceptions and Feelings in the Peer Culture,** *Gary W. Ladd and Nicki R. Crick, Purdue University.* **The Nuturance of Motivation Attention in the Daily Experience of Children and Adolescents,** *Reed Larsen, Mark Ham and Marcela Rafaelli, University of Illinois at Urbana-Champaign.* **Goal Perspectives and Behavior in Sprot and Exercise Settings,** *Joan L. Duda, Purdue University.* **The Dynamic Interplay of Student Motivation and Cognition in the College Classroom,** *Paul R. Pintrich, University of Michigan, Ann Arbor.* **Cooperative Learning and Student Achievement: Six Theoretical Perspectives,** *Robert E. Slavin, Johns Hopkins University.* **Motivational Consequences of a Supportive Work Environment,** *Thomas N. Martin, John R. Schermerhorn, Jr., and Lars L. Larson, Southern Illinois University, Carbondale.* **School Culture, Motivation and Achievement,** *Martin L. Maehr, University of Michigan, Ann Arbor and Leslie J. Fyans, Jr., State Board of Education, Springfield, Illinois.* **Leadership and Learning: A Measurement-Based Approach for Analyzing School Effectiveness and Developing Effective School Leaders,** *Samuel E. Krug, MetriTech, Inc., Champaign, Illinois.*

Also Available:
Volumes 1-5 (1984-1988) $63.50 each